Delphi GUI Programming with FireMonkey

Unleash the full potential of the FMX framework to build
exciting cross-platform apps with Embarcadero Delphi

Andrea Magni

BIRMINGHAM - MUMBAI

Delphi GUI Programming with FireMonkey

Commissioning Editor: Kunal Chaudhari
Acquisition Editor: Alok Dhuri
Content Development Editor: Rosal Colaco
Senior Editor: Rohit Singh
Technical Editor: Gaurav Gala
Copy Editor: Safis Editing
Project Coordinator: Francy Puthiry
Proofreader: Safis Editing
Indexer: Rekha Nair
Production Designer: Aparna Bhagat

First published: October 2020

Production reference: 1281020

Published by Packt Publishing Ltd.
Livery Place
35 Livery Street
Birmingham
B3 2PB, UK.

ISBN 978-1-78862-417-6

www.packt.com

I've always loved technology and computer programming. Thanks to my father, I had access to computers when it was neither easy nor popular to have. This, together with my personal inclination to problem-solving, made me a software developer way before I graduated from university as a computer engineer. For me and Delphi, it was love at first sight, even when I was still a kid. The Italian Delphi community (strongly backed by Marco Cantù, the Delphi guru since forever and the current RAD studio product manager at Embarcadero Technologies) is the cradle where I started my growth into the professional that I am today.

Besides Marco, I really have to thank many people who helped me a lot. Among all of them, I'd especially like to mention two: Uberto Barbini, who was the first one to believe in me and offer me a job, and Nando Dessena, who has been (and still is) my mentor and an irreplaceable source of knowledge. I also owe a lot to my customers over the years, who trusted a very young guy (in the past, at least) when there were not many evident reasons for doing so.

During the last 5 years or so, I've opened up a great deal to the worldwide Delphi community, starting in Europe. There are so many Delphi gurus and talented developers out there that it is simply impossible to mention them all. All of them have brought some light to my path to becoming a better software developer, and to them I pay much respect. I also want to thank Jim McKeeth (chief developer advocate and engineer at Embarcadero Technologies) for all the effort he puts into promoting Delphi worldwide and coordinating MVP activities.

Now that I am an experienced Delphi developer, it is my turn to give back to the community some of the knowledge I've tried to collect over the years. This is the main reason I've written this book, adding this to my regular activity as Embarcadero MVP (technical blog, conferences) and an author of Delphi-related Open-Source Software projects.

Writing a technical book proved to be quite an effort for me, and this makes my admiration for all those prolific authors of Delphi-related books out there greater and greater.

This book is especially dedicated to these people:

> My wife, Marta, for the love, support, and inspiration through all these years; and my lovely daughter, Federica: I hope that you always keep your happiness and curiosity.

– Andrea Magni

Foreword

For many years since its release, Delphi development was tied to the Microsoft Windows platform and based on the VCL library, which is deeply rooted in the Windows API. As Embarcadero started attempting a foray into mobile development, it became clear that the challenge of building single-source, multi-device applications required a rethink of the user interface controls library, while keeping the core foundations of Delphi and its runtime library made sense.

The original solution was to create a library that represents components in terms of their primitive graphical elements, so that the same component could draw itself with different graphical elements depending on the platform, making it almost identical to the platform controls. In this way, you create a button, which looks like a classic button on Windows, an Android one on the Google mobile OS, and an iOS element on the Apple OS. As operating systems evolve their UI style, the library can keep up and be updated. This is the essence of FireMonkey and its styling architecture.

The second core element of the architecture is that its **Graphical User Interface** (**GUI**) rendering is mapped to the **Graphical Processing Unit** (**GPU**) with drivers that use the optimal GPU solution for each platform (at times offering more than one). This is the direction all the cross-platform frameworks are embracing today, so we can say that FireMonkey was ahead of time in its design. Finally, the library uses its styling architecture to allow mapping controls to native platform user interface components (such as the web and maps, but also input controls).

Given that the foundation of FireMonkey is in its styling architecture, it is really impossible to understand FireMonkey without delving into it. One element of this book I deeply appreciate is the fact it starts by introducing FireMonkey styles and goes deeper and deeper into this architecture with the high level of detail and information required to unleash the full potential of FireMonkey, as the subtitle indicates.

FireMonkey indeed has a large, partially hidden potential and it has been lacking a detailed book explaining it extensively from the ground up, both in terms of offering details about its large number of controls and in terms of going deep into their underlying structure. Andrea's book really fills a very important gap in the Delphi documentation, providing guidance for anyone moving from VCL to FireMonkey, but also for someone starting with Delphi for mobile.

As a personal note, when FireMonkey was released, I did plan on writing a book on it, but later I joined Embarcadero as a product manager and this became impossible in terms of the time required. It looks like this volume has the structure and the focus of the book I could have written, and I'm very happy it was Andrea who wrote it. When he mentioned this to me that he was up for this task, I encouraged him: I have known Andrea for a long time (since he was still at University), we worked together in the past, and I know his focus on and care for technical details and accuracy. They can be clearly seen in this book.

It is also relevant to notice that Andrea is not an author sitting alone at his research desk, but is deeply involved in practical projects and the information in this book certainly comes from his real-world experience using Delphi since its early days and using FireMonkey for many years, building many different types of applications, both for and with developers in different industries. He also started speaking at different Delphi conferences, sharing his expertise, as well as being an active Embarcadero MVP and actively engaging with the developer community.

Going back to the book, I like the way it starts with an overview of FireMonkey (setting up the technical tone from the beginning), covers the main components the library provides, delves into a discussion of styles, and doesn't try to cover concepts like the FireUI designer and Live Previews until the reader is able to appreciate its power, as Andrea knows about styles and the platform architecture.

Another key element of the book is that, while it focuses on FireMonkey, it isn't restricted solely to the user interface controls, but touches on other key runtime library areas and libraries that are relevant to use along with FMX, including FireDAC for database access, and the Parallel Programming Library for modern multithreading support.

The third key element that makes this book precious is that it doesn't limit itself to presenting merely what the components can do, but helps to provide the bigger picture, touching on user interface design principles and tackling directly the common requirements for building responsive user interfaces, given the myriad of screen device sizes and resolutions an application might run on.

As I've already mentioned, I've personally known Andrea for many years, I know his expertise, and I'm very happy to see this book out. I'm happy as a friend, because of his nice work, but I'm equally happy as RAD Studio Product Manager focused on Delphi, because this book fills a gap and I'm certain it will help countless programmers learn how to use FireMonkey at its best, and will help us to drive the adoption of this powerful, modern, multi-device user interface library.

Delphi has a huge opportunity in the multi-device space with FireMonkey, but even if you are building for just one target operating system, the library is nice to use and offers great power that this book helps discover and tap into. I'm certain you'll learn a lot from this book and enjoy reading it.

Marco Cantù
RAD Studio Product Manager, Embarcadero Technologies

Contributors

About the author

Andrea Magni is an Italian computer engineer (with a degree in artificial intelligence and robotics from the Polytechnic of Milan, 2007) living near Monza. He is a freelancer who has gained 2 decades of experience in the industry as a software developer and consultant. He has trained many development teams to design software architectures and models, acquire knowledge, introduce source and project management tools, and perform troubleshooting. He has been an Embarcadero MVP since 2014 and he runs a technical blog and some OSS projects on GitHub. He regularly takes part in major Delphi conferences, such as EKON and DCC (DE), Embarcadero DelphiCon, PasCon, SDN (NL), Be-Delphi (BE), DAPUG (DK), ITDevCon (IT), DelphiDay (IT, until 2015), DelphiDay (PL), and other events.

I want to thank Bruce McGee (Glooscap Software) for all the support and hints he shared with me during the process of writing this book. I also have to thank my editors at Packt a great deal for the patience and all the effort spent to improve this book as much as possible. A big thank you to all the people who spent their time giving feedback on the book.

About the reviewer

Abduraimov Muminjon is a growing and talented developer from Khorezm, Uzbekistan, and has great experience with Delphi, C/C++, and Python. He has produced more than 100 articles and tutorials on Delphi and C++. He is also the author of the *Mastering Delphi* video course for Packt. He is active in the programming world and loves to give back to the community, supporting several open source projects in his free time. Furthermore, he has done several workshops online and offline at a number of conferences and meetups. He is pursuing his computer science and engineering bachelor's degree in Uzbekistan. Currently, he is a Microsoft Learn Student Ambassador from Amity University Tashkent.

I would like to express my special thanks to the project coordinator, Francy Puthiry, as well as Packt Publishing, for the golden opportunity to do this wonderful project with Andrea Magni. I am truly thankful to them! Furthermore, I would also like to thank my parents and siblings, who have always been by my side.

Packt is searching for authors like you

If you're interested in becoming an author for Packt, please visit authors.packtpub.com and apply today. We have worked with thousands of developers and tech professionals, just like you, to help them share their insight with the global tech community. You can make a general application, apply for a specific hot topic that we are recruiting an author for, or submit your own idea.

Table of Contents

Section 3: Pushing to The Top: Advanced Topics

Table of Contents

Preface

FireMonkey (FMX) is a cross-platform application framework that allows developers to create exciting **user interfaces (UIs)** and deliver applications on multiple operating systems. This book will help you learn visual programming with Delphi and FMX.

This book has been written with a classical approach. Topics are introduced by first examining the context that they belong to, and then adding some practical examples to showcase the features or capabilities under discussion. Examples are kept simple yet significant (and full code is provided with the book). We are going to cover essential components and advanced concepts, both of which will be clearly explained and used as building blocks for developing real-world applications.

In order to acquire the ability to deliver modern applications with a **graphical user interface (GUI)** on multiple platforms with a single code base, you will learn about FMX's UI-related features and capabilities, together with many useful techniques. Taking advantage of them all will make your applications stand up in terms of **user experience (UX)**.

We are going to start with an overview of the FMX framework, including a general discussion of the underlying philosophy and approach. We'll then move on to the fundamental components and the deeper architectural details of FMX. Then we'll compare FMX and **Visual Component Library (VCL)**.

We are going to address how to achieve visual responsiveness through alignment strategies, layout components, and built-in FMX technology (to deal with multi-resolution images, for example). Also, you'll learn how to enrich the UX with the help of transitions and visual animations. You'll get to grips with data access, visual data binding, and techniques to implement responsiveness effectively on desktop and mobile platforms. An entire chapter of the book is dedicated to the TFrameStand and TFormStand components, which are useful for properly modularizing your applications in terms of UI elements, promoting the reuse of UI views, and improving the UX through visual continuity.

The book covers the main FMX components (both simple and complex ones), but it also covers style-related concepts and explains how they are used to deliver consistent UIs while targeting different platforms. To address one of the most relevant issues in modern application development, the book provides you with a general introduction to parallel programming, specifically targeting UI-related aspects thereof, in order to achieve application responsiveness.

Later, we'll explore the most important cross-platform services in the FMX framework, which are the crux of delivering your application on multiple platforms while retaining the single code base approach. Finally, you'll learn about FMX's built-in 3D functionalities.

By the end of this book, you'll be familiar with the FMX framework and be able to build effective cross-platform visual applications.

Who this book is for

This book is for Delphi developers who are looking to discover the full potential of the FireMonkey framework in order to build interactive cross-platform GUI applications and achieve an optimal UI/UX. Basic familiarity with Delphi programming and the VCL will be beneficial, but are not mandatory.

What this book covers

Chapter 1, *Introducing the FireMonkey Framework*, provides a general overview of the FMX framework, including fundamental aspects, architecture details, and general aims of the framework.

Chapter 2, *Exploring Similarities and Differences with VCL*, discusses cross-platform development. Many Delphi developers are experienced VCL users and are now looking to FMX in order to achieve the main promise of the FMX framework: cross-platform development. FMX is a brand-new application framework, while VCL has always been the framework for Delphi.

Chapter 3, *Mastering Basic Components*, explains how some of the most widely used UI components can be used in a real application. After gaining confidence with each component, we will see how to combine them to build a consistent UI.

Chapter 4, *Discovering Lists and Advanced Components*, covers the various kinds of list controls available in FMX and explains how to efficiently use and customize their appearances. Every application manages data, but on mobile platforms the natural way to present data is by using lists. You'll also learn about using container components to properly organize your UI elements.

Chapter 5, *Using FireDAC in FMX Applications*, explains that when building data-centric applications, FireDAC is the best companion included in RAD Studio. As a rich-featured Data Access Component library, it provides access to many RDBMSes and data sources through a unified programming interface. Also, even when an external data source (an RDBMS or similar) is not involved, FireDAC provides data storage and manipulation for every Delphi application through powerful in-memory dataset capabilities and local persistence features.

Chapter 6, *Implementing Data Binding*, helps you understand the new data binding approach (which is different from the traditional TDataSource approach) is essential for leveraging Delphi's RAD capabilities and delivering your application more quickly. Data presentation is done through data binding techniques and technologies such as **LiveBindings**, a powerful element in the Delphi toolset.

Chapter 7, *Understanding FMX Style Concept*, helps you understand that the concept of style is fundamental for every FMX developer, and it is at the root of the framework's ability to build cross-platform applications by abstracting the visual aspects of each component from its behavior. Each FMX visual component is built from two separate angles: behavior and representation. The first is built by the code, while the second is built through styles.

Chapter 8, *Divide and Conquer with TFrameStand*, focuses on the TFrameStand component. TFrameStand is an open source component for FMX that enables developers to modularize the UI of an application and achieve visual continuity in the entire application. It combines the power of the standard TFrame component with the flexibility of FMX styles to let developers concentrate on the content and how it is presented. A twin component (TFormStand) is discussed to achieve the same results when dealing with TForm elements.

Chapter 9, *Building Responsive UIs*, helps you understand one of the most important aspects of a modern UI, which is the ability to adapt to different screen resolutions. The FMX framework has some interesting features in this area, but the two most effective ones are the alignment models of the components and the ability to use layouts (and, eventually, nested layouts) to achieve a relative alignment of visual components in each view.

Chapter 10, *Orchestrating Transitions and Animations*, helps you master modern UI animations and transitions to enrich the UX of an application. A deep explanation of the built-in animation model will enable you to properly take advantage of the various types of animation and the functionalities provided.

Chapter 11, *Building Responsive Applications*, covers responsiveness. The responsiveness of the UI is by far the most coveted feature of every app and, at the same time, one of the most difficult achievements for a developer. While parallel programming can be used to achieve responsiveness, it has some implications regarding the UI implementation.

Chapter 12, *Exploring Cross-Platform Services*, helps you understand that FMX is much more than just a visual framework. Important aspects of applications are conveniently wrapped into FMX services, and this is a crucial element of retaining a single code base while delivering cross-platform applications.

Chapter 13, *Learning about FMX 3D Capabilities*, covers the FMX 3D functionality that can be combined with 2D functionality. In this chapter, you will find an overview of FMX 3D functionality, including the ability to deal with third-party 3D models.

To get the most out of this book

Generally speaking, for the whole book, you need a computer with Delphi set up and a few additional libraries installed (such as **Radiant Shapes** (https://getitnow.embarcadero.com/?q=radiant+shapes) and **CodeSite Logging** (https://getitnow.embarcadero.com/?q=codesite)). Having other devices and setting up multiple platforms (iOS, Android, OS X/macOS, and Linux) other than Windows is a plus, but not strictly needed to follow the flow of the book.

You will need a version of **Delphi** installed on your computer—**version 10.3** or later is recommended. All code examples have been tested using **Delphi 10.4**. However, they should work with future version releases too. Mobile examples have been tested on **Android** physical device (**Nexus 5X**, **Android 8.1**), and **iOS** physical device (**iPhone 6**, **iOS 12.4.8**). **Windows** environment is a **VMWare Fusion** virtual machine with **Windows 10** running on a **Apple MacBook Pro** with **macOS Catalina 10.15.7**.

Here are the software requirements for this book:

Software/hardware covered in the book	OS requirements
Delphi 10.4 Sydney	**Windows 10** and above, **.NET Framework 4.5** or later

You should be able to run most of the examples with every Delphi edition including FMX (this also includes the Delphi Community edition).

If you are using the digital version of this book, we advise you to type the code yourself or access the code via the GitHub repository (link available in the next section). Doing so will help you avoid any potential errors related to the copying and pasting of code.

Download the example code files

You can download the example code files for this book from GitHub at https://github.com/PacktPublishing/Delphi-GUI-Programming-with-FireMonkey. In case there's an update to the code, it will be updated on the existing GitHub repository.

We also have other code bundles from our rich catalog of books and videos available at https://github.com/PacktPublishing/. Check them out!

Download the color images

We also provide a PDF file that has color images of the screenshots/diagrams used in this book. You can download it here: https://static.packt-cdn.com/downloads/9781788624176_ColorImages.pdf.

Conventions used

There are a number of text conventions used throughout this book.

CodeInText: Indicates code words in text, database table names, folder names, filenames, file extensions, pathnames, dummy URLs, user input, and Twitter handles. Here is an example: "A second way to customize your items (exactly as described for TListBox items) is to inherit your own class from TTreeViewItem and provide extra functionality or on-board components directly via code."

A block of code is set as follows:

```
TMyTreeViewItem = class(TTreeViewItem)
  private
    FPerson: TPerson;
  protected
    procedure SetPerson(const Value: TPerson);
  public
    property Person: TPerson read FPerson write SetPerson;
  end;
```

When we wish to draw your attention to a particular part of a code block, the relevant lines or items are set in bold:

```
procedure TMyTreeViewItem.SetPerson(const Value: TPerson);
begin
  FPerson := Value;
  Text := Person.ToString;
end;
```

Bold: Indicates a new term, an important word, or words that you see onscreen. For example, words in menus or dialog boxes appear in the text like this. Here is an example: "The exact specifications of these boundaries are shown in the top toolbar of the **BitmapLinks** editor, in gray text: **TBounds (4,00,168,00)-(84,00,197,00) TBounds (3,00,3,00)-(3,00,3,00)**."

 Warnings or important notes appear like this.

 Tips and tricks appear like this.

Get in touch

Feedback from our readers is always welcome.

General feedback: If you have questions about any aspect of this book, mention the book title in the subject of your message and email us at customercare@packtpub.com.

Errata: Although we have taken every care to ensure the accuracy of our content, mistakes do happen. If you have found a mistake in this book, we would be grateful if you would report this to us. Please visit www.packtpub.com/support/errata, selecting your book, clicking on the Errata Submission Form link, and entering the details.

Piracy: If you come across any illegal copies of our works in any form on the Internet, we would be grateful if you would provide us with the location address or website name. Please contact us at `copyright@packt.com` with a link to the material.

If you are interested in becoming an author: If there is a topic that you have expertise in and you are interested in either writing or contributing to a book, please visit `authors.packtpub.com`.

Reviews

Please leave a review. Once you have read and used this book, why not leave a review on the site that you purchased it from? Potential readers can then see and use your unbiased opinion to make purchase decisions, we at Packt can understand what you think about our products, and our authors can see your feedback on their book. Thank you!

For more information about Packt, please visit `packt.com`.

1
Section 1: Delphi GUI Programming Frameworks

This section will introduce you to the FMX application framework and explain some of its capabilities in relation to another Delphi product: the **Visual Component Library** (**VCL**). We are going to explore the context in which FMX has been designed and implemented in order to understand how its peculiarities suit a product such as Delphi (or RAD Studio).

The comparison with VCL will be extremely useful if you are already familiar with Delphi and VCL, but also, if you are using Delphi for the first time, many fundamental concepts are summarized in this section and you will see how these concepts fit together.

This section contains the following chapters:

- Chapter 1, *Introducing the FireMonkey Framework*
- Chapter 2, *Exploring Similarities and Differences with VCL*

Introducing the FireMonkey Framework

1

Welcome to the first chapter of this book! We are at the beginning of a journey to gain knowledge about a great application framework, that is, the **FireMonkey (FMX)** framework. These days, developers face a hard-to-solve problem—building effective cross-platform applications. From a project management point of view, one of the most wanted features is to achieve this goal through a single source code base, not, for example, having a different code base for each supported platform.

The introduction of the **FireMonkey** framework represented a crucial point, putting Embarcadero Delphi in a magic spot in the global software development scenario. Developers are enabled to design and build native applications for the most popular platforms, including both desktop (**Microsoft Windows**, **Linux**, and **Apple OS X**, now also known as **macOS**) and mobile (**Google Android** and **Apple iOS**), using a single toolset and language (thus reducing the effort needed).

This chapter will go through the following topics, to provide some background about what FMX is, why it was created, and its most evident strengths:

- Approaching FireMonkey
- Abstracting the visual part of your apps
- Looking beyond the UI
- Back to the metal
- Understanding the strengths and weaknesses of the FMX approach

After reading this chapter, you will be familiar with the general context in which this framework has been developed, including a general understanding of the underlying philosophy of the chosen approach.

Technical requirements

Here is the source code used in this chapter: `https://github.com/PacktPublishing/`
`Delphi-GUI-Programming-with-FireMonkey/tree/master/Chapter%2001/HelloWorld`.

Generally speaking, for the whole book, you need a computer with Delphi set up and a few additional libraries installed (such as **Radiant Shapes** (`https://getitnow.`
`embarcadero.com/?q=radiant+shapes`) and **CodeSite Logging** (`https://getitnow.`
`embarcadero.com/?q=codesite`)). Having other physical devices and setting up multiple platforms (iOS, Android, OS X/macOS, and Linux) other than Windows is a plus but not strictly needed to follow the flow of the book.

Approaching FireMonkey

In this section, we will explore the general background we need to properly introduce the FMX framework. **Delphi** is a longevous environment and it existed way before the FMX framework. We need to delve a bit into the roots of the Delphi tool to understand FMX in a better way.

When I was still a teenager, Delphi was the best development environment to build Microsoft Windows applications. I had some **Turbo Pascal** background knowledge and someone told me to give **Borland Delphi** a try in order to easily get into visual application development. That was during the time of **Windows 95** and the world, from an IT point of view, was much simpler than today. **DOS** and Windows had a very large share of personal computer coverage. The remaining part of the world was running **Linux** or **Macintosh** but with a limited share and only in very specific contexts. Even though the mainframe (such as **IBM AS400**) was still a thing, business companies were mostly running Windows.

Given that I had limited DOS programming knowledge, I spent a lot of time learning how to build a Windows GUI application and also experimented with other languages (such as **Visual Basic**, **Java**, and **Visual C++**) but Delphi has been my favorite right from the start.

The ability to easily build beautiful Windows applications through a designer is still a great plus and I really think this has been one of the key factors of Delphi's success. The following screenshot shows the **Delphi 10.4.1** Sydney splash-screen:

Figure 1.1

Apart from the convenient GUI **Rapid Application Development (RAD)** approach, built into an effective IDE, **Object Pascal** was a great language showcasing full **Object-Oriented Programming (OOP)** support, great C compatibility (perfect for Windows API calls), and featuring a very fast compiler. Generated applications also had outstanding runtime performances.

Looking at Delphi as a whole product, what surfaces is a fantastic tool, capable of letting developers focus on their application code while building fast, good-looking, modern applications – a shiny gem to easily deliver proper and curated GUI applications for the Microsoft Windows platform. In other words, the product performed very well by being more abstracted than raw C/C++ programming and proving to be way more powerful than Visual Basic (just to cite two of the biggest Delphi competitors over time).

This has been possible thanks to a framework shipped with the product: the **Visual Component Library (VCL)**. It acted as a sort of abstraction over the standard Windows controls, wrapping them in a more suitable and easy-to-use programming interface. A big difference with respect to other products has been that all this provided the ability to go back to being low-level and interact with the primitive control whenever needed.

Using the VCL was convenient and the library naturally evolved over two decades (at least!) of development by covering more and more Windows features and capabilities. Every Delphi developer felt at home while dealing with VCL components and most applications never needed to breach into low-level code. This meant higher productivity for the developer and I myself have seen several projects started with other technologies then being abandoned due to running over time for the project execution. Developer teams struggled to deliver functionalities in years while the same project revamped with Delphi came to a successful conclusion within months.

Today, the general scenario is much more complex than what it looked like in the late 1990s. We have seen the rise of mobile platforms and at the time I am writing this, a mobile **Operating System (OS)** (that is, **Android**) is now the most used OS worldwide. Also, the desktop platforms scene has seen some changes and now **Apple**'s **Mac OS X (aka macOS)** has much more widespread adoption than before (even if this is not equally true in every part of the world). **Linux** somewhat lost the race for desktop user adoption (I am not considering Android as a Linux family member, even though it is Linux kernel-based) but got a relevant position as a server-side platform (driving the web, one could say).

In the following graph, you can see OS distribution over time (period starting January 2009 to January 2020 – data source: `https://gs.statcounter.com`):

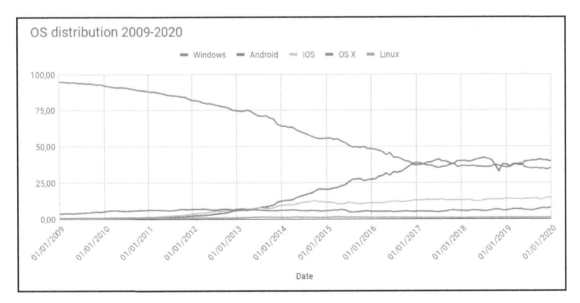

Figure 1.2

From the preceding graph, it is easy to spot the decline of Windows (the dominant platform from 2009 up to 2017) and the corresponding rise of Android (with it overtaking around 2018).

Generally speaking, today, multi-tier architectures have become the *de facto* standard for real projects that have to deal with a (possibly high) number of heterogeneous clients and need to provide users with proper interfaces in very different scenarios (desktop, mobile, web platforms across different device families). Due to this fact, it's more and more challenging to see applications as single projects, built for a specific platform (as it was for decades). The availability of an application across multiple platforms has become a very demanding feature (it has almost become an intrinsic standard requirement).

To build and maintain multiple (one per supported platform) development projects, just to deliver the same functionalities to all involved final users, is costly from several points of view. It is hard because developers will have to learn platform-specific behaviors, technologies, APIs, programming languages and deployment toolchains. This requires several different, demanding skills. It will likely mean more than a single development team will be required to accomplish the mission. This also quickly leads to maintainability issues over time, with a huge impact on the total cost and time-to-market of the product you are building. Even if building a specific application for each platform sounds too expensive, the other option (to build a single cross-platform application) has to address some not so evident issues.

First of all, nobody really wants to have a cross-platform application framework that only enables the developer to rely on the common shared part of all platforms. Obviously, this approach (the greatest common divisor) would fall short as platforms are diverging in terms of functionalities and even those capabilities available on all platforms usually have some interface/implementation details that make them hard (or expensive/inefficient) to abstract.

At the same time, nobody needs a framework that is a composition of specific functionalities gathered from all supported platforms as this would result in something actually enabling developers to build applications relying on all functionalities of all platforms but forcing them to write different code (in the same language, though) for each platform (that is, the general problem the framework has been built to solve).

The solution (as often happens) is something in between these two opposites. **FireMonkey** is in a nice spot, thanks to its mixed strategy. Being a sort of compromise, it goes without saying that this also translates into a list of related strengths and weaknesses.

In the following screenshot, you can see the Delphi IDE while designing a multi-platform application. The Android style is selected for use in the form designer, an iOS style preview is available through the **Multi-Device Preview** window (docked into the IDE on the right side) and an instance of the application is running on the Windows platform, just in front of the IDE itself—three styles visible at the same time, one per platform; three different binaries using the same (single) source code:

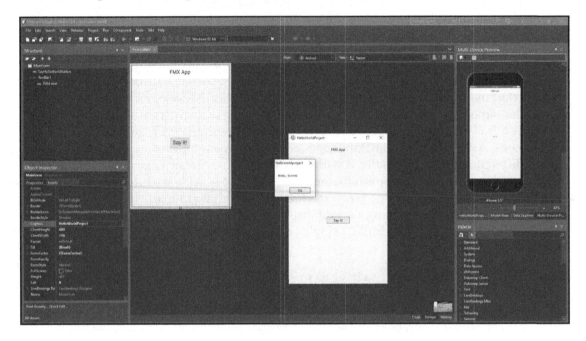

Figure 1.3

As you can see, the cross-platform capabilities of Delphi are highlighted in the preceding screenshot. You are building your application (using a single programming language: Delphi), addressing multiple platforms easily. You can design your app in the IDE, select one of the supported styles (each style being associated with a specific platform—Android, as shown in the previous screenshot) to preview the result in the form designer, seamlessly. At the same time, you can also have a look at **Multi-Device Preview** (part of the IDE set of functionalities named **Fire UI**). There, you'll get a realistic preview of how your application will look on other (multiple, eventually) platforms (iOS, which is also shown in the preceding screenshot).

Note that neither of the two mentioned platforms (Android and iOS) is the one that your IDE is running (Windows) and that your app will also be able to be executed, no code changes needed, on Windows (and Linux and OS X/macOS). *Doesn't sound great enough?* Then you can go even further and have your forms previewed, live, on a mobile device through another technology named **Live Preview** (still part of the Fire UI set, http:// docwiki.embarcadero.com/RADStudio/en/FireUI_Live_Preview). This time, you'll be able to preview (without having to wait until the compilation time) your UI on actual physical devices, without effort, with the screen of the device acting as an extension of your IDE.

In this section, we discussed the current scenario of software development, describing how and why we are facing the need to deliver multi-platform applications. We also introduced the FMX framework approach, with respect to the difficulties of the implementation of the same application using different tools to address different platforms.

In the next section, we are going to focus on the strategy FMX takes in order to provide different UI visuals to match the current platform of the running application.

Abstracting the visual part of your apps

The first version of the FMX framework was released in 2011 and already had one of its fundamental features, that is, the rendering of the UI was done completely from scratch, using the GPU. At the time, the GPU already supported technologies such as **shaders** (https://en.wikipedia.org/wiki/Shader), opening up a way to implement high-quality vector graphics, also considering the CPU growth in terms of computational power.

It became possible to build complex UIs, decorated with stunning effects and transitions, reaching the same appealing visuals typical of technologies such as **Flash** (the leading technology in modern and good-looking UIs, at the time). Given that **WinAPI** (thus, the VCL) and the new (at that time) **.NET** alternatives - **Windows Presentation Foundation (WPF)** were not covering the capabilities, the development team of FMX saw a great opportunity to build a new framework and, thankfully, they decided to take the chance.

This was the beginning of the framework having the opportunity to control every aspect of the UI implementation, opening the possibility to strongly abstract the UI from platform-specific controls and capabilities, but the number of controls available was limited and the first version of FMX was not really able to catch up with the same level of functionalities offered by the VCL on Windows.

The major new feature added with FMX 2 was bitmap styles: building a rich vector-based UI had a huge impact on performance and, at the same time, it was hard to implement some of the required components and peculiarities of the UIs. Adding the bitmap style capability moved FMX into the position to build effective, good-looking (*pixel-perfect* was the motto at the time), and performant applications, still keeping strong abstraction (through the style concept).

Even though it may seem a step backward (from pure vectors to bitmap styles), one should consider that most computer graphic evolution over the decades has gone in a direction where bitmaps were a central part of the game, thus most operating systems and drawing technologies are very familiar with bitmap (raster images) handling and have been optimized for that.

In the next couple of sections, we'll explain why the FMX framework is to be considered an application framework rather than a merely visual framework. It is important for you to properly understand that the general approach toward cross-platform application development has a lot to do with the visuals (we are focusing on visual applications), but there's much more to consider.

Looking beyond the UI

Even though many current prototyping tools tend to see an application as a bunch of views, we all know that a real application is not made only of a set of mere visual assets.

While building a cross-platform application, you obviously wish your visual application framework (FMX in the case) to deal with visual aspects but at the same time, to provide actual functionalities. This is because you will end up needing some level of interaction with the platform your application is running on.

Modern applications have to provide advanced functionalities, including some that are really basic (not always trivial, though), such as (multi-)touch support, and interaction with the system clipboard or with the filesystem. There are some possibly more specific topics, such as sensor integration (camera and positioning, for example), or other device-/platform-specifics such as notification systems, voice recognition, text-to-speech, and other advanced capabilities.

What I am trying to say is that FMX (and the Delphi RTL parts added by Embarcadero in recent years, available both for FMX and VCL) is much more than a visual framework, that is, it provides powerful abstractions that a developer can use to implement functionalities in a real cross-platform way.

This is true and evident in many areas we will cover throughout this book. Starting from *behavioral services*, with the aim of abstracting some device-/platform-specific behaviors (such as tab positioning in tab control or the default presentation mode of some components such as `TMultiView`, commonly used to implement mobile app menus). We could also abstract audio/video services, where a single, shared interface lets you access device cameras, microphones, or other common (but specific) aspects related to the multimedia area.

Just as a simple example, iOS and Android use different file formats for audio and video, thus to have a single `TMediaPlayer` component leveraging this difference is very convenient for the developer, that is, just ask the component to play or record audio/video with the same code.

Accessing the storage of the device (the *camera roll* for iOS or the *Gallery/Photos* apps for Android) is another great example. There are many functionalities (the device contact list to name another one), and it is hard to provide an exhaustive list.

You may think this list would represent the playground for the app developer but this is only partially true, that is, the VCL has a great level of abstraction over most Windows controls and APIs. Though, you always had a chance to go *back to the metal*, breaking this generally convenient abstraction and tweaking your code, adding low-level Windows API calls (without confining your possibilities to what the framework offers) and this is true also in the FMX framework, as we will see in the next section.

Back to the metal

Each strong abstraction can easily become a golden cage for its user. This also applies to software development and frameworks where you may obviously like the fact the framework is hiding the complexity underneath and providing a simple, clean, and comfortable place where the developer can live with fewer worries with respect to a more raw approach where everything is the developer's responsibility (embracing the subsequent complexity as much as they can afford).

At the same time, this kind of safe playground (always) has some boundaries and the developer can sometimes reach one of these boundaries and will go (or need to go) further.

Delphi always shined in this, letting you stay warm and safe with your VCL components wrapping Windows controls but, at the same time, letting you directly call whatever external function was available, including, of course, all WinAPI functions. When coming to FMX, as I said, I considered it to be more than a visual framework but rather an application framework; this is still true because, even if you can't handle FMX controls using APIs designed for native controls, you can still have your FMX (and RTL) Delphi code with platform-specific calls to the underlying APIs of the currently running OS.

This means you (from your Delphi code) can call any iOS library functions (as you would do in **Objective-C** or **Swift**). The same applies to Android where you can wrap (there is the **Java2OP** tool available for Embarcadero's registered users) the Java code you want to reach into Delphi classes and functions and have it available for your application developer. Even though this may seem like a kind of *last refuge* for the developer, it also represents a guarantee that your framework (FMX) is not closed and you are actually able to get back to the metal as much as you like or need.

For example, it is not unusual, when writing Android apps on custom devices (that is, those including industrial-level optical or **NFC/RFID** readers) to have the manufacturer of the device provide it with a standard Android OS image with the addition of some external **JAR files** with the libraries needed to properly interface with some device-specific features. Also, it guarantees that if Embarcadero is not providing you this or that API wrapper, you may proceed and generate it (manually or with a tool such as Java2OP) without having to wait for official support for that functionality.

In the next section, we'll try to consider the good and the bad coming from the peculiarities of the FMX approach.

Understanding the strengths and weaknesses

So far, we have simply introduced the FMX framework, exploring both the surroundings in which an FMX application should live and the context the technology was created in.

In this section, we will discuss how the FMX framework performs in the context that it is intended to be used in (the development of cross-platform applications). We'll consider some topics representing the strengths and weaknesses of the FMX approach. This should help you understand where in the big picture of multi-platform development tools we are.

Even though I think this introduction is relevant and should always be considered when evaluating FMX, there are some more practical aspects you may be interested in as well.

At first, consideration is given to the available continuity from VCL to FMX. At first sight, you can appreciate the fact that an experienced Delphi (VCL) developer has been provided with a chance to reuse part of their knowledge and experience while moving from a single (very specifically, Windows) platform development environment to a multi-platform (and/or cross-platform). The existence of FMX has enabled all those Delphi developers to not have to start from scratch (possibly doing this multiple times, one for each platform to address) while making their first steps into new scenarios (such as mobile platforms).

This is far better than having completely different toolsets, especially if you are building a project supporting multiple platforms and also if you are a developer of several projects targeting different platforms. Today, we are starting to diffusely see software (applications) as the backbone of industries and, more generally, today, everything seems to have a somewhat software core to it, with the IT industry gaining more and more consideration and respect. At the same time, this means a huge increase in the demand for software with sustainable costs in terms of money and delivery time, with more and more demanding quality factors.

As we already addressed earlier in this chapter, enabling existing developers (with their valuable experience baggage) to cover new platforms instead of having to raise new (inexperienced) developers, from scratch, on each new platform is obviously a game-changer opportunity that we should try to catch as much as possible. Just to name a clear example where this whole system shines, think about the data access components (and their knowledge) you can naturally use within applications of both the FMX and VCL frameworks. Every business application I've seen in 15 years (and counting) of consulting in the IT world had some data-centric part somewhere (often, the most relevant one). We will give an overview of this topic in `Chapter 4`, *Discovering Lists and Advanced Components*, covering FireDAC utilization within FMX applications.

Another strength factor FMX has is the possibility to add support for new platforms on the go. Just before the **Apple iPhone** launch (2007), nobody would have ever guessed that **Nokia's Symbian** OS would become a dead platform so quickly. The story of Microsoft mobile operating systems has also been subject to lots of change and with some bumps (think about Nokia acquisitions and Nokia X device families that are commercialized by Microsoft but with a custom Android OS on board).

Generally speaking, the mobile world has seen some new entries and some unexpected passings for a while. Today, we can reasonably think of the mobile world as having a substantial split between Android and iOS but, at the same time, we should always consider the fact that a new platform may arise tomorrow. Even though it is not really a *new* platform, the recent addition of Linux as a target platform for FMX GUI applications has been seen as a new conquest by the whole Delphi community. This addition has been possible thanks to the new implementation provided by a third-party vendor named **KSDev** (embodied by the original FMX authors, Eugene Kryukov and Alexey Sharagin) and the effort by Embarcadero to deliver a new compiler for the Linux (**Intel**) platform.

Together with the **LLVM compiler technology**, the inner architecture of the FireMonkey framework obviously is responsible for this accomplishment, which puts Delphi in a position to build effective UI applications on up to five different platforms, namely, **Microsoft Windows** (32-bit and 64-bit), **Apple OS X**, **Apple iOS** (and its simulator), **Google Android**, and **Linux** (**Ubuntu** and **RedHat** are officially supported by the compiler). From a strategic point of view, knowing the set of tools your IDE uses to actually build your applications is extensible (from the compiler to the UIs, including RTL and main DAC libraries) has a lot of value, especially if you are building large applications or you have an estimated lifespan for your projects of more than a couple of years.

Obviously, there are also some drawbacks. There always are, especially in such a high-demanding and dynamic environment made of moving targets (such as mobile platforms). The first obstacle is caused by the high-level abstraction I have described in this chapter. That is, Embarcadero's whole cross-platform solution is made of abstractions of services and functionalities where the construction of the UI is one of the most relevant in terms of the user experience (more and more of a central success factor for every piece of software out there, from the user's (and customer's) point of view). The key strengths of FMX (such as styles and the ability to perfectly mimic a native application's visual and interactive pattern fundamentals) should strongly mitigate the distance from the top of the abstraction and the bare metal on the ground, but this still remains a challenge.

The speed in innovation, especially in mobile platforms, we are perceiving today can be hard to handle and integrate into a highly abstracted framework. Embarcadero has some opportunities to solve (or at least mitigate) these problems and the first example in this direction has been the introduction of the `ControlStyle` property, with the platform option to let FMX use a corresponding native control where the developer decides it is worth doing so. This means that if the underlying OS has some advanced features (think about a device-wide orthographic corrector or an advanced dictation system) built into native controls, even cross-platform applications built in FMX can rely on them and not lack behind other apps.

In the same area, relatively young mobile platforms are continuously evolving, trying to improve their performance and so the FMX framework (and Embarcadero's ecosystem of technologies) will have to improve over time to catch up with native applications (whatever native *applications* might mean—you should read *native* here as in *non-cross-platform* applications).

There is a strange point in my mind and it isn't so easy to state whether it is a strength or a weakness, that is, Embarcadero is a relatively small player compared with Apple, Google, and Microsoft. This means they obviously have to strive to follow the major decisions of those big players (who all make money from things other than developer tools) and at the same time, it means they have a chance to be more agile and less extremist than them. They have the opportunity to provide a common path to all platforms (a very ambitious goal).

Summary

In this chapter, we introduced the FMX framework, including the historical reasons behind its creation and the context of where it all began. The philosophy of the framework (and its inner evolution) should act as support for the rest of the book and should provide you with some basic understanding for the rest of the content of the book.

If you are an experienced Delphi developer, this chapter should have provided you with a non-technical bridge from classic Delphi to the newer versions, now including this second application framework, other than the original VCL. At the same time, if you are a developer addressing Delphi for the first time, a little background information should help you go through the rest of the content of this book.

In the next chapter, we will explore differences and similarities with respect to the VCL. This will serve experienced developers to learn how many of their skills they can reuse and what they need to keep in mind for their new projects. If you are new to Delphi and will start with FMX, you will nonetheless find some useful basic information about how FMX works, so turn the page and go ahead!

2
Exploring Similarities and Differences with VCL

In the previous chapter, we covered a bit of the conceptual and historical context of the **FireMonkey Framework** (**FMX**) and its evolution. In this chapter, we will get our first direct contact with FMX, learning some basic concepts and covering some of its peculiarities using the **Visual Component Library** (**VCL**) as a meter of comparison. If you are an experienced Delphi developer (with some understanding of the VCL framework), you'll find this overview useful, where the usual pillars of your development life are translated into their use in the new FMX framework. You'll learn what topics/technological details remain untouched and which ones are different.

If you are new to the Delphi world, this is a convenient chance to learn about some peculiarities of this powerful development environment. Many times throughout the (long) history of Delphi, we have seen the same concepts borrowed by more recent (and sometimes more popular/hyped) technologies, proving that **Borland/CodeGear/Embarcadero** made steps (many times) in the right direction way ahead of other competitors.

In this chapter, we will cover the following topics:

- Understanding RTL for everyone
- Learning about component streaming
- Understanding the Style Designer
- Learning about components
- Handling the placement and sizing of components
- Understanding actions
- Learning about data bindings

After completing this chapter, you'll be familiar with most of the basic functionalities of the Delphi IDE in conjunction with the FMX framework. We'll learn about some very fundamental internal mechanisms of RTL, component streaming, the concept of style and corresponding support in the IDE, and so on. We'll also introduce some initial visual-related functionalities, such as anchors and alignments. *Take a deep breath and let's get started*!

Technical requirements

Here is the source code used throughout this chapter: `https://github.com/ PacktPublishing/Delphi-GUI-Programming-with-FireMonkey/tree/master/ Chapter%2002/NestedLayouts`.

Generally speaking, for the whole book, you need a computer with Delphi set up, and a few additional libraries installed (such as **Radiant Shapes** (`https://getitnow. embarcadero.com/?q=radiant+shapes`) and **CodeSite Logging** (`https://getitnow. embarcadero.com/?q=codesite`)). Having other devices and setting up multiple platforms (iOS, Android, OS X/macOS, and Linux) other than Windows is a plus, but not strictly needed to follow the flow of the book.

Understanding RTL for everyone

When we use the name Delphi, we often tend to mix the language (**Delphi** or **Object Pascal**, as you prefer) with the IDE (including all related tools). Sometimes, this gets extended to the libraries that come alongside the (main) product.

Moreover, it is not so unusual to push the concept even further and consider everything included, even third-party libraries (open source and commercial libraries from vendors).

This happens because we identify Delphi as a toolset to build applications and not merely just a language. This is true, to some extent. You are not going to execute a SQL query using the Delphi language; you'll use a **Data Access Components (DAC)** library for Delphi. This library will provide you, through the Delphi language and IDE (that is, providing convenient components to be used in the IDE), with the ability to execute SQL statements while returning some Delphi-compatible data structure (that is, a `TDataSet` descendant or equivalent) representing the result set.

There is one special library that comes with Delphi, the **Run-Time Library** (RTL, http://docwiki.embarcadero.com/RADStudio/en/Using_the_RTL_(Run-Time_Library)). It represents the foundation of every Delphi application. It provides core functionalities, such as type definitions, basic string manipulation routines, stream type definition and management facilities, and base classes such as TObject (the root class of Delphi object-oriented hierarchies) and TComponent.

A lot of classes and functions are made available to each Delphi developer through the RTL; let me name just a few unit names (a unit is a container for Delphi type and code definitions) that every experienced Delphi developer will have seen in almost every Delphi project out there: Classes, SysUtils, Math, DateUtils, and StrUtils.

A huge set of classes and functionalities are implemented in these units; even after 15 years (and counting) of my journey in learning Delphi, I am still amused when, I am looking for functionality that I need, I find it already implemented in the RTL. Let me name a very ubiquitous class: TStrings (or, more practically, TStringList). When we talk about string manipulation, obviously the first thought is to look at the language capabilities (*which operator is needed to concatenate two strings?*). But as soon as you move from theory to real code, you'll find yourself asking, *how do I deal with a list of strings? How do I sort them? How do I look for a specific entry? How do I save or load it to/from a file?* All these functionalities are built into the RTL of Delphi, just waiting for you to use them, regardless of the context in which you are going to run the final application.

If you are an experienced Delphi developer, you will already know this and will have loved it for many years. The high proficiency you get as a developer with Delphi is also due to its powerful RTL. We have all used TStream descendants, collections, the TList class and its siblings, and many more.

Over the years, RTL has kept growing, and many new functionalities have been added from version to version. Starting with Delphi 2010 version, we have seen the introduction of **generics**, as well as **JSON** format support, filesystem functionalities (IOUtils), network-related routines and types (**Net**), and **regular expressions**. Other features that were more recently built into RTL are **sensors, tethering, parallel programming, HTTP native interface**, **Bluetooth**, and **Beacon** support. All of these can be considered as building blocks that you can use to build your applications, regardless of whether you are using the VCL or FMX framework.

Once again, I'd like to stress how powerful and convenient for the developer this is. Having the chance to reuse a large part of developer knowledge even across such a transition (from a Windows-only framework such as VCL to a cross-platform multi-device-enabled framework such as FMX) is a huge added value for the Delphi product and its users (that is, us developers).

A very powerful aspect that has been part of the Delphi product since the very beginning of its history is that the development environment is component-based (actually, you are not forced to use components everywhere, but there is an evident inclination toward them throughout the entire Delphi development experience). In the next section, we are going to understand how components work in Delphi applications and uncover some internals about them.

Learning about component streaming

Talking about the **Rapid Application Development** (RAD) aspect of a product such as Delphi, we surely have to start with the TComponent class. The main concepts of RAD are based on the idea of pluggable, reusable, and configurable building blocks combined to implement complex applications easily while keeping the developer in an affordable complexity zone.

Back in the early days, it was easy (and quite popular) to divide Delphi into two big layers – namely, RTL and VCL. VCL was (and still is) a collection of components built to wrap Windows controls in a Delphi-friendly interface, adding uniformity for many functionalities across different components (that is, font settings, positioning, and alignment settings). It also enables the possibility to have them in the Delphi IDE at design time, allowing developers to actually visually design their applications (dragging components from the tool palette to a form or a frame and editing their properties through the **Object Inspector**).

This way, the developer can visually compose the UI of the application, adding custom code where needed, implementing what we now call delegates (event handlers), and then deploy the application as a (usually standalone) executable.

When this executable is run, the structure of components designed by the developer is properly created thanks to a feature called **component streaming** (which is the ability to represent a component tree and their properties in a binary or text format, embedded into executable resources).

FMX follows the same approach and the same streaming system but with some peculiar aspects. The main concept behind FMX is that the visual characteristics of components are closed into a style object – that is, a structured hierarchy of elements (primitives or composed themselves) stating how objects are nested and keeping a record of their property values as well.

So, the equivalent of VCL's **DFM** files are FMX's **FMX** files (yes, the file extension is **FMX**, like the framework's acronym). The same textual format used in FMX files is also used to store (uncompressed) style objects.

Styles in FMX are used to provide a proper platform-compliant visual definition for each UI element of the application. The style mechanism can be used to deliver a coherent application-wide custom style or to provide customized style definitions for specific classes or even specific instances.

Let's have a closer look. We can create a blank FMX application and drop TEdit and TButton instances on the main form. Then, we can switch from the visual designer to **Text View** (right-click on the Form Designer, then select **View as Text**; or just hit *ALT + F12*). You will see the textual representation of the form you are designing. The visual representation is straightforward and intuitive, as you can see in the following screenshot:

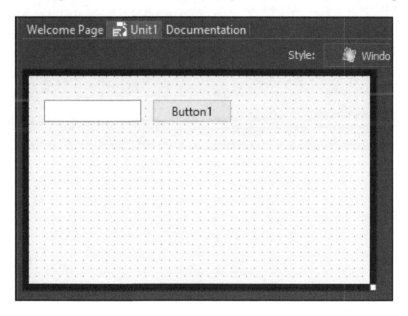

Figure 2.1

The visual representation is actually implemented by the Delphi IDE by creating (on purpose) a form instance with components on it. It is built reading a textual representation that is less human-friendly but is a more accurate definition of components as it includes more information (and not only those related to the visual aspect). In the following screenshot, you can see what the textual definition of our form looks like:

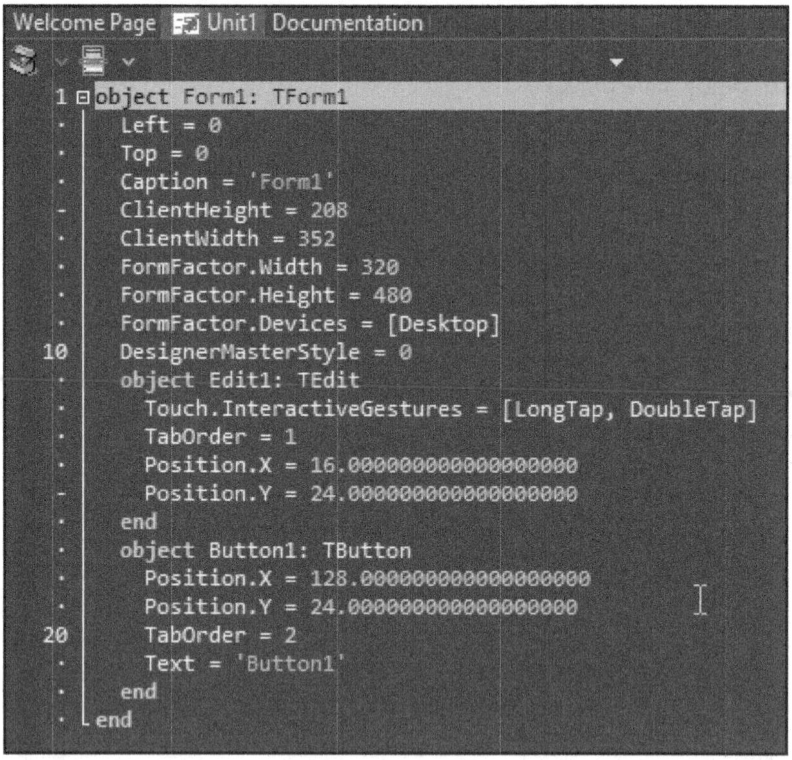

```
Welcome Page    Unit1  Documentation

 1 □object Form1: TForm1
 ·      Left = 0
 ·      Top = 0
 ·      Caption = 'Form1'
 -      ClientHeight = 208
 ·      ClientWidth = 352
 ·      FormFactor.Width = 320
 ·      FormFactor.Height = 480
 ·      FormFactor.Devices = [Desktop]
10      DesignerMasterStyle = 0
 ·      object Edit1: TEdit
 ·        Touch.InteractiveGestures = [LongTap, DoubleTap]
 ·        TabOrder = 1
 ·        Position.X = 16.000000000000000000
 -        Position.Y = 24.000000000000000000
 ·      end
 ·      object Button1: TButton
 ·        Position.X = 128.000000000000000000
 ·        Position.Y = 24.000000000000000000
20        TabOrder = 2
 ·        Text = 'Button1'
 ·      end
 · └ end
```

Figure 2.2

If we do the very same thing but with a VCL application, we can have a look at the differences across VCL and FMX. Let's set up the same simple form (using VCL this time) through the visual designer of the IDE, as we did before with FMX.

It should look as in the following screenshot:

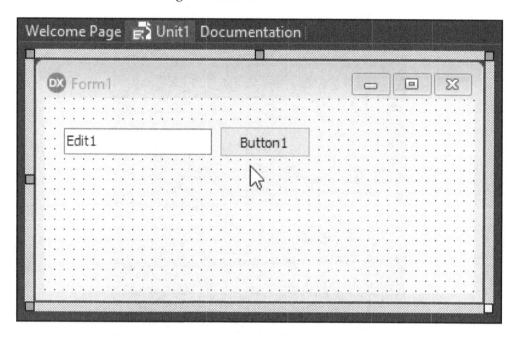

Figure 2.3

Then, we can switch to its textual representation, as we did for FMX. You may notice that switching from *code* (not Pascal code but the DFM text) to visual may take more time than the opposite operation as the IDE needs to actually build all the components and set all the properties according to the definition. In the following screenshot, you can see the text version of our Delphi VCL form:

```
Welcome Page    Unit1  Documentation

 1 ⊟ object Form1: TForm1
 ·      Left = 0
 ·      Top = 0
 ·      Caption = 'Form1'
 -      ClientHeight = 154
 ·      ClientWidth = 353
 ·      Color = clBtnFace
 ·      Font.Charset = DEFAULT_CHARSET
 ·      Font.Color = clWindowText
10      Font.Height = -11
 ·      Font.Name = 'Tahoma'
 ·      Font.Style = []
 ·      OldCreateOrder = False
 ·      PixelsPerInch = 96
 -      TextHeight = 13
 ·      object Edit1: TEdit
 ·        Left = 16
 ·        Top = 24
 ·        Width = 121
20        Height = 21
 ·        TabOrder = 0
 ·        Text = 'Edit1'
 ·      end
 ·      object Button1: TButton
 ·        Left = 143
 -        Top = 22
 ·        Width = 75
 ·        Height = 25
 ·        Caption = 'Button1'
30        TabOrder = 1
 ·      end
 ·   end
```

Figure 2.4

There are a lot of similarities and, at first sight, you may think the formats are identical. But there are differences, and some are significant and easy to spot:

- Components no longer have `Left` and `Top` properties, in favor of `Position.X` and `Position.Y` values; these values are now floating-point values (single type), instead of integer values. Please note that this does not apply to forms, though; they are still using `Top/Left` properties, as you can see.
- There is a global trend to replace `Caption` properties with `Text` properties (see `TButton.Caption` for VCL versus `TButton.Text` for FMX). Experienced Delphi VCL developers will take some time to get used to this change.

Once again, we are facing a concept (component streaming) that has been there for decades in VCL and now is also present in FMX. If you are going to learn about FMX and you already have a VCL background, you can benefit a lot from these similarities. A lot of things and functionalities (let's say alignment, anchors, actions, and many others) you will be immediately familiar with, effortlessly. Moreover, having basic functionalities shared across the two application frameworks also means that the general concept is not extremely different.

Nonetheless, there are some new high-level functionalities and differences with respect to VCL:

- Components can now be nested at will. This means you can put a `TLabel` component in a `TButton` instance or `Button` in a `TEdit` instance, or put a `TLabel` component in a `TButton` instance and put that button in a `TEdit` instance. There is no longer a clear distinction between components that can act as a container and others that cannot (as in VCL, where you can put a `TLabel` instance in a `TPanel` component, but not the other way around).
- Many properties have been enhanced (for instance, the `Align` property can now assume many more values with respect to VCL, enabling new features and placement fine-tuning).
- Generally speaking, FMX offers a much more modern approach to features such as filling (including gradients and bitmaps), stroke definition, opacity, and rotation of each component, enabling the developer to easily build modern, good-looking UIs.
- FMX has built-in support for animations and effects.

We will look at most of these functionalities in detail, but I want to also highlight that the IDE itself has changed through recent Delphi versions to help developers build cross-platform applications with FMX.

As I mentioned previously, one of the fundamental elements of FMX is the concept of **Style**. We will expand more on style in the next section (we'll also return to the topic for a deeper understanding in the following chapters), but for now, we can say that style is a definition of the visual aspects of a structure of components.

Understanding the Style Designer

A style object definition contains enough information to describe the organization of a set of components. It also includes the values of the components' properties. In practical terms, you may think of style as a (portion of a) Delphi UI definition without code and event handlers implementation. From a certain point of view, you may see the **Form Designer** (the IDE central window) as an editor for the style of your application.

There is another tool introduced specifically to manipulate FMX styles (and/or portions of them) within the Delphi IDE, which is the Style Designer.

In the previous section, I have shown you what FMX files look like and told you that styles are stored in the same format. If you drop a `TStyleBook` component on your form and activate the editing mode (double-click on it), the Style Designer will pop up.

The key parts of the IDE that are involved are as follows:

- The **Structure View** (which will list the contents of `StyleBook`)
- The **designer area** (where you will see a visual preview of the currently selected item, according to the Structure view)
- The **Object Inspector** (which will let you see and modify the actual values of the properties of the current item)
- The **Tool Palette** (where you will find components to be used in your composition)

I am not going to delve too much into the Style Designer functionalities here, but I want to bring to your attention that this new part of the IDE is there because of the ability of FMX to let you customize the visual aspect of a component (or a set of them) by simply editing the style definition for that component.

To get your first contact with the **Style Designer**, simply drop a `TLayout` component (kind of like `TPanel` but invisible) to create a container, give it some sizing, then add a `TEdit` instance, and a `TButton` instance. You should see something as in the following screenshot:

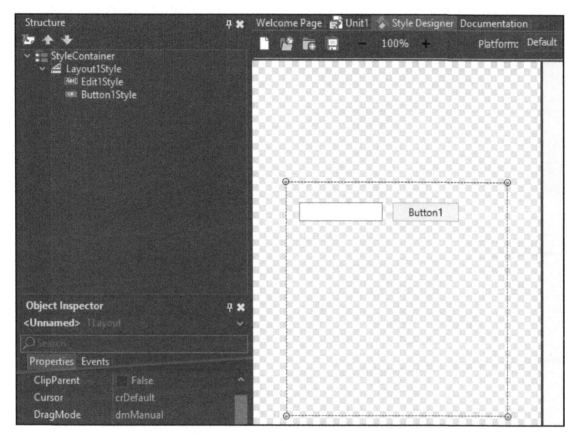

Figure 2.5

Now that you have content, you can close the Style Designer and its content will be stored within the `TStyleBook` component, in the FMX file of the form where it has been dropped.

The Style Designer also provides you with a way to save (export) this content to an external file. Two different file formats are available: **FireMonkey Style** (*.style) and **FireMonkey Style Binary** (*.fsf). This is an easy way to have a look at both the cleartext version and the binary version of your Style definition. The following code snippet shows our Style definition serialized in a human-readable (yet inefficient in size/memory consumption) way:

```
object TStyleContainer
  object TLayout
    StyleName = 'Layout1Style'
    Align = Center
    Size.Width = 268.000000000000000000
    Size.Height = 273.000000000000000000
    Size.PlatformDefault = False
    TabOrder = 0
    object TEdit
      StyleName = 'Edit1Style'
      Touch.InteractiveGestures = [LongTap, DoubleTap]
      TabOrder = 0
      Position.X = 16.000000000000000000
      Position.Y = 24.000000000000000000
    end
    object TButton
      StyleName = 'Button1Style'
      Position.X = 128.000000000000000000
      Position.Y = 24.000000000000000000
      TabOrder = 1
      Text = 'Button1'
    end
  end
end
```

You can see the nested structure of the textual representation, matching the *contained in* relationship rendered through the **Structure View** IDE window (in the previous screenshot): TStyleContainer is at the root, then you can spot the TLayout instance, containing both TEdit and TButton. For each object, properties (within their actual values) are represented through <Name> = <Value> pairs, as already discussed.

The same piece of information is actually stored in the executable resources (and in the FMX file where `TStyleBook` is described) in a more compact (yet human-unreadable) binary format, which can be represented in the familiar hex representation, as follows:

```
464d 585f 5354 594c 4520 322e 3501 060c
4c61 796f 7574 3153 7479 6c65 0378 0100
5450 4630 0754 4c61 796f 7574 0009 5374
796c 654e 616d 6506 0c4c 6179 6f75 7431
5374 796c 6505 416c 6967 6e07 0643 656e
7465 720a 5369 7a65 2e57 6964 7468 0500
0000 0000 0000 8607 400b 5369 7a65 2e48
6569 6768 7405 0000 0000 0000 8088 0740
1453 697a 652e 506c 6174 666f 726d 4465
6661 756c 7408 0756 6973 6962 6c65 0808
5461 624f 7264 6572 0200 0005 5445 6469
7400 0953 7479 6c65 4e61 6d65 060a 4564
6974 3153 7479 6c65 1954 6f75 6368 2e49
6e74 6572 6163 7469 7665 4765 7374 7572
6573 0b07 4c6f 6e67 5461 7009 446f 7562
6c65 5461 7000 0854 6162 4f72 6465 7202
000a 506f 7369 7469 6f6e 2e58 0500 0000
0000 0000 8003 400a 506f 7369 7469 6f6e
2e59 0500 0000 0000 0000 c003 4000 0007
5442 7574 746f 6e00 0953 7479 6c65 4e61
6d65 060c 4275 7474 6f6e 3153 7479 6c65
0a50 6f73 6974 696f 6e2e 5805 0000 0000
0000 0080 0640 0a50 6f73 6974 696f 6e2e
5905 0000 0000 0000 00c0 0340 0854 6162
4f72 6465 7202 0104 5465 7874 0607 4275
7474 6f6e 3100 0000
```

Now that you are able to recognize how style is defined and stored, we can easily make some considerations about how it works and its peculiarities. For example, you may want to note the following:

- You cannot assign event handlers through the Style Designer; this makes no sense because, as I said, a style only has something to do with visual aspects of the components (so no code is allowed in the definition).

- Components do not have a name (so you see `object TEdit` and not something such as `object Edit1: TEdit`) but they do have a `StyleName` property that is used to bind an actual instance of the component with this or that style object (through naming conventions and the use of the `StyleLookup` property each time `TFmxObject` is provided).
- Quite obviously, the binary representation tends to be much smaller in size (around 62% in this small example) than the equivalent cleartext representation; this is the reason why `TStyleBook` (and the executable resources) always contains styles in the binary format.
- The outer `TStyleContainer` object is just there as a convenient root for the Style Designer.

Now that we have covered the background about the similarities and differences between VCL and FMX, we can step a bit further and see how common tasks are achieved in FMX (with some links to how it is done in VCL).

In the next section, we are going to introduce what components are and which are the most commonly used. You will also learn about the hierarchy of classes implementing components in the FMX framework.

Learning about components

We can think of a UI as a set of components put together to build a visual unit that the user can interact with to perform some task or get some information.

The components are the building blocks of our UI, and FMX (and VCL as well) has plenty of components (usually a bit complicated). Let's start with three very common components – `TLabel`, `TEdit`, and `TButton`. The following diagram will help you consider the position of these three classes in the general Delphi component hierarchy, for the FMX version:

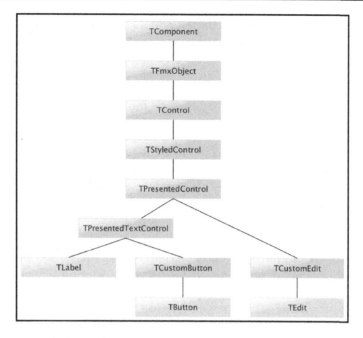

Figure 2.6

At the same time, these three classes have a corresponding version in VCL, and the following diagram provides a representation of the significant portion of the VCL class hierarchy around TEdit, TButton, and TLabel:

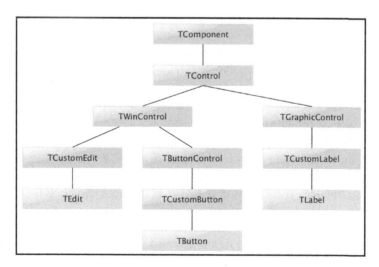

Figure 2.7

You can see, in *Figure 2.6* and *Figure 2.7*, the class hierarchy structures for FMX and VCL. For convenience, we can assume TComponent as the root class and you can easily spot some homonyms in the two representations – that is, TComponent, TControl, TCustomButton, TCustomEdit, and the three leaves, TLabel, TEdit, and TButton.

Some considerations around this topic may include the following:

- TFmxObject is the common ancestor for all FMX controls and adds some functionality, such as hold and manipulate (add, remove, search) children objects, clone capability, and the first level of support for styles; it also adds minor utilities, such as TagObject, TagFloat, and TagString properties (handy sometimes even if not properly elegant in every situation) that are indeed available for all subclasses.

- TControl, in FMX as well as in VCL, is the base class for components featuring a visual implementation; therefore, this class encapsulates a TCanvas component and introduces many properties related to the positioning, visibility (with opacity factor in FMX), and sizing of a component, including concepts such as margins and paddings (and rotation in FMX). Most of FMX's components are TControl descendants and they are divided into primitives (TShape and descendants, such as TLine or TRectangle) and styleable components (TStyledControl and descendants, such as TButton, TEdit, or TLabel).

- TStyledControl implements the style mechanism, which is truly fundamental in FMX; each component has a style object, which is built by looking up available styles collections (TStyleBook of the current scene, application-wide style, and platform styles) through a simple (and overridable, when needed) naming convention.

- The TPresentedControl class introduces a central concept in FMX – that is, components are internally seen as a model (data) with a presentation. We will delve into this concept more deeply in Chapter 07, *Understanding FMX Style Concept*, but basically, this is what enables different ControlType value selection in FMX objects (enabling the developer to choose from a style-based presentation and a native, OS-provided one).

- TLabel and TButton seem much closer in the FMX hierarchy; this somehow can be reduced to the fact that, with great approximation, a label is just text to be shown to the user and a button is text that the user can click (or tap). This is not really significant, but it is a good hint that FMX has a more radical abstraction level in its UI with respect to the behavior of the components. This results in (or at least should enable) more flexibility and separation between what a component does (behavior) and what it looks like (presentation).

I decided to pull you through this very general comparison between the FMX and VCL component hierarchies seeing as they have such simple (yet essential) components, such as `TEdit`, `TButton`, and `TLabel`. Even in this basic scenario, without complex components, you can clearly understand how VCL was designed based on Windows native controls. For example, we can consider the `CreateParams` method of `TCustomButton` and `TCustomEdit` to understand that they differ simply by creating a different subclass of Windows controls.

From a general point of view, these two VCL classes are a clear example of how the Windows API has been wrapped into Delphi components to improve the ease of use. On the other hand, FMX has been designed to completely abstract the presentation details of its components. In recent versions of the framework, the ability to implement the presentation through the use of native control has also been introduced. This provides a convenient shortcut for those situations where you really want to benefit from having native control instead of a lookalike style-based implementation.

Now that we have introduced some background about components and how VCL and FMX relate to each other (spotting some resemblances and some diversities), we can take it another step further. Each UI view is a composition of components that can be wrapped in two kinds of containers: a form (`TForm`) or a frame (`TFrame`) descendant.

This statement has been true in Delphi (VCL) for a very long time (**version 5**, which means around the summer of 1999), back when frames were introduced. Once you have a set of components in a container, the problem of positioning and aligning them arises. This seemingly innocent problem can be very hard to solve if you want to keep a decent and functional composition regardless of the container changing size or orientation.

One of the hardest problems in software development for decades has been the difficulty of adapting a UI to different screen sizes or resolutions, or, in modern terms, achieving a responsive UI.

There are different recipes to approach and possibly achieve this goal. We aim at having a single, adaptive yet functional and good-looking UI, but the problem is way harder to solve than it seems at a first glance.

Let's see what the functionalities are that can help us to deal with such a difficult task. As often happens, we can soften the problem if we learn about the tools we can use to address it and split it into simpler tasks. In the next section, we are going to introduce some topics around the concept of the placement and sizing of visual components – a crucial aspect to achieve a modern-looking and responsive UI.

Handling the placement and sizing of components

One of the central topics about visual components is obviously how they are placed and arranged in the view. There are many different strategies available and, historically, many technologies (other than Delphi, I mean) have tried to address the problem to provide a placement and sizing strategy that fits well even when the surrounding environment (that is, the main container of the view – the window) changes in size or aspect ratio.

Several attempts have been made over the years, but we as developers are still struggling to achieve a truly visually responsive UI. Some approaches were code-based, trying to describe through code some model of the positioning/sizing of components that would dynamically adapt to changes at runtime. Some other approaches were event-driven, with many subsequent calculations to fit the whole set of components onto the available screen space. There are drawbacks to each approach, of course.

Delphi's choice has been to stick to a sort of absolute positioning of components at the base, but with the addition of features to enable some sort of relative positioning and sizing (anchors and alignments) together with the introduction of a chain of parenthood to make every component relative to its parent (simplifying nesting and elastic UI structures). All this retains the ability to design UIs in the IDE, a great simplification for the developer, who is not forced to imagine their UI reading (possibly not intuitive) code lines.

In the next section, we are going to introduce **anchors** and talk about how their use can greatly simplify the relative positioning of controls.

Understanding anchors

The first way to obtain a responsive UI is to avoid absolute positioning (and, when it makes sense, avoid absolute sizing). In this section, we will learn about anchors and the functionalities that they enable. Even if it may seem (and probably is) the most natural approach, you should not think of having `TEdit` at a certain point (see the `Position.X` and `Position.Y` properties in FMX, and `Left` and `Top` in VCL) and of a certain size (`Width` and `Height`).

The main problem with this approach is that, usually, the container of your `TEdit` component may change its size over time. This may happen because we are talking about a form that the final user is resizing at runtime. The same happens when we are dealing with a mobile application, and the size of the form (that is, tied to the size of the device's display) is different according to the specific device the user has (for example, a phone with a 5-inch screen or a 10-inch tablet). Moreover, even assuming that we are all using the very same device, the form may be forced to change its size (swapping width and height) just because of a change of orientation of the device.

The fact is that you would like your components to nicely accommodate the container's new size. We can take a login form as a simple example, as follows:

Figure 2.8

As you can see, this form is 250 x 125 in size and the components have been disposed to properly fit its area in a typical login layout. The only property used so far is `Position`, which has been set for all the components on the form. Now, think about what you would consider natural to happen when the form is resized and try to experience yourself to see what actually happens. The following screenshot shows the situation after you have augmented the `Width` value of the form:

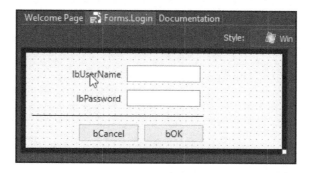

Figure 2.9

In the previous screenshot, some space is left unused on the right side of the form. Components are not changing their position nor their size. In the following screenshot, we can see similar behavior when changing the Height value of the form. The unused space is now at the bottom of the form and components are left in their original position:

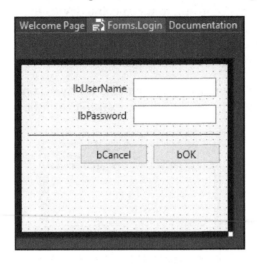

Figure 2.10

Obviously, this is not the kind of user experience you want to deliver to your end users/customers, and I would not be surprised if this turns out to be the reason why so many login forms out there are not resizable, cutting the problem at the root. Anchors is a property available in each TControl descendant to determine how the component is pinned (anchored) to its parent.

A first enhancement to our login form would be to set the **Anchors** property (you can spot it, fully expanded, in the **Object Inspector** window, visible in the following screenshot) of the two TEdit instances in order to have their width automatically changed as the form is resized horizontally:

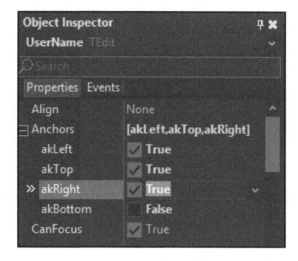

Figure 2.11

As you can see in the previous screenshot, just include **akRight** (TAnchors is a set of TAnchorKind values) through the **Object Inspector**, and they will always follow the right edge of the form. The same change can be made for the TLine instance used to draw a divider between the two edits and the two buttons on the form.

If you resize the form horizontally, now, you will see a more intuitive behavior, but what about the buttons at the bottom and what if we change the height of the form? The following screenshot shows how the edges of the edit boxes are kept at a fixed distance from the right border of the form:

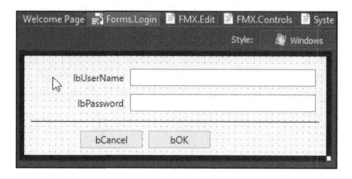

Figure 2.12

We may also want to change the Anchors property for the two buttons, anchoring them to the bottom and right edge of the parent (instead of the default, which is the top and left edges). The TLine instance should be anchored to the Left, Right, and Bottom edges. The resulting behavior is visible in the following screenshot:

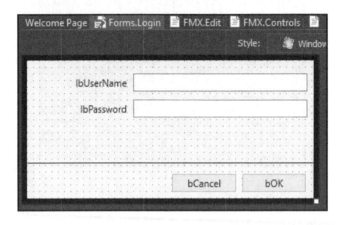

Figure 2.13

Now, our user is free to resize the form, and we'll see the position and size of the contained controls dynamically adjusted accordingly.

A lot of other small changes can be made to this form to improve the UX, starting from setting the initial position (by setting the Position property to the poScreenCenter value, for instance) to applying some size constraints (this only applies to desktop platforms, of course, and can be easily done through the Constraints property in VCL). I obviously agree that this form is still quite basic, but it should give you a basic understanding of how useful the Anchors property (available both in FMX and VCL) is.

If anchors are a straightforward way to determine how a component is stretched accordingly to its parent's dimensions, alignments are another possibility (with some overlaps with anchor behavior) to implement the dynamic positioning and sizing of your UI controls.

Learning about alignments

The `Align` property, once again available in all `TControl` descendants, can be set to determine how the component should align inside its container. It is available both in VCL and FMX, but the set of available values in FMX is much larger than in VCL (please refer to the documentation of the `Vcl.Controls.TAlign` and `FMX.Types.TAlignLayout` types for a comprehensive overview, available at `http://docwiki.embarcadero.com/Libraries/en/Vcl.Controls.TControl.Align` and `http://docwiki.embarcadero.com/Libraries/en/FMX.Controls.TControl.Align`, respectively).

Some possible values for `Align` are quite straightforward – that is, `Top` (`alTop` in VCL) will let your component be positioned in the top part of its parent and it is more or less equivalent to positioning it at the top-left corner of the parent, setting `Width` the same as its parent, and `Anchors` to (`akLeft`, `akRight`, `akTop`). You are then free to decide the height of your component, but it will always stick to the higher part of its parent.

Of course, you can set the `Align` property to `Top` for more than a single component inside the same parent and they will pile up starting from the top of the container. It is quite straightforward to see (or imagine) how the `Left`, `Right`, and `Bottom` values for the `Align` property act (spoiler – they will behave exactly how you would expect and how you have seen with `Top`).

The `Client` value means *fit all the available space in the parent* – in other words, fill the area of the parent not already occupied by other components with the `Align` property set (for example, to the side of the parent), and it is more or less equivalent to manually positioning and sizing your component in order to cover all the available space and setting all four anchors.

`QuickEdit` (a functionality introduced since version **10.1 Berlin**) provides (for both FMX and VCL) the opportunity to quickly set the `Align` property of a component, and provides a visual representation of the available options. In the following screenshot, you can see the VCL flavor and notice the visual representation of available values for the `Align` property:

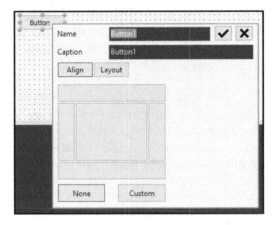

Figure 2.14

The same functionality is available in FMX and, if you start `QuickEdit` over an FMX component, you may notice that the same dialog pop ups but with several more available values for the **Align** property. See the following screenshot and notice that the dialog will, at the same time, provide the ability to change the current value for the property and provide a visual explanation of most of the available values:

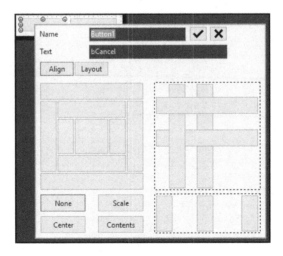

Figure 2.15

As you can see, FMX has a lot more options; let's have a quick look at some of them:

- **Contents**: Your component will fit its parent without considering any other sibling alignment. They also can be useful to set up an overlay of the parent.
- **Fit** (plus **FitRight** and **FitLeft**): Your component will fit the parent area, but preserving its aspect ratio, the `Right` and `Left` variants allow you to also determine which side of the parent stick to.
- **Center**: Your component center will always be in the center of the available area of the parent; no anchors are set, so the size of your component will not be affected by this setting.
- **Scale**: Your component will preserve its aspect ratio and its relative positioning with respect to the parent – that is, all anchors are set.
- **Vertical** (and **Horizontal**): Your component will fit the height (`Width`) of the parent but will not be affected by changes in the width (`Height`) of it. This can be quite useful to create column (row)-based layouts. Anchors, in this case, are set to `[Top, Bottom]` (`[Left, Right]`).

As said, alignment (set through the `Align` property) can use anchors to implement the specific behavior, and when this happens, it has a higher priority on whatever value you may set for those anchors interested by the `Align` setting. This does not mean that in other cases you may still want to change anchors, and it does actually affect the final result. For instance, you may want to add a left or right anchor to a component having `Align = Vertical` and have, in this way, a column that will follow the edge of its parent.

Anchors and alignments (in addition to margins and paddings) represent the best ways to determine a component position and size in a dynamic way. This will help you build UIs that are more prone to fit in different scenarios (such as different screens or screens with different densities). However, there is another important step you will have to learn in order to be effective in this area – that is, to learn about FMX's `TLayout` and its descendants. Basically, this will let you compose different alignment and anchor settings by nesting components and containers at your will. We will see more on this topic in `Chapter 9`, *Building Responsive UIs*.

If the concept of alignment is shared across FMX and VCL, FMX seems far more advanced in this area, not only because of the larger set of values you can choose for the `Align` property but also because of the intrinsic capabilities to nest components one inside the other. This is illustrated in the following screenshot:

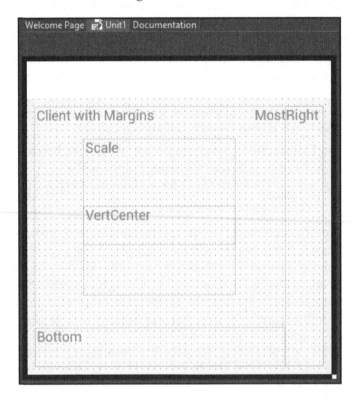

Figure 2.16

So, you can nest layouts to achieve the desired alignment by composition and the capability of FMX objects to have content that is also outside their boundary (it is difficult to achieve something similar in VCL, where you can easily paint whatever you like inside your component, but it is hard to have some content overflowing outside the area of it).

Next, let's move on to understanding one of the most powerful Delphi features – actions and action lists.

Understanding actions

Actions and action lists were introduced in **version 4**, and I have used them largely in VCL projects. Actions are a great yet simple way to properly divide application code from the presentation layer, providing an abstraction of something that can be executed and an easy way to bind the execution trigger to one or more UI elements.

The fact that abstraction is available for manipulation at design time is a great benefit in terms of the RAD approach. But at the same time, it keeps your code cleaner than having it spread out through event handlers of your UI elements.

Additional features include the ability to define a **hint text** and an image of the action (helping to achieve a visual continuity throughout your UI) and to define when the action is enabled and/or visible in a single code point (the OnUpdate event handler).

If you are an experienced Delphi developer, you will be happy to know that actions have been refactored in order to be shared across VCL and FMX. This means you can continue using this approach in your applications and get the same benefits. The following screenshot exemplifies this for you:

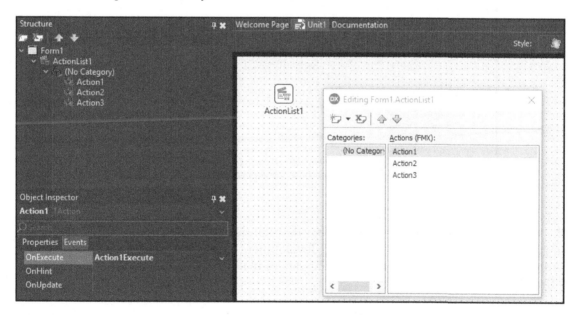

Figure 2.17

One thing that has changed in this area is `TImageList`. It has been completely re-implemented in FMX in order to properly support some very common functionalities, such as the ability to have a single image as a source of several different sub-images (seen as a portion of the main image), layering capabilities, and proper support for multi-res bitmaps, which greatly simplifies having the same application in execution across a wide range of devices with possibly very different resolutions. The following screenshot exemplifies `TImageList`:

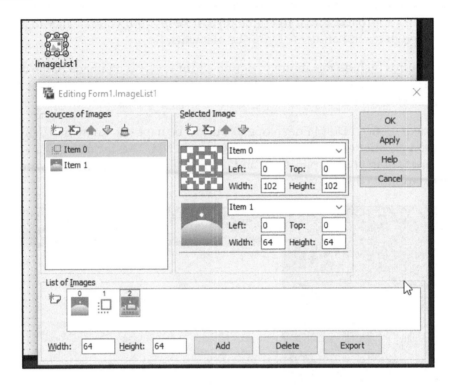

Figure 2.18

Back to actions, it is important to remember that standard actions are available, and some of them are important especially for mobile development. For example, let's say you need to prompt the user to select a picture from the device media gallery; there is an action for that – that is, `TTakePhotoFromLibraryAction`.

So, what to do when we want a fresh picture? `TTakePhotoFromCameraAction` comes to the rescue. Once you have the picture and you have added something to it (maybe applying some of the available effects or filters that FMX comes with), you may want to use `TShowShareSheetAction` to share the picture on your favorite social network site or instant messaging app.

The following screenshot shows this example:

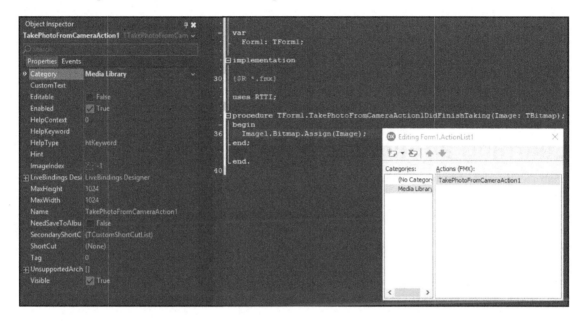

Figure 2.19

These three actions (`TTakePhotoFromLibraryAction`, `TTakePhotoFromCameraAction`, and `TShowShareSheetAction`) enable the Delphi mobile developer to focus on the application code and have a completely cross-platform (iOS and Android) abstraction of some very common tasks on a mobile device. Starting the default camera app and grabbing the new photo only takes a snap – that is, simply adds the standard action to a `TActionList` instance, links a button to that action, and implements the `OnDidFinishTaking` event handler (to copy the obtained bitmap in a `TImage` control, for example).

Mobile platforms have strict regulations for software to access the device's capabilities. Delphi provides support to manage this aspect (**Project** | **Options** | **Application** | **Uses Permissions**). This covers the declarative part of the issue. On some systems (Android, for example) you may also need to interactively ask the user to grant permissions to your app. This is the case of camera access and you can see in the included demo how to deal with it.

At this point, we have seen that FMX offers a quite coherent scenario with respect to VCL. Some functionalities are present in both frameworks and, in some cases, they act exactly the same way or have been enhanced or extended in some way. This is not true when it comes to the **data binding** strategy: the two frameworks here have a very different approach (and I can see the pros and cons of both).

Learning about data binding

Historically, data binding in VCL has always had a `TDataSet` instance as subject. The data has always been stored in a `TDataSet` descendant and manipulated through the `TDataSet` interface (every experienced Delphi developer can list most of the method names of `TDataSet`, such as `Edit`, `Post`, `Cancel`, `Prior`, and `Next`). A `TDataSet` instance can be seen as a list (or array) of records, representing some dataset with a rectangular shape (rows and columns). The dataset has a state (a current record, a modality such as browsing versus editing, some filtering and/or sorting conditions, and so on) and acts like what today would be called a model for the data (including extended metadata and constraints).

Once we had a place to store data, the problem of surfacing this data to the UI became apparent. Delphi had a set of standard components used to manipulate strings, dates, multiple-choice selections, and a set of classes (components) to compose the UI in order to present and enable interaction with the user. These were `TEdit`, `TLabel`, `TComboBox`, `TListBox`, `TStringGrid`, and many other components available in the **Standard** and **Additional** palettes of the Delphi IDE.

So, you could easily build a UI with those components and with some custom, application-specific code, provide functionalities to move data from `TDataSet` (probably after loading the dataset from a database) to the controls (to let the users see and edit them) and vice versa (to store the modified or newly entered data back to the database, through `TDataSet`). Cleverly, and with great impact on the RAD capabilities of the product, a high-level abstraction was introduced decades ago, with a mediator component between `TDataSet` and the set of controls developed to build the UI of a data-driven application.

Its name is TDataSource, a nonvisual component that provides bidirectional access and notifications across the two ends of a data link. Several kinds of data links are available, the most common being dataset-wide (think about a grid with data from the dataset and syncing the dataset's current record with the grid's current row, or dispatching information about the state of the dataset to the grid) or field-wide (think about an edit control showing the content of a specific field of the current record of the dataset and letting the user change that value).

This strategy led to the introduction of a set of components built to surface data of a dataset to the UI layer – that is, most standard Delphi controls (TEdit, TLabel, TComboBox, and so on) got a sibling control with the same name and TDB as prefix (TDBEdit, TDBText, and TDBCombobox). This means that the control would have been linked to some data stored in a dataset (thus, most of the time, coming from a database), passing through the TDataSource mediator. For decades, VCL developers built data-driven UIs using data-aware controls, and this approach proved to be successful and efficient as long as data was accessible through the TDataSet interface and components designed for the actual content of the fields were available.

In more recent times, the concept of binding got wider, and today, we tend to consider binding as a general concept that does not specifically involve a dataset, or at least not always a conventional one. Modern applications can have several data sources (think about databases, remote services, onboard sensors, and so on), so we can see a lot of frameworks and techniques arising to address the binding problem (how to tie data to a UI element, eventually in a two-way relationship) in a more general way.

FMX comes without data-aware components, embracing a new binding technology that is expression-based, and it is known by the name **Live Bindings**. The idea is that you can write an expression involving one object and another one to bind the properties of the two objects together.

A minimal example is to bind the `Text` property of a `TEdit` component to the `Text` property of a `TLabel` component – that is, we are defining a simple one-way relationship (since the `TLabel` does not provide a way to modify its value), basically meaning we want to see the content of the edit control copied into the label control each time it is modified. You can see this in the following screenshot:

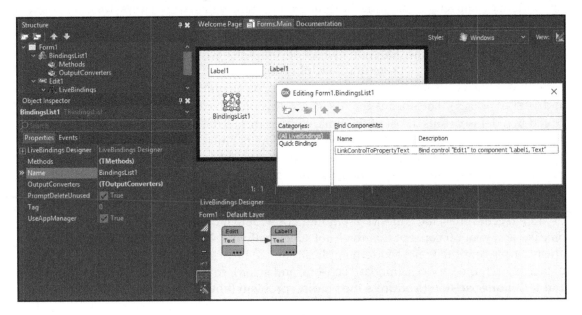

Figure 2.20

The mechanism is completely standalone and can be set up even at runtime (as you would do with any other component in Delphi). However, the IDE provides you with a convenient way to define Live Bindings at design time through the **LiveBindings Designer** and through some shortcuts that you can trigger on bindable components (for example, for a `TDataSet` descendant, just right click on it, in the Form Designer, and select the **Bind visually** item). The expressions are stored in a nonvisual component (`TBindingsList`) holding a list of bindings (there are different kinds of bindings, according to the nature of the values and the controls involved) that can be manually configured or manipulated through the LiveBindings Designer.

The LiveBindings Designer consists of an IDE window where you can see represented all the bindable components (more precisely, you initially see the most relevant ones and you can always add any others) in a visual way (see *Figure 2.20*). The bindable objects and their properties are represented with rectangles listing the available members, while binding expressions are represented by connectors (lines) between the members. This visual representation (which can grow a lot if you have many controls involved) can be organized in layers for your convenience and sometimes can be useful as a sort of documentation of how the data flows into the application (of course, this may be suitable only for developers and end users or project managers).

To create a new binding, simply drag a member of an object onto the member of the destination object. In our example, drag the Text property of the Edit1 component onto the Text property of Label1; refer to *Figure 2.20*. A new TLinkControlToProperty binding will be added to a TBindingList object (created on the purpose if not available) and you are set – though, at runtime, if you set the Edit1.Text value to something, you will see the same value in the Label1.

The same mechanism is used to bind datasets or a list of objects to controls (grids or, more likely on mobile applications, lists). I will cover this topic extensively in Chapter 6, *Implementing Data Binding*, dealing with list components (TListView, to name one) and datasets (data binding).

As a note on Live Bindings, please remember that this powerful technology is available both in FMX and in VCL, and, although an experienced VCL developer can be totally acquainted with the traditional data binding approach of data sources and data-aware components, it may represent a nice and quick solution in several circumstances, especially when dealing with bindings across visual components, not involving datasets at all.

Summary

In this chapter, we acquired a general overview of how FMX works, building some bridges with the pre-existent VCL approach where available. Some concepts explained in this chapter will act as a background for the coming chapters, where these basics will be used all together to build modern UIs with FMX.

It is always hard to compare two frameworks, especially when their chronological distance can be measured in decades, but, given some common traits and some evident effort (in FMX) not to completely disrupt the past Delphi experience, I hope you finished this chapter with more confidence about FMX and its philosophy.

In the next chapter, we will get to know some other FMX components, especially the most common and used ones.

Section 2: The FMX Framework in Depth 2

This section takes us for a deep dive into the most important FMX capabilities and concepts. They are discussed in detail and with the help of many useful examples. We are going to address commonly used components and technologies in order to deliver modern, responsive, and effective applications on multiple platforms.

Apart from visual topics, other related technologies and concepts are explained. Most applications rely on data access and data binding in order to effectively implement functionalities for the final user; we will discuss how this relates to FMX in this section.

This section contains the following chapters:

- Chapter 3, *Mastering Basic Components*
- Chapter 4, *Discovering Lists and Advanced Components*
- Chapter 5, *Using FireDAC in FMX Applications*
- Chapter 6, *Implementing Data Binding*
- Chapter 7, *Understanding FMX Style Concept*
- Chapter 8, *Divide and Conquer with TFrameStand*
- Chapter 9, *Building Responsive UIs*
- Chapter 10, *Orchestrating Transitions and Animations*

3
Mastering Basic Components

In the previous chapter, we provided an overview of the main similarities and differences between FMX (the main focus of this book) and VCL (the other long-standing application framework for Delphi). In this and the next chapter, we will cover the main FMX components that you are going to use while building real-life applications.

In this chapter, to get the most out of your FMX applications, you will learn how components work and familiarize yourself with the most commonly used ones. There are two big sets of components: simple elements (usually single, independent components) and more complex elements that can handle larger amounts of data.

In this chapter, we will cover the following topics, all of which are related to the first set of components (simple ones):

- Understanding the TText component
- Understanding shapes
- Managing images effectively
- Learning about buttons

The second set of components (those that handle more data) will be covered in the next chapter, where we will introduce Lists, Treeviews, Grids, Drawers, and Panels. Even if there are several other components available in the FMX framework, they are usually ubiquitous, and some of the mechanisms you will learn about in this and the next chapter are generic. Mastering them is a requirement if you wish to deliver the best user experience through your applications (either for mobile or desktop platforms).

Let's get started!

Technical requirements

The following link will take you to the source code that will be used throughout this chapter: `https://github.com/PacktPublishing/Delphi-GUI-Programming-with-FireMonkey/tree/master/Chapter%2003`.

Generally speaking, for the entirety of this book, you'll need a computer with Delphi set up and ready to go, as well as a few additional libraries installed (such as **Radiant Shapes** (`https://getitnow.embarcadero.com/?q=radiant+shapes`) and **CodeSite Logging** (`https://getitnow.embarcadero.com/?q=codesite`)). Having other devices and setting up multiple platforms (iOS, Android, macOS/OS X, and Linux) other than Windows is a plus, but not strictly needed to follow the flow of this book.

Understanding the TText component

Text is, without a doubt, one of the most fundamental elements of every application. In this section, we will take a close look at the `TText` component, along with another ubiquitous and related component known as `TLabel`.

Before GUIs became prominent in the UI scenario, text was there to build the most basic human-computer modern interactions available (you may want to consider blinking a LED, emitting a beep sound, or controlling a switch as one of the most basic **Human-Computer Interactions** (**HCIs**) ever).

This doesn't mean dealing with text is always simple. A lot of features and details become available when text is your subject. For example, the text should have a size, a typeface (or font family), a color, and a wide set of options available (including bold, italic, strikeout, and underline, all of which are popular examples).

After this, you will find yourself considering how to properly align the text with respect to some boundaries, how to—and whether you should—trim it if there's not enough room to print it out completely, or whether to apply word (or character) wrapping. Sometimes, you may want to stretch it to fit a space, while other times, you will need it to automatically grow in size so that it represents a string as a whole. You may also need to control its visibility, rotate it or change its opacity, or – last but not least – control its level of interaction with the user (so that it responds to a click or having the user tap on it rather than having it transparent with respect to user interaction).

The following screenshot shows the properties you can use to align the text with respect to various parameters (the following is two screenshots merged into one since the list of properties is pretty long):

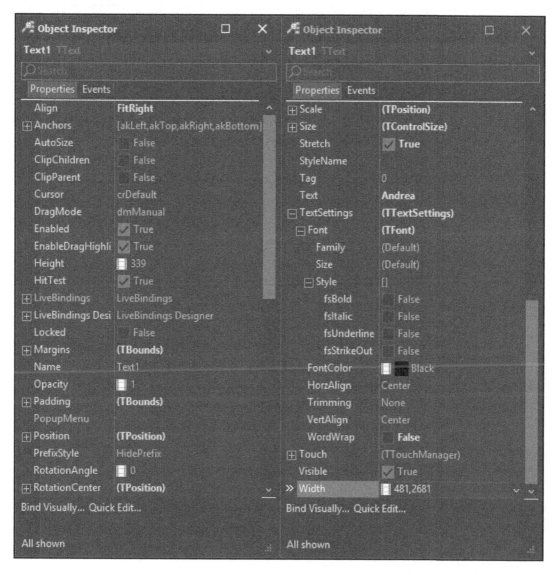

Figure 3.1

As shown in the preceding screenshot, all these functionalities are available and ready to use thanks to the `TText` component, the building block that's used in FMX to represent text and its options. In the preceding screenshot, you can see all the component properties available in the IDE's **Object Inspector** window for a `TText` object. Most of the properties should be straightforward and allow the developer to have full control of every aspect of the text's visuals in any modern application.

The following image shows some of the capabilities of `TText`, including some (specifically clipping) capabilities that are available for every `TFMXObject` but particularly helpful when dealing with text:

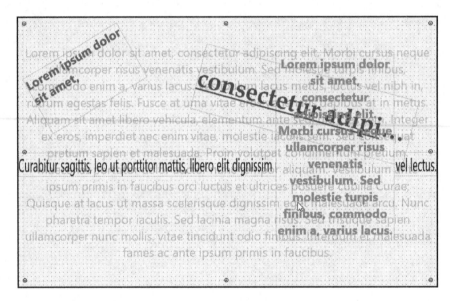

Figure 3.2

Moreover, you may want to apply other graphic effects to your components so that you can, for example, apply a shadow or reflection effect to your text. These (and other effects) will be used throughout this book, and their usage is generally very straightforward: just add them as children of the item (component) you want to target and enable them by setting the **Enabled** property to **True**.

The following screenshot shows some of the properties that are available:

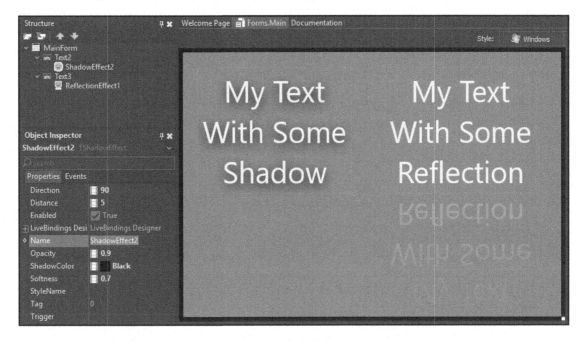

Figure 3.3

You should know that every effect has its own properties so that you can tune them appropriately.

If you are an experienced VCL Delphi developer, you may think TText is the equivalent of VCL's TLabel component, but that's not the case. TText is to be considered a primitive text object, more or less how a TRectangle shape is typically viewed as a primitive for a button object.

Next, we'll look at the TLabel component.

Learning about the TLabel component

The FMX TLabel component is a style-enabled component (a
TPresentedControl component, as explained in Chapter 2, *Exploring Similarities and
Differences with VCL*), which means you should not blindly overlap the concept of TLabel
with the usual TText-based implementation.

For the **Windows** platform, the standard TLabel style is only composed of a TText object
named *text*. This is used to provide a visual representation of the TLabel.Text property's
value. But actually, a TLabel is a TPresentedTextControl, just like TButton,
TCheckbox, and TRadioButton are.

TPresentedTextControl is abstracted from the actual implementation. This means
TPresentedTextControl has its own properties (that is, Font, FontColor, WordWrap,
Trimming, TextAlign, VertTextAlign, and so on) that can be used to fully describe how
the text should be displayed. It uses these properties to configure a style object that is
supposed to implement an ITextSettings interface. You can check out (if you have a
Delphi edition that includes FMX sources) the implementation of
the TPresentedTextControl.ApplyStyle method in the FMX.StdCtrls unit for
yourself.

In the case of TLabel, when used on the Windows platform, a TText object perfectly fits
the style implementation. However, nothing prevents you from switching to a more
elaborate style definition, such as substituting the TText element with a TButton one,
thereby making all the labels look (and behave) like buttons. The following screenshot
shows the new style implementation; note the TButton instance being used with
the Anchors property. It's been set to all edges to properly resize the TButton instance
according to the TLabel component:

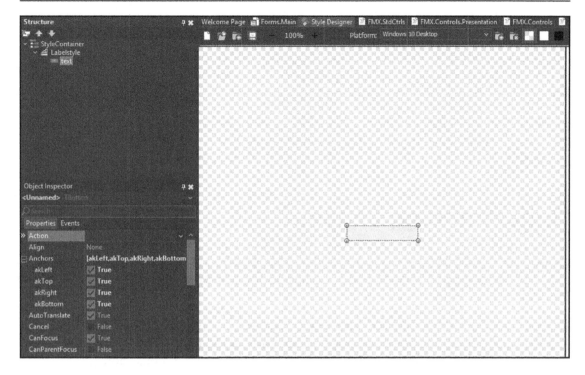

Figure 3.4

In the following screenshot, you can see the result of applying these effects. Here, you can see a simple form with three labels and the new style applied. Note that you can change the properties of the TLabel component and see the corresponding changes that were applied to the underlying TButton component. You can do this because, as we explained previously, you are actually manipulating the TLabel object so that the property's values are then sent to the underlying component through the ITextSettings interface:

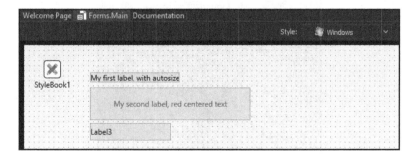

Figure 3.5

Some `TLabel` functionalities are built on top of the mere text representation. A typical example is the `AutoSize` property, which automatically sets the `Width` and `Height` properties according to the current value of the `Text` property. Beware that this capability only works if your `TLabel.Align` property is not set to the `Client` or `Contents` value and you have set the `WordWrap` property to `False`.

In this section, we learned about the `TText` component and its properties. We then focused on `TLabel`, a popular component that's used to render text but is also a style-enabled component. In the next section, we will learn about shape components.

Understanding shapes

In this section, we will learn about shapes. The shapes that are provided represent basic geometrical figures and can be used as building blocks for more complex compositions. We will also look at the properties that are available for these components since they are introduced by a common ancestor: the `TShape` class.

Shapes are the primitives of FMX components. They are not provided with a style object and they are the building blocks for many visual parts of FMX's UIs. They are listed on the **Shapes** page of the **Component** palette, as shown in the following screenshot:

Figure 3.6

In the preceding screenshot, you can easily spot `TLine`, `TRectangle`, `TRoundRect`, `TEllipse`, `TCircle`, `TArc`, `TText`, `TImage`, and `TGlyph`. Your use of them may vary but in my experience, `TRectangle/TCircle` and `TImage/TGlyph` are the most commonly used in FMX applications.

They are all descendants of `TShape`, which itself is a descendant of `TControl` (the `FMX.Objects` unit). You can consider a `TShape` descendant as an abstraction of something that is painted on `Canvas` and has a rectangle as a boundary (not necessarily a clipping boundary). Two properties determine the details of the `Stroke` and `Fill` properties of these objects. Other properties are added by each class to help you achieve some specific behavior.

The following screenshot shows an example of some `TShape` descendants on a form:

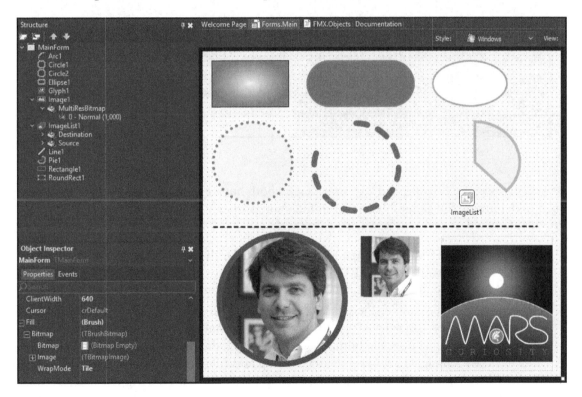

Figure 3.7

Let's have a closer look at the `Stroke` and `Fill` properties. They control the borders and the fill of a shape object, respectively, and provide several (modern and advanced, with respect to the VCL counterparts) capabilities for developers. The following screenshot shows these properties:

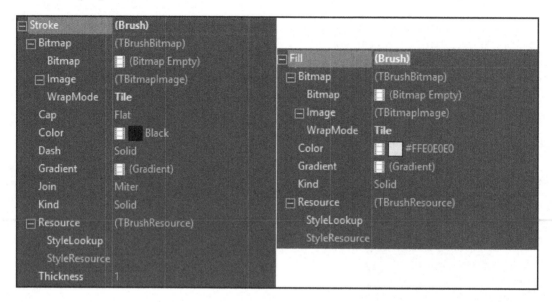

Figure 3.8

As you can see, the `Stroke` and `Fill` properties both have a `Kind` sub-property that is used to determine the general behavior of the main property. The allowed values (and a brief explanation of each) for `Kind` are as follows:

- `Solid`: The fill of the shape will be a solid color that can be selected through the component editor in the **RGBA** space (support for alpha blending is built in). You can use the `Color` sub-property to specify the actual color to use.
- `Bitmap`: This enables the `Bitmap` sub-property (a `TBrushBitmap` instance) and is where you can set a `Bitmap` (the `TBitmap` instance) to be used as a **Brush**. You can also adjust how the bitmap is used through the `WrapMode` property. You can choose among `Tile`, to repeat the bitmap and fill all the available space; `TileOriginal`, to use the bitmap only once with its original size; or `TileStretch`, to use the bitmap once but so that it's stretched to fill the available space.

- Gradient: When the Kind property is set to this value, the fill of the shape will be achieved through the use of the Gradient sub-property, which represents a linear or radial color gradient. You can set the direction of linear gradients and define one or multiple color segments (again, with a full RGBA color space available).
- None: This value means that Stroke or Fill will not be painted at all (this is equivalent to being transparent).
- Resource: Select this value to delegate the brush definition to an external object that can be referred to by name. This is because it follows the same search schema that style objects do (more on this will be covered in Chapter 7, *Understanding the FMX Style Concept*, which is dedicated to the concept of Style).

  Let's say you want to define a brush in a TStyleBook object associated with the parent form of the shape object – that is, by filling the Resource.StyleLookup sub-property with the name (style) of the brush that will be used to paint the content. This can be very powerful as it provides visual consistency through different elements and also enables cross-platform flexibility and application-wide styling opportunities (in other terms, it is another application of the **Don't Repeat Yourself (DRY)** principle, given that you may have several graphic elements sharing the same visuals and using a shared resource, which is a convenient way to centralize changes to a single point).

The Stroke property has some specific sub-properties that drive some peculiar aspects of a border:

- Cap: This chooses a value for the property to determine whether the head of the brush has to mimic a squared (Flat) or round brush.
- Dash: This property controls how the trait of the lines is drawn (continuous, dotted, dashed, or some combinations of these values are provided).
- Join: The value of this property sets the kind of joints that are used to connect different segments of lines. The available values are Miter (sharp corners), Round (a circular joint that uses arcs to connect segments), and Bevel (segments are connected by diagonal corners). The Delphi Library Reference for FMX.Graphics.TCanvas.StrokeJoin provides a visual representation of these three values (alternatively, you can just try them out and see the difference for yourself).
- Thickness: The value of this property determines the thickness of the contour of the shape; the value can be a floating (Single) number so that you can set, for example, 1.5 units and fine-tune the result at your leisure.

You can easily play with the `Stroke` and `Fill` properties to achieve several combinations. Some of these combinations are shown in the following screenshot:

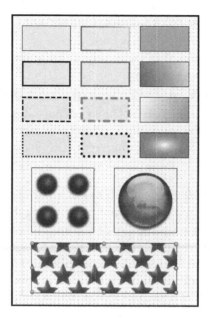

Figure 3.9

Now, let's take a deeper look at some of the shape components in order to learn about some of their peculiarities. The components we'll be looking at in the upcoming sections are `TLine`, `TRectangle`, and `TCircle`.

Often, you will find yourself composing shapes to achieve a desired visual result, so being confident about how they work is highly recommended. We'll start by looking at the `TLine` class.

Learning about the TLine class

We're mentioning `TLine` here because, for a long time, Delphi developers had no simple way to draw a line on a form (with the standard components and without painting on the `Canvas` directly, of course). Now, you can simply drop a `TLine` on a form or frame and set its properties to achieve what you are looking for.

The `Stroke` and `Fill` properties are there to help you out with this! We covered them extensively in the previous section, so if you want to learn more, please take a look at that section.

Let's focus on three specific properties that were introduced by the `TLine` class:

- `LineType`: This property deals with the fact that, like all `TShape` descendants, a `TLine` is actually placed like a rectangle, and you may want to determine where to put your line inside this rectangle. The values you can assign to this property are quite straightforward:
    - `Bottom`/`Top`/`Left`/`Right`: Use these values to draw the line on the corresponding edge.
    - `Diagonal`: When this value is selected, the line is drawn from one corner to the opposite one. By default, this line is drawn from the top-left corner to the bottom-right corner, so you may want to play with the `RotationAngle` and/or `RotationCenter` properties to obtain the other diagonal form or, in general, to obtain an oblique line at your leisure—even for values for `LineType` other than `Diagonal`.

- `ShortenLine`: If the value for this property is `True`, the line will be shortened to half of its `Thickness`, but this will not affect the `TLine.Width` value (this can come in handy if you don't want the edges of the line to be really in touch with the boundaries of the `TLine` rectangle).

- `LineLocation`: Your line lives in a box (a rectangle) and you may want to specify the exact position and behavior with respect to the boundaries of the rectangle. You can choose from three modalities:
    - `Boundary`: The line lies on the boundary of the rectangle. This means that if you increase the value of the `Thickness` property, you will see the line grow and keeping center-aligned with the boundary of the rectangle.
    - `Inner`: The line lies inside the rectangle and is free to grow past its thickness (it can overflow the boundaries of the `TLine` rectangle).
    - `InnerWithin`: The line lies inside the rectangle and is constrained inside the rectangle (it will be clipped inside the rectangle if it were to exceed it).

To better understand the `LineLocation` property, take a look at the following screenshot, which shows three lines vertically aligned:

Figure 3.10

As you can see, the one at the top-left corner has `LineLocation` set to `Boundary`, the middle one is set to `Inner`, and the bottom-right one is set to `InnerWhitin`. Selecting the lines (in the IDE) will show the boundaries of the `TLine` rectangle around the line. Note that the line at the bottom shows a constrained `Thickness` due to the `Height` property of `TLine` itself (all three lines have the same value for the `Thickness` property).

Understanding the TRectangle class

Rectangles are quite ubiquitous in modern **user interfaces** (**UIs**). Most buttons are rectangles (with some variations), and controls and containers are often rectangular in shape. The `TRectangle` shape can come in handy in a number of situations. In the *Understanding shapes* section, we covered how to use the `Stroke` and `Fill` properties to deeply customize the visuals of `TRectangle` with ease.

As a descendant class of `TShape`, `TRectangle` introduces some properties we will now focus on:

- `Sides`: This property's value represents a set of `TSide` (`Top`, `Left`, `Bottom`, and `Right`) that can be used to determine which sides are actually to be drawn for the rectangle.
- `Corners`: This value is a set of `TCorner` (`TopLeft`, `TopRight`, `BottomLeft`, and `BottomRight`) that can be used to determine which corners will actually be drawn for the rectangle.

- `CornerType`: The value for this property can be one entry of the `TCornerType` type (`Round`, `Bevel`, `InnerRound`, or `InnerLine`) and determines the kind of corner that will be drawn for the rectangle. You will see differences across these values, as shown in the following screenshot.
- `XRadius` and `YRadius`: The values for these two properties are two floating-point values (`Single`) that are used to determine the distance of the contour's corners from the boundaries of the containing rectangle.

Obviously, `CornerType` only has meaning if `XRadius` and `YRadius` are set to a value greater than zero and the corresponding corner is included in the `Corners` set.

A large number of combinations are available. Some of these can be seen in the following screenshot:

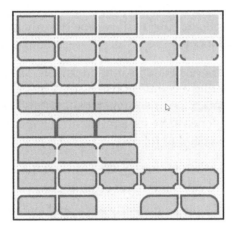

Figure 3.11

It seems quite straightforward to me that having confidence with these options can be a real time-saver when you are building your UI and need some of these elements. Remember that shapes can be seen as natural building blocks for more complex elements and can play a fundamental role when you're building or customizing FMX style objects.

Also, remember that all the common features (properties such as `RotationAngle`, `RotationCenter`, `Opacity`, `HitTest`, `Align`, and `Anchors`) are available and can come in handy in a number of circumstances where a `TRectangle` can save you from more complex solutions. Think about adding an overlay to your form to make users believe that the application is busy.

A very simple solution would be to drop a TRectangle onto your form, bring it to the front, remove all Sides, select a black Fill color, set Opacity to something lower than 1, set Align to Contents, and then play with the Visible property to show/hide the rectangle at your will. With the HitTest property, you can determine whether the rectangle should capture user inputs (touches on a mobile device). You may also want to add some text (or other components, such as TAniIndicator) that's aligned to the center of the rectangle. *With that, this first rudimentary example of wait form is completed!*

Learning about the TCircle component

The TCircle component doesn't really add any relevant to the TShape implementation. As the intermediate class known as TEllipse, it only overrides the Paint method (and the PointInObjectLocal function) in order to properly draw the circle. It responds if a coordinate pair is actually inside or outside the shape (mostly to properly handle user interaction, such as clicks or touches).

However, circles are very common elements in modern UIs, so I thought it was worth having a closer look and covering a couple of use cases. Circles can be used to, for example, hold a profile picture (in a contact list or equivalent situations). By combining the Stroke and Fill capabilities, it is super easy to implement a UI element that shows a profile picture. Here are the steps you need to follow:

1. Drop a TCircle component onto your form, set the Align property to Top, and set some Margins to get some space around your circle.
2. Set the Stroke.Thickness property to 10 and choose a good-looking Color value.
3. Set the Fill.Kind property to Bitmap and add a profile picture inside the Fill.Bitmap.Bitmap property; set Fill.Bitmap.WrapMode to TileStretch if necessary.
4. You may want to drop a TShadowEffect component onto your TCircle and adjust the shadow since it will be added to your profile picture holder.
5. Feel free to add some TLabel components (you may wish to achieve a bit of responsiveness by playing with the Align or Anchors properties) to show some basic contact data (in my example, this data is just the user's forename and surname, their country of origin, and their spoken languages).

Given what we have learned so far, it should be very easy to achieve a good-looking result simply by playing with the component property values. Specific components are available so that you can provide images of certain components (such as the flags that are used to render spoken languages in a graphical way). We will delve into them shortly. The following screenshot shows an example that I created – this should be something you can also replicate:

Figure 3.12

There's a lot of room for improvement regarding this contact form. However, all the main elements are already there, with most of them being composed of very simple components that are powerful and easy to use. There's a huge set of configuration options available for you to play around with.

In this section, we learned how a simple shape instance, such as a `TCircle` or a `TLine`, can be tweaked and made into a nice-looking UI element simply by playing with its properties and adding a simple effect. FMX capabilities allow even simple shapes to become important elements of your UI. In the next section, we are going to take a look at image components.

Managing images effectively

Every UI has to deal with images sooner or later. Images can be part of the data you need to handle in the application or part of the UI's elements. Today's minimalistic trend pushes UI toward icons and glyphs with respect to text since a (well-chosen) image is usually more immediate to the user, can be quite convenient in terms of occupied space, and is usually less impacted by language switches.

In this section, we will learn about the components and capabilities the FMX framework offers so that you can effectively deal with images in your applications.

In FMX, we can deal with images through different functionalities and components. A TImage component (collocated on the **Shapes** page of the **Component Palette** section, even if it is not a descendant of TShape) is designed to show a single image and provide some typical functionalities (see the WrapMode property) to properly display the image on the screen.

A TImageViewer component can be used to present an image to the user and let them navigate a portion of it or even zoom into it (this is only supported on desktop). As the number of images grows in an application, there's a need to optimize and centralize them. The TImageList component is designed exactly for this since it stores and provides images to other components and has some nice functionalities built in (such as image composition and proper scale handling).

The images stored in the TImageList component can be used in several UI components of the FMX framework, including lists and the TGlyph component. You can choose one and easily move from the burden of switching images to the far easier task of dealing with corresponding image indexes.

Before we provide an overview of the most common FMX components related to images, we'll take a minute to consider where modern apps live.

A wide variety of devices with different graphic capabilities are now the playgrounds of our applications, and the problem of providing the perfect graphical resources for each and every device is far from simple to address.

Learning about the MultiResBitmaps unit

For decades, the computer graphics world has strived to find a way to have graphic resources (images) in a proper format so that they can scale on different resolutions or screen densities without impacting the resource space/memory side too much.

Today, since this scenario is evolving faster and quickly adding diversity (and thus, complexity), we cannot rely on the old-fashioned idea of a single bitmap that fits all situations. Today's graphic resources need to be provided in different versions so that they're used according to the real capabilities of the target device running the application. This is the reason the `FMX.MultiResBitmap` unit exists.

The basic idea is to provide a collection of different versions of the image, each suited to a different scale (or pixel density, as you may prefer to call it), as opposed to there being a single version. Having an automatic mechanism to deal with dynamically selecting the best option in terms of quality and computational cost is a great idea. It is a must-have, not only for mobile platforms where, even on the same platform, you may face devices with very different capabilities and computational power, but also for desktop platforms due to the advent of high **dots per inch** (**DPI**) monitors. The same problem also affects responsive designs, where the same graphic item may be resized according to the device's current capabilities or to the will of the user, thus resizing windows or panels to adjust the user experience.

So, from now on, always consider that everything (read every scene) has a scale value and that we can use it as an indicator of the graphical capabilities of the actual device (that is, if we set the default scale value to 1 for standard resolutions and DPI, we can ensure that the scale value becomes 2 or 3 on a very high DPI screen). So, when we provide a graphic resource (let's say a picture), we can (this is not a must) provide several versions of it and associate each one with a scale value.

Typically, we do this to provide the correct resolution according to the screen density and size of the destination target for the picture. However, nothing prevents you from providing very different versions of the same graphics that match the final target. For example, you may want to use a decent quality photo for your user account's profile picture (typically shown on the top-right corner of most applications) but use a stylized icon on mobile devices or when the placement for the picture is very small.

The following screenshot shows the different profile picture formats you can choose from, along with their different scale factors (see how the **Width** and **Height** values differ from entry to entry):

Figure 3.13

The `TImageMultiResBitmap` (the `FMX.Objects` unit, a descendant of `TFixedMultiResBitmap`) class provides you with a convenient way to manage a collection of different versions (in the preceding screenshot, you can see different resolutions for the same profile picture). Design time support is included (you can see the component editor in the preceding screenshot) and several use cases are covered.

It is mandatory to provide a *standard* (that is, **Scale** factor 1) version of the graphic. By doing this, you can add other versions by clicking the first button of the editor's toolbar, input the scale factor (if it differs from the one that's automatically suggested), and provide a different file to get the actual content. To explain how this works, I have watermarked the profile pictures with red text stating the widths of the different images.

Different files means different resolutions and, consequently, more or less weight of the picture in terms of bytes (on disk and in memory). However, this also means you will not end up in situations where you are using a very high resolution picture to draw a small glyph for a button or, the other way around, where you're using a low resolution picture with consistent quality (and user experience) loss.

As shown in the preceding screenshot, you can also set a transparency color and choose how the size of the image is determined. The **SizeKind** combobox lets you choose between three options:

- **Custom size**: When this option is selected, you can enter (in the two edit controls, on the right, with respect to the combobox) the **Width** and **Height** properties of the image you provided as *standard* (**Scale** = 1). The size of the per-scale factor images is calculated by obtaining this standard size and multiplying it by the scale factor; then, when you provide a source file for the picture, if the size doesn't match the calculated one, the image will be fitted according to the calculated size.

- **Default size**: Regarding this configuration, the size of the parent image (a `TImage`, for example) will be used to determine the size of the resulting bitmaps. This will be multiplied for the `Scale` factor of each item. The size of the per-scale factor images will also be determined by multiplying the standard size of the scale factor so that the source file provided will be fitted into the calculated size. The following screenshot shows the **MultiResBitmap** editor configured with the **Default size** value for **SizeKind**:

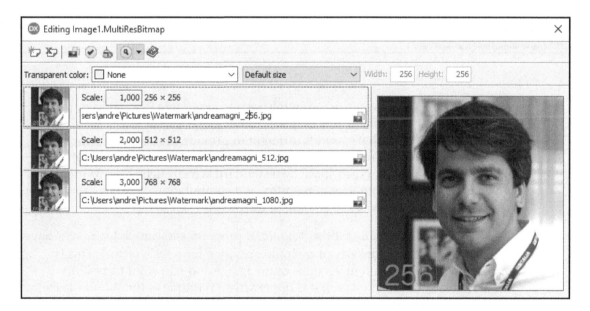

Figure 3.14

The following screenshot shows the result that's obtained on three different platforms/devices (Windows VM with a standard screen density, **MacBook Pro** with a **Retina** display, and an **Android** phone with a very high screen density):

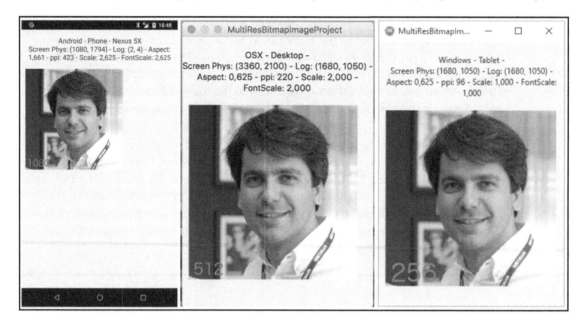

Figure 3.15

As you can see, the image is drawn while keeping the same logical size (apart from the size of screenshots, the images actually look the same size on the screen). However, the version that's used is different to provide the best user experience possible. At the same time, this saves resources for the system (using a full HD picture in such a small screen space on a standard screen such as the **Windows VM** would mean wasting a lot of memory and computational cost to gain a worse result than using the 256 x 256 version of the picture).

- **Size by image**: This value for the `SizeKind` property is meant to let images have different sizes (the actual size of each file provided for a scale factor). This is handy if you have different versions of the image and you want to assign a version to a scale factor (even if it is not exactly a multiple of the standard size); that is, the different (even in size) version will be used according to the scale factor of the current scene.

`MultiResBitmap` units are used in several FMX controls. You will see this mechanism built into the framework in various places since it applies to different situations. Now, let's have a look at four different components that are used to deal with images in FMX.

TImage

The `TImage` component is very common in a lot of FMX applications. Basically, it is a container for `MultiResBitmap` and lets you render a graphic resource by selecting the most appropriate one for the device running your application. This means the scale factor that's selected to match `MultiResBitmap` only depends on the scale factor of the form where the `TImage` instance resides.

The main properties of this component are as follows:

- `MultiResBitmap`: The value of this property will provide the actual content of the image. As we mentioned previously, this represents a very modern and effective way of handling graphic resources.
- `DisableInterpolation`: When this property is set to `False` (the default) and you are in a situation where a bitmap is drawn to a target size greater than its actual size, you automatically get an interpolated version that smooths the picture to make it look better. If you set the value of this property to `True`, you will probably gain some performance but at the cost of seeing the typical pixelate effect when the bitmap resolution is lower than needed.
- `WrapMode`: This is the main property and it affects how the image is drawn. Here, you can select one of the following values:
    - `Center`: When this is the value of the property, the image is shown in the middle of the `TImage` component. The image is never resized or cropped, so it can exceed the `TImage` component's boundaries (if the `ClipChildren` property is `False`, of course).
    - `Fit`: The image is resized (if needed) to fit the `TImage` dimensions, keeping the aspect ratio. This is the default value for the `WrapMode` property.
    - `Original`: The image is displayed with its original dimensions, in the top-left corner of the `TImage` component. The image will be cropped to fit the container's size if needed.

- `Place`: Similar to what happens when the `Fit` value is used, but the image is never made larger than its original size (only smaller to fit the container, when needed).
- `Stretch`: The image is stretched to fit the container (regardless of its aspect ratio).
- `Tile`: The image is repeated (keeping its original size) so that it fills the container.

- `BitmapMargins`: This property lets you set a margin value for each side of the image.
- `MarginWrapMode`: This is only effective when `BitmapMargins` has been set. It lets you determine how to implement the margins of the image and can be useful for implementing bitmap buttons and having them maintain the corners and edges, even when the `TImage` component's size varies.

The following screenshot exemplifies most of the available options for `TImage`:

Figure 3.16

Next, we will have a look at the `TImageViewer` component.

TImageViewer

`TImageViewer` is a simple component that can provide basic manipulation functionalities to the user. Basically, it shows an image (see the `Bitmap` property) in a scroll box so that if the image exceeds the viewer's dimensions, scrollbars will appear and the user will be able to pan the image (via the mouse or touch) to view a portion of it.

The image can also be scaled by setting the `BitmapScale` property (there is also support for user interaction on the desktop since the user can scale the bitmap by rolling the mouse wheel when the `MouseScaling` property is set to `True`). The component provides a convenient background for the picture (see the `BackgroundFill` property, which is implemented with a `TBrush` object – this means it has the same capabilities we covered for the `Fill` and `Stroke` properties of `TShape` descendants, previously in this book). There is also basic support to let the user change the actual content of the image (an `OpenDialog` component appears when you click on the image).

This component is not very cross-platform due to some of its functionalities but can come in handy for desktop and mobile applications (maybe with some coding so that you can implement the pinch-to-zoom gesture on mobile, for example). Another option would be to go for a simpler `TImage` inside a `TScrollbox`, though this would probably require some more code.

TImageList

Modern applications tend to have a lot of graphic resources in their UIs. Images are used to implement backgrounds, glyphs of buttons, tabs or list items, icons, and so on. The `TImageList` component (a name familiar to Delphi VCL developers) implements a collection of images to be used once or multiple times in your application. You can have multiple image lists, and each implements a very effective set of functionalities.

A `TImageList` instance has the following capabilities:

- Acts as a **centralized repository** for multiple images (and each entry is implemented with `MultiResBitmap` so that it's like a table where the rows are the different images and the columns are the scale factor versions provided for each image).
- Supports **multi-layer images**, meaning you can compose an image through overlapping layers, with each one containing a different image.

- Enables **caching**, meaning once you have defined your source images (`MultiResBitmaps`) and destination images (possibly multi-layered composition), you can use them in different places (and eventually with different sizes). Recreating the same size-specific bitmap can obviously be a resource-heavy operation, so having a (configurable) caching mechanism can greatly improve performance.

Image lists is a very well-known concept (and has been available in VCL for decades), but the FMX implementation is fairly more advanced. Due to this, the component editor is a bit more complex than the corresponding VCL one, as shown in the following screenshot:

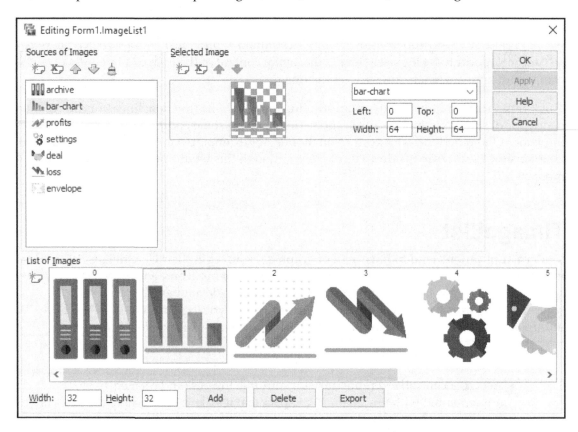

Figure 3.17

As you can see, the editor is composed of three different panels:

- The top-left panel is where source images are defined. You can have several entries (each one being `MultiResBitmap`) and you can use the toolbar at the top of the list to manage entries. Every entry has a name and you can double-click on it to open the **MultiResBitmap** editor (covered previously).
- The lower panel shows the images that have been made available through the `TImageList` component to the outside world (that is, other components). There is a toolbar to the left of the panel with a single button (**Add new item into List of Images** is used as a hint). Once you've selected an entry from the source images list, in the top-left panel of the window, a new entry will be created using the source image as a source for the first layer of the final image.

  You can add other layers and manage them using the top-right panel of the window; at the bottom, you will find two edit boxes so that you can specify a **Width** and a **Height**, as well as three buttons (**Add**, **Delete**, and **Export**). The size (**Width** and **Height** values) is used to export/import the image list (as a single image). Once you have set up your image list, you may want to fix a size (that is, 32 x 32) and export the list as a single image. To do this, simply click on the **Export** button once the list is ready.

If you want to do the opposite and you have a single file where all your images are adjacent to one another (this is a very common practice since it can be handy for a graphic designer to manipulate an image set coherently when all the images are in a single file), just input the actual size of each image in the **Width** and **Height** edit boxes and click **Add**. Then, select the single file containing all the images. A popup will ask you if you wish to have the file split into separate images or whether you want to keep them together.

If you choose to split the file, a single entry will be added to the source images list, but several images will be added to the **List of Images** collection. Each image is a portion of the source image (the image's boundaries are defined through the top-right panel when you're defining layers), as shown in the following screenshot:

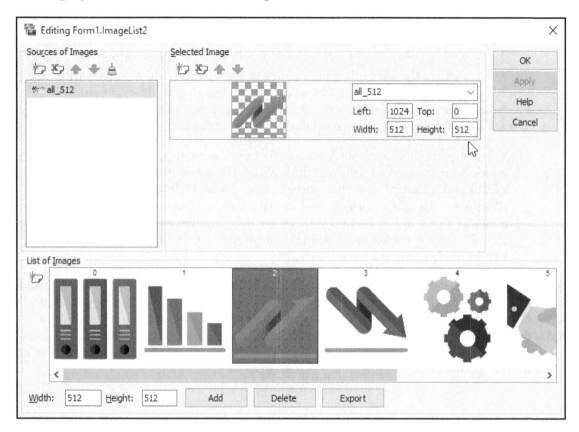

Figure 3.18

You can also use the **Add** button to import a single image (the size should match the size of the other images in the image list). The **Delete** button will delete an entry from the **List of images** collection.

The top-right panel allows you to manage the layers within an entry of your image list (one item of the **List of Images** collection). Each final entry of your image list can be seen as a composition (overlap) of one or more layers, and each layer is defined by one of the source images and a set of coordinates (Left, Top, Width, and Height). This means that the corresponding portion of the source image is used to fill the layer (please note that coordinates always refer to a scale factor of 1.0, even if the source image has several scale versions available). If the source image is greater than the portion specified, you can use the two black arrows visible near the layer preview to jump to the adjacent portion of the same size, as shown in the following screenshot:

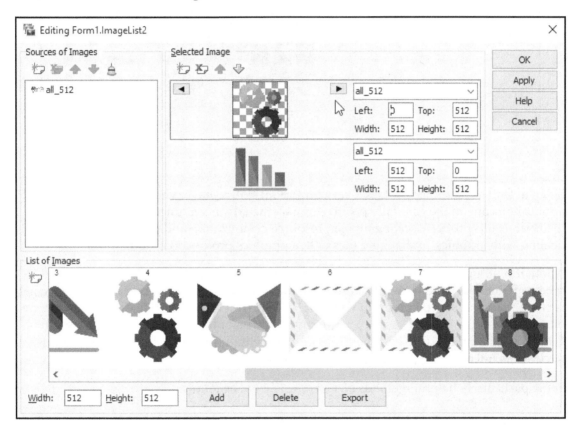

Figure 3.19

Another way to define the portion of the source image that will fill the layer is to double-click the layer preview. This will open the **MultiResBitmap** editor, which provides a selection editor that you can move and resize if needed. This is shown in the following screenshot:

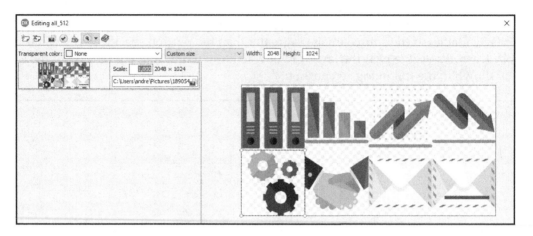

Figure 3.20

Being able to master image lists is a very important skill to have when you're building FMX applications due to the generally positive impact the advanced functionalities will have on the final result (properly scaling images, resource optimization and productivity when dealing with graphics, exchanging files with a graphics professional, and so on).

Another built-in feature is the caching mechanism, which makes your application avoid repeatedly building the same bitmaps over and over just because an entry for the image list is being reused in several places in your application. You can control this caching behavior through the TImageList.CacheSize property (the default value is 8, with a minimum of 1 and a maximum of 1,024) and the ClearCache method (it has an argument you can use to clear the full cache or only the cache entries relative to a specific image index).

Some particularly helpful methods of TImageList are as follows:

- Bitmap: Once called, it will return a TBitmap reference of the specified image index that matches the size that has been passed. The result is actually a reference to the eventually cached bitmap for that size/index, so you should treat this reference as very volatile.
- Draw: This method can be handy for drawing an entry (see the Index argument) to a target Canvas (exactly within the Rect destination) with a specific opacity (the default is 1).

- `BitmapItemByName`: This is useful for retrieving a reference to an entry of the image list (source images) and, for example, gaining access to its `Width` and `Height` properties without actually touching the Bitmap (see the `Dormant` property help entry).

 A nice and effective project about `TImageList` is available at `https://github.com/EtheaDev/SVGIconImageList` and also has some support for FMX framework. Carlo Barazzetta leads this open source project that has been very well received by the community.

Now that you've learned how to use the `TImageList` component, let's take a look at the simplest component you can use to expose an entry on your UI: the `TGlyph` component.

TGlyph

We've already learned how the `TImage` component can hold `MultiResBitmap` and show the most appropriate scale version according to the capabilities of the device running the application. The `TGlyph` component pushes this concept further and allows you to show the best version of your application. It does this by considering not only the screen density of the device but also the size of the desired image, as shown in the following screenshot:

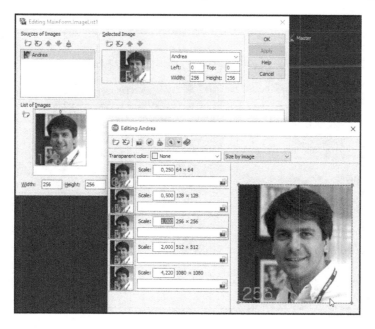

Figure 3.21

The preceding screenshot shows that if you have an image list (`ImageList1`), it provides an entry with a default size of **256 x 256** and bitmaps for scale factors 0.25 (**64 x 64**), 0.5 (**128 x 128**), 1.0 (**256 x 256**), 2.0 (**512 x 512**), and 4.22 (**1080 x 1080**)..

Once you've done this, you can add a `TGlyph` component. Note that it implements the `IGlyph` interface (defined in the `FMX.ActnList` unit), which basically consists of a couple of properties (`Images` and `ImageIndex`), and the `ImagesChanged` method (this should be called when one of the two properties changes value). Set the `Images` property of your `TGlyph` component to `ImageList1` and then have a look at the property editor for the `ImageIndex` property.

It's easy to select images from the image list. Once you have set the `Images` and `ImageIndex` properties, you will see your bitmap drawn inside the `TGlyph` component using the scale version that best fits the screen density of your device and the size of the `TGlyph` component. You may want to set the `Align` property of your `TGlyph` component to `Client` (for covering the whole form), run your application, and play with the form's size. Once you've done this, you will see the bitmap change to the size of the `TGlyph` component accordingly. I have prepared the image list with the watermarked profile picture set and implemented an `OnResize` event handler for the form so that it prints the `ClientRect` values – `Width` and `Height` – in the `Caption` area of the form. The following screenshot shows what happens when you resize the form (and the glyph as a consequence):

Figure 3.22

The main properties of the `TGlyph` component are as follows:

- `AutoHide`: When its value is `True`, the glyph will always be visible at design time but will only be visible at runtime if an actual image is available to be shown (this will actually determine the `Visible` property's value, so the behavior of `Align` will be affected). If you want to manually manage the visibility of the glyph component, set this property to `False`.
- `Images` and `ImageIndex`: As we mentioned previously, you can use these properties to select an image from an image list.
- `Stretch`: When set to `True`, the image will be fitted to the size of `TGlyph` (similar to a `TImage` with `Fit` as the value for the `WrapMode` property). When `False`, you will still see the image change size (if you have provided multiple entries for the image in the image list), but you will see the exact size of each version (in the preceding example, the sizes were 64, 128, 256, 512, and 1,080 units, respectively) without continuity in size variations.

`TGlyph` is a very common component in FMX and is used in a lot of other controls (such as buttons, tabs, list and tree view items) and many of them have a `TGlyph` instance in their style object, usually named `glyphstyle`, as a building block.

At design time, specific support is provided to highlight the current index of the image shown (printed in small characters in the top-left corner of the glyph), mark the boundaries of the glyph (with a greenish dashed border), and provide feedback on the control's visibility at runtime (with an `X` character printed in the top-left corner in red if the image is not available or in gray if the image is set but empty).

In this section, we learned a lot about image management in FMX applications. Several components are available that allow you to deal with images (multi-resolution images), all of which cover the most important cases where UI elements are used in modern applications.

In the next section, we are going to look at buttons. These are the fundamental elements of most user interfaces since they are the most common way to let the user execute code inside your application.

Learning about buttons

In this section, we will learn about various kinds of buttons and their capabilities. **Buttons** are, of course, a vital part of any application out there on the internet. They represent one of the most elementary and effective ways of interacting with the user.

Even though the concept of a button may sound elementary (something I can click/tap on in order to execute a piece of code), a lot of functionalities have been built around this aspect. Buttons can have (or not) visible text, hints, or images, they can be customized to have a specific color (or tint), they can have a state (pressed, active, focused, hovering, and so on), and they can be very different in terms of shape and visual representation.

`TButton` is the component that implements the standard button in FMX. It inherits from `TCustomButton`, which in turn inherits from `TPresentedTextControl` and implements the `IGlyph` interface. Basically, this means a button is also a `TPresentedControl`, so it actually has a `ControlType` property. However, it does not have an effect on buttons since they aren't in the list of **Firemonkey Native Controls** (for any platform), so you can consider them to always be implemented through an FMX-style mechanism. This enables a very high level of customization.

For example, you can have a custom button text color according to its state, which means you can have a different color for the text button when it is focused, pressed, hot (mouse hovering), or in a normal state. Embarcadero supplies button styles for each of the supported platforms (Windows, Android, iOS, and macOS/OS X at the moment), so you will always have a button implementation that's visually very close to the native one.

Let's have a look at the main capabilities and properties of the `TButton` component:

- `Action`: Through this property, every button can be linked to a `TAction` instance (we briefly covered actions in `Chapter 2`, *Exploring the Similarities and Differences of VCL* – they are great mechanisms that each Delphi developer should master) and when this property is set, the `Text`, `Hint`, `Enabled`, and `Visible` properties will be managed by the subsequent action link. This basically means the button will fire the action when clicked and that it will reflect any changes that have been made to the action (that is, the button will be enabled/disabled according to the `Enabled` property of the action and so on).
- `ModalResult`: Modality is a way of showing forms that are quite common on desktop platforms (while completely avoided in mobile applications). This property lets you determine the modal result of the form being shown when this button is clicked. It represents a handy way to implement buttons for the **OK/Cancel** functionalities of modal dialogs.
- `StaysPressed`/`IsPressed`: Each FMX button can be held down when it is clicked, making it act like an on/off button. This can be handy when you're using buttons to toggle options or modifiers.

- `RepeatClick`: When this property is set to `True` and the user holds down the respective button when it's been clicked, the `OnClick` event will fire every 100 ms (after an initial half-second wait). This can be useful for implementing buttons (even with touch UIs) that increment/decrement values quickly.

- `Images/ImageIndex`: These properties enable the use of an image (taken from the specified `TImageList`) as a glyph of the button. Most styles already include a `glyphstyle` element for buttons that you can use or customize further.

- `Cancel/Default`: These boolean properties set the button so that it responds to very common keyboard shortcuts (usually `Esc` and `Return`) and, like the `ModalResult` property, are very effective when you're implementing modal dialogs on desktop platforms.

- `StyleLookup`: As we introduced in `Chapter 2`, *Exploring the Similarities and Differences of VCL*, and as we will have a chance to explore in detail in `Chapter 7`, *Understanding the FMX Style Concept*, we know that the visuals of a component are driven by its `Style` definition. The `StyleLookup` property lets you specify a custom style name that will be applied to a specific instance of a `TButton`, opening it up to heavy customization capabilities. Embarcadero provides a set of predefined styles suitable for buttons on different platforms so that you can implement common use cases (such as the *hamburger icon* for menus, camera buttons to initiate image acquisition, and simple next/previous behaviors). The list varies, depending on the current style being applied to the scene (form) of the button.

- `TintColor/IconTintColor`: Even though the `Style` mechanism is powerful and flexible, sometimes, you just need to make a small adjustment, such as changing the color of a single button to make it stand out from the others or giving it a specific accent. `TintColor` (and the corresponding `IconTintColor` for when the `StyleLookup` property refers to an iconized button style) is there for you (note that the style must be tint-aware, so this feature is not always available; you can give it a try with the Android default platform style provided by Embarcadero. Check out `http://docwiki.embarcadero.com/RADStudio/en/Using_Styled_and_Colored_Buttons_on_Target_Platforms` for details). Simply assign a color to these properties and you'll get a custom coloration for your button.

The following screenshot shows some of these capabilities and properties being utilized on the Windows platform. There are 11 `TButton` instances on this form. They are as follows:

- The standard behavior (`Btn1`).
- Some different visuals changing the `StyleLookup` property (`Btn2` to `Btn6`; the second row in the following screenshot).

- An instance with `StayPressed` and `IsPressed` set to `True` (`Btn7`).
- A button with `FontColor` set to orange (`Btn8`).
- A button with the `Font` property changed so that it has bold text and is a different size (`Btn9`).
- A button with a custom value for the `FontColorForState` property (`Btn10`, where the `Hot` color is set to `Tomato` but obviously does not print in the following screenshot). The `FontColorForState` property (only available in `TextSettings` in some circumstances, depending on the actual component and style applied) can be very handy in conjunction with the `TintColor` property as it always makes text stand out from the background.
- A button where the `Images` and `ImageIndex` properties have been set to show a glyph on the button itself (`Button1`).

The following is a screenshot of the entire form, with all the buttons shown:

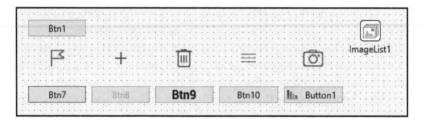

Figure 3.23

Obviously, the actual design of the buttons is style-dependent, so by switching style (that is, switching to a different platform), you will get a different result. The following screenshot shows the same form after selecting the Android platform in the Form Designer section of the IDE:

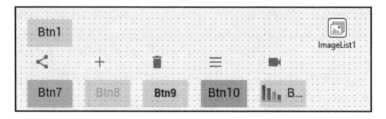

Figure 3.24

As you can see, the standard button is quite different from the Windows version, as well as that the icon buttons on the second row look totally different and are coherent with the Android platform's typical representations. On the other hand, the customization that's been made still holds (see Btn8 and Btn9) and Button1 is now showing the same glyph (it's larger here to meet the platform's conventions). Btn10 now reveals that its TintColor property has been set to a Slateblue color (the Android platform style is a tint-enabled style, while the Windows one isn't).

TSpeedButton

Another very common component is TSpeedButton. Its main difference compared to a standard TButton is that it does not capture focus (this means you can click on it without moving the focus from another component). This can be very useful when you're implementing toolbars since you may want to perform some actions on a previously selected piece of text (that is, in a memo component) or on a row of a grid/list control.

TSpeedButton usually looks different (somewhat less important) from a standard button, but you can easily change its appearance by setting its StyleLookup property to the buttonstyle value. Other styles come in handy when you want to implement the typical **segmented control** (sometimes named **scope bar**) that you can find in several applications. You can think of it as a set of buttons, one adjacent to the other, with some visual peculiarities for the first and last buttons of the set. From a behavior point of view, you can configure it to have independent buttons (clicking one does not affect the state of the others) or to implement the only-one-pressed behavior (clicking one makes it become pressed and releases the others).

To implement this segmented control UI element, simply drop some TSpeedButton instances onto your form and change the StyleLookup property. To do this, select segmentedbuttonleft for the first button on the left, segmentedbuttonright for the last button on the right, and segmentedbuttonmiddle for all the other buttons in the middle of the set.

The following screenshot shows how the buttons will look on the four different platforms (Windows, macOS/OS X, iOS, and Android, from top to bottom):

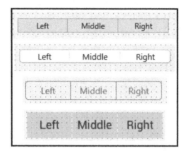

Figure 3.25

This is a very common UI element (to implement, filter, or change the options in many situations) because it is simple and effective. This is easy to achieve thanks to FMX's predefined styles. You can also easily customize these styles (as we will see in `Chapter 7`, *Understanding the FMX Style Concept*), even if they are mostly equivalent to the standard button ones (this means you can effortlessly add a glyph through the `Images` and `ImageIndex` properties, associate a `ModalResult`, set `RepeatClick` as needed, associate actions (instances of `TAction` class), and so on).

In this section, we learned about buttons in FMX applications. Apart from their basic functionalities, we covered how to tweak button components with respect to their font color, tint color, grouping them, and so on. Almost every application has at least one button in it, so it goes without saying how important it is for you to be familiar with these components. Often, user interaction is driven by buttons, even in touch-enabled applications where you would think gestures are more important.

Summary

In this chapter, we covered the most essential FMX components available, as well as some very common capabilities they share (for example, text settings, fill and stroke definitions, and so on). It is almost impossible to build an FMX application without having to deal with the topics that were covered in this chapter. By now, you should be comfortable with them.

By reading this chapter, you are now one step closer to being able to build rich and effective UIs, thus getting the most out of the FMX framework.

In the next chapter, we will learn how to master lists, trees, and grid controls.

4
Discovering Lists and Advanced Components

In the previous chapter, we started a detailed overview of the most common and important FMX components. Every component has its own peculiarities and fits different use cases, so having a good knowledge of what is available within the FMX framework will enhance your ability to select the right component while building your UI.

In this chapter, we will focus on those components suited to providing the user with some (possibly large) amount of structured data (lists, trees, and grids), as well as on visual components (drawers and panels), which are useful when dealing with the visualization of large amounts of data or information on smaller screens.

In this chapter, we will cover the following topics:

- Learning about lists
- Exploring treeviews
- Using grids
- Mastering drawers and panels

You may dream about a perfect component, suitable for every possible situation. If such a component were to exist, we would not have the variety of choices we are going to see in a moment. Keep in mind that the scenario in question can heavily affect the choice of the right component, in conjunction with the need to also consider performance and general usability (a difficult matter this one, as it tends be a bit subjective and to change over time).

By the end of this chapter, you will have familiarized yourself with many different and complex components, useful in the common task of presenting non-trivial data to the user. List controls, treeviews, and grids can be crucial in delivering the user with data, while we'll look at drawers and panels later in the chapter, they will help you correctly and effectively organize your UI components, thereby improving the UX.

Technical requirements

The source code used in this chapter is available at `https://github.com/PacktPublishing/Delphi-GUI-Programming-with-FireMonkey/tree/master/Chapter%2004/MultiView`.

Generally speaking, for the whole book, you need a computer with Delphi set up, a few additional libraries installed (such as **Radiant Shapes** (`https://getitnow.embarcadero.com/?q=radiant+shapes`) and **CodeSite Logging** (`https://getitnow.embarcadero.com/?q=codesite`)). Having other devices and setting up multiple platforms (iOS, Android, OS X/macOS, and Linux) other than Windows is a plus, but not strictly necessary in order to follow the flow of the book.

Learning about lists

In this section, we are going to explore list controls in FMX, specifically, two components that implement list controls: `TListBox` and `TListView`. We'll learn when to favor one over the other and how to master their powerful features.

List controls (a concept usually distinct from grids) are very important in almost every application, but it is especially true that lists are the most frequently used way to deliver a large amount of data to the user on mobile platforms. Screens of mobile devices are usually smaller and the interaction is usually not mediated by a high-precision device (a mouse or a physical keyboard, for instance). Especially on mobile phones, it is quite natural to interact with the screen with a finger while holding the device with the same hand, making it naturally comfortable to consume information in the form of lists of items instead of grids with bi-directional scrolling.

The importance of list controls is assumed on mobile platforms, in conjunction with the high expectations regarding responsiveness and fluidity that users tend to have, making the performance of these controls a critical point for every app. We genuinely want the user to scroll lists with hundreds of elements with a perfect user experience (mostly meaning smooth scrolling) but, at the same time, these lists may be complex, possibly with additional controls on each item, and not just a mere text entry.

This introduces a problem in implementing these lists and, at some point, two components emerged to address the two main issues associated with list controls – that is, customization of items (including scenarios where each item looks very different from the other) and general performance.

While it is clear that in order to have ideal scrolling performance, the ideal scenario is to have items of the same predetermined height, which is also a major showstopper for highly customized lists. It is also generally true that when high customization is a must, you rarely need to handle many items in the list, while the opposite is also true; that is, when you require performance, you are generally handling a long list of very similar items.

To address these two different use cases, we have `TListBox` and `TListView` components available in FMX. We will look at both in the following sections.

TListBox

`TListBox` is the ideal component for relatively short lists that may require highly customized items. Basically, it inherits from `TScrollBox` and manages a collection of items (`TListBoxItem`, inheriting from `TTextControl`).

Each item, being a `TFmxObject` descendant, can easily contain other components, so you can basically put whatever you want inside each `TListBoxItem` instance. Also, each item can have a specific style (you can set it individually, giving a value to `TListBoxItem.StyleLookup`, or change the default for the whole list box through the `TListBox.DefaultItemStyles` property). Hence, you are free to customize every aspect of the items.

Apart from standard items, you can have separator items (enabling item grouping), such as `TListBoxGroupHeader` and `TListBoxGroupFooter`, with specific styles implemented to have a different visual aspect (this again you can change).

You can see an implementation of `TListBoxGroupHeader` and `TListBoxGroupFooter` in the following screenshot:

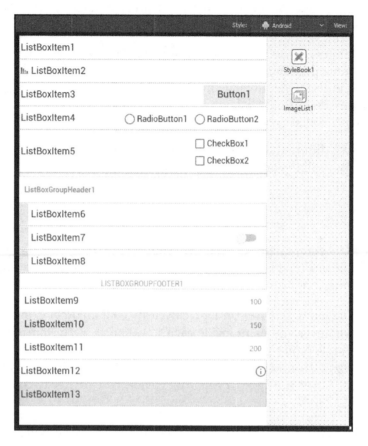

Figure 4.1

Items can be created at design time, so you can manipulate them directly in the IDE designer (and edit the style through **Style Designer**), giving the developer a true RAD experience (which is really a plus in terms of productivity).

Another way to get a customized list box item is to inherit your own class from `TListBoxItem` and basically treat it as another component (where you can obviously add sub-components and implement behaviors via code). Remember to register it (calling `RegisterFmxClasses`) in order to get it listed among the available list box item types at design time.

Let's now have a closer look at the main `TListBox` properties:

- `AllowDrag`: Set this property to `True` to enable item drag/drop reordering for the user (at runtime); the default setting is `False`.

- `AlternatingRowBackground`: This property enables/disables the alternating background color of the item; the default setting is `False`. The color to be used is determined by accessing a style resource of the `TListBox` style, named `AlternatingRowBackground` (a `TBrushObject` instance where you can manipulate the `Brush` property in order to achieve fills with solid colors, bitmaps, or gradients).

- `AutoHide`: This property determines whether scrollbars are shown automatically only when content overflows the visible area.

- `Columns`: Through this property, you can determine the number of columns to lay down items in the list. You can set this property and consequently have items resized to match the value or the other way around (see the `ItemWidth` and `ItemHeight` properties).

- `DefaultItemStyles`: Set this property's value to specify, in a single place, the default value for the `StyleLookup` property of the items (where not overridden on the specific item). The three available sub-properties are `GroupFooterStyle`, `GroupHeaderStyle`, and `ItemStyle`. These are used to set different values for footer, header, and regular items, respectively.

- `GroupingKind`: Use this property to determine whether or not items should be grouped, basically meaning that there will be an evident separation of items when a group header item is encountered. The default value is `Plain` (no extra space) and you can set it to `Grouped` to see the difference.

- `ItemHeight`: This property lets you force the item's height (all items) to a specific value. It can be handy to have all items the same height, but this option cannot be overridden (so it's an *all or nothing* setting).

- `ItemWidth`: This property acts exactly the same as the `ItemHeight` property, but with respect to the width of the item. If you set the `ItemWidth` property, it will cause items to be re-displaced on columns (where possible) and you can read the resulting column count through the `Columns` property.

- `Items`: This property initiates an old-fashioned way (similar to VCL) of setting list items. Basically, you define a string list where no customization is possible on specific items (setting this property will clear the list box and provide content that is a collection of unique text items, one for each row of the `Items` property). If you are looking for the traditional `VCL.TListBox` behavior, this is the way to go.
- `ListStyle`: This property lets you determine whether the list should flow vertically or horizontally.
- `MultiSelectStyle`: This property determines how the multi-selection of items works, with three possible options; that is, `None` (multi-selection is disabled), `Default` (in Windows, for example, you can select multiple items by holding down `Ctrl` and clicking on items), or `Extended` (clicking on an item toggles the selection of that item, so you can click multiple items and compose a multi-selection this way).
- `ShowCheckboxes`: Set this property's value to show/hide checkboxes provided for each item so that it is easy to check them (please note *selected* and *checked* are two different topics).
- `Sorted`: The default value for this property is `False`. When you set it to `True`, the items are sorted (by default using the `Text` property). It works better when the list is used as a string list (see the `Items` property), since sorting by an item's text does not take account of the item's type (group header/footer). In order to fix this behavior, you may want to call the `TListBox.Sort` method, where you can provide a custom comparer function.

When `TListBox` is acting like a collection of `TListBoxItem` (and not as a collection of simple string items), you can also set some of the item's properties, such as the following:

- `ImageIndex`: Set this value if you are brave enough to associate an image with the item (see also the `TListBox.Images` property to assign the `TImageList` instance).
- `IsChecked`: This property determines the state of the associated checkbox (only visible according to the `TListBox.ShowCheckboxes` property).
- `IsSelected`: This property determines whether the item belongs to the actual selection.

- `ItemData`: Each instance of `TStyledControl` has a property named `StyleData`, which is a dictionary with `string` as the key and `TValue` (from the `System.Rtti` unit) as the value entries. This property lets you access and set a value (any type, thanks to the ability of `TValue` to box every Delphi type) of any child control property of the styled control (including those belonging to the `Style` object used to provide a visual representation of the control, not necessarily accessible through regular properties of the class). By way of an example, with the following code you can access and change the color value used to implement the `TListBox.AlternatingRowColor` behavior:

```
ListBox1.StylesData['AlternatingRowBackground.Brush.Color'] :=
TAlphaColorRec.Red;
ListBox1.NeedStyleLookup;
```

Be aware that access violations may occur if the string is not a valid path to an actually existing object. Many aspects of the item are style-driven and `ItemData` provides you with a shortcut to style data that is also available at design time:

- `Accessory`: This property lets you specify the kind of accessory (the extra sign you can spot on many list controls, usually on the right) for the item. You can choose from between `aNone` (no accessory), `aCheckmark` (a check sign), `aDetail` (an info icon), or `aMore` (an angle bracket). The actual implementation may vary depending on the current style used because setting `ItemData.Accessory` simply changes the visibility of three style objects named `'accessorymore'`, `'accessorydetail'`, and `'accessorycheckmark'`. The implementation is entirely customizable through style.
- `Bitmap`: This property provides a handy way to set a `TBitmap` value to be used as an item's glyph.
- `Detail`: This property value will be used as an extra line of text, usually shown in a second line with respect to the `Text` property or on the right (the actual implementation depends on the style applied; here, you can simply define the string to be used).
- `Text`: Set this value to define the main caption of the item. Again, here you define the string to be used while every visual aspect is determined through the corresponding (`stylename = 'text'`) style object.

- `Selectable`: When its value is `True`, the item can be selected (or added to a multi-selection), otherwise not.
- `StyleLookup`: You can select a specific style name for each individual item. Some are already available out of the box, such as `colorlistboxitemstyle`, which is intended to add a sub-item to show a color associated with the item in some way. Keep in mind that you can set the actual color associated in two ways: by providing a value for the item's `StyleData['color.Fill.Color']` property or by accessing the underlying style implementation (that is, a `TRectangle` named color) through a call to `FindStyleResource('color')` and setting whatever property you wish. We will cover more on styles in `Chapter 7`, *Understanding FMX Style Concept*.

Now that we have covered the main functionalities and capabilities of `TListBox`, we have learned how to customize (through properties or style objects) many aspects of this control (we will cover styles in greater detail in `Chapter 7`, *Understanding FMX Style Concept*). The real key factor regarding `TListBox` versatility and ease of use entails two elements: you can easily add and manipulate items at design time and these items can contain any other component, acting as containers. As has already been said previously, this leads to a very RAD experience while designing your UIs, but does involve some performance limitations when dealing with long lists (and their scrolling performance).

TListView

The second list control we'll cover in this book is the `TListView` control. The general concept behind this control (a representation of data in list form) is quite different from that of `TListBox` (a collection of visual items).

`TListView` is a `TStyledControl` descendant. It is not a direct descendant; we have some layers of inheritance between the two, including `TListViewBase`. It is the first real UI control in the chain, able to use an adapter to mediate between data and its representation, and implementing basic functionality, such as scrolling and drawing `TPresentedListView`, which enables native control implementation, and `TAppearanceListView`, which enables dynamic appearances for list items (basically enabling the developer to fully customize an item's appearance and build one directly in the IDE or by code).

`Listview` controls have a really advanced implementation, and covering too many internal mechanisms and capabilities of these controls is far beyond the scope of this book. I really want to focus on functionalities that the application developer can use in order to get the most from this component. We will look at few functionalities in the following sections.

Providing data for the list

Before starting with some basic examples, we have to deal with the fact that you can't manually create list view items at design time. `TListview` has been designed to work well with the **LiveBinding** technology (I briefly introduced LiveBindings in Chapter 1, *Introducing the FireMonkey Framework*, and will go into more detail on this in Chapter 6, *Implementing Data Binding*. If something is unclear at this point, please explore LiveBindings in more detail in Chapter 6, *Implementing Data Binding*, and then come back). So basically, we have some source of data providing a list of items and then we have to manipulate its representation to build our UI element.

I am going to use the `TPrototypeBindSource` component to have a data source available at design time. If you are unfamiliar with this component, you can think of it more or less like an in-memory dataset of randomly generated data.

In *Figure 4.2*, you can see a `TListView` instance (on the left), a >`TPrototypeBindSource` component (named **ContactsPBS**) with some fields configured, a `TBindingList` component (that's where LiveBindings definitions are stored), the **LiveBindings Designer** (an IDE window providing visual editing of LiveBindings), which shows that I have linked the list view, and the data source with two relations.

The first relation (`Synch <--> *`) will keep the two in sync (the selected item on the list and the current item in the data source will always correspond), and the second states that I want the content of the `Name` field of the data source to be used to fill the `Text` property of my items.

Here is a screenshot of a portion of the Delphi IDE showing the most significant players in this scenario:

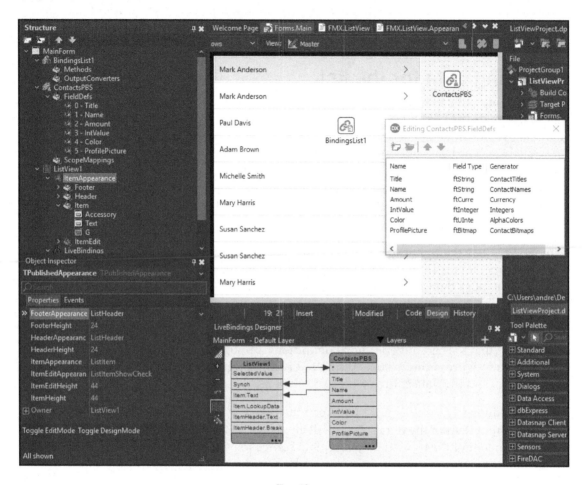

Figure 4.2

This configuration immediately leads my list view to build items for each entry in the data source and you can actually see the list view already populated at design time.

In the preceding screenshot, looking at the **Structure** view and the **Object Inspector** window, you can spot the ItemAppearance property of TListView. This data structure is where you define which appearance has to be used to actually render items (standard items refer to the ItemAppearance sub-property, having a ListItem value in the previous screenshot). In the **Structure** view, you can also see that this appearance comprises three items: Accessory, Text, and G(lyph).

An item appearance can be seen as a definition for a collection of drawable items representing some portion of the data associated with the item. FMX has a base class for all the drawable elements that will compose the final view of each item: TListItemDrawable.

The commonly used examples of descendants are TListItemText, TListItemImage, TListItemAccessory, TListItemGlyphButton, and TListItemTextButton (you can easily guess by the name of these classes what kind of content they will enable for painting). Each one also has a corresponding TObjectAppearance descendant (that is, TTextObjectAppearance), which is used as an element of TItemAppearanceProperties of each registered item appearance (I warned you beforehand that TListView implementation details are not straightforward).

In simpler terms, an item of a list view will be rendered as a set of drawable items (TListItemDrawable descendants), the composition of these items is known as an ItemAppearance, and the details (settings) concerning each drawable that are stored within ItemAppearance are made available at design time through TObjectApperance descendants.

Item appearances

Some of these item appearances are built-in and you can simply select one of them to change the layout of your TListView items. Different appearances can be set according to the item's type (header, footer, regular item, and edit item where the last one is a different version of the item used when TListView is put in Edit mode), and there is a registry (TAppearancesRegistry in the FMX.ListView.Appearances unit) so you can add your own if you like.

Back to our example, you can select the `Text` item in the **Structure** view (the type is `TTextObjectAppearance`) and change `TextColor` (or other `Font` properties) to configure how the text of the list item will be painted. You can configure almost any aspect of the text and it is fairly simple: text alignment (vertical and horizontal), text trimming, wrapping, and similar ones are all there. The following screenshot shows the **Object Inspector** window when the `Text` object is selected:

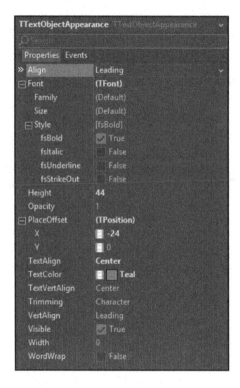

Figure 4.3

You can edit these properties and see what the final result will look like, or enter the `TListView` Design mode and have `ItemApperance` represented in a sort of designer inside `TListView` (you actually also have some visual editing capabilities as you can resize items and move them inside the item).

The following screenshot shows both situations, that is, on both sides you are looking at `TListView` in the Delphi IDE's form designer, but on the left, Design mode is off, while on the right-hand side, I have enabled it. Note I made the font *bold* and set `TextColor` to `Teal` (you can see the exact state in *Figure 4.3* where the **Object Inspector** window is shown):

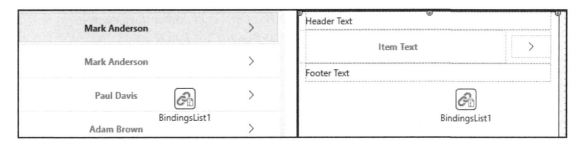

Figure 4.4

As I said, there are several built-in appearances available (implemented in the `FMX.ListView.Appearances` unit). Once selected, you will see different published object appearance entries (in the **Structure** view, in the **Object Inspector**, and in **LiveBindings Designer**) enabling different aspects of each appearance. Let's have a quick look at what you can easily achieve this way (we will focus on the regular item's appearance, `ItemAppearance`):

- `ListItem`: This is the simplest `ItemAppearance` instance available. It is composed of `TText` and `Accessory` objects.

- `ListItemRightDetail`: This appearance adds a secondary `TText` object to each item. A `Detail` property is added to the item (so you can easily provide a value for the new text line).

- `ImageListItem`: With respect to the appearance of `ListItem`, this also adds an image for each item. Also, two properties are added to the item: `Bitmap` and `ImageIndex`. You can either provide an image index (see the `TListView.Images` property to set the source image list) or provide a regular bitmap (that is, if you have a blob field in a dataset containing some graphics).

- `ImageListItemBottomDetail`: This appearance extends `ImageListItem` by adding a second `TText` object (`Detail`) positioned right at the bottom of the regular `Text` object.

- `ImageListItemRightButton`: This appearance extends `ImageListItem` by adding a `TTextButtonObjectAppearance` entry, resulting in a `TListItemTextButton` drawable for each list item, which is handy for linking some action to all or some objects (you will see further on in this chapter how to deal with the visibility of these objects and how to handle their events).

- `ImageListItemBottomDetailRightButton`: This appearance combines the `ImageListItemBottomDetail` and `ImageListItemRightButton` appearances, resulting in making a detail (on the bottom of the item) and a button (on the right side of the item) available for each item.
- `Custom`: This appearance makes available all the typical elements of a `TListViewItem` instance, such as `Text`, `Accessory`, `Detail`, `Image`, and `TextButton`. You are free to configure them as you see fit (including visibility of course).
- `DynamicAppearance`: Select this appearance to manually define your item's appearance through the Delphi IDE; that is, you can add as many drawables as you like and configure them through **Form Designer** and **Object Inspector**. This is the most advanced customization technique with design-time support.

As the following screenshot summarizes, you have nice support for a number of situations simply by using the built-in item appearances, but it is very powerful to have a chance to build a dynamic appearance from scratch. We'll see in the next paragraph how to deal with the creation of a dynamic appearance and this will allow us to focus on a couple of general topics relating to `TListView` appearances, too:

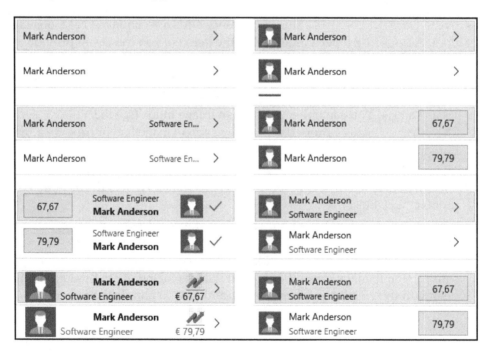

Figure 4.5

The previous screenshot shows eight different setups of the same `TListView` instance (and with the same data). In the first column of the screenshot, starting from the top, you can see `ListItem`, `ListItemRightDetail`, `Custom`, and `DynamicAppearance`. In the second column, from top to bottom, you can see `ImageListItem`, `ImageListItemRightButton`, `ImageListItemBottomDetail`, and `ImageListItemBottomDetailRightButton`. All the screenshots are taken at design time (in the IDE's form designer) and with the Windows platform style selected. There is no code so far in this example.

Custom appearance

`Custom ItemAppearance` lets the developer determine the visibility of each available item and control its position. The placement of a drawable is achieved through some of its properties (inherited from `TCommonObjectAppearance`), given as follows:

- `Height` and `Width`: These properties dictate the size of the drawable. When the value is zero, the drawable will assume the same size of the parent item (individually for width and height, so you can set one and leave the other at zero), otherwise you may specify the actual size of the drawable.
- `Align` and `VertAlign`: Both these properties assume values from the `TListItemAlign` type defined in the `FMX.ListView.Types` unit. Three values are available: `Leading`, `Center`, and `Trailing`. We can regard the list item as a rectangular shape and we can determine the desired alignment both horizontally and vertically. These three values mean *at the beginning, in the center,* and *at the end* of the item, respectively. Obviously, this setting only affects drawables with a specified size (non-zero values for `Width` and/or `Height` properties).
- `PlaceOffset`: This property has `TPosition` as a type (defined in the `FMX.Types` unit), so two sub-fields are available, named `X` and `Y`. You can use these to set a horizontal and/or vertical offset from the positioning otherwise determined (through the `Align`, `VertAlign`, `Width`, and `Height` properties).
- `Opacity`: This property's value determines the opacity of the drawable.

You can set these properties in the **Object Inspector** window once the corresponding item appearance object is selected (you can do this in the **Structure** view, in **Form Designer** when `TListView` is in Design mode, or inspecting the current item appearance through the **Object Inspector** window itself). Other properties (specific for each drawable item) are available (for example, text objects have a number of properties to drive font and text color behavior).

Dynamic appearance

Setting DynamicAppearance value for ItemAppearance provides you with a similar experience to the Custom one, but you can determine the collection of drawables implementing the appearance. This means that you may add three or four text items, a number of images, and one or more accessory items implementing a very tailored representation of your data.

The following screenshot shows a portion of the Delphi IDE while editing the dynamic appearance used in the previous example:

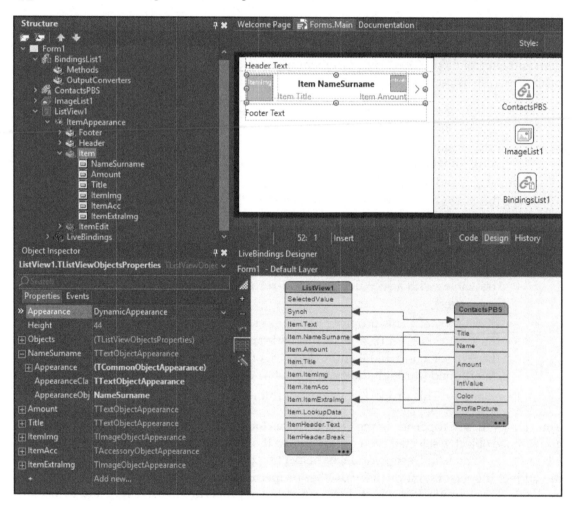

Figure 4.6

As you can see, the (regular) Item node of the appearance is selected in the **Structure** view and its properties are shown in the **Object Inspector** window. In **Form Designer** (the upper-right portion of the preceding screenshot), you can see the list view with Design mode enabled and, in **LiveBindings Designer**, you can have a representation of how the data is provided to the list view.

The preceding screenshot contains some meaningful peculiarities:

- **Object Inspector** (while inspecting a list view item appearance) represents a collection of objects instead of a collection of properties of a single object (standard case).
- You can spot the last row in the list showing a plus sign and an Add new... combo box, where you can select the type of the drawable you want to add to the collection.
- **LiveBindings** are set up across the data source (our ContactPBS object, TPrototypeBindSource) and the list view items using names of the item appearance as a target. These names can be set through the **Object Inspector** changing the AppearanceObjectName property of each entry. You will find them as Item.<Name> entries in the **LiveBindings** editor window corresponding to the list view.
- The list view Design mode provides you with a visual representation of the item's structure, resulting from the collection of drawables set by the item appearance. Some editing capabilities are available, however, through **Form Designer**, but usually you may want to change the values of the properties in the **Object Inspector** window.

- You can spot two details, one in *Figure 4.5* and another one in *Figure 4.6*:
    - The Amount value (lower-right corner of the list item) is formatted (with a **Euro** sign preceding the value). This is done through the CustomFormat property of LiveBindings (we will cover more on this topic in Chapter 6, *Implementing Data Binding*).

- `ItemExtraImg` seems to be bound to the `Amount` value of the data source. Again through the `CustomFormat` property of LiveBindings, I entered an expression to implement a threshold behavior, something along the lines of *If the Amount value is greater than 50, use ImageIndex 2, otherwise use ImageIndex 3*. This is very handy for transforming a value (the currency value of the amount) into a corresponding visual icon. Please note that you can either assign an `Integer` value to `TListItemImage` and it will try to retrieve the image from the `TImageList` instance associated with `TListView` (the `Images` property) or provide an actual bitmap (as is done with the `ItemImg` field of the same list item). The `CustomFormat` expression is evaluated on the fly, so again, no code is needed for this demo.

Now that we have covered a significant part of `TListView` `ItemAppearance` capabilities (standard, custom, and dynamic flavors included), we can take another step in this direction and have a look the list view style object.

TListView's style customization

As I wrote at the very outset of this `TListView` overview, this is a `TStyledControl` descendant, meaning its visual representation is implemented through a style object.

This also means you can customize this `Style` object and change some visual aspect of the component to meet your needs. A detailed overview of FMX styles is provided in `Chapter 7, Understanding FMX Style Concept`, but for convenience, I want to address a simple customization for `TListView`. As you have seen, a text button drawable is available for use in the item's appearance. Even if you can't think of it as an actual `TButton` instance (because it is not), it is style-enabled and its definition is part of the `TListView` style object.

Select your `TListView` instance in **Form Designer**, right-click on it, and select **Edit Custom Style...** from the pop-up menu. **Style Designer** will be shown and a copy of the default style for the `TListView` component (specific for the currently selected platform) will be added to the editor. Refer to the following screenshot, which shows the **Structure** view (listing style contents when **Style Designer** is active) with the **button** element (a `TStyleObject` instance) selected.

You can also see the **Object Inspector** window listing properties of the **button** element:

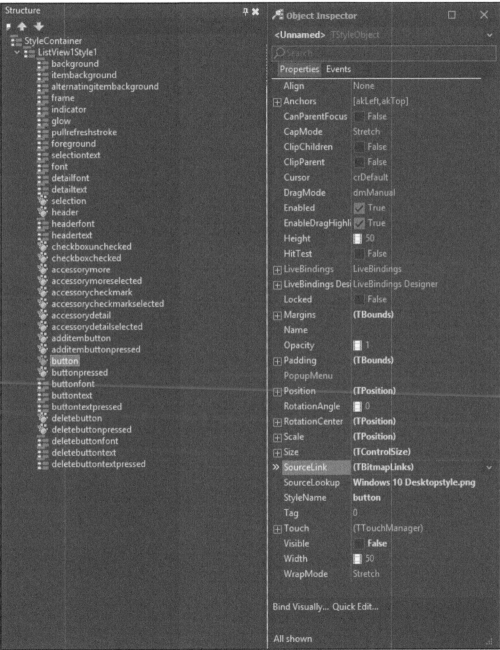

Figure 4.7

The `TStyleObject` button is part of an FMX bitmap style (refer to `Chapter 7,` *Understanding FMX Style Concept*). Thus, the visual aspect of the button is defined as a bitmap that actually is a portion of a larger one (refer to the `SourceLink` and `SourceLookup` properties of `TStyleObject`) and Delphi provides an editor for the definition of this bitmap, that is, the **BitmapLinks** editor, shown in the following screenshot:

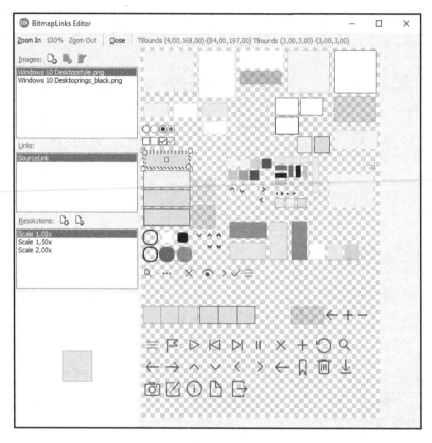

Figure 4.8

As you can see, the **BitmapLinks** editor highlights with a selection marker the portion of the diagram used to implement our button. It is a rectangular gray shape with a border (see the preview in the bottom-left corner of the diagram).

`TBitmapLinks` is not only a mere rectangle definition, but it also allows a definition of the insets of the rectangle (meaning you can select a rectangular area and then define what part of this area can be tiled to implement the fill and the borders of the resulting diagram.

As you can see in the preceding screenshot, there is a kind of smaller rectangle marked inside the bigger one). The exact specifications of these boundaries are shown in the top toolbar of the **BitmapLinks** editor, in gray text – **TBounds (4,00,168,00)-(84,00,197,00) TBounds (3,00,3,00)-(3,00,3,00)**.

What you need to know here is that you can grab the selection using the central green square and move it to another part of the source diagram, let's say the blueish rectangle in the upper-right corner. Then you can resize the selection, grabbing the yellow squares to match the desired size, as shown in the following screenshot:

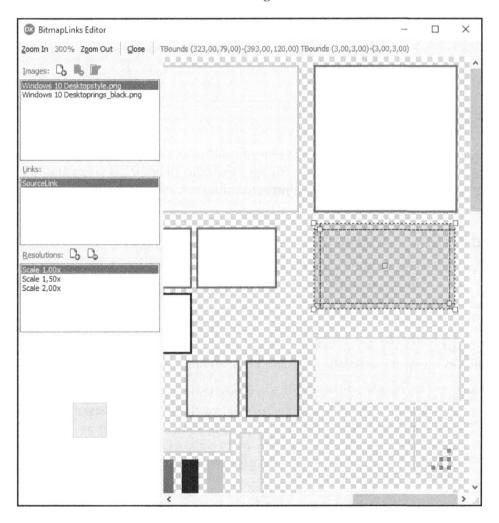

Figure 4.9

Note that the preview is now showing a nicely bordered square (even if the source is a rectangular area) and boundaries have been updated (see the top toolbar of the editor) with respect to the previous screenshot. We can now close the **BitmapLinks** editor and get our style definition updated (close **Style Designer** to apply the changes). The IDE has added a `TStyleBook` component (a style container component) to our form, set it as a value for the form's `StyleBook` property, and set the `StyleLookup` property of `TListView` to the newly created style (`ListView1Style1`) with the result that our list view looks now different, as you can see in the following screenshot:

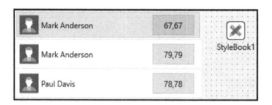

Figure 4.10

The button has changed from grayish to blueish, and this would apply to all `TListItemTextButton` objects in your list view (and all other list views sharing the same style through the `StyleLookup` property value).

Basic event handling

As we have talked about buttons on list view items, you may now ask how event handling should be dealt with, for example, to react to the user clicking or tapping on an item's text button.

Generally speaking, you are always clicking on the item, even if you are aiming to click on a specific part (a specific drawable) of it. The `TListView` class provides you with some convenient events you can handle in order to implement the desired behavior:

- `OnClick` / `OnDblClick`: These are very standard events to capture the click/double-click on the whole `TListView` component. No specific information is provided within the event handler, so you can only rely on properties such as `TListView.Selected`, but beware of timing (at the point when you are clicking on an item, the `Selected` property will still refer to the previously selected one).

- `OnItemClick`: The event handler for this event will be supplied with a reference to the clicked item (the one you actually clicked/touched). This is the basic event to respond to the user interaction within a list view.

- `OnItemClickEx`: Providing a handler for this event will give you more detailed information about the user action; for example, the clicked item's index in the list, the actual location where the user clicked in the list item, and a convenient reference to any drawable at that location. This will enable the developer to properly discriminate whether the user clicked on the item's main text object, on a secondary text object, or, for example, on an image of the item (providing full support for the various item's appearances we have seen previously in this chapter).
- `OnButtonClick`: Use this event to specifically handle click events of an item's button. It will fire whenever the user clicks/taps on a text button or on a glyph button of an item. A reference to the item and to the actual button component are provided within the event handler's arguments.

Naturally, `TListView` has several other events defined to deal with other aspects of the component but, most of the time, you simply need to handle direct user interaction with the component.

Search capabilities

Every `TListView` component has a built-in search capability to let the user quickly filter the items in the list. Simply set the `SearchVisible` property to `True` to see a search box on the top of your list view where the user can input some text and have convenient filtering of the list items. An event, `TListView.OnSearchChange`, is provided to be notified when the search text is changed, just in case you need to know that the list has been updated after the user changed the search text, as shown in the following screenshot:

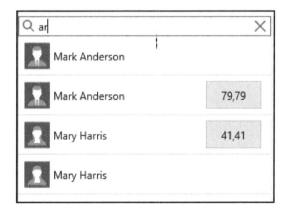

Figure 4.11

The preceding screenshot shows the search box provided by `TListView` to filter list items.

 If you don't want to rely on built-in search capabilities, you can use the `OnFilter` event handler and implement your own UI elements to collect input from the user and implement the filter function.

Filtering is done against the `Text` value of each item, so you might need to implement some other advanced search but, for the typical use case, this proves to be very effective in most situations.

Pull to refresh

One of the most universally accepted UI patterns on mobile devices involves the way in which the user can call for a data refresh, that is, pull down on the screen with a finger and have some visual feedback linked to the actual gesture of the user. If a threshold is reached, update the content and hide the visual feedback.

This kind of interaction is very common in a wide variety of applications (mail, social networks, and more) and can be applied to lists, grids, and other controls. The `TListView` component makes it very easy to implement this behavior, which is, in fact, built in and, on mobile platforms, can have some native integrations (that is, platform-specific animations). To enable *pull-to-refresh* (which is *off* by default), you can set the `PullToRefresh` property of `TListView` to `True` and implement the `OnPullRefresh` event handler.

In the following screenshot, you can see the steps involved in a pull-to-refresh interaction:

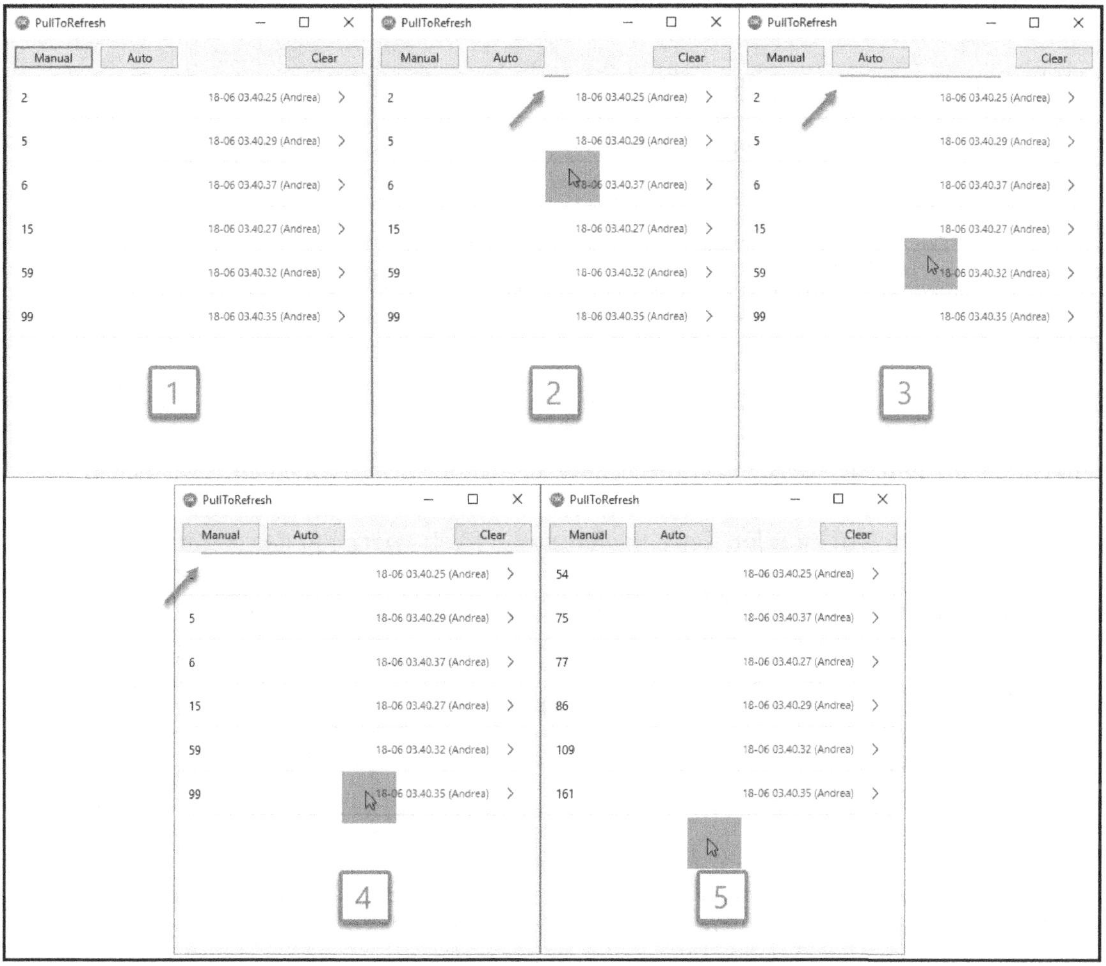

Figure 4.12

As you can see, starting with the list containing some data, the following steps can be performed:

1. The user can start the refresh request (step **1**) by pulling down the list (with the mouse on desktop platforms or with a finger on mobile devices).
2. In step **2**, visual feedback appears (on the top of the list, implementation details may vary depending on the platform).

3. If the user keeps pulling (steps **3** and **4**), the `OnPullRefresh` event is fired and the developer has a chance to update the data underlying the list view and have the new data presented to the user (step **5**).

In this example, the `Text` element of the list view shows an integer number (the list is sorted with respect to this value), while on the right, you can read the timestamp of the initial creation of the item and the owner's name. When the user performs a pull-to-refresh operation, values are updated (and the list is reordered accordingly).

It is important to fully understand that the `OnPullRefresh` event is fired in the main thread context. If refreshing data is a time-consuming operation (that is, you need to wait for a **REST** call to retrieve data from a remote server), you may want to use the event handler just to start the refresh operation.

The `TListview.PullRefreshWait` property can be set to `True` to instruct the list view that we are going to manually notify it once the refresh operation has completed. This way, you can take advantage of **parallel programming** techniques (we'll cover this topic in `Chapter 11`, *Building Responsive Applications*) to trigger a data refresh operation in the `OnPullRefresh` event handler. Once the lengthy refresh operation has completed, you simply need to make a call to the `TListView.StopPullRefresh` method. In the time between the refresh request and completion of the operation, the main thread has been able to keep your UI responsive.

> A full example is included among the book's examples. Refer to `https://github.com/PacktPublishing/Delphi-GUI-Programming-with-FireMonkey-/tree/master/Chapter%2004/TListViewPullToRefresh`.

Pull-to-refresh is very important on mobile devices as it represent the *de facto* standard to refresh the current view. Users consider it natural to interact with lists this way, so consider implementing this feature in your applications when needed (meaning whenever automatic refresh is not feasible or is lacking in effectiveness).

This lengthy section has been dedicated to `TListView`, probably the most important list component for modern applications (where lists are preferred to treeviews and grids). We have seen how to populate the list, how to customize the list appearance, and how to deal with the most commonly used events provided by the component, including search capabilities and gestures.

The next section is about treeviews, a classic component for presenting data to the user. It is particularly effective when the data to be presented has a hierarchy.

Exploring treeviews

In this section, we are going to learn about treeviews, a commonly used component in many UI examples (a classical example being the on-disk folder structure in many operating systems' shells).

A very common data structure is the **tree**. Basically, data is provided with a hierarchical relationship between items so each item can be seen as a parent of other items. A typical example of this kind of nested list structure is how filesystem objects get represented (some filesystem entries that are used to call folders or directories can have children, that is, files or folders entries).

FMX has a `TTreeView` component suitable for representing such data structures. Basically, you can see it as a scrollable list of items where each item can contain other items. Sub-items are generally indented horizontally more than their parent and parents are generally expandable and collapsible. These characteristics make the hierarchy across items very evident to the user.

The implementation relies on the capability of each FMX object to be a parent for other FMX objects (`TFMXObject`). More specifically, each `TTreeViewItem` object has a `Content` field of the `TTreeViewItemContent` type, inherited from `TControl`, that acts like the parent of sub-items. By overriding some `TFmxObject` methods (that is, `DoAddObject`), `TTreeViewItem` uses the `Content` field to store and manage sub-items.

`TTreeView` is not a LiveBindings-enabled component, so items have to be manually created and added to the component. At design time, a component editor is provided to facilitate the management of items. Aside from adding items, a classical IT topic concerns **traversal of the tree** (the process of visiting all nodes of the tree once).

> This is far beyond the scope of this book, but just keep in mind that you may want to traverse the tree in depth or in breadth.

The `Items` indexed property of the `TTreeViewItem` class will easily provide you with access to sub-items of each item (it is up to you how to traverse the tree). `TTreeViewItem` is basically a `TTextControl` object (so it is `TStyledControl` with a caption) with the ability to contain other FMX objects (as it implements `IItemsContainer`), actually the sub-items, and have a glyph associated (supports the `IGlyph` interface). Let's have a look at its main properties:

- `Items[const Index: Integer]`: This indexed property provides you with access to sub-items of the item. You can refer to the `Count` property to know the boundaries for `Index`; each entry is a `TTreeViewItem` instance itself, so you can conveniently use this property to traverse all the trees.

- `Index`: This property is inherited from `TFmxObject`, but acquires a different meaning in `TTreeViewItem` since the class is overriding the `DoAddObject`, `DoInsertObject`, and `DoRemoveObject` methods in order to specifically handle children objects that are `TTreeViewItem` instances (managing them through the `FContent` sub-object). The value of the `Index` property is the index of each item with respect to the `Content` object of its parent item; that is, the difference is that this value is not affected by the presence of other objects that may have been added to the parent item (which can still have children of different classes with respect to `TTreeViewItem`, such as a button or an extra image).

- `GlobalIndex`: `TTreeView` maintains a list of all visible nodes of the tree, from top to bottom. Each item has an index in this list and you can use the (read-only) `GlobalIndex` property to get access to its value. Keep in mind that this value may change when some nodes of the tree get expanded or collapsed (collapsed items are not visible and so are not listed in the global list).

- `Level`: This isn't exactly a property but rather a function, that is, it returns the nesting level of the item. This can be handy when determining where in the tree the item is located.

- `ParentItem`: This function returns the first parent item, that is, `TTreeViewItem`. This means that it will return the parent item for a child node or `nil` for the root node of the tree.

- `TreeView`: Similar to the `ParentItem` function, this function will traverse the parenthood chain to find the first `TCustomTreeView` instance in the chain. This can be a useful reference when implementing your own `TTreeViewItem` descendants and you need to access the parent tree view.

- `ChildrenOffset`: This is the space between the left side of `TTreeView` and the left side of `TTreeViewItem`. It is generally calculated by considering the nesting level of the item and the visibility of some accessory elements of the item (the associated checkbox, the expand/collapse button, and the glyph). This is a read-only property, but you can affect this value by setting the `CustomChildrenOffset` property.

- `CustomChildrenOffset`: This property lets you specify a custom offset value for the item's children item (sub-items). Take note that if you set this value manually, no further considerations will be made to adjust the offset with respect to the accessory elements of the items. You can even set it to zero and see children items at the same indentation level of their parent.

- `Enabled`: This Boolean property determines whether the item is enabled. If set to `False`, the item will not be selectable by the user and will usually have a different visual representation (most of the time, the item will be dimmed, but it depends on the actual style used).

- `IsChecked`: This property reflects (and lets you assign) the state of the checkbox associated with each item. The checked state of each item can be manipulated by the user only when the `TTreeView.ShowCheckBoxes` property is set to `True` (thus, checkboxes are visible), but you can use it programmatically even when checkboxes are not shown to the user. Please keep in mind that this has nothing to do with the selection topic.

- `IsExpanded`: This property's value is `True` when the node is expanded and `False` when it is collapsed. You can actually even expand a node with no children (sub-items), but usually this property is used when dealing with sub-items. The user can easily expand/collapse a node by clicking on the expander button (that can be customized through the `TTreeView` style object). You can set this property programmatically as well.

- `IsSelected`: This property's value is `True` when the item is included in the current selection (multi-selection is controlled by the `TTreeView.MultiSelect` Boolean property), or `False` otherwise. The user can easily select items from the tree view or you can set this property programmatically as well.

- `ImageIndex` / `Images`: These two properties (as seen many times in this book) are used to determine the source of images to be used as glyphs for items and, for each item, the actual index of the image to be used.

In the following screenshot, you can see a `TTreeView` component with several items, defined at design time, with the **Windows** style applied:

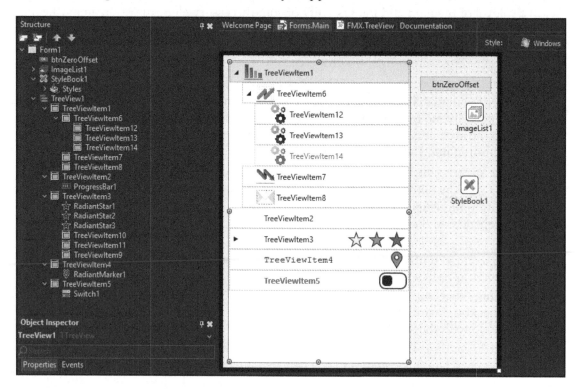

Figure 4.13

As you can see, items defined at design time are also visible in the **Structure** view windows of the Delphi IDE. The first item (`TreeViewItem1`) has three children (`TreeViewItem6-7-8`) and one of these children itself has three children (`TreeViewItem12-13-14` are sub-items of `TreeViewItem6`). You can clearly see that I have linked the tree view to an image list (`ImageList1`) and assigned the `ImageIndex` property of some of the items, now showing a glyph alongside their captions. `TreeViewItem1` and `TreeViewItem6` are expanded (the `IsExpanded` property value is `True`) and you can actually see their children, while `TreeViewItem3` is collapsed (notice how the expander button appears different and you can spot the children of `TreeViewItem3` in the **Structure** view of the IDE – `TreeViewItem9-10-11`).

`TreeViewItem14` is disabled, so slightly dimmed out (and the user won't be able to interact with this item at runtime), and a button has been dropped on the form in order to set the `CustomChildrenOffset` value of the first item of the tree view to zero (you have to run the demo in order to see the behavior).

`TreeViewItem3-4-5` also shows nested components, that is, three stars, a position marker, and a switch component have been dropped on these items (as we did with the `TListBox` component previously in this chapter). This way, it is really straightforward to customize items and add functionalities whenever you wish.

`TreeViewItem4-5` also proves how you can customize the caption's settings, defining a different font family, size, or color (and much more besides, as we have seen in `Chapter 3`, *Mastering Basic Components*, dealing with text objects).

 The stars and position marker components are from the **Radiant Shapes** set, by **Raize** software (`www.raize.com`). You can easily download these through **GetIt Package Manager** in most circumstances, or purchase them directly from **Raize** software. I really like these components and they can significantly improve your FMX UIs.

The last thing I'd like you to notice is that I customized the item's height (changing the `ItemHeight` property of the tree view) and, in order to have the item's glyphs better fit the new height, I have customized the style of the items, changing the position and size of the glyph).

Customizing TTreeview's items

Similar to what we have seen with the `TListBox` component (previously in this chapter), we can easily customize `TTreeView` items by dropping other components inside them. Adding an extra button to a specific item merely requires selecting the items and double-clicking on the `TButton` entry in the **Component Palette** of the IDE.

A second way to customize your items (exactly as described for `TListBox` items) is to inherit your own class from `TTreeViewItem` and provide extra functionalities or onboard components directly via code.

The following code snippets show how to implement a simple tree view item that is able to hold some extra data (specifically, a TPerson record data structure):

```
TPerson = record
    Name: string;
    Surname: string;
    DateOfBirth: TDate;
    function Age: Integer;
    function ToString: string;

    class function Andrea: TPerson; static;
  end;

{ TPerson }

function TPerson.Age: Integer;
begin
  Result := -1;
  if DateOfBirth > 0 then
    Result := YearsBetween(DateOfBirth, Now);
end;

function TPerson.ToString: string;
begin
  Result := string.join(' ', [Name, Surname]);
  if Age > 0 then
    Result := Result + Format(' (%d)', [Age]);
end;

class function TPerson.Andrea: TPerson;
begin
  Result.Name := 'Andrea';
  Result.Surname := 'Magni';
  Result.DateOfBirth := EncodeDate(1982, 05, 24);
end;
```

The preceding code contains the definition of the TPerson record data structure, including implementation of the Age and ToString method functions. The Andrea class function is there to provide an instance of this data structure. Now that we have introduced the data structure that we aim to embed as data on TTreviewItem, we need to define our item class, as you can see in the following code snippet:

```
TMyTreeViewItem = class(TTreeViewItem)
private
  FPerson: TPerson;
protected
  procedure SetPerson(const Value: TPerson);
```

```
  public
    property Person: TPerson read FPerson write SetPerson;
  end;
```

```
(...)
```

```
{ TMyTreeViewItem }
```

```
procedure TMyTreeViewItem.SetPerson(const Value: TPerson);
begin
  FPerson := Value;
  Text := Person.ToString;
end;
```

The preceding implementation of a TTreeViewItem descendant class (TMyTreeViewItem) sets the Text property of the treeview's item inside the SetPerson method code. This will cause the item to reflect data changes (triggered when the Person property gets written) and always provide an up-to-date caption. This is obviously just an example, and you may want to implement more complex behaviors or use data throughout other event handlers of the components involved.

Now that we have defined the TPerson and TMyTreeViewItem data types, we can make use of them, as shown in the following code snippet:

```
(...)
```

```
// code to add a new item as child of TreeViewItem1
var
  LItem: TMyTreeViewItem;
begin
  LItem := TMyTreeViewItem.Create(TreeView1);
  try
    LItem.Person := TPerson.Andrea;
    TreeViewItem1.AddObject(LItem);
  except
    LItem.Free;
    raise;
  end;
end;
```

The preceding code creates a new tree view's item (TMyTreeViewItem class, with TreeView1 as the owner of the object instance) and assigns the Person property of the newly created item to the result of the TPerson.Andrea class function. Then, the item is actually added to the tree view item that will be its parent (TreeViewItem1).

Last, but not least, always remember that TTreeView is a styled component, so you can customize almost every aspect of the tree view and its items by editing their style objects. Just right-click on the tree view in **Form Designer** and select **Edit custom style...**, the **Style Designer** window will pop up and a copy of the default style for the selected platform will be made available for your customization.

As stated previously, the items shown in *Figure 4.13* have been customized in order to enlarge the glyph of the items, to better fit the augmented item's height. This has been achieved by editing the style of the tree view and manipulating the glyphstyle component that is located inside the Layout component of the TreeViewItem1Style node.

The following screenshot shows **Style Designer** with the **glyphstyle** component selected:

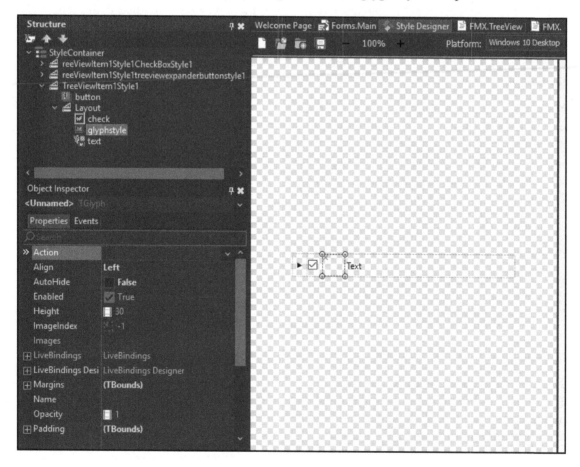

Figure 4.14

Many elements of the tree view can be customized this way, including the expander button (either in the expanded or collapsed state) and the checkbox used when the `TTreeView.ShowCheckBoxes` property is set to `True`.

Note that the style has been split to implement `button` (expander) separately. You can check this by having a look at the `StyleLookup` property of the `button` element of the `Layout` component of the `TreeViewItem1Style` entry.

Always remember to edit the style for each platform that you want to address at runtime.

In this section, we learned how to deal with tree views, a very powerful component for data presentation, and how to effectively customize a tree view's items. In the next section, we are going to introduce grids, another useful tool for presenting datasets to the user.

Using grids

In this section, we are going to discuss a classic element of traditional user interfaces: the (data) grid. We are going to learn how to use it, bind it to data, and customize its visual appearance.

Every desktop data-centric application out there has a data grid somewhere. For a long time, the default data structure has been the rectangular shaped dataset and its natural representation is a grid.

A **grid** is a collection of rows, each consisting of a collection of columns. The number of rows is variable, while the number of columns is fixed for each dataset. When we are dealing with (relational) databases as a source of data, the number of rows is usually linked to the number of records of a result set and the number of columns depends on the table structure (or structure of tables involved in a query). Aside from the database-related datasets, a very common example of a grid component is a spreadsheet, something that has been available in the IT world for decades. In this case, the number of rows and columns is much more flexible and the modern look and feel of spreadsheets tends toward an infinite number of rows and columns.

Anyway, the basic unit of a grid is a cell, and we usually identify (and refer to) it using its row and column indexes. Cells usually contain a value in the form of a text representation of a string or a number, but it may also contain graphics or specific controls to render specific contents.

FMX comes with two component entries for grids: `TGrid` and `TStringGrid`. They share a common ancestor (the `TCustomGrid` class) that basically implements most of the functionalities. The abstraction of `TCustomGrid` involves a `TGridModel` instance that enables aspects such as column management, editing in grids, and cell drawing.

The grids are, in fact, `TPresentedControl` descendants, hence many aspects of their UI implementation are driven by a presentation factory that provides a presentation according to the value of the `ControlType` property of the grid component. Presentations for styled grids are defined in the `FMX.Grid.Style` unit and mostly based on a shared `TStyledGrid` implementation. `TStyleGrid` has the ability to define the classes used to render cells (selected through a call of the `GetCellClass` method) or the ones used to provide the corresponding editors (selected through a call of the `GetEditorClass` method). Native implementations of presentations for the grids are available for the iOS platform and are defined in the `FMX.Grid.iOS` unit.

Detailed coverage of the internals of grid presentation implementations is far beyond the scope of this book, although it would be a very interesting topic to delve into if you are interested in these kinds of details. As an aside, if you are an experienced Delphi developer, you may find it cumbersome that grids do not have a central role in the FMX framework as they have in the VCL. In fact, the scenario seems a bit polarized and this is the case because, especially on mobile platforms, grids are no longer the most popular component.

Lists have somehow won the battle in this area, presumably because of their better fit in terms of usability on touch-enabled devices. If you really need to show a large amount of data, or if you need a higher level of customization, I would try to achieve the result through a list component instead of delving too much into grid customization. Given this, grids can still play a role (for example, on FMX desktop applications), so it is worth covering the available functionalities and base concepts surrounding them.

Live Binding support is baked into `TCustomGrid` and `TGridModel`, but you can choose to populate the component through LiveBindings or manually, with different opportunities.

If you proceed manually, you can define a collection of columns for your grid by using the component editor in the Delphi IDE (right-click on the grid, select the **Items editor...** entry from the pop-up menu, and the editor will appear).

The following screenshot shows the grid's **Items Editor** with some columns defined. Notice the combo box over the **Add Item** button that will let you select the kind of column to add (you can obviously mix types in the same grid):

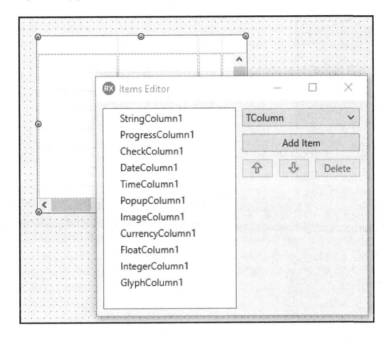

Figure 4.15

As you can see, several kinds of columns are available, including TStringColumn, TIntegerColumn, TFloatColumn, and TGlyphColumn. As you can easily guess from the class names, each column has been specialized to properly render its content according to the data provided. This same editor (shown in the previous screenshot) is available both for TGrid and TStringGrid and is used when the LiveBindings approach is not used to provide data to the grid.

A different editor (the **Columns** editor) becomes available (through the pop-up menu you get by right-clicking the grid component in **Form Designer**) when LiveBindings are used. You can see this in the following screenshot:

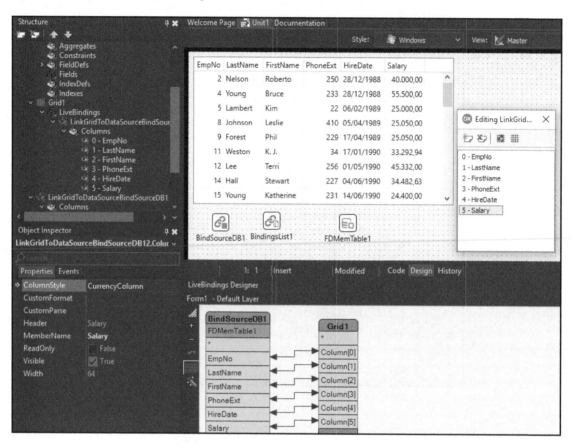

Figure 4.16

Please note that the two scenarios are quite different, as the first one (manually created columns) results in a collection of controls (`TColumn` descendants) added to the grid control. `GridModel` will then be used to provide data to the grid (and, hence, to the single columns). The second scenario (LiveBindings) will automatically create columns according to the bind source. These columns will be held by the `TLinkGridToDataSource` object and you can decide whether or not to persist them and consequently have a chance to tune their properties at design time (in the preceding screenshot, you can see the **Column** editor, on the right-hand side, with the **Salary** entry selected, and **Object Inspector**, on the left, which provides you with access to column-specific properties and details of the live binding mechanism, such as the `CustomFormat` and `CustomParse` properties we will discuss in detail in `Chapter 5`, *Using FireDAC in FMX Applications*).

Available column classes are defined and registered in the `FMX.Grid` unit; you can register your own descendant of `TColumn` if necessary. Basically, the grid uses a presentation object (styled or native) to render each cell and manages the visible cells in order to optimize the creation of controls when dealing with large datasets.

The implementation usually relies on cell objects and editors implementing the `IDrawableCell` or `IDrawableObject` interfaces so that the grid can easily handle the drawing of the cells on the `Canvas` object. When the LiveBindings mechanism is used, you can select the kind of column through the `ColumnStyle` property of the column itself (hint: if you are looking for the `TProgressColumn` correspondent, it is missing in **Delphi 10.4.1 Sydney**, but you can manually input `ProgressColumn` as a value for the `ColumnStyle` property and have it correctly applied).

Now that we have introduced some shared concepts, we can have a closer look at `TGrid` and `TStringGrid`, respectively.

TGrid and TStringGrid

`TGrid` and `TStringGrid` are very similar from the functionality point of view, but there is a significant difference in terms of the data to be displayed; that is, `TGrid` does not hold the data it is showing. To provide data for each cell, you must implement the `OnGetValue` event handler.

This handler will be called each time the grid needs a value for a cell, but it will not actually be stored within the grid. There is a caching mechanism to improve performance and avoid multiple unnecessary requests to the OnGetValue implementation, but the cache only contains data for the visible cells and it is cleared as soon as the cell goes beyond the scope of visibility. If you need to solicit the grid to refresh data shown to the user, you will have to instruct the grid model that some data has changed. The following code block shows a simple implementation of the OnGetValue event handler, providing (mostly random) values for a grid with three columns where you will find a description, a progress bar, and a glyph, respectively:

```
procedure TMainForm.Grid1GetValue(Sender: TObject; const ACol, ARow:
Integer;
 var Value: TValue);
begin
  case ACol of
    0: Value := 'Task n. ' + (ARow + 1).ToString;
    1: Value := Random(100);
    2: if Random(100) >= 50 then Value := 2 else Value := 3;
  end;

  CodeSite.SendFmtMsg('Providing data for (%d, %d): %s', [ACol, ARow,
Value.ToString]); // include CodeSiteLogging unit to compile
end;
```

As you can see, the number of rows in the grid is regulated by the RowCount property of the grid itself. The event handler will be called as long as the grid needs values for visible cells in the grid. In the code block, I've added a call to the CodeSite logger (another Raize product I like and which I have used in many situations; the **CodeSite Express** edition is easily available from Embarcadero's GetIt package manager) to keep track of how many times the event handler is called.

Let's say our grid has 50 as a value for the RowCount property and has 12 items visible (you can control the item's height through the RowHeight property of the grid). Running this simple example, you will see 36 log entries in the logs (through the **CodeSite Live Viewer** window, for example) because the grids need to fill the 3 cells for 12 rows in order to properly render the grid for the first time. The data values, as said, will be cached in order to get a chance to repaint the same cells without firing the OnGetValue event too often but, obviously, if you scroll the grid (vertically), you will see new rows in the log viewer as the grid is fetching data to render the cells of the newly visible rows. The cache is freed as soon as the cells are no longer visible, so only a portion of the data is kept in the cache, that is, the part corresponding to the visible cells of the grid.

If you need to force the grid to re-fetch data and reflect changes in the data, you will need to notify the grid model that data has changed. You can do that by calling the `TGridModel.DataChanged(ACol, ARow: Integer)` method (that is, calling `Grid1.Model.DataChanged(1, 1);`) or by instructing the grid to update a cell of a specified column through the `TColumn.UpdateCell(ARow: Integer)` method (that is, by calling `Grid1.Model.Columns[1].UpdateCell(1);`; this will internally trigger the `DataChanged` method as well) and the `OnGetValue` event will be fired again for the cell. In our example, updating the cell at the (1, 1) position will result in a change in the corresponding progress bar's value of the second row (**Task n. 2**). Data is randomly generated, so you will see it changing every time you call the `UpdateCell` method by pressing the button for example.

The following screenshot shows how the grid appears at runtime and also reports the log viewer window:

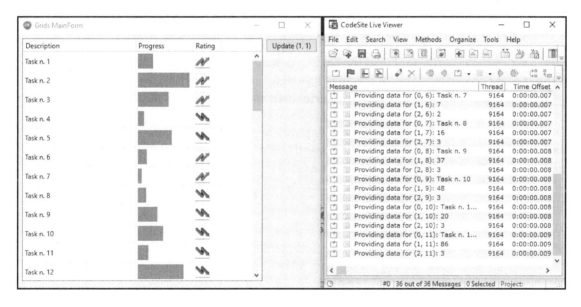

Figure 4.17

Even if I am not really a fan of this behavior, grids are often used to let the user edit data directly. The FMX grids will provide an *editors* object for the cells (according to the actual presentation of the grid) so that the user is able to change the value of the cell. Symmetrically with respect to the `OnGetValue` event, this will fire an `OnSetValue` event, called each time the value for a cell is updated by the editor (read by the user). You can implement a handler for `OnSetValue` to gather the new value and apply it to the actual data model. Subsequently, a new call of the `OnGetValue` event will occur, fetching data back to the grid to inform the user.

So, given the grid has events to fetch data for a cell and to post data changes back to the underlying data model, you are definitely able to implement whatever binding you choose between the grid and any kind of your data structures. Or, if you want, you can opt for LiveBindings to actually bind your data to the grid and back, almost automatically.

Basically, you can choose to have a separate data structure and somehow bind it to a grid (manually through `OnGetValue` / `OnSetValue` events or through LiveBindings technology) or go for a different approach and use `TStringGrid`.

`TStringGrid` has a different grid model that actually holds the data for the grid (hence, its `DataStored` property is `True`). The grid model is implemented by a `TStringGridModel` where, basically, the cache is used as a permanent storage for cells' values. The indexed `Cells[const ACol, ARow: Integer]: string` property is exposed by the grid model (and republished by `TStringGrid`) and is publicly available to set and read the value of each cell from the outside. Internally, the grids hold a `TGridValues` instance (basically, a dictionary of `TValue` entries, accessed by a cell's coordinates) but, as you can see from the definition of the `Cells` properties (of the model and the grid), only string values are allowed.

Again, the definition of column collection is made at runtime via code or at design time through the **Items Editor** we have seen before, while the number of rows is determined by the value of the `RowCount` property. Then, you can access the `Cells` property to set values for individual cells (even non-visible ones).

When it is time to render the grid, values stored in the `Cells` property will be used (trying some conversions if the chosen column type needs them). For example, you may have `TStringGrid` with `TGlyphColumn` and set its value to a string representing the image index you would like to see drawn in the cell (that is, 3) and have it converted to an integer and used as is. Otherwise, you may want to implement a handler for the `TGlyphColumn.OnGetImageIndex` event and perform any kind of mapping across the cell's value and the resulting image index to be used.

In the following code snippet, you can see how to assign content values through the double-indexed `Cells` property, as well as an example of `OnGetImageIndex` event handler implementation, as discussed previously:

```
// you can set the value for the row 1 and column 3 through the Cells
property and using a string representation of the index
StringGrid1.Cells[3,1] := '2';

// you can set the value for the row 1 and column 3 through the Cells
property and using any kind of string
StringGrid1.Cells[3,1] := 'sold-out';

// OnGetImageIndex event handler: will translate sold-out to an image index
procedure TMainForm.GlyphColumn1GetImageIndex(Column: TColumn;
    const Value: TValue; var ImageIndex: TImageIndex);
begin
  if Value.AsString = 'sold-out' then
    ImageIndex := 3;
end;
```

`TStringGrid` can also be bound to data through LiveBindings. It is basically implemented by disabling internal data storage and relying completely on the bound data source.

In the next section, we are going to briefly address customization of `TGrid` and `TStringGrid` components.

Customizing TGrid and TStringGrid

Customization of `TGrid` and `TStringGrid` can be done in the standard FMX way: by editing the style of the objects (when `ControlType` is set to `Styled`). This will allow you to change the general aspect of the components and possibly add some other element to the list. Another way to provide some customization to grid controls is to register your own column classes or handle the `OnDraw*` events they expose.

A much more advanced customization would be to provide other presentations for the grids or customize the style of controls used in the standard columns but, as already said, this is an advanced topic and a bit beyond the scope of this book.

In this section, we discussed grids, which are popular components (especially with respect to desktop platforms) for presenting data to the user in a visual manner. In the next section, we are going to encounter components acting as containers of other visual components, thereby improving and facilitating the general organization and management of the UI as a whole.

Mastering drawers and panels

In this section, we are going to learn about drawers and panels. These are some very commonly used containers for organizing UI elements in modules. In most situations, UIs are focused on a main content and the current trend (especially on mobile) is to split each activity (or task) the user should accomplish into a separate, dedicated, UI module (mobile apps are often modeled as state machines where each state has a corresponding view).

This means you will find yourself designing your form (or frame as we'll see in Chapter 8, *Divide and Conquer with TFrameStand*) with a specific target in mind and trying to focus the user's attention on that. However, even if we strive much to reduce our UIs and keep the user focused on the main topic, we often need places to put secondary UI elements, settings, menus, and similar things. Sometimes it is useful to also have a container for a group of UI elements to keep them in the same context, improving the overall user experience (finding a break even across a minimalistic and functional/rich UI).

FMX has a component that can be considered as a *smart panel*: the TMultiView component. It makes it really straightforward to implement drawers, docked panels, or pop-up panels. Aside from the actual implementation of these different kinds of containers, what really makes TMultiView a nice addition to the FMX component family is that it uses the so called behavior services of FMX to react differently on different platforms/device classes.

This basically means that the same instance can act differently according to the actual device your application is running on, or even react at some device-specific parameter that may vary at runtime (that is, device orientation).

One of the main use cases of this component is the implementation of a master/detail view. A typical example is on mobile, where the master view can be implemented as a list of items (using a TListView) and the detail view can be a collection of components to edit the data of each entry in the list (let's say a panel with edits, buttons, combo boxes, images, and so on). On a smartphone, where the available screen space is limited, you may want to focus user attention on the detail view, while having a secondary way to change the currently selected item.

Having a side drawer that can slide in (when the user slides his finger from a side of the touchscreen or by pushing some button in the detail UI), showing the master list can be very effective as it provides a way to select a different entry without reducing the screen size available to place all the necessary controls to present and allow the editing of data for the user. The same scenario on a tablet may take advantage of the extra screen space by having the master (list) view always visible as a docked panel right beside the detail (controls) view. This can be more effective (at a screen space cost that is intolerable on smaller screens) as the user always has the master list (with evidence of the current selection) in sight. TMultiView is the perfect component to easily implement this cross-platform scenario.

In fact, TMultiView has several Mode options, each one with its own peculiarities. Let's have a look at them, one by one.

Drawer mode

A drawer is a container for other controls that is generally not visible and can be activated by sliding one edge of a touchscreen from the outside to the inside of the screen. This triggers a gesture that will bring the drawer (now visible) in the current view by following the user's finger on the screen. It is a very common UI element as it adds some available space for UI controls without losing focus on the main content of the current view and without permanently stealing space for other controls. A typical usage is for menus or navigational items that the user can use to change/tweak the current view's content or switch to another view of your application.

Apart from a gesture, it is usually associated with a button you can press to trigger an animation mimicking the gesture behavior. It is not mandatory, but most people will look for a button with the *hamburger* icon (*three horizontal lines stacked up, or three bullets stacked up*) that is now universally recognized as the icon for accessing settings or other details of your current view.

The following screenshot shows TMultiView in Drawer mode:

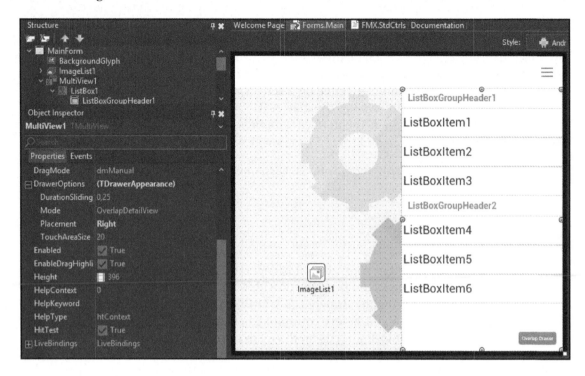

Figure 4.18

As you can see, the drawer will be shown using a light-box effect (you can fine-tune this effect through the ShadowOptions property of the TMultiView component). The main content of the current view (form) will be dimmed out and the drawer will slide in on top of this dimming surface. Clicking (or touching) the dimming surface will cause the drawer to close automatically. To associate a button with the drawer, in order to control the drawer through the button, simply set the MasterButton property of the TMultiView component.

Object Inspector (on the left-hand side of the preceding screenshot) shows a DrawerOptions entry that allows you to fine-tune some aspects of the drawer behavior, through properties including the following:

- DurationSliding: This property specifies the duration of the animation that occurs at the opening and closing of the drawer.

- `Mode`: This property will determine the actual behavior of the drawer with respect to the detail view (see the `TargetControl` property of the `TMultiView` component). You can set two values for this property:
  - `OverlapDetailView` (default): When the `Mode` property is set to this value, the drawer will overlap the detail view. The drawer will partially cover the detail view.
  - `PushingDetailView`: When this value is selected for the `Mode` property, the detail view will be jointly moved with respect to the drawer. The detail view is always visible, but the sliding part of it (in the direction depending on the drawer position) can leave the actual visible space.
- `Placement`: This property determines which edge of the screen the drawer should be associated with. The common values are `Left` or `Right`, but you can also choose `Bottom` or `Top`.
- `TouchAreaSize`: This property lets you adjust the size of the virtual *knob* of the drawer. The larger the value, the easier it is to grab it, but with a higher likelihood of tampering with controls nearby.

You can have several `TMultiView` instances in your form or frame and I would suggest avoiding having more than one per edge.

NavigationPane mode

A navigation pane is a collapsible panel that, when closed, occupies a relatively small screen space but, once opened (take note that it is not mandatory to open it in order to interact with its content), can display a larger content and capture user focus through a light-box effect. As stated previously, you can fine-tune the effect through the `ShadowOptions` property of the `TMultiView` component.

It is very effective to implement some kind of master selection when the master can be easily identified with a small amount of screen space (that is, through the use of an image) but, at the same time, you may want to provide a more detailed description of the items if needed. The following screenshot showcases precisely this scenario, where each item has a unique image and the user can get acquainted with the sole image in order to select an entry from the list:

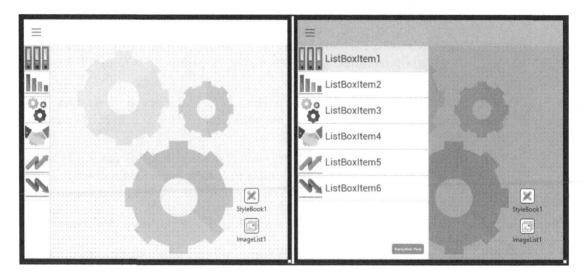

Figure 4.19

Another use case for this mode can be found when the master content includes a main selection (the selected item in a list represents the master data item), but there are other minor elements or options linked to the master that can be tweaked in order to drive the detail view (that is, you are editing master data, and you may find it handy to provide a checkbox or switch component to set a characteristic of the master item that has some consequences for the detail view).

The only specific property available for this mode is the `CollapsedWidth` property (you can find it in the **Object Inspector** window under the `NavigationPaneOptions` sub-property). The default value is `50`, but you can obviously change this value to set the size of the `TMultiView` component when this `Mode` is selected and the component is closed.

Panel mode

The (docked) panel mode will make `TMultiView` act like a standard panel component. No animation or gesture will play a role in this mode and the only parameter you may want to tweak in this mode is defined through the `Placement` property of the `SplitViewOptions` sub-property of the `TMultiView` component. Basically, you can select where the panel will be aligned when this mode is selected, choosing between the `Left`, `Right`, `Top`, and `Bottom` values.

The following screenshot shows how the component will look (at design time, but also at runtime) and, on the left-hand side of the screenshot, you can spot the `Placement` property highlighted in the **Object Inspector** window of the IDE:

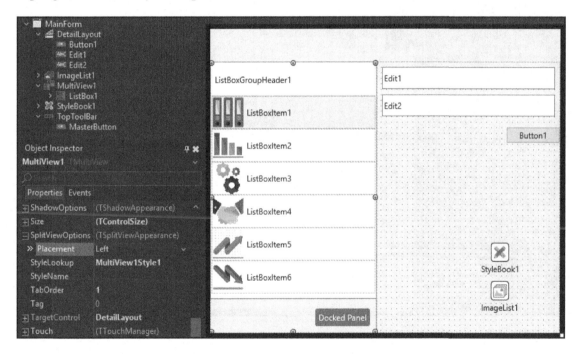

Figure 4.20

Even if this behavior seems really basic and you may consider using a simpler `TPanel` component to achieve the same effect, please consider the fact that you can actually switch across different mode values at runtime (manually or through the automatic selection mechanism we will discuss later in this chapter).

Popover mode

The final mode implemented for the `TMultiView` component is the popover one. This mode implements the master view as an external (pop-up) panel that will float over the detail view. This mode is effective when the master view is wholly unnecessary when the user is focusing on the detail view (the opposite with respect to Navigation Pane mode or Panel mode and more akin to what happens with Drawer mode).

You can trigger the popover show through a button, which is easy to set up through the `MasterButton` property of the `TMultiView` component itself. In the following screenshot, you can see what it looks like at runtime (on the Windows platform):

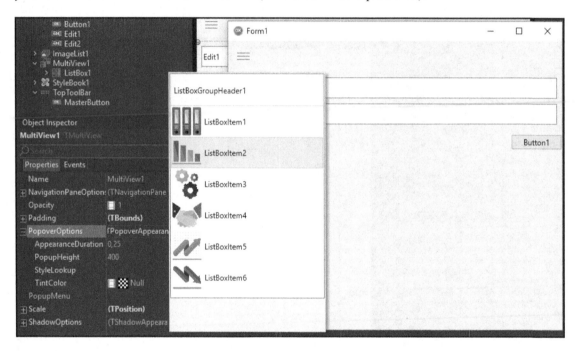

Figure 4.21

As with the Drawer mode, you can tweak some appearance details of this mode through the `PopoverOptions` sub-property, which includes the following properties:

- `AppearanceDuration`: This property lets you define the duration of the show/hide animations for the popover.
- `PopupHeight`: This value determines the vertical size of the popover panel.

- `StyleLookup`: This value can be set to override the visual aspect of the popover panel, through a `Style` object.
- `TintColor`: You can set this value to define a color for the popover button. Be aware this will have an effect only when the current style is a tint-enabled FMX style.

Popover mode is quite handy when you need to implement panels with several options that are only needed from time to time in your application usage and when you don't want to waste screen space on secondary controls.

In a master/detail view mechanism, a popover can be effective if the selection of the master requires some space (for example, because the master items have a long description), but it is unlikely that the user will switch across masters very often.

PlatformBehavior mode

We have seen that `TMultiView` offers several pre-implemented modes that you can use directly by setting the `Mode` property of your `TMultiView` instances. However, this is not the best use case for this component because it has been specifically designed to offer cross-platform behavior by switching automatically from one mode to another, according to the actual platform/device class/orientation the application is running on.

So, apart from the convenience of having a simple way to align this kind of panel and provide advanced functionalities such as gesture response and interactivity through other components (remember the `MasterButton` property), the real game-changing functionality of this component is that it will be super easy to implement master/detail views that properly adapt to the actual scenario the user is immersed in.

More specifically, you can refer to the following schema to know how the component behaves in different situations:

Mobile	Phone		**Drawer**
	Tablet	Landscape	**Docked Panel**
		Portrait	**Drawer**
Desktop	Windows 10		**Navigation Pane**
	Windows 8 and earlier		**Docked Panel**
	OS X (macOS)		

Table 4.1

As you can see in the preceding table, depending on the device family (mobile/desktop), the device class (phone/tablet) or the OS version, and the device orientation (landscape/portrait), a convenient mode is selected (on the right of the table, in bold). For example, if we run the application on a phone (Mobile/Phone), we'll get the **Drawer** mode selected. If we run the application on a tablet being held landscape (horizontally), we'll get the **Docked Panel** mode selected.

So, if this fits your needs, simply select `PlatformBehavior` as a value for the `Mode` property of your `TMultiView` component and let the component switch to the correct mode each time.

Custom mode

If none of the pre-implemented modes for `TMultiView` fit your needs, you can provide a custom implementation by implementing a `TMultiViewPresentation` descendant and setting the `CustomPresentationClass` property of your `TMultiView` component.

Summary

In this chapter, we have seen how to effectively use some very important components of the FMX framework: list controls, tree views, grids, and multi views. These components are very common in most applications and are the key building blocks of your UIs. Some of them are very rich in functionalities and provide a high level of customization opportunities and it is very important that you have a general understanding of how they work and what functionalities are available in order to build effective and rich UIs for your applications.

At the same time, having good knowledge of the individual building blocks is generally not enough to deliver a decent user experience. The upcoming chapters will focus on several traversal aspects of programming with FMX.

The next chapter will cover FireDAC, the data access component library included in Delphi since the **XE3 version**, covering basic concepts and typical usage in FMX applications.

We'll discuss another important topic, in `Chapter 6`, *Implementing Data Binding*, but that has already been encountered sporadically in this chapter and in the previous one, is the LiveBindings technology, which we'll discover together.

5
Using FireDAC in FMX Applications

In Chapter 3, *Mastering Basic Components*, and Chapter 4, *Discovering Lists and Advanced Components*, we covered an overview of the most fundamental and commonly used visual components in the FMX framework. Many applications are actually data-centric, meaning that the **User Interface (UI)** is a way to present some data to the user. This data can be from different sources and must be accessed and managed accordingly.

In this chapter, we will have a look at the default (and included) **Data Access Components library** for Delphi, that is, **FireDAC** (https://www.embarcadero.com/products/rad-studio/firedac). It is a powerful, feature-rich, robust, performant, and well-architected library that comes from decades of development and tuning, mostly by its original author, Dmitry Arefiev.

This chapter will focus on the fundamentals of FireDAC to get you started with this library but also with some specific highlights of peculiar features useful in FMX (especially mobile) applications.

We will cover the following topics in this chapter:

- Learning about the FireDAC library
- Understanding the options system
- Working with macros and parameters
- Taking advantage of memory tables
- Connecting to a database
- Introducing Tables, Query, StoredProc, and Command
- Understanding dataset persistence
- Implementing an onboard database
- Exploring the LocalSQL feature

Even though an in-depth disquisition of FireDAC would be largely out of scope for this book, covering fundamentals and some key concepts will provide you with capabilities to handle data in applications and, consequently, have a chance to build a user interface around data.

Technical requirements

Here is the source code used in this chapter: `https://github.com/PacktPublishing/` `Delphi-GUI-Programming-with-FireMonkey/tree/master/Chapter%2005`.

Generally speaking, for the whole book, you need a computer with Delphi set up and a few additional libraries installed (such as **Radiant Shapes** (`https://getitnow.` `embarcadero.com/?q=radiant+shapes`) and **CodeSite Logging** (`https://getitnow.` `embarcadero.com/?q=codesite`)). Having other devices and setting up multiple platforms (iOS, Android, OS X/macOS, and Linux) other than Windows is a plus but not strictly needed to follow the flow of the book.

Learning about the FireDAC library

In this section, we are going to discuss FireDAC, the data access library shipped with Delphi. We'll discuss the general architecture as well as some key points that make this library very effective for every Delphi developer.

There are many things I love about FireDAC, and they are as follows:

- It is a well-designed library, with a neat separation across functions, classes, and component layers; given this separation and another kind of separation, across functionalities, you can pick what you need and leave the rest out of your applications.
- The base concept of this DAC library is to provide access to a wide variety of database servers through the same programming interface, with a non-limiting approach that enables cross-database system programming as well as direct access to each system's peculiar features.

- It enables high-level features (such as in-memory datasets, filters, grouping, **local SQL**, persistence, **macros**, **array DML**, fetching and locking strategies, connection pooling, and many other capabilities) without effort and providing fallback implementations where these features are not available natively.

- It provides a migration path from the **Borland Database Engine (BDE)** technology, now deprecated, but still used in many (aged) Delphi projects that can be easily upgraded to a more modern approach without heavy refactoring. At the same time, many Delphi developers are familiar with the **BDE-like DAC approach** so having some common ground with it also means a more gentle learning curve. FireDAC also has a way to (re)use **dbExpress** (the previous *default* DAC library in Delphi) drivers.

- It is a full Delphi source code library, meaning everything in this library can be compiled on each supported platform (**Windows**, **Linux**, **OS X/macOS**, **Android**, and **iOS**). This implies you can use this library everywhere (standalone, client/server, multi-tier, desktop, and mobile applications), that is, a single skill set to rule them all.

- It has a long history behind it and it is a mature product that has been around for a decade or more. You can immediately feel how FireDAC has been designed and grown on real case scenarios and its main author, **Dmitry Arefiev**, has been very active through the years in improving the library's quality and robustness.

As I have already written, I am not going to even attempt full coverage of the FireDAC library. It comes with very broad documentation, and there are many samples that come with the Delphi installation. There are forums where excellent support is provided by Dmitry himself (and others) and there are books from experts written specifically to provide in-depth knowledge of the library (for example, Cary Jensen's *Delphi in Depth: FireDAC*, 2017).

Understanding the library's composition

The following diagram (source: https://www.embarcadero.com/products/rad-studio/ firedac) summarizes the architecture of the **FireDAC** library and you can clearly see how the library is layered, that is, on the top, there are FMX and VCL applications, using the library to implement data access and management:

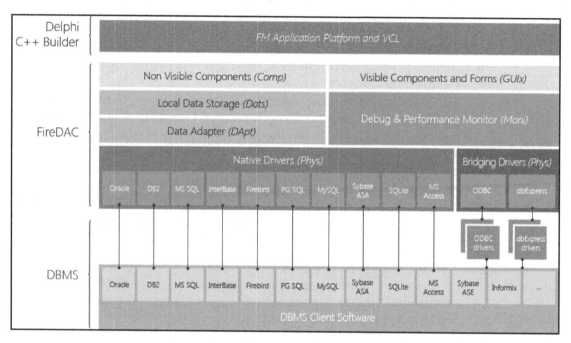

Figure 5.1

As you can see, at the bottom, there are the **DBMS** client libraries (provided by each vendor and part of the DBMS software itself) and in the middle, there is **FireDAC**, itself layered from drivers (physical or bridging) to interface with the DBMS client libraries up to the higher-level components (non-visible and visible).

The most important and most used components, such as those implementing a database connection, transaction handling, **SQL** execution, and result-set fetching, are all situated in the **Non Visible Components (Comp)** layer and take advantage of capabilities and functionalities implemented in the underlying layers.

As you can see in the preceding diagram, FireDAC has the capability to connect to several different DBMSes (the list is impressive and, moreover, you can reach almost every other database through the bridging drivers, eventually paying a performance or functionality cost). However, I want to start from the real core of each DAC suite, that is, the **dataset** – the object wrapping data in order to present it and perform some operations on it.

A detail I really appreciate in FireDAC is that all datasets (that is, TFDTable, TFDQuery, TFDStoredProc, and TFDMemTable) have a common core that implements most of their functionalities. This means FireDAC datasets are easy to handle as they are actually relative to one another (as an example, cached update functionality is implemented at the TFDDataSet level so is available to all FireDAC datasets). The following diagram depicts the inheritance relationship across some of the named components:

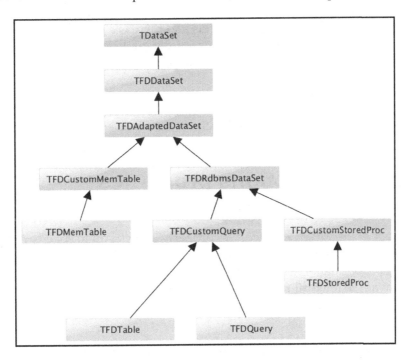

Figure 5.2

In the next section, we are going to introduce how options work in FireDAC. A great plus of this library is the huge amount of configurable options exposed. You can literally tweak most aspects of the library, making it effective in your very specific use case.

Understanding the options system

Four fundamental properties introduced in `TFDDataSet` (thus, available in every one of its subclasses) are `FetchOptions`, `FormatOptions`, `ResourceOptions`, and `UpdateOptions`.

These property sets model the majority of FireDAC behaviors and their values are used to fine-tune how each component instance actually works. A nice thing to note is that the options system of FireDAC is multi-level with fallback definition, meaning that in a real use case you probably have a dataset (that is, `TFDQuery`) that is making use of a connection (`TFDConnection`) that has been created from a definition by the FireDAC manager (`TFDManager`).

Each of these three elements can specify options and there is a fall-back mechanism that will enable you to define the default behavior once per application (setting the option sets of `TFDManager`) and then eventually override each option item at the connection and dataset levels.

Let's have a closer look at some of these properties and, while you're reading the descriptions, you will notice a number of functionalities FireDAC offers out of the box.

Exploring FetchOptions properties

The `FetchOptions` property has the following sub-properties:

- `Mode` and `RowsetSize`: The `Mode` property allows you to specify how FireDAC should implement the fetching of records for a result set. If you are doing some batch processing or some data transformation involving the whole dataset, you may want to fetch all records in a single shot, to reduce network time (if any, as FireDAC can work both with local and remote databases), especially when the latency is not minimal.

  In a perhaps more common scenario for regular applications, you may want the fetching to be incremental to improve the user experience as the user is not forced to wait for the whole dataset to be loaded before starting to see/work with the data. Different values of the `Mode` property will let you determine the exact behavior of the fetching strategy, ranging from completely manual handling to automatic or semi-automatic. There are a number of secondary aspects involved in fetching and you can fine-tune most of them through FireDAC's options.

For example, the `RowsetSize` property will determine how many records will be involved in each single fetch operation. The larger the value of `RowsetSize`, the lower the number of fetches needed to load the whole dataset will be but, at the same time, the longer each fetch operation may take (determined by the bandwidth this time). Other options (like `RecsMax` or `RecsSkip`) will help you impose some limits on the total number of records fetched (useful in a situation where you want to show the first X records of a result set or when you are implementing the pagination of a result set).

- `RecsMax` and `RecsSkip`: There are a number of situations in modern scenarios where the pagination of data is needed. If this is scarcely used in desktop applications (apart from a situation where the total amount of data is huge, of course), mobile and web applications tend to be more careful about the amount of data presented to the user in a single dataset.

This means my query returning 1,000 rows may need to be split into 20 pages of 50 records each so the frontend (web or mobile) can consume it easily and the process is optimized for the user (who is not supposed to be in need of the whole dataset immediately). FireDAC offers you a built-in implementation of pagination by letting you specify (through the `RecsMax` property) the size of the page (meaning the length in records) and the number of records to skip from the beginning of the dataset.

In our previous example, the dataset would have `RecsMax` set to `50` and, to load page number three, you could set `RecsSkip` to `100` (as the result of `(3-1) * 50` corresponding to the general formula `(PageNumber-1) * PageSize` where `PageNumber` is 1-based) and have the dataset containing records from 101 to 150.

FireDAC will implement this behavior efficiently by taking advantage of the capabilities of the underlying DBMS or, if these capabilities are not supported, by providing an equivalent implementation (note, this is a very good feature of FireDAC as it will save you from a hard error if you switch to a less featured database system).

- `RecordCountMode`: According to the selected fetching strategy, you may be in a situation where the number of records in the dataset is not corresponding to the number of records your result set is composed of. Let's say you have a database table and you are trying to access it.

If you configured (through the `Mode` property) the dataset to fetch all records at dataset opening, the dataset will contain an amount of records that matches the amount of records in the table. *But what if your database table is large and you are using incremental fetching to improve the user experience to avoid load time at database opening?* Let's say your `RowsetSize` property is set to `50`, so FireDAC fetches 50 records at a time.

What should the `RecordCount` property of the dataset represent? Will it represent the number of records fetched into the dataset, or the total number of records in the table? The `RecordCountMode` property value will determine how FireDAC should implement the `RecordCount` property and, for example, may automatically perform a `select COUNT(*) from ...` to read the total number of records on the server side (thus, letting you have an incremental fetching strategy and at the same time mimicking some behavior, think about progress or position indicators as if the records are all already available, read and fetched, to the client).

Exploring FormatOptions properties

The `FormatOptions` property has the following sub-properties:

- `MapRules`: A dataset may be seen as a sort of abstraction over some data storage format (in the case of a classic DBMS, it may represent a table or query result set). This abstraction is based on rows (records) and columns (fields) and each column is usually associated with a specific data type (a string, an integer number, memo text, and so on).

  The way a data access library binds the native type of data to a column type can have a very significant impact on the application development and also on the evolution of the data storage through time. If you are an experienced developer, you surely have faced this before and you know how handy it can be to have a way to fine-tune the mapping rules your DAC library applies to construct datasets.

Sometimes the database architect uses some conventions to mark all integer fields with a name starting with `B_` that are in fact Boolean values or uses some specific numeric definition for currency values stored in the database and so on. `MapRules` are a collection of rules (once again, with the **FDManager** / **Connection** / **Dataset** fallback chain) FireDAC uses to map a native (storage) data type to a column (field) type of the resulting dataset. Simply add a new `TFDMapRule` to the `MapRules` collection and specify `SourceDataType` and `TargetDataType` to drive all columns that would result in `SourceDataType` (as the current driver would suggest) to an eventually more friendly for the application `TargetDataType`.

You can make the rule stricter by specifying a `NameMask` value to address only fields matching a specific name pattern. Typical examples of use are mapping `smallint` columns to Boolean fields, or numeric (BCD) columns to currency fields, but there are a lot of situations where this capability can step in to lend a hand to the developer (to address changes in the driver rules impacting existing applications or when moving from one database to another).

Exploring ResourceOptions properties

The `ResourceOptions` property has the following sub-properties:

- `CmdExecMode` and `CmdExecTimeout`: A very common issue I have seen developers asking about on forums is about how to avoid the application from *freezing* while performing a time-consuming SQL operation (opening a large table or executing a not-so-fast query). Around the same topic, there is a second question, *how do you cancel a long SQL operation from the client side?*

  Both questions deal with the command execution mode and the fact that most data access libraries are blocking and single-threaded. We'll learn about parallel programming in `Chapter 11`, *Building Responsive Applications*, and how to achieve responsiveness in blocking scenarios, but there is a very handy feature that FireDAC has. Through `CmdExecMode`, you can choose among some built-in implementation that may help you avoid UI blocking and at the same time give you a chance to cancel a long-running SQL operation from your application code.

The default value is `amBlocking` (thus the operations are blocking and your code will wait for long operations locking the calling thread needed all the time, also meaning that if the calling thread is the main thread of your application, where the UI lives, your UI will freeze as well). Other possible values are `amNonBlocking` or `amCancelDialog`, both using a secondary thread to avoid blocking the calling thread (with the latter option also presenting the user with a cancel dialog to interrupt the operation, if the underlying driver allows operation termination) but keeping your code synchronous, meaning the call (to `Open` or `Execute` methods) will not return until the operation is finished, even if your application will be able to process GUI messages (but discarding mouse and keyboard related ones to avoid the user messing up during operation execution).

The last option for `CmdExecMode` is the `amAsync` value, which will make the operation execution actually parallel and asynchronous, using a secondary thread with the call to the dataset's method returning immediately, and you will have to rely on event handlers (that is, `AfterOpen`) to respond to the fact the operation has been completed (or failed).

In the following screenshot, you can see the provided demo project, `Chapter 05\CmdExecMode_amAsync` (**GitHub repo:** `https://github.com/PacktPublishing/Delphi-GUI-Programming-with-FireMonkey/tree/master/Chapter%2005/CmdExecMode_amAsync`). The `FDQuery1` component has been configured, setting the `CmdExecMode` property value to `amAsync` and a proper handler for the `AfterOpen` event will be fired when data is available (the query statement has been written to be slow, on purpose, and takes at least a second on my machine):

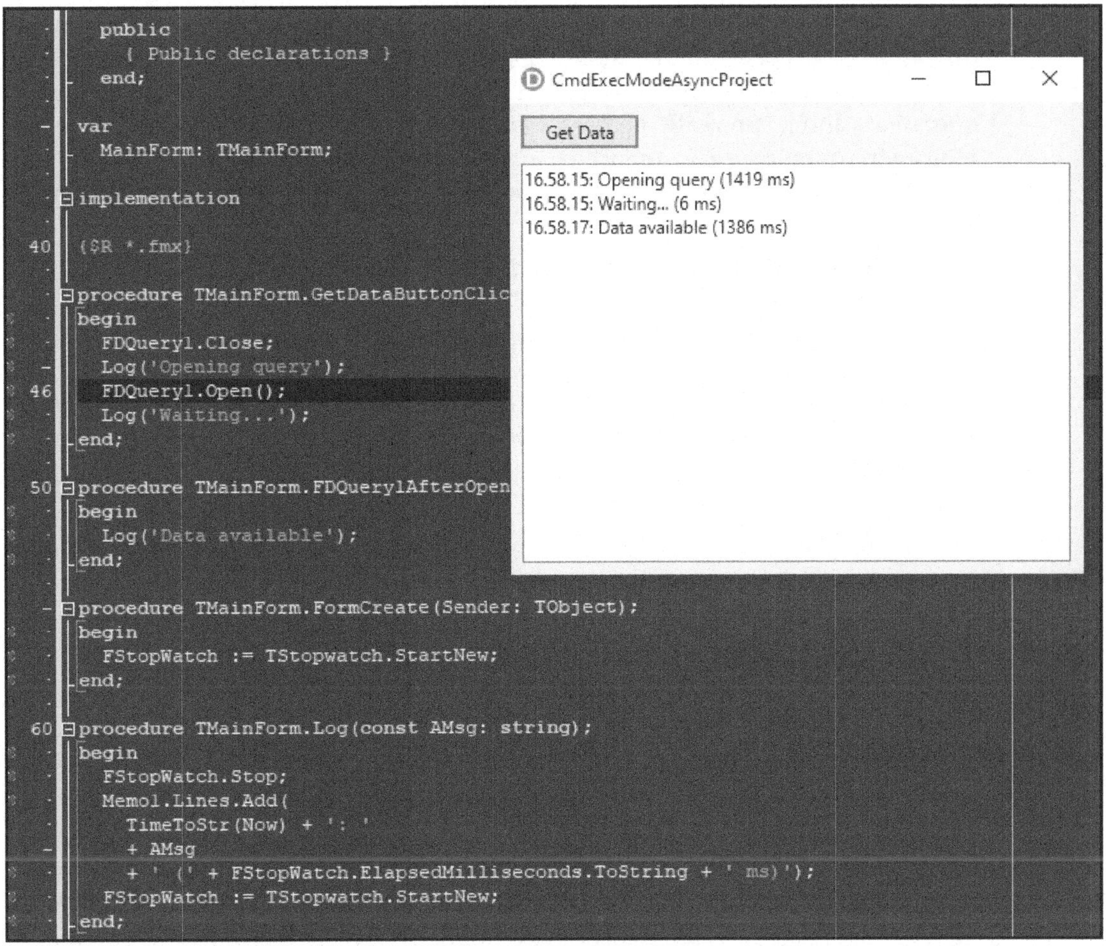

```
    public
       { Public declarations }
    end;

 var
    MainForm: TMainForm;

implementation

 {$R *.fmx}

 procedure TMainForm.GetDataButtonClic
 begin
    FDQuery1.Close;
    Log('Opening query');
    FDQuery1.Open();
    Log('Waiting...');
 end;

 procedure TMainForm.FDQuery1AfterOpen
 begin
    Log('Data available');
 end;

 procedure TMainForm.FormCreate(Sender: TObject);
 begin
    FStopWatch := TStopwatch.StartNew;
 end;

 procedure TMainForm.Log(const AMsg: string);
 begin
    FStopWatch.Stop;
    Memo1.Lines.Add(
      TimeToStr(Now) + ': '
      + AMsg
      + ' (' + FStopWatch.ElapsedMilliseconds.ToString + ' ms)');
    FStopWatch := TStopwatch.StartNew;
 end;
```

CmdExecModeAsyncProject — □ ✕

Get Data

16.58.15: Opening query (1419 ms)
16.58.15: Waiting... (6 ms)
16.58.17: Data available (1386 ms)

Figure 5.3

As you can see looking at the trivial code in the preceding screenshot, the
Waiting... line gets printed in the log before data is actually available. The
execution of the Open() method, though, is asynchronous and will not prevent
the **Waiting...** line from being delayed just because the query takes 1.386 seconds
to execute.

In this same area, you may want to make sure data operations always succeed or
fail within a certain amount of time and you can specify this by setting
CmdExecTimeout, which will raise an exception when the running operation
takes too long (more than the specified timeout) to fulfill.

- `SilentMode`: FireDAC has a built-in mechanism to notify the user when some operation is occurring on datasets. This includes, for example, changing the mouse cursor to an hourglass when the dataset performs some potentially long operations and it can really be useful and nice for a better user experience. However, for better performance or to avoid distracting the user when not necessary, you can switch this behavior off by setting this property's value to `True`.

- `StoreItems`: A great functionality each FireDAC dataset has relates to persistence capabilities. You can easily save (to file or to a stream, so basically to whatever) and load datasets in several formats (**XML**, **JSON**, and **binary**). *What does saving a dataset to a file mean exactly?* A dataset is basically a collection of data records but also contains some metadata and, given that every FireDAC dataset has the ability to implement cached updates, possibly a log of the changes made to data locally. The `StoreItems` property will let you fine-tune exactly what to store in the external file/storage with the possibility to include (or not) data, delta, and metadata.

Exploring UpdateOptions properties

The `UpdateOptions` property has the following sub-properties:

- `LockMode`, `LockWait`, and `LockPoint`: If you are building an application (or part of it) where concurrency happens, you may want to specify the lock strategy and some parameters to fine-tune it. For example, if the underlying database supports the `SELECT FOR UPDATE` (or the like) statement (for example, in **Oracle**, **Firebird**, **MySQL**, and many more), you can set `LockMode` to the `lmPessimistic` value in order to obtain FireDAC to lock a record before editing it. Furthermore, you can specify (through the `LockPoint` property's value) whether the lock should be acquired at the moment the dataset starts editing the record (that is, when the `State` property of the dataset goes from `dsBrowse` to `dsEdit`) or when the changes are posted (that is, when the `TDataSet.Post` method gets called). But there's more: if the lock strategy is pessimistic and the record is already locked (so acquiring the lock will fail at the first attempt), you may want to determine whether this should cause an exception or whether it is better to wait some time to see if the record becomes available. You can decide this by setting the `LockWait` property's value to `True` or `False` (that is the default).

- `UpdateMode`: Probably the most important property to determine how updates are written back to the database from the dataset is the `UpdateMode` property. You can select a value among `upWhereAll`, `upWhereChanged`, and `upWhereKeyOnly` to determine how the `where` clause of the generated `UPDATE` statement is built and, consequently, what updating policy you want to enforce, that is, a conservative one, a mixed strategy, or a *last-one-wins* strategy.

  Your first option (`upWhereAll`) will cause all the fields to be included in the `where` clause (meaning the update will succeed only if no fields of the record have been changed by some other update that occurred in the time between the fetching of the record in the dataset and the moment where updates are trying to be applied back to the database). The second option (`upWhereChanged`) will only include fields that actually have been changed in the dataset (so you can be assured you are changing values that no other user/agent has changed in the meanwhile, but other fields of the same record may have changed).

  The last option (`upWhereKeyOnly`) will only try to locate the record to update by including the primary key fields in the `where` clause. This is a more permissive concurrency configuration as you are allowing the last update to supersede each other update that occurred in the meanwhile (even though this may sound a bit too permissive). In my experience, a lot of scenarios will benefit from this setting, but obviously, there is no general rule to choose the best value for the `UpdateMode` property, so it varies from case to case.

- `RefreshMode` and `RefreshDelete`: Once you have data loaded (fetched) into your dataset, you can make modifications and it is quite straightforward that you will see changed values immediately (they are local values). *But what if some fields are affected by some server-side mechanisms like calculated fields or auto-incrementing fields?* Moreover, the issue of deciding whether to refresh (read back) a record once changes to it are posted to the DBMS is quite general and applies to very simple situations (that is, the field has a default value in its server-side definition) and more complex ones (that is, a trigger is manipulating data after the insert or update of the record).

  FireDAC offers a useful functionality here because you can decide whether you want to manually control record refresh or let the library decide when it's a case to refresh the record after posting some changes to it; for example, if there are auto-incremented or calculated fields and the library is aware of them (it depends on the available metadata, but for most situations, this is true). It may automatically trigger a refresh after changes are applied (automatically handling a long-standing issue about retrieving the primary key of the record when this is implemented by an auto-incremental field or the like).

To deal with situations where the refresh is unfeasible, possibly because the server-side version of the record has been deleted, there is a `RefreshDelete` property to let you specify what to do when the `RefreshRecord` method is called and the remote record is not found (if the value is `True`, as the default, the local version of the record is deleted too, otherwise it remains untouched in the dataset).

FireDAC is a very enhanced data access component library, with a number of precious functionalities available for the developer to address some very common situations while building data-centric applications (client/server especially). As we have seen through this brief overview of some commonly used options, most of the time, you can rely on the default configuration of the library but, if needed, you can specify even tiny details of the applied mechanisms and automation. This is, without a doubt, great added value to keep complexity low where it is not needed and achieve the effectiveness of a product like Delphi, which has always shined in data-centric application development.

Once again, I want to state clearly that there are several other functionalities and options in FireDAC, but it is far beyond the scope of this book to delve too deeply into the library. In the next section, we will cover two functionalities that are quite peculiar, with respect to the average data access library and some basic usage examples and details.

Working with macros and parameters

While dealing with SQL statements, the complexity of these statements tends to grow. Aside from academic examples, the average SQL statement consists of a quite large fields list, some joins, filter criteria listed in the `where` clause, sorting, and possibly grouping.

For decades, in every programming forum I've been in, I have seen people manually concatenating SQL statements as strings in order to provide values for filter criteria or similar tasks. This is bad for a number of reasons, starting from some evident opening up to SQL injection vulnerabilities, down to possible performance penalties. However, basically, often there is the need to dynamically build (parts of) SQL statements, and FireDAC comes to the rescue with two handy functionalities: **parameters** and **macros**.

Parameters are quite a common feature among modern DBMSes and FireDAC correctly provides an interface to access them and populate them with values (as other DAC libraries do); macros are quite a peculiar capability that is built into FireDAC.

With parameters, you can give a pseudo name to a value (so you can, for example, write a SQL where clause like where ID = :ParamID) and then refer to this param through the Params collection. Each param is usually tied to a name (or, less commonly, accessed by position) and a data type. The param can be used as an input value or an output/result value of a SQL statement and FireDAC will properly handle most aspects of the param seamlessly against many DBMSes.

Using parameters can, in addition to letting you write more secure SQL statements, avoiding SQL injection pitfalls, come in handy to avoid the specific formatting of values (for example, passing a date/time value as TDateTime instead of the peculiar, database/OS/language/whatever-specific string format required by the underlying DBMS). Moreover, they will let you easily specify a NULL value for the parameter without having to have a separate case if/when needed. And they will surely open to performance speedups when you need to fire several syntactically identical statements over a number of a set of different values (batch processing – in this same area, please deeply consider the Array DML support FireDAC enables over many DBMS).

This is all good and I think most experienced developers are (or should be) familiar with parameters in SQL statements. **Macros** are a similar concept but they can be used to parameterize parts of the SQL statement – usually hard to manage without messing up string concatenation.

Let's have a look at the simplest example I can think of: *how do you select all fields and all records from a variable table? Something like* select * from TheTable *where* TheTable *is actually a variable and not the exact name of the table?* Most people would simply concatenate strings (or use a Format call) to compose the final SQL statement, but this can be bad in terms of readability and future maintenance.

Macros come to the rescue with the following syntax:

```
select * from !TheTable
```

You are actually defining a new macro name (TheTable) and you can provide a value for the macro before executing/opening the SQL statement by accessing the macro by name via code (FireDAC comes with a rich set of design-time editors so you can accomplish the task to provide values for parameters and macros even at design time).

Simply double-click on a `TFDQuery` component and you will see the component editor in your IDE, as in the following screenshot:

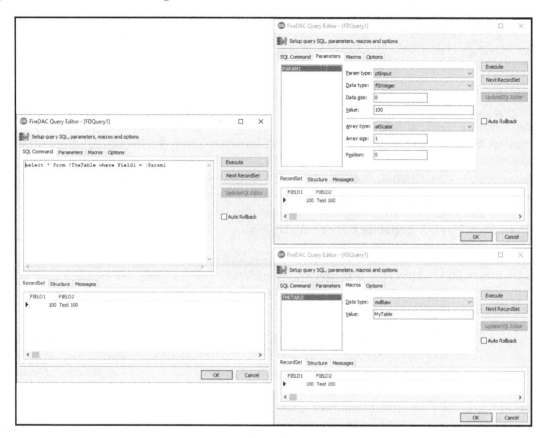

Figure 5.4

As you can see, the design-time experience is great and you can easily write your SQL statements, including macros and parameters, and have a chance to provide values before executing the query even at design time. Macros can be raw parts of the SQL statement (thus, you can really parameterize every part of the statement, including the kind of the statement and or other syntax portions of it), or you can define a data type and use them more or less as parameters. There are two modalities to define a macro in FireDAC:

- Using the exclamation mark, `!`, for which you are going to have a raw string substitution (no data type transformations – basically the same as concatenating strings).

- Using the ampersand, &, for which you are going to have a data type enabled (including conversions to the specific format of the underlying DBMS) value substitution (more secure and handy to cover different data formats).

Macro substitution is part of FireDAC preprocessing command capabilities and comes together with a number of other goodies you can combine to reach a very high level of flexibility; for example, you can use **escape sequences** (in curly braces) to pass a value and inform FireDAC how to properly format it.

For example, you can write {d '1982-05-24'} and it will be expanded as the proper date conversion function of the underlying DBMS), or you can write {ucase(Field1)} and have it expanded as the corresponding syntax equivalent of the underlying DBMS to uppercase values of the specified field. A number of escape functions are available (that is, {NOW()} to get the current date-time or {YEAR({NOW()})}) and they greatly simplify cross-database development (as they are actually an abstraction over the underlying SQL syntax) and enhance developer productivity.

The preprocessing engine is quite powerful and supports even the if statement, as follows:

```
select * from MyTable {if !Criteria} where !Criteria{fi} order by Field1
```

This will expand into an actual where clause only if the Criteria macro has a non-empty value) and the iif statement to implement case-like choices (with a final fallback) as in {iif (MSSQL, Microsoft, FIREBIRD, Firebird, Other)}, which will expand into the following:

- Microsoft when the underlying DBMS is **Microsoft SQL Server**
- Firebird when the underlying DBMS is **Firebird**
- Other for all other cases

Functions and statements can be nested at will with the only (personal) warning being not to add too much complexity this way, otherwise, you will experience a loss in readability (thus, going against the fundamental aim of these constructs).

In this section, we learned about macro and parameter capabilities. They can be very powerful and ease the building of complex statements or improve multi-database compatibility.

In the next section, we are going to introduce in-memory datasets, a powerful feature of the DAC library. There are in fact a number of scenarios where data needs to be collected, modified, or presented without being extracted, stored, or managed by a DBMS.

Taking advantage of memory tables

Even if most DAC libraries were born to provide you with the basic capabilities to read, manipulate, and store data from/into a DBMS, this is not always the case. **Memory tables** (in-memory datasets) are a very multi-purpose capability that may often change the way you deal with data in your applications.

There are a number of situations where an in-memory dataset can be useful. Let's cover some of the most common:

- **Handling data that does not come from a DBMS**: Sometimes you need to handle or collect data and the data source is something different from a DBMS. For example, you may want to collect data from sensors or other devices you can reach through networking or other communication channels. When the amount of data reaches a certain point, you may actually want to treat it as a dataset and possibly still use all the goodies you are familiar with (like filtering, sorting, aggregate functions, and so on). Also, having data in a format that is basically the same as when dealing with a DBMS means that you can use the same data-binding techniques to surface your data to the UI.
- **Efficiently transforming or manipulating a large amount of data (even when it comes from a DBMS)**: We already covered FireDAC's capabilities regarding the fetching and tuning possibilities of this (often critical) point when dealing with large data. Also, this use case sounds perfect for a stored procedure object, where all data is efficiently available to a piece of code running directly in the DBMS (I am not really a fan of stored procedures, for a number of reasons, mainly centered on maintainability and architecture design, but this is greatly out of scope).

However, this does not mean you may actually need to modify large sets of data in a batch, possibly having to deal with partial computations or multi-pass algorithms over the same datasets. Having an in-memory dataset here means you can actually read data (from a DBMS and/or some other source, with the only physical limit being the RAM you can actually address), then actually disconnect from one or all data sources to perform some long or difficult processing on that dataset. Think about dealing with data from a traditional DBMS that needs to be integrated with data from a different data source.

Once again, you'll have the best of two worlds: a consistent, handy, familiar approach to common data-related functionalities combined with the high-speed performance of in-memory operations. Once finished, you may even want to store the result back to a DBMS or to some other form of persistency.

- **Caching data to improve the performance of some algorithm**: Every time you need a caching layer in your application, you will end up looking for proper storage for your data and implementation for basic functionalities (the lookup of a value and similar). *Why not get the work done by reusing the already built functionality of your DAC library?*
- **Prototyping your applications**: In terms of RAD, a great advantage comes when you can anticipate the building of some parts even when they strongly rely on some other parts of the system itself. Think about the capability to prototype a mobile application part of a larger system that includes the backend for the mobile app itself.

As we will see, having a non-empty, live dataset in your IDE can really shorten the development time to build the UI of your mobile (but this also applies to desktop) application. In memory datasets, it is a good option to have some data (*snapshotted*, fake, or generated data) even when the data source is not (yet) available. You can achieve this by loading data from files (sample files or actual datasets you have previously saved to file) using the **Load From File...** entry in the component context menu, or even copy the data (and structure) of a live dataset into your TFDMemTable by using the **Assign DataSet...** entry of the same context menu, as you can see in the following screenshot:

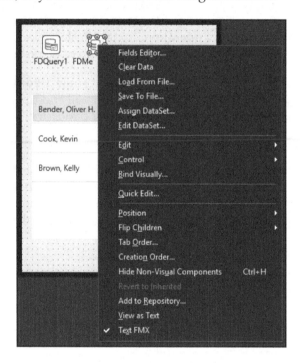

Figure 5.5

There are several other similar situations where the in-memory option can be a game-changing choice for your performance, functionalities, or development time. FireDAC really shines here because it includes the TFDMemTable component, which is feature-rich, like every other TFDDataSet descendant (including dataset navigation, filtering, sorting, aggregate and calculated fields, local SQL compatibility, persistence capabilities, and many others). It shares the same interface as all other datasets in FireDAC and provides an easy way to read and write data across other FireDAC datasets – and it is really fast and robust!

As I've already said, a great plus is that FireDAC depends on the fact the actual core of its datasets is shared and, consequently, it is easy to use it *standalone* in an in-memory dataset component without losing the interface consistency. This means that the developer can be immediately familiar with this component if they've already used the library to deal with a DBMS, providing a very effective additional functionality to traditional data-access-driven applications. Actually, you may think TFDMemTable is built as the core of every FireDAC dataset and, for example, enables the cached update mechanism that is nonetheless ubiquitously available in FireDAC.

 Cached updates are a powerful feature that enables developers (and thus users) to make data changes to a dataset without immediately translating to SQL statements and committing those changes to the actual backend. Changes are tracked and stored in a proper data structure (commonly referred to as the **delta**). The original values (as they were fetched from the backend) are also stored so you can always roll back to them if you need to (punctually inspecting the original value or zeroing the delta of the whole dataset).

A convenient method (ApplyUpdates) is available to actually process the dataset's delta and execute the corresponding SQL statements against the actual backend. A mechanism is available to deal with eventual conflicts that may occur due to data changes on the backend side.

Cached updates are useful in a number of scenarios, including the so-called briefcase-mode (connect, fetch data, disconnect, continue editing data during the disconnected period, and once the backend is available again, commit changes). They also represent a kind of alternative to transactions as changes are actually collected over time and then executed against the backend in a single shot (providing a sort of atomicity). This may be helpful to relieve the backend from long-lasting transactions and is completely tolerant of connection disruptions.

I personally have experience on a project basically crunching some large datasets (coming from sensor devices) to adjust the data according to different expert-selected criteria. This is often something related to time gaps or time-shifting due to sensor locations, to get back an actual significant meaning and an in-memory dataset proven to be a great solution (with respect to storing data locally in some file-based database) delivering results in a bunch of seconds (sometimes minutes) and retaining the capability to let the user manually edit the data during the process, where needed.

With the latest Delphi versions (**10.1 Berlin** and later), you even get the capability to actually see and modify data at design time (through the component editor) aside from loading datasets from files or copying existing datasets. This can represent an easy way to provide some sample data for your application or even one-shot data for consultation (as if data were an image you add in your form/frame and store in the corresponding **FMX** file). The following screenshot shows the new **Edit DataSet...** functionality, showing the actual dataset content you can refer to and edit at design time:

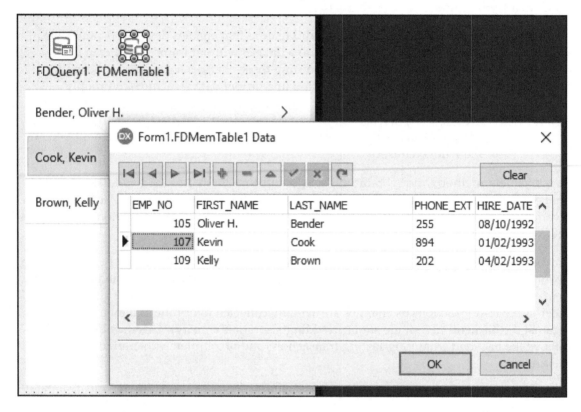

Figure 5.6

Another interesting use case involving an in-memory dataset relates to the use of local SQL functionality (more on this later in this chapter), enabling the use of SQL even above non-DBMS-originated datasets. In fact, you may write SQL operations (including set-oriented operations like `update MyTable set Field1 = 'XXX' where Field2 > 100`) against data stored in `TFDMemTable` components (and/or other datasets even belonging to other DAC libraries).

Last, but not least, in-memory datasets can play a central role in a multi-tier architecture as they can be used to represent datasets on the client side regardless of the communication layer used to retrieve them.

Also, powerful capabilities like cached update support (that is, the capability to track changes to a dataset and build a change log sufficient to replicate those changes back to the data source) are automatically available as well as persistence capabilities. These are perfect to implement a full *briefcase* experience within your application, that is, to connect and consume a backend to retrieve data, edit data locally, even through multiple local sessions and with the opportunity to save it locally on disk, then collect changes and send them back to the backend (either in a raw format, possibly applying them by relying on FireDAC on the server side too or processing the change log to perform backend operations accordingly).

Connecting to a database

Now that we have covered some ways to use FireDAC even without an underlying DBMS, we can step back to what is probably the main (but not exclusive) focus of this library: dealing with a DBMS (a traditional one like an **RDBMS** or even modern ones like **NoSQL**).

The first task you need to accomplish is usually to set up a connection to the data source (the DBMS). Either for historical or practical reasons, there are a number of ways to define connections.

The first great distinction is between defining a connection through its set of parameters rather than using a connection definition name. The following screenshot shows the component editor available for TFDConnection, including the list of configuration parameters composing the connection definition:

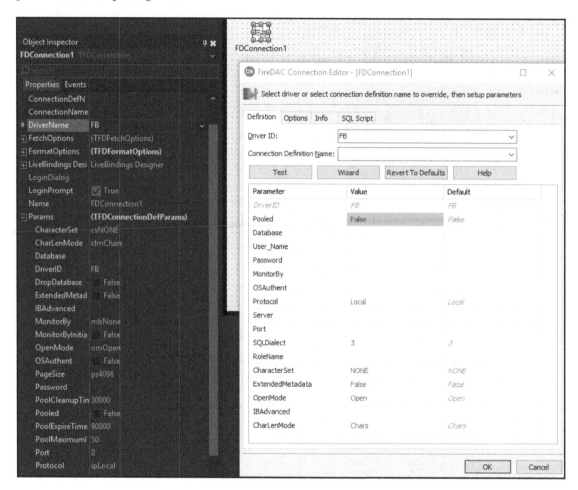

Figure 5.7

As you can see, you can drop a TFDConnection object on your form/frame/data module and start configuring it. On the left of the screenshot, you will notice the **Object Inspector** IDE window showing the properties of your FDConnection1 object. The first thing to set is the DriverName property value to be used, to address a specific database driver corresponding to the underlying database management system.

Selecting the driver will cause the IDE to include the corresponding unit of the driver in your source code (that is, the FireDAC.Phys.FB unit for the **FB**, Firebird, driver) so that it is actually compiled within your application and available at runtime. This also determines the set of parameters meaningful for this driver.

You can set these parameters through the TFDConnection.Params property (basically a name-value list, implemented with the TStrings descendant) at runtime or at design time through the **Object Inspector**. A third, convenient, option is to double-click on the TFDConnection component and use the component editor (named **FireDAC Connection Editor**, visible in the preceding screenshot, on the right).

For each parameter, you can see the default value and set a value to be used. Once you are done configuring the required parameters, a handy **Test** button is available to trigger a connection attempt to the data source. Using the **FireDAC Connection Editor** will also enable you to set the options (covered in a previous part of this chapter), access the **Info** tab where details about the connection are provided (that is, the actual client library used to perform the connection, its version, and some other useful information for immediate troubleshooting), or enter the **SQL Script** tab and execute some SQL statements.

The connection definition is basically composed of the DriverName (**Driver ID**) value and the collection of parameters' values defined. FireDAC provides an indirection mechanism to let you refer this information through a name: the connection definition name (ConnectionDefName).

You can store connection definitions in multiple places, managed by the TFDManager component that is able to retrieve them and let them be available to your application. I don't want to cover every detail of connection definitions (as it is well explained in the FireDAC documentation already), but it is important to know there are three kinds of connections you can refer to: **Persistent**, **Private**, and **Temporary** connections. Let's briefly expand a bit on these topics:

- **Persistent connections** have their definitions stored in a file (by default, an .ini file). So, basically, they can be *per-machine* or *per-application* and you can set the name of the file containing definitions to control this mechanism. The TFDManager class/component can be used to manage these connection definitions. You can also use the FireDAC Explorer administration tool to manage/edit the connection definitions (there is a shortcut to run it under the **Tools | FireDAC Explorer** menu entry).

- **Private connections** are not stored in connection definition files but they can be defined through the TFDManager component and their definition is available application-wide. Basically, this means you may have some dynamic behavior (or external configuration file) to determine the connection definition, create it through TFDManager and make it available (through a ConnectionDefName value) to the whole application.

- **Temporary connections** are defined locally, basically adding a TFDConnection component and populating its Params property with the required parameters. This kind of definition is very specific and can't be reused automatically, even within the same application.

Depending on the specific scenario, you may want to go for a persistent, private, or temporary connection definition, but keep in mind that this directly affects the availability of one of the most significant enterprise-level features built into FireDAC: the **connection pooling** capability (not available for temporary connections).

If it is true that most client/server applications deal with a single connection to the main data source (usually a DBMS) and that this connection is often initiated at the program startup (or user login) and kept alive till the end of the program (or logout).

This is not the most common scenario for multi-tier applications. Given that the REST approach has become the *de facto* standard for multi-tier solutions, the typical scenario is the client will have several, possibly frequent but isolated, contacts with the backend application server and this one will need to fulfill requests from clients against the database, acting as a mediator between raw data and clients (and implementing the application logic). So, in an application server context, you will find yourself dealing with requests that need to use a database connection but only for a fraction of time (the time needed to provide a result to the specific request).

This naturally evolves into a continuous connect-read/write-disconnect cycle that can strongly affect the general performance of the system (for example, because the DBMS may have a connection/disconnection cost or because *cold* connections may perform worse than *hot* connections on the specific DBMS). The connection pooling feature built into FireDAC comes to the rescue and will let you define how the DAC library should handle all these connect/disconnect requests to the DBMS, enabling the possibility to implement a pool where connections can live for a while after being created, waiting to be reused by the next incoming request.

The performance boost can be astonishing but it is not the only benefit you will get from this mechanism. In fact, you can define the maximum number of active connections in the pool (using a parameter as well so you can tune other aspects of the connection pooling mechanism such as the cleanup and expire timeout), basically avoiding stressing out the underlying DBMS over a certain point. This can be an easy way to implement a peak handling strategy (for example, allowing 100 connections to the DBMS and rejecting the others without affecting the first 100 connections).

Apart from the multi-tier scenario, most applications usually deal with a single data connection. FireDAC greatly simplifies the developer work as every supported database (from local file-based ones, like **SQLite**, to classic C/S DBMSes like Firebird, **MS SQL**, and **Oracle**) has the same steps to configure the connection (those described in this paragraph and, for some targets, a wizard guiding the developer through the required steps is available – just click on the **Wizard** button visible in *Figure 5.7*). This characteristic, together with the unified SQL preprocessing capabilities, the huge options set, and feature fallback mechanisms (that is, for features like `ArrayDML`) makes cross-database (eventually cross-platform) applications a reasonable possibility instead of a nightmare.

Once the connection object is available (directly through an instance of `TFDConnection`, properly configured, with explicit parameters or referring to a connection definition name or implicitly managed by the library, for example, by setting the `ConnectionName` property of a FireDAC dataset like `TFDQuery` to a corresponding connection definition name). You can start executing statements and access the underlying DBMS. There are a number of other features around FireDAC connections (such as automatic connection recovery, offline mode, and more) and their configuration options, but with the information gathered in this chapter, you should be able to easily define your first connection and use it.

Some of the fundamental components in the FireDAC library are those suitable to access data and present it in the form of a `TDataSet` descendant. We already met `TFDMemTable` but there are some more classic kinds of datasets of course.

Introducing Tables, Query, StoredProc, and Command

`TFDTable`, `TFDQuery`, and `TFDStoredProc` provide a dataset interface to data retrieved from a database system, each with some peculiarities. They are obviously very common components in data-centric applications, together with `TFDCommand`, which can be used to execute SQL statements and is largely used in the implementation of FireDAC adapters (the intermediate objects that translate dataset-like operations to SQL-like statements).

All the typical functionalities, such as master/detail mechanisms, macros and parameters, cached update support, local filtering and sorting capabilities, metadata retrieval, persistence capabilities, aggregates, and advanced functionalities such as the LocalSQL technology, are available to all FireDAC datasets (`TFDTable`, `TFDQuery`, and `TFDStoreProc`). Some of them are also available for `TFDMemTable` and `TFDCommand` (which slightly diverge from the other components).

We will cover some considerations about the TFDTable, TFDQuery, TFDStoreProc, and TFDCommand components, trying to provide you with knowledge of the peculiarities of each one, as follows:

- TFDTable: Historically designed to mimic the **BDE (Borland Database Engine)**'s TTable (designed for local file-based databases, substantially) and to move the same concept in the new **Client/Server (C/S)** era, without breaking all the existing code interfaces used by many applications. The concept of opening a table to access it from the first to the last row may sound quite anachronistic in the network-everywhere era. Everyone who experienced the years where first file-based databases gave access to data through networks are unlikely to have nostalgic thoughts.

  However, FireDAC once again comes in with a great compromise: keep the old TTable interface (so most of existing code of old applications won't break), but use a new SQL query-based implementation with some goodies like the **Live Data Window** capability. This will basically give the end user (and the developer) the same feeling as the old file-based paradigm, with the benefits of the new C/S approach (seamlessly loading data when needed and fetching only the most convenient portion of the table to provide a nice user experience).

  If you are starting a new C/S or multi-tier project, I would not start with this component as, even though it has been a great opportunity for migration, it represents an old-way approach and I would go for TFDQuery all the time. This, however, is not true for those modern applications that may need a local database, such as mobile apps with an onboard database to manage data locally (**SQLite** and **Interbase** are easy to use for this purpose). In this scenario (and some others, where local data is relevant), you may still want to go for the table-based approach and TFDTable is there for you.

- `TFDQuery`: If you are familiar with C/S architectures, running a query should be an everyday task. Most of the time, C/S applications use `TFDQuery` objects to retrieve, store, modify, and apply changes to result sets. Queries can naturally make use of macros and parameters and they have the capability to process changes made to the data stored in the dataset through the generation and execution of corresponding SQL update/insert statements. This process is highly automated but still highly customizable by the developer through the use of another companion component named `TFDUpateSQL`, where the developer can directly dictate how the SQL statement should look in order to apply changes made at the `TDataSet` level (from basic update commands to full control over locking and fetching mechanisms). This mechanism basically hooks into the underlying dataset adapter and is available at the `TFDAdaptedDataSet` level but is published only by `TFDQuery`, `TFDTable`, and `TFDStoredProc`.

- `TFDStoredProc`: There are a number of database architects fond of stored procedures, as there was a time where a consistent portion of the IT industry was pushing for extensive use of stored procedures in the attempt to centralize application logic (rather than spreading it through several applications of systems) and push performance (reducing network usage). Given that there is less hype than there used to be some years ago but they are still largely used, we are happy FireDAC has a corresponding component, enabling you to deal with stored procedures (including input/output/result parameters and multiple result sets where supported by the DBMS) and represent result sets through the usual familiar and consistent interface of a `TDataSet` descendant.

- Last, but not least, `TFDCommand`: It can be seen as a basic executor of SQL statements but with no `TDataSet` relationship. In other terms, it has all the features related to processing, parsing, and executing SQL statements but it is more useful to execute commands (through the name) than retrieving and manipulating data in a dataset object. This object is used internally by the other components as it wraps the fundamental interaction with the underlying DBMS.

As I said, the well-thought-out architecture of FireDAC makes it a very powerful and flexible library, making it, at the same time, easy to use. The balanced hierarchy of dataset descendants as well as good reuse of the command executor class and the common availability of the same functionalities (and options) across FireDAC components, makes it really comfortable to use FireDAC and the developer really can save a lot of development time because of the qualities of this library (at the same time, keeping full customization capabilities and keeping an eye on performance as well).

Understanding dataset persistence

At first, it may seem a bit strange to talk about dataset persistence within a data access component library. One might think data is in the database and you simply need to retrieve it, use it, and save it back. But there are a number of situations where these three basic steps get something in between that somehow interrupts this very simple cycle.

Nowadays, when systems are often distributed and your software solution may consist of some client applications (desktop, mobile, or web), one or more application servers (usually REST), and some final storage (still usually an RDBMS), you may find yourself in need of managing a dataset's life in not-so-classical ways.

Let's think about a client mobile application that retrieves data from the server and then has to work out of reach of the server itself. The chance to keep the dataset in memory is gone since mobile applications have their own lifecycle, usually managed by operating systems. Manually saving the dataset to file can be complicated as soon as you start making changes to the data.

FireDAC has built-in capabilities to save and load datasets to and from a file (or stream) in several formats. The operation will preserve every aspect of the dataset, including applied filters, options, and the change log of modifications made to data. Basically, this means you can actually persist the dataset to reload it back when you need it, as many times you will. In our example, you can retrieve data from the server, save it locally (running multiple editing sessions to the user) and load it back when the server returns as available. The cached updates mechanism will provide you with a way to apply changes back to the original data source in one shot.

FireDAC natively supports three storage formats: **XML**, **JSON**, and **Binary**.

The XML format looks like the following excerpt (beautified):

```
<?xml version="1.0" encoding="utf-8"?>
<FDBS Version="15">
  <Manager UpdatesRegistry="True">
  <TableList>
    <Table Name="FDQuery1" SourceName="EMPLOYEE" SourceID="1" TabID="0"
     EnforceConstraints="False" MinimumCapacity="50">
      <ColumnList>
        <Column Name="EMP_NO" SourceName="EMP_NO" SourceID="1"
        DataType="Int16" Searchable="True" Base="True" OInUpdate="True"
        OInWhere="True" OInKey="True" OriginTabName="EMPLOYEE"
        OriginColName="EMP_NO"/>

        <Column Name="FIRST_NAME" SourceName="FIRST_NAME" SourceID="2"
        DataType="AnsiString" Size="15" Searchable="True" Base="True"
```

```
                OInUpdate="True" OInWhere="True" OriginTabName="EMPLOYEE"
                OriginColName="FIRST_NAME" SourceSize="15"/>
    (...)
        </ColumnList>
        <ConstraintList/>
        <ViewList/>
        <RowList>
          <Row RowID="0">
            <Original EMP_NO="2" FIRST_NAME="Robert" LAST_NAME="Nelson"
             PHONE_EXT="250" HIRE_DATE="19881228T000000" DEPT_NO="600"
             JOB_CODE="VP" JOB_GRADE="2" JOB_COUNTRY="USA"
             SALARY="105900" FULL_NAME="Nelson, Robert"/>
          </Row>
          <Row RowID="1">
            <Original EMP_NO="4" FIRST_NAME="Bruce" LAST_NAME="Young"
  HIRE_DATE="19881228T000000" DEPT_NO="621" JOB_CODE="Eng" JOB_GRADE="2"
  JOB_COUNTRY="USA" SALARY="97500" FULL_NAME="Young, Bruce"/>
          </Row>
    (...)
        </RowList>
      </Table>
    </TableList>
    <RelationList/>
    <UpdatesJournal>
      <Changes/>
    </UpdatesJournal>
    </Manager>
</FDBS>
```

You can easily spot, in the preceding XML document, that the `<ColumnList>` element contains metadata information about each column in the dataset, while data is stored through a set of `<Row>` elements, children of the `<RowList>` element. The change log would be represented inside the `<Changes>` element.

The **JSON** format for the same dataset looks like the following excerpt (beautified):

```
{
  "FDBS": {
    "Version": 15,
    "Manager": {
      "UpdatesRegistry": true,
      "TableList": [
        {
          "class": "Table",
          "Name": "FDQuery1",
          "SourceName": "EMPLOYEE",
          "SourceID": 1,
          "TabID": 0,
```

```json
    "EnforceConstraints": false,
    "MinimumCapacity": 50,
    "ColumnList": [
      {
        "class": "Column",
        "Name": "EMP_NO",
        "SourceName": "EMP_NO",
        "SourceID": 1,
        "DataType": "Int16",
        "Searchable": true,
        "Base": true,
        "OInUpdate": true,
        "OInWhere": true,
        "OInKey": true,
        "OriginTabName": "EMPLOYEE",
        "OriginColName": "EMP_NO"
      },
      {
        "class": "Column",
        "Name": "FIRST_NAME",
(...)
        "DataType": "AnsiString",
        "Size": 15,
(...)
      },
(...)
    ],
    "ConstraintList": [],
    "ViewList": [],
    "RowList": [
      {
        "RowID": 0,
        "Original": {
          "EMP_NO": 2,
          "FIRST_NAME": "Robert",
          "LAST_NAME": "Nelson",
(...)
        }
      },
      {
        "RowID": 1,
        "Original": {
          "EMP_NO": 4,
          "FIRST_NAME": "Bruce",
          "LAST_NAME": "Young",
(...)
        }
      },
```

```
(...)
              ]
          }
       ],
       "RelationList": [],
       "UpdatesJournal": {
         "Changes": []
       }
     }
   }
 }
```

You can see and easily locate the `ColumnList`, `RowList`, and `Changes` pairs of the preceding JSON document. As you can easily see, the two formats are equivalent and, in fact, they both fully represent the dataset, its metadata, and the eventual log of changes. You can determine what information is to be stored through the `StoreItems` sub-property of the `ResourceOptions` property.

I am not going to paste the third available format here, the binary one, as it would not be that useful, but please note that on my disk, the XML and JSON formats are about the same size (12.3 KB and 12.8 KB, respectively – before beautifying them of course) while the binary format is only 7.56 KB (nearly 40% less) so it is inherently more concise for obvious reasons.

This persistence feature can save you a lot of development time and works perfectly in many scenarios (even outside mobile development of course). However, this is not the equivalent of having a local database onboard, which we will see in the next section.

Implementing an onboard database

In the previous section, we had a look at the persistence capabilities built into every FireDAC dataset. This is a really useful technique when you need to save and load back your datasets, possibly keeping the actual state (including local modifications).

However, this is not the equivalent of having an onboard or local database you can use to store a larger amount of data (the persistence mechanism is not incremental so you can actually save a large dataset, but you'll deal with it with a *none-or-nothing strategy* and you may spend some time waiting for the full dataset to load) or when you need to perform queries and extract (or store) data with datasets that can actually vary in shape (the columns or relation involved).

This is not really a FireDAC feature but it is the result of the combination of Delphi cross-platform support and FireDAC connectivity features; however, to add an onboard database to your applications is actually very easy.

The choice is not limited but is usually across SQLite (ubiquitously available for many platforms) and **InterBase** (**IBLite** or **IBToGo**, depending on the feature set that you need).

Let's say you want to use SQLite on an Android device. You can simply configure your connection object with the SQLite driver (available in the form of a statically linked object) and set the name of your database file. Depending on the OpenMode parameter value (CreateUFT8 by default) you may simply need to attempt a connection in order to have your database automatically created on disk and start working.

Obviously, you have to keep in mind that the database position on disk will differ on different platforms and you may want to programmatically set it in order to always have a valid path to the database. The BeforeConnect event of your TFDConnection object seems a suitable place to set the Database parameter, as shown in the following snippet:

```
procedure TForm1.FDConnection1BeforeConnect(Sender: TObject);
begin
{$IF DEFINED(iOS) or DEFINED(ANDROID)}
  FDConnection1.Params.Values['Database'] :=
TPath.Combine(TPath.GetDocumentsPath, 'MyDataBase.sdb');
{$ENDIF}
{$IF DEFINED(MSWINDOWS) or DEFINED(MACOS)}
  FDConnection1.Params.Values['Database'] :=
TPath.Combine(TPath.GetHomePath, 'MyDataBase.sdb');
{$ENDIF}
end;
```

There are a few things to note in the previous code snippet: I am actually changing the Database value only for mobile platforms (iOS and Android), so this will not affect my application when I run it on Windows, for example, (this may be useful to ease debug and development runs as you can continue defining the database location through the TFDConnection object properties).

Another thing to note is I am using the TPath record (the System.IOUtils unit) to retrieve the name of the user's documents path (the TPath.GetDocumentsPath function) and properly combining this folder name with my filename ('MyDataBase.sdb'). Given that each platform has its own convention about the filesystem, Embarcadero provided the IOUtils unit with a lot of function and data structures conveniently wrapping most filesystem related objects and functionalities, enabling true cross-platform code for your application.

Finding the proper location for your application files can be challenging and severely depends on the actual targeted platform but the **Deployment** page of the IDE can be very useful with regard to this topic.

Once we have determined the database location and given that we configured that on the first connection attempt the database will be created, we still have to consider that the database will be empty. So, we have a choice between incorporating some SQL script to rebuild the database structure (and possibly the initial data) from scratch or building a template database file and bundling it together with the application. Depending on the actual complexity, your choice may vary.

If you want to deploy an existing database file, you simply need to prepare it and add it to the deployment list of your project (select the **Project | Deployment** option from the Delphi IDE's main menu). Then, select the target platform and add a new entry in the list (depending on the target platform, the destination folder may change; for Android, usually the '.\assets\internal' value is fine). Then, you will need to find out the actual path on the target device (the files copied in '.\assets\internal' are copied in the application's writable folder during installation so you can reach them using the TPath.GetDocumentsFolder function).

Otherwise, if you prefer to have your application capable of setting up its own database from scratch, you can add a TFDScript component, populate its SQLScripts collection and execute them right after the connection has been set up (the AfterConnect event of TFDConnection would fit). Just beware that you'll need to either write scripts that are safe to be run on an already existing database (that is, using the IF NOT EXISTS syntax for the creating table) or find a way to initialize the database only once and not on each connection (that is, check for the existence of a specific table and make your assumptions consequently).

Once you have your database ready, the rules to develop your application are the same as they would be with any other local database, including restrictions about the maximum number of active connections or considerations about how the database handles concurrency and locks.

To have a database onboard is quite a sophisticated feature your (mobile) app may need. FireDAC and Delphi make it easy to handle this painlessly but keep in mind whether this is the right option and when to avoid it. If you are looking for a way to have a (relatively) large amount of data at your application's disposal (even offline or outside the reachability of your backend providers) and/or you need to perform complex SQL operations on data, possibly involving privacy protection issues (read: you may need encryption for some of your data), then an onboard database seems to be a good solution.

On the other hand, once you have data on the device, you should consider what would happen if the device got lost or broken or the user uninstalled the application or similar. If you need to keep data safe (that means synchronizing it back to the backend from time to time), you will face a problem that is often seen on most programming forums: *how can you keep two databases (client and server) in sync?* There are a number of solutions here but none of them is trivial and without considerations. My suggestion here is always to design the mobile (client) database as separate storage, built purposely to serve the mobile application, and keep the logic and mechanism to send data back to the backend separate. **Automatic synchronization** is just a *chimera*, in my opinion, and replicated databases get complicated quite soon.

Exploring the LocalSQL feature

The last powerful feature I want to address in this chapter dedicated to FireDAC is the LocalSQL functionality.

Ever wanted to load some data in a dataset (let's say you are parsing some data from a file and storing it in a memory table) and perform a SQL join statement across that standalone dataset and some data in your real database? Or, in a more modern scenario, *ever wanted to collect some data from sensors and find a match against some data in your database or in some other available dataset?*

In other words, some time ago, there was a neat distinction between the SQL world and other data-oriented manipulation techniques. SQL is great for set-oriented operations, joins, Cartesian products, aggregates, filtering, and similar while other data-manipulation approaches were usually heavily based on code implementations of loops, lists, and temporary data structures to collect data. *Now you can easily mix the two worlds!*

LocalSQL is functionality built over the SQLite engine (thus, when using LocalSQL you are actually embedding an SQLite engine in your application) feature known as **Virtual Table API**. Basically, from a SQL statement point of view, you are simply referring to a table as all the others but operations are carried out calling callbacks of a compiled object available to the engine. This way, you can use SQL (well, the SQL language as implemented by SQLite of course) to query your datasets. It is not limited to FireDAC datasets but it is open to every `TDataSet` descendant out there (also meaning this can be an easy way to integrate other DAC libraries with FireDAC to mitigate migration trauma or to mix the functionalities of other libraries).

Let's build a simple example:

- Assume we have a database (look for the `DataConnection` object, a `TFDConnection` instance) with a list of people (I will use the usual `EMPLOYEE.FDB` database from the FireBird standard installation) and we have a query (`EmployeeQuery`, a `TFDQuery`) to select them (`select * from EMPLOYEE`, *nothing special*).

- Assume your application in some way puts together a list of items ordered by someone, including information such as a quantity and a unit price. We stored that information in a convenient `TFDMemTable` named `OrdersMemTable`.

- We want to build and present a list of active orders (people in the first dataset, `EmployeeQuery`, with the items they ordered, stored in `OrderMemTable`). Basically, we want to make an inner join between `Employees` and `Orders` and, by the way, calculate the total price (`UnitPrice * Quantity`) for each order entry. In SQL words, we want to run the following query:

  ```
  select
    E.FULL_NAME,
    O.*,
    O.UNITPRICE * O.QUANTITY TOTAL
  from EMPLOYEES E
  inner join ORDERS O on E.EMP_NO = O.EMP_NO
  ```

  As you can see, `EMPLOYEES` is our first dataset (`EmployeeQuery`) and our second, in-memory dataset (`OrderMemTable`) is `ORDERS`.

We can achieve this result with the help of a `TFDLocalSQL` component where we can register two datasets in the `DataSets` collection (`EmployeeQuery` with `EMPLOYEES` as the value of `Name` and `OrderMemTable` with `ORDERS` as the value of `Name`). Then, we will have to add a new `TFDConnection` (let's name it `LocalSQLConnection`) and set the `Connection` property of the `TFDLocalSQL` component to it. Now, we can use this connection to execute SQL statements against an environment, provided by the `TFDLocalSQL` component, that is, a *virtual* database where `EMPLOYEES` and `ORDERS` are valid relation names, tied to our two dataset instances.

Simply add a `TFDQuery`, set its `Connection` property to `LocalSQLConnection`, and enter our SQL statement, that is, you will see your result set exactly as it would work within a single database. The following screenshot summarizes this example and shows two listviews and a grid to render the datasets' contents:

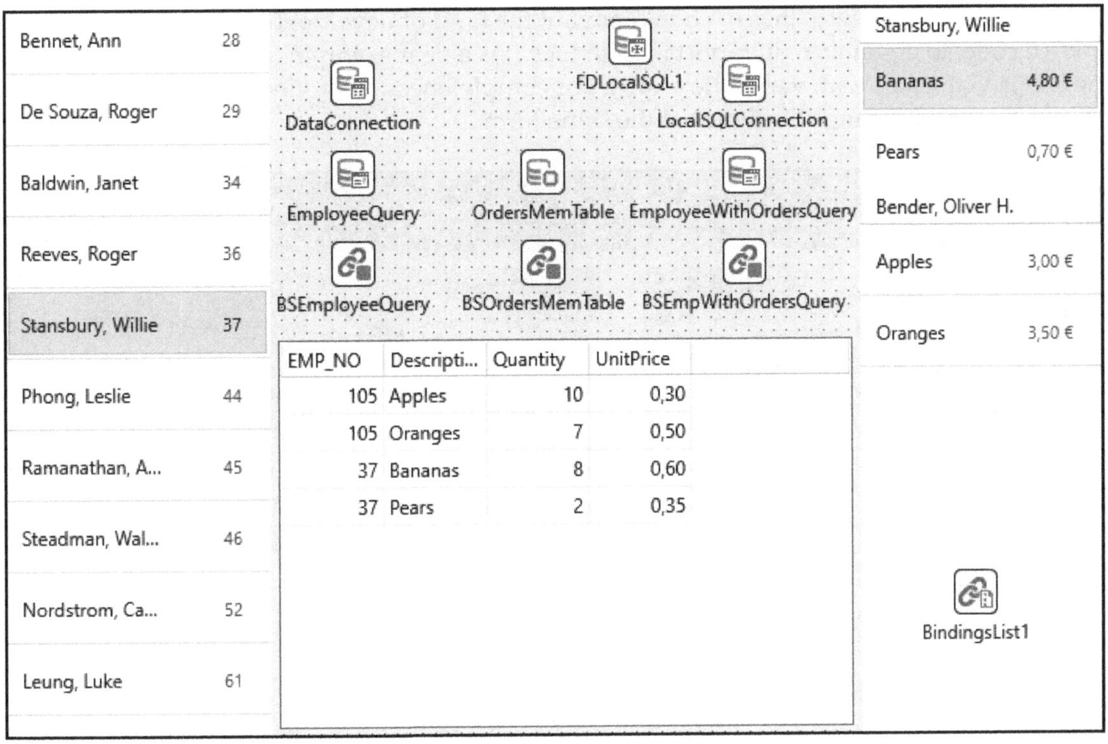

Bennet, Ann	28	
De Souza, Roger	29	
Baldwin, Janet	34	
Reeves, Roger	36	
Stansbury, Willie	37	
Phong, Leslie	44	
Ramanathan, A...	45	
Steadman, Wal...	46	
Nordstrom, Ca...	52	
Leung, Luke	61	

FDLocalSQL1
DataConnection   LocalSQLConnection
EmployeeQuery   OrdersMemTable   EmployeeWithOrdersQuery
BSEmployeeQuery   BSOrdersMemTable   BSEmpWithOrdersQuery

EMP_NO	Descripti...	Quantity	UnitPrice
105	Apples	10	0,30
105	Oranges	7	0,50
37	Bananas	8	0,60
37	Pears	2	0,35

Stansbury, Willie
Bananas   4,80 €
Pears   0,70 €
Bender, Oliver H.
Apples   3,00 €
Oranges   3,50 €

BindingsList1

Figure 5.8

The `TListView` instance on the left is bound to the `EmployeeQuery` dataset (through the `BSEmployeeQuery` bind source component), the central `TGrid` shows the contents of the `OrdersMemTable` dataset (through the `BSOrdersMemTable` bind source component) and, on the right, another `TListView` instance renders the results of the executed join, including the `TOTAL` calculated field (properly formatted to a currency value through the LiveBindings `CustomFormat` property, `Format('%%.2f €', Value+0)` – the plus zero part is a way to let the evaluator properly determine the format's second argument value).

The application has zero lines of code (I am not the kind of developer particularly scared by source code, to give this real importance; in fact, it is a neat example of how to achieve a not-so-trivial result with very little effort). For completeness, the following screenshot shows the **LiveBindings Designer** of the same form:

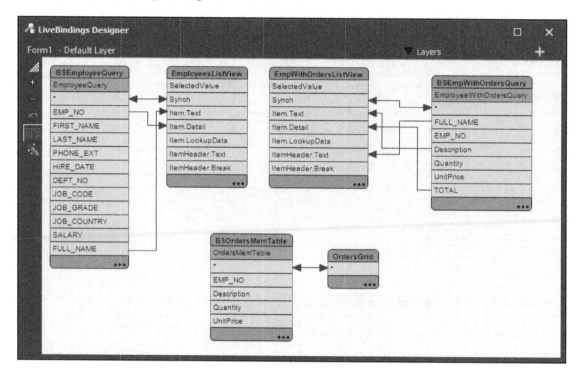

Figure 5.9

I really like the LocalSQL feature in FireDAC as it enables you to easily solve some recurrent scenarios that are harder to solve with different approaches. Particularly, it has been of great help in performing cross-database queries (reading datasets from different databases and/or data sources and then performing SQL over them, more or less as we did in our example with TFDQuery and TFDMemTable), and in situations where all datasets were actually in-memory datasets (to run join and aggregate queries that would have required for loops and intermediate calculations easily carried out via SQL). I am pretty sure every experienced Delphi developer reading this book has encountered at least one use case for LocalSQL during their career.

Summary

In this chapter, we had an overview of FireDAC, the *standard* data access component library for Delphi. Being a very solid library with a long history, it has a lot of powerful and interesting features and, even if a complete overview is far beyond the scope of this book, you should have acquired all the necessary background to start using it profitably. Delphi is a very wide-ranging product, enabling developers to write a huge variety of applications including data-centric ones. FireDAC is the perfect solution for local, C/S, and even multi-tier solutions, with full support for a great number of data sources (DBMSes) and natural support for cross-platform applications as it is a pure Delphi library (thus, compiling on every platform supported by Delphi itself).

Having the chance to learn about a single DAC library (included in the product) and use it to build server, desktop, and mobile applications is a huge advantage over other technologies out there. As already stated in this chapter, I can't recommend anything better than Cary Jensen's book (*Delphi in Depth: FireDAC*, 2017) as a reference guide for FireDAC. The author is a real *guru* of data access technologies (and much more) and the coverage of the book is very comprehensive.

In the next chapter, we will discover how data binding works in FMX applications, covering the LiveBindings technology (also available for VCL).

Implementing Data Binding 6

In the last few chapters, we learned about the capabilities of many of the visual components available in the FMX framework, as well as the fundamentals of the data access component library **FireDAC**, which is included with Delphi. In this chapter, we are going to cover a natural follow-on concept; that is, data binding between data access components and visual controls.

In this chapter, we will cover the following topics:

- Introduction to data binding
- Approaching LiveBindings
- Binding datasets to lists and grids

By the end of this chapter, you will be familiar with the LiveBindings technology and some of its peculiarities. You'll be able to bidirectionally bind properties of components and know how to bind datasets to list components and grids (this is a very common topic in data-centric applications). You'll also know how LiveBindings can be extended and used outside its most common use cases.

Let's get started!

Technical requirements

The following link will take you to the source code that will be used throughout this chapter: `https://github.com/PacktPublishing/Delphi-GUI-Programming-with-FireMonkey/tree/master/Chapter%2006`.

Generally speaking, for the entirety of this book, you'll need a computer with Delphi set up and ready to go, as well as a few additional libraries installed (such as **Radiant Shapes** (`https://getitnow.embarcadero.com/?q=radiant+shapes`) and **CodeSite Logging** (`https://getitnow.embarcadero.com/?q=codesite`)).

Having other devices and setting up multiple platforms (iOS, Android, macOS/OS X, and Linux) other than Windows is a plus, but not strictly needed to follow the flow of this book.

Introduction to data binding

Once you have data available in some form (that is, datasets) and you are ready to build a UI-enabled application, you need to find a way to let the user consume this data, modify it through visual controls, and post changes to the original data source. This sounds simple at first, but finding a general approach to solving this problem elegantly and efficiently is far from trivial.

Data may differ in size, kind, or availability. Their visual controls greatly differ, as we have seen in earlier chapters, both in terms of their visual aspects and loading strategies/capabilities. Moreover, you may want to apply some transformations to the data before presenting it to the user (that is, formatting values) and apply some inverse transformation when storing it back in the data source.

Historically, Delphi has shined (*and continues to do so today!*) at being an effective tool for large data-driven applications, and every experienced Delphi developer should be familiar with the traditional data binding approach built into the VCL framework, wherein the TDataSource component acts as a mediator between datasets and data-aware controls. Data-aware controls used to be one of the two twin sets of standard controls and were designed to respond to changes in a data source (through a notification system known as a data link), provide a proper visual representation of the data, manage user interaction so that modifications could be collected, and notify the user of updated values in the data source.

With the advent of the FMX framework, another technology has been added to the Delphi product known as **LiveBindings**. This new, modern-oriented approach is also available for use in the VCL framework. We'll take a look at it in more detail in the next section.

Approaching LiveBindings

The FMX framework comes with a piece of technology known as LiveBindings. It's expression-based and designed around the observer pattern. Expressions can involve different kinds of members, including data sources (object-oriented or dataset-oriented) and **user interface** (**UI**) elements (controls).

The LiveBindings engine holds expression definitions and gathers and dispatches events. It does this by, for example, collecting a member's value change notification and reevaluating every expression where the member is involved. This same technology is also available in VCL, and design-time support has been added to the IDE on purpose (we already looked at the LiveBindings Designer earlier in this book in Chapter 2, *Exploring the Similarities and Differences of VCL*, and Chapter 4, *Discovering Lists and Advanced Components*).

LiveBindings is quite a broad technology that's simple in theory but has some layering and peculiarities you must consider if you wish to fully master it. The aim of this chapter is to help you learn how to use it in a wide variety of common situations. Even though its use isn't mandatory (for example, you can build your own data binding strategy/technology or simply go raw and manually handle the relationships across your data and UI), I really think understanding the official (and supported) data binding technology is important because once you become familiar with it, you can save a lot of development time and effort.

LiveBindings is basically an expression-based mechanism where there is usually a **Source** component and a **Target** component, and the aim is to bind one or more expressions involving Source members to one or more properties of the Target. To achieve this, the system needs somewhere to store the collection of binding expressions (the TBindingList component) involving components (in a form, frame, or data module). To make data available to the expression engine, you will need to use intermediate components (BindSources) to mediate between the expression engine and the actual data storage.

Later in this chapter, we will see that a number of different bindings are available that fit different Source and Target control capabilities. However, before we do that, we need to make a general distinction between **managed** and **unmanaged** bindings.

Introducing managed bindings

As we've already mentioned, a **binding** is basically made up of an expression that ties a Source and a Target control together. Typically, it evaluates the expression against certain properties of the Source control in order to assign the result to certain properties of the Target control. Let's start with a simple example. Here, we will try to tie the Text property of a TEdit instance to the Text property of a TButton instance.

Follow these steps in your IDE:

1. Create a new, blank FMX application.
2. Drop a `TEdit` and `TButton` component onto your form (we'll keep their default names of `Edit1` and `Button1`).
3. Drop a `TBindingList` component onto your form.
4. Add a new binding expression to your binding list (double-click on the `TBindingList` component and click on the **New binding** button, the first on the left in the component editor toolbar).
5. Find the `TBindExpression` entry in the list shown in the **New LiveBinding** dialog that appears. This is located in the **Binding Expressions** node of the tree view, as shown in the following screenshot:

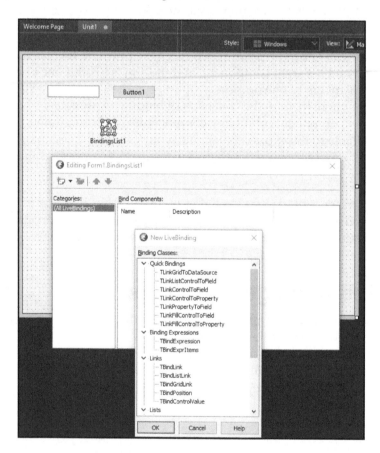

Figure 6.1

6. By doing this, a new `BindExpression1` entry will be added to the binding list editor. Now, you can change its properties through the **Object Inspector** window of the IDE:
   1. Set `ControlComponent` to `Button1` and set `ControlExpression` to `Text`.
   2. Set `SourceComponent` to `Edit1` and set `SourceExpression` to `Text`.

With that, our configuration for this expression is now complete. However, nothing has actually happened; you'll still see that your edit box is empty and that your button showing **Button1** is being used as the `Text` property's value, as shown in the following screenshot:

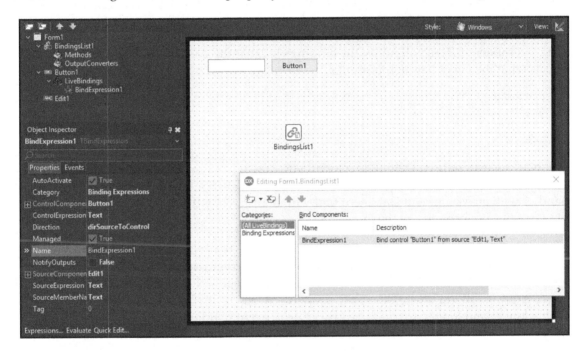

Figure 6.2

What's missing here is something that fires the expression evaluation in order to produce an output value that can be used against `ControlComponent`. You can trigger expression evaluation manually by clicking on the `Evaluate` shortcut, which can be found at the bottom of the **Object Inspector** window.

Once you've selected `BindExpression1`, click on it. You will see the `Text` property of `Button1` assume the value of the `Text` property of our `Edit1` component (thus, a blank string). You can set the `Text` property of the edit component and reevaluate it to see how the binding mechanism brings the same value to the `Text` property of the button. This is what we call a managed, single expression binding. This means we are defining an expression that will populate a property value with the result of the evaluation. Note that we need an explicit (external to the involved components) trigger to start the evaluation process.

To have your binding expressions evaluated at runtime, notify the `BindingList1` component that a value potentially involved in part of its binding expression has changed value and that you expect this to trigger all the involved expressions to reflect this change. To achieve this, we can add an event handler for the `OnChangeTracking` event of our `Edit1` component. This will notify the bindings list that the `Text` property has changed. This is what the event handler looks like:

```
procedure TForm1.Edit1ChangeTracking(Sender: TObject);
begin
  BindingsList1.Notify(Sender, 'Text');
end;
```

If you are an experienced Delphi developer, you may not be impressed by this mechanism and think it would have been much easier to simply implement the preceding event handler with an assignment statement that will, in turn, copy the value of the `Edit1.Text` property to the `Button1.Text` one.

However, there is a slight yet significant difference here that's invisible in an example as simple as this one; that is, this pattern (basically an observer pattern) typically shows its advantages when things become more complicated. Imagine that you have several expressions involving the `Edit1.Text` property, which means you will quickly end up with a longer and longer `Edit1ChangeTracking` event handler implementation with assignment statements (or equivalent statements) proliferating in your code.

Binding expressions are actually interpreted and are stored in a proper container (our binding lists). The only conjunction point that's needed is the notification code to trigger expression reevaluation.

Another argument in favor of the LiveBindings approach is that these expressions can be represented visually (in fact, you can easily open **LiveBindings Designer** by right-clicking the form in **Form Designer** and selecting **Bind visually...** from the contextual pop-up menu. This will allow you to view a visual representation of our expression).

The following screenshot shows **LiveBindings Designer** (I have undocked it from the IDE here) rendering our binding expression between the `Edit1.Text` and `Button1.Text` properties:

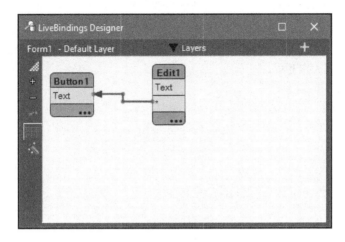

Figure 6.3

In the preceding screenshot, the link direction (from `SourceComponent` to `ControlComponent`) can be seen by the arrow going from `Edit1` to `Button1`. The `Direction` property of the binding expression regulates this.

In this section, we learned how to set up a simple, manually managed data binding across two components' properties. What we are doing here is defining an expression that needs to be evaluated at some point in the execution to produce a new value for the target property. The underlying technology includes an expression manager (an evaluator) that takes a string representation of the expression and uses it to produce the actual resulting value. We'll look at this in more detail in the next section.

Understanding what happens under the hood

The `System.Bindings.*` set of units is where this mechanism has been implemented. It is a far from trivial implementation and includes a relevant number of functionalities and capabilities (scope definition, method implementations, object wrapping, constants and operator definitions, and more). This final convenient behavior is made available to developers through a number of abstraction layers and goes up as far as the high-level abstraction we saw in the previous section. This abstraction can be easily handled at design time in the IDE – and even through the support of a visual designer.

The expression evaluator supports constants, variables, wrapping objects, functions (methods), and operators. The basic concept of **scope** represents the building blocks of the expression evaluator; that is, you can define several kinds of scopes (that is, dictionary scopes such as TDictionaryScope, which can be found in the System.Bindings.EvalSys unit) and combine (nest) them.

With a few lines of code, you can take advantage of this built-in technology to calculate (at runtime) a simple expression:

```
uses
    System.Bindings.EvalSys, System.Bindings.EvalProtocol,
    System.Bindings.Evaluator;

var
    LScope: IScope;
    LExpr: ICompiledBinding;
    LDictScope: TDictionaryScope;
    LResult: TValue;
begin
    LDictScope := TDictionaryScope.Create;
    LDictScope.Map.Add('firstNumber', TValueWrapper.Create(2));
    LDictScope.Map.Add('secondNumber', TValueWrapper.Create(2));

    LScope := TNestedScope.Create(BasicOperators, LDictScope);

    LExpr := Compile('firstNumber + secondNumber', LScope);
    LResult := LExpr.Evaluate(LScope, nil, nil).GetValue;
    ShowMessage(LResult.ToString);
end;
```

Even if the preceding example looks trivial to you, please consider the following:

- The expression we are calculating is determined by the 'firstNumber + secondNumber' string value, which can easily be replaced with a variable (user input or maybe a variable that's been read from a configuration file).
- The same applies to the values of firstNumber and secondNumber. These have been set to a decimal constant (2) in this example, though they can be substituted with variables or function return values.
- The evaluated value is actually typed (it is not a string). The LResult variable is of the TValue type (the System.Rtti unit). This is a Delphi type (a record type) similar to a box as it can hold any kind of data type (no automatic conversions; that is, what you put in stays the same type when you extract it).

- Once the expression has been compiled, you can evaluate it as many times as you wish and retrieve the output values before changing them to input values (this is not the case for this simple example as firstNumber and secondNumber are const values).
- Note the BasicOperators function, which provides IScope where common operators (+, –, *, /, not, =, <>, >, <, >=, and <=) are already defined.

As I mentioned previously, the evaluator is rich in features, and you can define your own functions (methods) by registering a new method through the TBindingMethodsFactory class. Let's say we want to introduce a custom function to our expression engine; that is, the Square function. Given a number, X, Square will return X squared, X*X:

```
var
  LScope: IScope;
  LExpr: ICompiledBinding;
  LDictScope: TDictionaryScope;
begin
  LDictScope := TDictionaryScope.Create;
  LDictScope.Map.Add('radius', TValueWrapper.Create(2));

  LScope := TNestedScope.Create(BasicOperators, BasicConstants);
  LScope := TNestedScope.Create(LScope, LDictScope);

  TBindingMethodsFactory.RegisterMethod(
    TMethodDescription.Create(
      SquareInvokable
    , 'Square', 'Square', '', True, 'Square(X) returns X * X', nil
    )
  );

  LScope := TNestedScope.Create(LScope,
  TBindingMethodsFactory.GetMethodScope);

  LExpr := Compile('Pi*Square(radius)', LScope);

  ShowMessage(LExpr.Evaluate(LScope, nil, nil).GetValue.ToString);
end;
```

Before compiling/evaluating the expression ('Pi*Square(radius)'), a TMethodDescription data structure is built that contains details about our function, including a reference to an IInvokable value, which is provided by the SquareInvokable function, and a name and description for the function. The data structure is the argument for the RegisterMethod call, which will make our function available in the scope maintained by the factory. This makes all registered methods part of our expressions.

The value of `Pi` is provided by another built-in scope known as `BasicConstants`, along with some other basic values such as `true`, `false`, and `nil`. Let's have a look at the `SquareInvokable` function's definition:

```
function SquareInvokable: IInvokable;
begin
  Result := MakeInvokable(
    function (Args: TArray<IValue>): IValue
    var
      LX: Extended;
    begin
      if Length(Args) <> 1 then
        raise EEvaluatorError.Create('Square: only one parameter
        expected');

      if not Args[0].GetValue.TryAsType<Extended>(LX) then
        raise EEvaluatorError.Create('Square: bad parameter');
      Exit(TValueWrapper.Create(Sqr(LX)));
    end
  );
end;
```

Through the use of an anonymous method (passed as an argument of the `MakeInvokable` function), we can delegate the implementation of our `IInvokable` instance, which is required for the method's registration. In other words, we'll need to provide a general implementation for a function with an arbitrary number of arguments (of any possible data type) that will return a certain value (again, of any possible data type).

The genericness of this mechanism is granted by the use of an `IValue` data type, which is a holder of the `TValue` type (we discussed this earlier). The actual implementation is quite straightforward in that after a minimum amount of precondition checking (a single numeric argument has been passed), the value is calculated through Delphi's standard `Sqr` function before being returned.

This set of capabilities surrounding expression evaluation can come in very handy and are powerful to developers, so you need to have a solid understanding of them to know how the LiveBindings technology works. A complete overview of the internals of LiveBindings is far beyond the scope of this book, so I am not going to delve any deeper. Just keep in mind that there are several other features and capabilities built into these basic building blocks (and/or around them).

The goal of any data binding mechanism is to provide us with a convenient way to bind data structures to the UI. In a typical FMX scenario (business applications), these data structures are either `TDataSet` descendants or object lists, and the UI controls involved are lists and (rarely) grids. Moreover, the definition of a *convenient way to perform the bind* has something to do with the intrinsic automation of the mechanism; that is, as a developer, I'd like to see my UI updated when my data structures change and vice versa.

Mastering real-world data bindings

So far, we have looked at a few examples of **managed** bindings, where the developer needs to explicitly trigger the evaluation of the binding in order to update the target. This kind of approach lets the developer have full responsibility and control over what happens in the application. This means that a normal-sized application may become hard to write/maintain because everything is left to the developer (reducing the advantage of a declarative versus imperative approach, whose simplicity is somehow the background concept for the entire thing), but also that the developer always has the opportunity to fine-tune the binding mechanism, thus keeping everything under control.

Apart from `TBindExpression` (and `TBindExprItems`), there are other kinds of LiveBindings available for different purposes. We'll provide an overview of the most significant use cases in the remainder of this chapter.

However, before we look at these LiveBindings, we need to briefly introduce the concept of BindSources.

Introducing BindSources

Earlier in this chapter, we looked at the concept of scope, which is tied to the ability of the LiveBindings expression engine and helps it deal with specific identifiers (such as constant names, variable names, functions, and other constructs that have a role in the expression). BindSource components can be used to implement a scope for the LiveBindings engine, thus making new identifiers available in expressions.

Let's say you have a `TDataSet` descendant and you want to show data from the dataset in the UI. What you are likely willing to do is write expressions involving the dataset and a certain UI element. As we mentioned previously, we need to make the dataset available to the expression engine through a specific scope. However, we are not talking about the static properties of the dataset itself.

Here, we need a more dynamic way to inspect the dataset and its specific structure in terms of data fields. Here's where `TBindSourceDB` comes to the rescue. By being a descendant of `TCustomBindSourceDB`, it implements a dataset binding scope, thereby making the values of the dataset's fields available in the scope (this can be seen in the following screenshot and can be found in the **LiveBindings Designer** window):

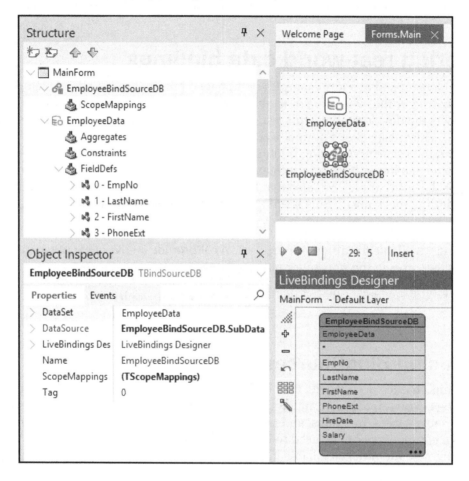

Figure 6.4

If you are an experienced Delphi (VCL) developer, you will have surely spotted the `DataSource` entry in the **Object Inspector** window. Here, the `TBindSourceDB` component has an internal `TDataSource` component (in the `Data.DB` unit) that implements the data link alongside the `TDataSet` descendant.

An additional opportunity to increase the number of identifiers available in the expression engine is provided through the `ScopeMappings` component properly. It may come in handy to provide some more entries to the scope, which will eventually refer to other components or provide punctual values (whether constants or not). Scope mappings are also useful when your expressions need to reference values from components other than the source and target of the specific binding.

Together with `TBindSourceDB`, the list of available BindSource components also includes two other entries:

- `TAdapterBindSource`: This implements a scope through an external adapter (for example, you may want to map a FireDAC `TFDQuery` component's parameters through a `TParamsAdapter` component or implement your own adapter to map some specific data structure of your own and make it available to the LiveBindings engine).
- `TPrototypeBindSource`: This is the equivalent of a combination of `TAdapterBindSource` and `TDataGeneratorAdapter`. Basically, it acts as a random data generator, which can be extremely useful if you wish to prototype your UI when you are still in the IDE (not at runtime).

  To achieve a similar capability (fake some data just to actually build UI elements and tie them together through LiveBindings), I tend to use an in-memory dataset (which, with recent Delphi versions, you can easily load and edit, even at design time) and a `TBindSourceDB` component. This gives you more control over data than a pseudo-random generator. However, this comes with the disadvantage that you have finite data available, whereas a generator has, theoretically, no limit.

One of the most basic tasks you'll need to accomplish when dealing with a dataset is to display the value of one of its fields in a visual element of your UI, such as a `TText` component. You may be thinking that the easiest way to overcome this would be to learn how to access the dataset field's value as a string value (`MyDataset.FieldByName('MyFieldName').AsString`) and assign this value to the `Text` property of the UI component (`MyTextComponent.Text`).

This does work, but the developer would then need to capture all the events around the dataset manipulation (navigation over the dataset, edit events, and more) to keep this information up to date for the user. Data binding mechanisms do exactly this; that is, they allow us to define relationships across data and other parts of the application (in this example, a UI element) in order to enforce this relationship through the lifetime of the data and the involved element. Let's take a look at some practical examples.

Binding a field value to a property – TLinkPropertyToField

Consider the following scenario: we have a dataset (`EmployeeData`), a corresponding `TBindSourceDB` component (`EmployeeBindSourceDB`), and a `TText` component (the `Text1` component). We want to bind the `Text1.Text` component property to the `FirstName` field of the dataset.

In the following screenshot, you can see the **LiveBindings Designer** tool window showing the bindable members of the `TBindSourceDB` and `TText` instances. The **New LiveBinding** dialog shows that the `TLinkPropertyToField` entry has been selected here:

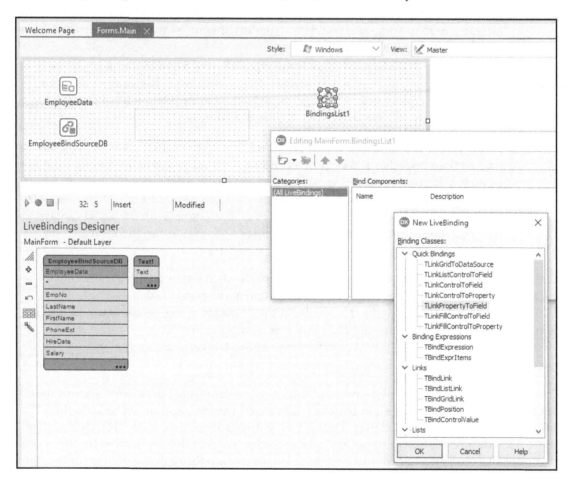

Figure 6.5

Here, we can add a `TBindingsList` component to the form, start the component's editor (by double-clicking on it), add a new binding, and select the `TLinkPropertyToField` entry from the list (the previous screenshot shows the **New LiveBinding** dialog with the `TLinkPropertyToField` entry selected). The IDE will add a new LiveBinding object named `LinkPropertyToField1` to the form (you can spot it in the **Structure View** window). This object has properties that can be used to define the binding. Specifically, you'll need to do the following:

- Set the `Component` property value to `Text1`.
- Set the `ComponentProperty` property value to `Text`.
- Set the `DataSource` property value to `EmployeeBindSourceDB`.
- Set the `FieldName` property value to `FirstName`.

All of these values can be set by typing them in directly or by choosing an entry from the drop down list provided by the **Object Inspector** editor, as shown in the following screenshot:

Figure 6.6

By doing this, you can view (immediately, at design time) the value of the `FirstName` field in the `Text1` component (used as the value for the `Text` property). Now, the LiveBindings Designer will draw a line, starting from the `EmployeeBindSourceDB` element (specifically, from the `FirstName` box), to the `Text1` element (the `Text` box), as shown in the following screenshot:

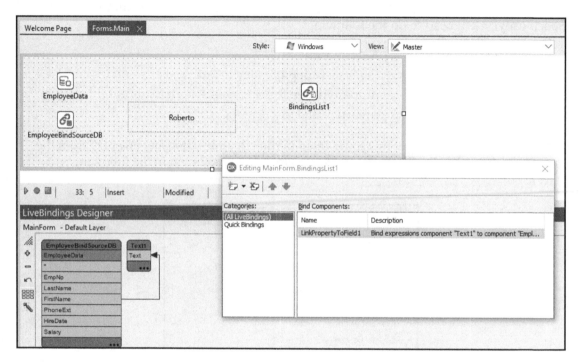

Figure 6.7

We now have a new binding expression involving the `Text1.Text` property and the `EmployeeBindSourceDB.FirstName` value. Once set, it's evaluated and the resulting value is assigned to the `Text` property (note that the relationship is unidirectional, which you can determine by looking at the connector between `EmployeeBindSourceDB` and `Text1` in the **LiveBindings Designer** window).

The evaluation here has been triggered automatically. Note that you can also change the current record of the dataset (an easy way to do this is to right-click the `EmployeeData` component, select the **Edit DataSet...** entry from the pop-up menu, and click on a different row of data). Once you've done this, you'll see the `Text1` component being updated with the corresponding `FirstName` field value for the newly selected record, meaning that the expression has been reevaluated. This is because the data source has changed.

This same process would trigger if we were to edit the EmployeeData dataset (that is, update the FirstName field's value for the current record or delete the current record). The dataset notifies the EmployeeBindSourceDB component about changes and triggers the LiveBindings expression engine, which will evaluate all the expressions involving the BindSource component.

Before we look at some other considerations, I want to show you how to achieve everything we have done so far in this section in a more RAD and visual way, through the use of the visual **LiveBindings** editor:

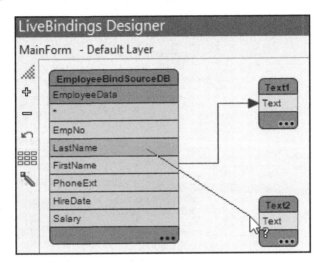

Figure 6.8

Using the preceding screenshot as a reference, we can summarize what we have done as follows:

- We have added a second TText component to the form (Text2).
- We have noted that this component appears in the **LiveBindings Designer** representation.
- We chose another BindSource field (LastName).
- We dragged the corresponding EmployeeBindSourceDB box onto the Text box of the Text2 component.

As a result, the component will be highlighted with a light green background color to reflect that it is a bindable member for the selected source. This can be seen in the preceding screenshot.

And with that, you're all set! What you previously set up manually for the `FirstName` field has been done automatically for the `LastName` field by the IDE in response to a single mouse gesture. This saves developers a considerable amount of time and effort (this is also known as boosting productivity). The final result can be seen in the following screenshot. Note that the values in the **Object Inspector** window have not been entered manually:

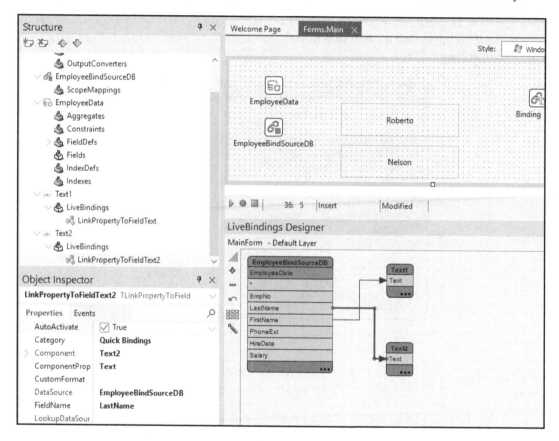

Figure 6.9

With that, we've learned how to quickly bind (**LiveBindings** are actually categorized, and this one will fall into the **Quick Bindings** category) a data field to a component property in a unidirectional way through a LiveBinding called `TLinkPropertyToField`.

The next few examples of bindings will make use of the same basic principles shown in this section, so please make sure you know the difference between what is done manually and what is done through the LiveBindings Designer. We will also explore some other functionalities surrounding this topic.

Binding a dataset field value to a control – TLinkControlToField

In the previous section, we learned how to unidirectionally bind a data field to a component's property value. The binding that was created to achieve the task was TLinkPropertyToField, while the target component that was used (TText) was a read-only one. *But what if we switch to a read-write component in order to let the user change data?*

In this section, we are going to use a bidirectional link between the data and target component since we want the component to keep reflecting changes on the dataset side (navigation over records, changes that have been applied to the record's content, and more). However, at the same time, changes may happen on the component side (because of user interaction, for example), and we want them to be applied to the dataset as well.

Here, we will try to use a TEdit component (Edit1) and bind it to the Salary field of the dataset. In the **LiveBindings Designer** window, simply drag the Salary box of the EmployeeBindSource element over the Text box of the Edit1 element. This will let the IDE create the quick binding for you, as shown in the following screenshot:

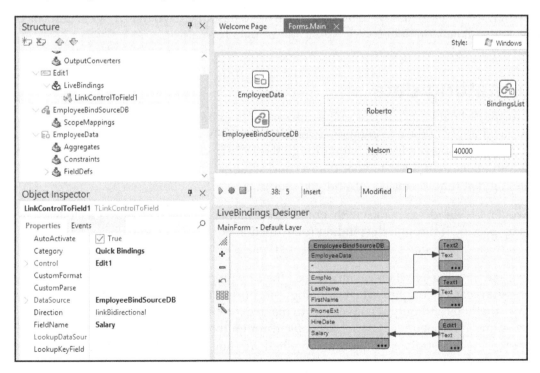

Figure 6.10

As you can see, the newly created `LinkControlToField1` object has a two-arrow representation in the **LiveBindings Designer** window. You should also be able to see a `Direction` property in the **Object Inspector** window stating that the link is bidirectional.

Note that the `Target` component is now defined through a `Control` property (instead of `Component`, as in the previous example); there is no `ComponentProperty` equivalent. That is, the binding is established across the field's value and the control as a whole (this leaves it up to the control to deal with specific internal aspects, such as what to do when a new value for the data field is available or what to do when the control's state changes). Once again, if you have a background in VCL, you'll be able to see the parallelism.

`Control` will not only show the field's value, as shown in the previous example, but will also keep its status in sync with the dataset's one. For example, if the field is `ReadOnly = True`, the edit will reflect this and will prevent the user from editing it. User editing will only be available if the dataset can be edited (that is to say, it has entered `dsEdit State` in some way, perhaps because the developer called the dataset's `Edit` method, or this can be done by the `DataSource` component aboard the `BindSourceDB` component, according to its `AutoEdit` property value) and so on.

Now that we've learned how to bind values from dataset fields to the UI, we will focus on a very common need in data-centric applications: **data formatting**.

Formatting data

The formatted data that's stored in the dataset may not be in the same format you want/need to use at the presentation level (UI). If you are confident with the VCL approach, you may think you can format data through the `TField.DisplayFormat` property (either by adding persistent fields to your dataset and setting `DisplayFormat` at design time or by accessing it at runtime via code), and you would be right.

However, LiveBindings comes with a more general mechanism that allows us to format data by passing it through the binding (unidirectionally or bidirectionally): using the `CustomFormat` and `CustomParse` properties.

As we saw previously when we introduced the LiveBindings expression evaluation engine, expressions can be complex. The technology supports a number of powerful functionalities, such as methods and output converters, to make expressions flexible and rich. The same expressions and functionalities are available through the `CustomFormat` and `CustomParse` properties, which apply a transformation when we transfer data to the `Target` component or vice versa, respectively.

If you have a number (`Salary` in the previous example) stored in a dataset, once you have established the data binding toward a UI element, you can set the `CustomFormat` property to have it formatted. This means that you can write a transformation expression of the value, which is much more powerful than formatting. Once you've performed a transformation from the data layer to the UI, if the binding is bidirectional, you'll need to provide an inverse transformation that will do the opposite. This is what the `CustomParse` property does.

Exploring CustomFormat/CustomParse expressions

Let's provide some background information about the `CustomFormat` format (*note that* `CustomFormat` *and* `CustomParse` *are twin properties*). As an example scenario, we'll keep our `Salary` field bound to the `Edit1` button:

- The `CustomFormat` format's default value is an empty string. The value is not formatted and is sent to the other end of the binding as is (this is the same value you would get by accessing the `TField.AsString` value).
- The following are the conventions and peculiarities of the expression:
    - `%s` is a placeholder for the textual representation of the current data value.
    - `Value` is a reference to the underlying `TField.Value` of the field that's associated through the binding. Its type is `Variant`.
    - `Self` is a reference to the underlying `TField` associated with the binding.
    - The expression engine supports **dot** notation, method invocation, and property access (including indexed ones), which means you can write `Self.ClassName()` so that it triggers a call to the `ClassName` method of the `Self` (`TField`) object. Note that the round brackets are mandatory for firing the method's execution (you may be used to omitting them in regular Pascal code).
    - You can access the dataset with expressions such as `Self.DataSet` (you can obviously omit the `Self` part, simply writing `DataSet` instead) or `Owner` since the underlying `TField` actually has a `DataSet` property. Usually, the dataset is also `Owner` of its `TField` objects.

- You can use any methods that have been defined for the corresponding bindings list (spot the `Methods` property of the automatically generated `TBindingsList` on your form or frame). As we have already seen, you can define your own methods if needed.
- Once your expression has been evaluated, the result (held in a `TValue` record) can be converted for use through `OutputConverters` (again, check the `TBindingsList` instance for a list).
- Operators and constants (as we saw earlier in this chapter) are available. Here, you can set the `CustomFormat` property's value to something like `'MyPrefix: ' + %s` for the unformatted salary value, and use a fixed textual prefix as the result (that is, use `'MyPrefix: 40000'` as the resulting string).
- For each dataset's fields, a corresponding identifier is added to the scope so that you can refer to the fields of the dataset by name (that is, `Salary.AsString`, `FirstName.Value`, `LastName.AsString`). This will save you from writing expressions such as `Self.DataSet.FieldByName('FirstName').AsString`.
- Every expression can include all the identifiers available in the associated scope, so even when the link we created has a main source value (for example, with respect to `TLinkControlToField` in the previous example, the value of the field whose name is set in the `FieldName` property of the link itself), you should think more generally regarding the associated scope (`TBindSourceDB`, in this case), as well as the collateral scopes that are available (operators, constants, methods, output filters, custom scope mappings, and more). This means it's possible, when thinking about our salary, to write an expression such as `'Current salary for ' + Dataset.FirstName.AsString + ' ' + Dataset.LastName.AsString + ' amounts to ' + %s`, where the evaluated value is `'Current salary for Roberto Nelson amounts to 40000`.

Once you have learned how to deal with the basics, you may need to do some more sophisticated data manipulation. In the next section, we will learn about LiveBindings methods.

Understanding LiveBindings methods

We've already seen that the `TBindingLists` component provides access to a set of methods you can use in your expressions (we also learned how to register our own methods in the system via the `SquareInvocable` example).

Methods are system-wide, so we need to refer to the `System.Bindings.Methods` unit (if your Delphi edition includes RTL sources, this can be a good place to look when you're in need of inspiration to define your own methods). A method can have arguments and return a value. Let's have a look at some built-in methods:

- `IfThen(Condition, Value1, Value2)` implements the inline `if` (**ternary**) operator. It requires all three arguments to be specified, and all of them can be values or expressions. If the `Condition` argument evaluates to `True`, the function returns `Value1`; otherwise (when `Condition` is `False`), `Value2` is returned. Obviously, if `Value1` and/or `Value2` are expressions, the result will be the evaluation result of that expression.

  Ternary operators can be very useful, but beware: if `Value1` and/or `Value2` are expressions, they get evaluated before it's decided which one should be returned. This implies that if these expressions have side effects, they will both be triggered (the same happens with the `StrUtils.IfThen` function in Delphi code since arguments need to be evaluated to be placed on the stack before the call to `IfThen` can take place). However, within the LiveBindings engine, if `Value1` and/or `Value2` don't need expression evaluation (that is, they are values or functions/properties returning the value, sometimes even with side effects), you can only get the system to trigger one of them (which one depends on the `Condition` value, of course). Here are some examples:

  - `IfThen(DataSet.Salary.AsFloat > 50000, 'High', 'Low')` will provide labels instead of salary values.
  - `IfThen(DataSet.Salary.AsFloat > 50000,DataSet.Salary.AsFloat, 'Low')` will provide a label for some salary values.
  - `IfThen(ListItemIndex(Owner.ComboBox1) <> -1, 'Select a value from ComboBox1', SelectedValue(Owner.ComboBox1) + ' ' + DataSet.Salary.AsString)` will use a prefix string from the selected item in `ComboBox1`, warning the user if one hasn't been selected.

- `IfAll(Condition1, Condition2, ..., Condition100)` returns `True` if all the passed conditions evaluate to `True` (an empty or non-boolean condition will be considered a `False` value). This is a utility function you can use to mimic an `AND` operator and its arguments, where some may not be provided (null). The maximum number of arguments you can have is 100 (hardcoded). Here is an example:

  - `IfThen(IfAll(Self.AsFloat > 0, Self.AsFloat < 10, Round(Self.AsFloat) <> 6), 'OK', 'ERR')` will show **OK** for all values greater than zero and lower than 10, excluding values that round to six.

- `IfAny(Condition1, Condition2, ..., Condition100)` returns `True` if at least one of the passed conditions evaluates to `True` (an empty or non-boolean condition will be considered a `False` value). This is a utility function you can use to mimic an `OR` operator and its arguments, where some may not be provided (null). The first condition that returns `True` will break the evaluation or subsequent conditions (this is a short circuit boolean evaluation, so keep this in mind for side effects). The maximum number of arguments you can have is 100 (hardcoded).

- `Format(FormatString, Value1, Value2, ..., ValueN)` provides a wrapper around the `SysUtils.Format` function (very popular and used in all Delphi applications). The `FormatString` parameter can be a string (or an expression returning a string) that is used as the first argument of the `SysUtils.Format` function call (please refer to Delphi's help guide for a complete overview: http://docwiki.embarcadero.com/Libraries/en/System.SysUtils.Format). The following arguments (`Value1` to `ValueN`) are used to build the open array of arguments for the `Format` function (that is, they represent the actual values that will replace the placeholders of `FormatString`):

  - `Format('Current salary: %m',DataSet.Salary.AsFloat)` will evaluate to `'Current salary: 40.000,00 €'`, but only if you are on a machine where € is the current currency.

  - `Format('%.2f',DataSet.Salary.AsFloat)` will evaluate to `'40000,00'`.

  - `Format('Employee number %d earns %m a year', DataSet.EmpNo.AsInteger, DataSet.Salary.AsFloat)` will evaluate to `'Employee number 2 earns 40.000,00 € a year'`.

- `FormatDateTime(FormatString, DateValue)` provides a wrapper around the `SysUtils.FormatDateTime` function, which allows us to format a date/time value as a string (please refer to the official documentation for all the possibilities: `http://docwiki.embarcadero.com/Libraries/en/System.SysUtils.FormatDateTime`). Here are a few examples (the value of `DataSet.HireDate.AsDateTime` is `December 28th, 1988` here):

  - `FormatDateTime('dd', DataSet.HireDate.AsDateTime)` will evaluate to `'28'`.
  - `FormatDateTime('yyyy-mm-dd', DataSet.HireDate.AsDateTime)` will evaluate to `'1988-12-28'`.
  - `FormatDateTime('ddddddd', DataSet.HireDate.AsDateTime)` will evaluate to `'mercoledi 28 dicembre 1988'` (this is the long date format for my machine, with **Italian** as the regional setting. In English, it would become something like `'Wednesday, 28 December 1988'`).

- `SubString(StringValue, Index, Length)` is a wrapper around the `SysUtils.TStringHelper.SubString` function and gets called when you write `'My string'.SubString(0, 2)` in Delphi code (where `'My'` is the resulting value). Basically, it extracts a portion of the given string. The first argument (`StringValue`) can be a string value or an expression, the second (`Index`) is the index of the first character in the string you want to copy, and the last argument (`Length`) is the number of characters you want to copy. The following is an example of this:

  - `SubString(DataSet.LastName.AsString, 0, 1)` will provide the initial of the user's last name.

As you can see, methods can be very effective when building complex expressions, and they add flexibility throughout the LiveBindings technology. We've already seen how easy it is to add a new custom method to the list of available ones.

If you want to register a new method and use it at design time or across several projects, you will need to create a new Delphi package and install it in the IDE. Let's say we want to wrap another RTL function called `SysUtils.FormatFloat`, which is used to format floating-point values by providing a format string and possibly a locale identifier (see the official documentation for a complete overview of the function: `http://docwiki.embarcadero.com/Libraries/en/System.SysUtils.FormatFloat`). We'll go through the steps required to create the package, add the new method implementation, register the implementation in the list of available methods, test our new methods at design time, and make the package available to an application at runtime in the following sections.

Creating the package (FormatFloatPackage)

Start by creating a new Delphi package by selecting **File** | **New** | **Package** | **Delphi** from the IDE's main menu. Once you have saved it using the name `FormatFloatPackage`, you need to add a unit to the package. This is where we'll add the required code:

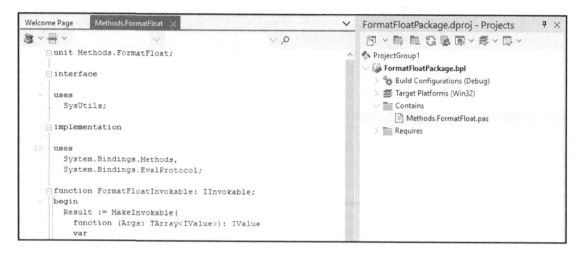

Figure 6.11

Once we've done this, we need to name the unit `Methods.FormatFloat` and save it. We'll need to add some unit names to the `uses` clauses of the unit so that we have visibility over the `SysUtils.FormatFloat` function and the LiveBindings infrastructure. Here are the units we are going to include:

- `SysUtils`: The `FormatFloat` function and the `TFormatSettings` type definition
- `System.Bindings.Methods`: The `MakeInvokable` function, the `TMethodDescription` type definition, and the `TBindingsMethodFactory` singleton
- `System.Bindings.EvalProtocol`: The `IValue`, `TValueWrapper`, and `IInvokable` type definitions

In the next section, we will learn how to implement the wrapper.

Implementing the wrapper (FormatFloatInvokable)

Providing an implementation for our new method basically means we need to provide an `IInvokable` implementor. The `MakeInvokable` function (in the `System.Bindings.Methods` unit) will accept an `anonymous` method as an argument and return an implementor of the `IInvokable` interface. The `anonymous` method will get the arguments (parsed from the actual expression) as input parameters in the form of a dynamic array of `IValue` (another interface type defined in the `System.Bindings.EvalProtocol` unit), and will then return another `IValue` instance containing the result.

We expect two or three arguments to be passed to our `FormatFloat` method in our LiveBindings expressions:

- `FormatString`: This is a string that's used to specify the desired format for the number.
- `FloatValue`: This is a floating-point (`Extended`) value that needs to be formatted.
- `Locale`: This is an optional string identifier of the desired locale settings to be used (that is, for decimal/thousand separators).

Our implementation can be split into five logical sections; that is, input recognition and validation, the actual call to the wrapped function, result value boxing, registering the method, and deregistering the method. This can be seen in the following code:

```
unit Methods.FormatFloat;

// uses clauses

implementation

function FormatFloatInvokable: IInvokable;
begin
  Result := MakeInvokable(
    function (Args: TArray<IValue>): IValue
    begin
      // 1 - Input recognition and validation
      // 2 - Actual call to the wrapped function
      // 3 - Result value boxing
    end
  );
end;

initialization
  // 4 - Registration of the method
```

```
finalization
  // 5 - De-registration of the method
end.
```

If you are not familiar with the `initialization` and `finalization` sections of a unit, all you need to know is that they're executed once (and only once, respectively) early on at the start of the program and then very late at the end of it. Let's discuss these five logical sections in detail:

1. **Input recognition and validation**: In this first section, we are basically checking that at least two arguments were passed. The following code exemplifies this section:

```
if Length(Args) < 2 then
  raise EEvaluatorError.Create('FormatFloat: two parameters
  expected');

if not Args[0].GetValue.TryAsType<string>(LFormatString) then
  raise EEvaluatorError.Create('FormatString: bad parameter');

LFormatSettings := FormatSettings;
if (Length(Args) > 2) and (Args[2] <> nil) then
begin
  if not Args[2].GetValue.TryAsType<string>(LLocale) then
    raise EEvaluatorError.Create('Locale: bad parameter');
  LFormatSettings := TFormatSettings.Create(LLocale);
end;
```

The first argument is going to be a `string` type. The third argument (if provided) should also be a `string` type and be used to load some regional settings. If not, this will default to using the current application-wide format settings.

2. **The actual call to the wrapped function**: In this section, we are simply calling the wrapped function (`SysUtils.FormatFloat`), as shown in the following code:

```
LFormattedString := FormatFloat(LFormatString,
Args[1].GetValue.AsExtended, LFormatSettings);
```

As you can see, we are accessing `Args[1].GetValue.AsExtended` to get the actual value we need to format (note that an exception will be raised if the provided value is not floating-point compatible).

3. **Result value boxing**: In this section, `TValueWrapper` will be created to hold the value we are returning as a result of our method call. This will make the result value available to the expression engine (for example, if it is involved in other expressions):

```
Exit(TValueWrapper.Create(LFormattedString));
```

The use of `Exit` with the explicit argument to set the return value of the function is just done to avoid a clash (for the programmer, not for the compiler) across the result of the `anonymous` method and the result of the `FormatFloatInvokable` function. As shown in the following code snippet, we could have used a more conventional (especially for young developers) assignment:

```
Result := TValueWrapper.Create(LFormattedString);
```

4. **Registering the method**: In this section, we will add the code that will add an entry in the global LiveBindings method register in order to make our new method listed and available:

```
TBindingMethodsFactory.RegisterMethod(
  TMethodDescription.Create(
    FormatFloatInvokable
  , 'FormatFloat', 'FormatFloat', '', True
  , 'SysUtils.FormatFloat wrapper. FormatFloat(FormatString,
  FloatValue [, Locale])'
  , nil
  )
);
```

As you can see, everything is done through a `TMethodDescription` record that contains all the details about the method to be registered (including its name, ID, a description, and the `IInvokable` parameter to be used for implementation).

5. **Deregistering the method**: This code will be executed right before the process is terminated. The code for this is as follows:

```
TBindingMethodsFactory.UnRegisterMethod('FormatFloat');
```

It is not really mandatory to have this code in a monolithic application, but it's useful in applications that have been built with packages (please remember that this package will also be used by the IDE at design time, so you should not make too many assumptions about the user's memory management strategy as this may lead to memory leaks, which is particularly disgraceful in an IDE that's used for hours at a time).

Now, we are ready to build our package.

Building and installing the package

You may want to specify a description (**FormatFloat LiveBindings method**) for your package in the **Project Options** dialog of the IDE. Build your package by clicking on the **Project | Build FormatFloatPackage** option in the main menu and install it (the IDE is a Win32 application, so that's your target platform).

Now, your new `FormatFloat` method will be available at design time (since the IDE will load your package, which will trigger the call for initializing/finalizing the code section of our `Methods.FormatFloat` unit. Once this happens, the method gets registered in the system).

Testing at design time and using it at runtime

Now, you can test your `FormatFloat` method. Just drop a `TBindingsList` component onto a form and open the editor for the `Methods` property to check whether your method is listed.

Just drop a BindSource (`TBindSourceDB` or `TPrototypeBindSource`) so that you have some data (with a floating-point value, of course) and try to use the `FormatFloat` function in a LiveBindings expression (beware that most parts of the LiveBindings expression engine are **case-sensitive**, even if this may sound unusual to a Pascal developer).

The following screenshot shows an example of how to use our newly introduced method:

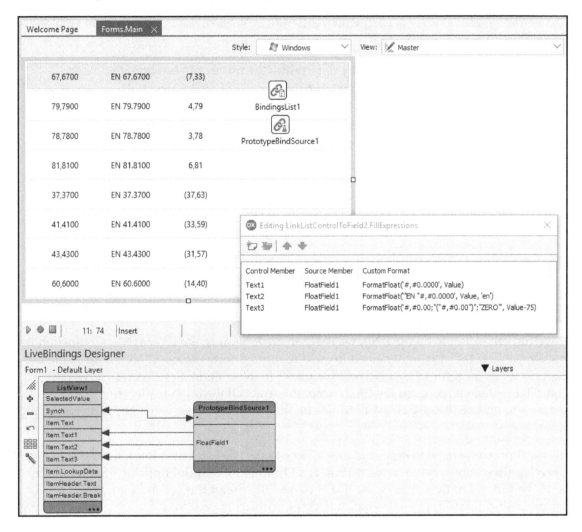

Figure 6.12

In the preceding screenshot, you can see that I've added three expressions to bind the value of `FloatField1` (a data generator within my `PrototypeBindSource1`) to three different text items in our `TListView`, each with a different `CustomFormat` property value making use of the `FormatFloat` function:

- The first (for `Text1`) simply determines the number to be formatted with thousands and decimal separators by using 4 digits for decimals.
- The second (for `Text2`) adds a constant `'EN'` prefix and specifies the use of English locale settings (for `Text1`, we are using the machine's default locale, which is Italian on my machine. As you can see, a different decimal separator is being used).
- The third (for `Text3`) provides three different format specifiers for positive, negative, and zero numbers (this is one of the capabilities of the `SysUtils.FormatFloat` function). Here, I am using the `Value - 75` expression instead of the raw value of the data field.

Our method is working fine at design time and we can happily see the results of our expressions by making use of it. However, here, the IDE is running our expressions. The method is available to the IDE's LiveBindings expression engine since we installed the package in the IDE itself. *But what about the applications?*

If we run our example (in the IDE), we'll get an error because the `FormatFloat` function is not available to the system. We need to include the `Methods.FormatFloat` unit in the use clauses of our form (or wherever you may prefer in the containing project) to have the compiler include its code for the final executable and call the initialization/finalization sections to update the global LiveBindings method register (this is what happens within the IDE).

You will probably need to make the unit visible to the compiler by adding its folder to the **Search path** section of your project (**Project** | **Options** | **Compiler options** | **Search path**) or to the **Library path** section of the IDE (I personally prefer this second option as it is a once-for-all-projects approach versus a once-per-project approach).

Methods can be very powerful additions to your LiveBindings experience, so please take the time to master them.

Making custom method calls available

Previously in this chapter, we saw that LiveBindings expressions allow you to access the main subject of the expressions (through the `Self` variable) to access its properties (that is, the `Owner` property, to access the underlying `TDataSet` of a `TField` component). You've also learned how to call methods using the same notation and expression engine. This mechanism is generic enough that you can usually reach the form (or frame or data module) you have put your BindSource on. This implies you are actually able to reach, for example, your form object (through the ownership chain) and call one of the methods of your form object within a LiveBindings expression.

If you have an expression that you need to bind to a field of a dataset (exposed through a `TBindSourceDB` component), you are in a situation where you can use the following:

- `Self`: This references an instance of `TField`.
- `Self.Owner`: This references the instance of `TDataSet` that is the owner of the field.
- `Self.Owner.Owner`: This references the owner of the dataset (possibly a form/frame or data module).

You can make a function call in all these cases (you can make a `try` instance using `Self.ClassName()`, but beware that the round brackets are mandatory for the function call to actually happen) and see the result of your expression change accordingly. You can actually call any of the methods of the objects you can reach in the LiveBindings expressions (remember that you can also expand the expression scope through the `ScopeMappings` component of most BindSource components), which is equivalent to a LiveBindings custom method.

The following implementation is equivalent to a `FormatFloat` wrapper using this approach instead of the methods one. In the same scenario (a `TPrototypeBindSource` component, along with a `TFloatField` data generator, on the form), we can add a public method to the form (`Form1` to `TForm1`):

```
TForm1 = class(TForm)
(...)
public
  function FormFormatFloat(const AFormat: string; const AValue: Extended;
const ALocale: string): string;
(...)
end;

implementation
```

```
function TForm1.FormFormatFloat(const AFormat: string; const AValue:
Extended;
  const ALocale: string): string;
var
  LFormatSettings: TFormatSettings;
begin
  LFormatSettings := FormatSettings;
  if not ALocale.IsEmpty then
    LFormatSettings := TFormatSettings.Create(ALocale);
  Result := FormatFloat(AFormat, AValue, LFormatSettings);
end;
```

The `FormFormatFloat` method is a simple wrapper of `SysUtils.FormatFloat`. I have also added some support to deal with the two available overloads as you can call the function with two or three parameters (making the last one optional). At the time of writing this book, the LiveBindings expression engine doesn't handle default parameter values, so I can't provide a default value for `ALocale`.

Our original expression (using the method approach) here is `FormatFloat('#,#0.0000', Value)`. However, now, we want to change this expression and address the `FormFormatFloat` function. By looking at the `Self` reference (a `TBindSourceAdapterReadWriteField<System.Single>` instance), we can go through the ownership chain:

- `Self.Owner`: This is an instance of the `TCustomDataGeneratorAdapter` class.
- `Self.Owner.Owner`: This is our instance of the `TPrototypeBindSource` class.
- `Self.Owner.Owner.Owner`: This is the `Owner` property of `PrototypeBindSource1` (the `Form1` form, in this case).

Now that we know how to reference the form, we also know how to call our `FormFormatFloat` method: the expression we are going to use is `Self.Owner.Owner.Owner.FormFormatFloat('#,#0.0000', Value, '')`, and the output will be equivalent to what we saw when using LiveBindings methods.

There are pros and cons to this approach, and I want to emphasize that I am not suggesting that you use form (or other) methods instead of LiveBindings methods in general. It is evident the last expression is *cursed* as it has too many indirection levels that may change unexpectedly over time and lead to maintenance difficulties.

Another argument against using this technique concerns optional parameters (something you may want to handle in a dynamic expression evaluation engine) that are not supported in this way. On the pro side, sometimes, a simple method in your form or data module can be powerful enough to solve some local manipulation of data (especially if it's tied to the UI).

So, keep in mind that this should not be abused, even though it provides you with an opportunity to address a number of real-life coding situations.

Now that we have learned how to use a few of the base mechanisms of the LiveBindings technology, we can address one of the most relevant kinds of binding you will be using in FMX applications (especially in the mobile scenario).

Binding a dataset to a list control – TLinkListControlToField

In previous chapters, we learned how lists are trending in terms of UI popularity in the mobile area with respect to grids (which used to be the key UI elements of most desktop applications). We also saw that there are two different components that implement lists in FMX: TListBox and TListView. The former can be customized easier (item per item), while the latter is more suitable for displaying several items (not identical but similar in structure).

When dealing with data binding against list controls, usually, you have a collection of data (a dataset, a list of objects, and so on) that you want to display in a single control. Each base unit of your data structure (a record, an object, and so on) will be rendered through an item of the list control. If the data structure item is complex, you may need the corresponding UI element to be rich and customize the aspect of each item according to the values of the underlying source data item.

If the source data structure changes, you'll want the UI to reflect this change (an item being deleted, inserted, and so on) and vice versa, especially if the user interacts with the UI control to make changes (from changing the current element to editing some of the rendered data). Here's where data binding (and LiveBindings specifically) comes in.

- The current element in the data structure should reflect the current element in the list control.
- The list control item count and the data structure item count should be the same (all the time).

You can define this kind of base link across a BindSource and a list control by creating `TLinkListControlToField` (by manually adding it to a `TBindingsList` component or by visually dragging the `'*'` box of the BindSource over the `'Synch'` box of the list control in the **LiveBindings Designer** IDE window), as shown in the following screenshot:

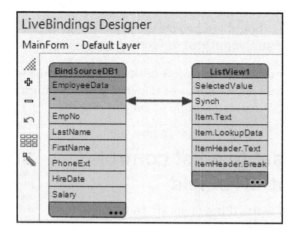

Figure 6.13

This newly created link will populate the list with a number of items that are equal to the number of rows in the `bindsource` component. From a traditional point of view, this is more or less like a piece of code iterating over the BindSource (or its dataset) to create list items:

```
var
  LItem: TListViewItem;
begin
  ListView2.BeginUpdate;
  try
    ListView2.Items.Clear;
    EmployeeData.First;
    while not EmployeeData.Eof do
    begin
      LItem := ListView2.Items.Add;

      EmployeeData.Next;
    end;

  finally
    ListView2.EndUpdate;
  end;
end;
```

The preceding piece of code fills the list using the dataset as a source. A `TLinkListControlToField` LiveBinding does the same thing but will automatically refresh the list (that is, refill the list) when needed (that is, if the dataset gets closed and reopened), while my manual code approach needs to be (manually) fired to keep the list and the dataset in sync.

So, with LiveBindings, we have the following:

- Zero code lines
- A **live** binding (meaning the binding can be unmanaged; that is, it can be automatically triggered when something changes on either of the two sides)
- A visual representation of the binding (through the **LiveBindings Designer** window)

Without LiveBindings, we have the following:

- Some code (I am not a lines-of-code person, but it's easy to understand that no code versus some code means you have to write it, possibly with some bugs, and maintain it later – possibly forever)
- A manual binding (this is similar to a managed binding, which is something we covered at the beginning of this chapter)
- Full control (the developer can decide when and how to trigger the binding)

There are different positions across the Delphi (or development in general) community regarding some topics related to these two big approaches to data binding. Some people love automatic bindings, while others hate them. I like (and strive) to be pragmatic: LiveBindings are powerful, easy, and quick in a number of situations and I tend to use them with no regrets. You may run into situations where you may need more control (over the expressions or over triggering them), but this doesn't happen to me very often (generally, you have some parallel code in the equation and the habit of binding the service data structure to the UI), so I won't delve into this debate any further.

Now, we need to fill the list items with data from the data source. Please refer to `Chapter 4`, *Discovering Lists and Advanced Components*, to visually configure your list and provide all the elements you need to show data from your data source. Since we are using data from an average-sized dataset, I am assuming you are using a `TListView` component. Due to this, next, we will go through some typical tasks related to data binding and management.

Filling items with data

Let's say we have prepared our `TListView` component with a dynamic appearance so that it can host multiple values on each item of the list. In the visual LiveBindings Designer, we can now see more bindable entries within the `ListView1` element that match the `Items.<ItemAppearanceElement>` naming pattern. The `LinkListControlToField` binding can hold several expressions to be used in different parts of the list control:

- `FieldName` and `CustomFormat` are useful when you need a simple binding across the data source and the list view, generally for addressing `Items.Text` (not many item appearance elements). The `CustomFormat` property is referred to when `FieldName` is specified.

- `FillExpressions` determines how each item is filled with data. If you have multiple item appearance elements to fill, you'll need an expression for each. For each item, you must specify a `ControlMember` instance, so that you can address the item's appearance element, and a `SourceMember` instance, so that you can select the source's field name. The `CustomFormat` sub-property is optional and lets you write a formatting expression for that specific binding.

- `FillHeaderFieldName` and `FillHeaderCustomFormat` let you define how the header for each item should be valued. Most of the time, you can rely on these two properties, but if you need multiple expressions (following the same pattern of `FieldName/CustomFormat/FillExpressions`), you can use `FillHeaderExpressions`, which is similar to `FillExpressions` (the same `ControlMember/SourceMember/CustomFormat` pattern is used).

- `FillBreakFieldName`, `FillBreakCustomFormat`, and `FillBreakGroups` are related to the grouping capabilities of `TListView`.

You can see the preceding expressions in the following screenshot:

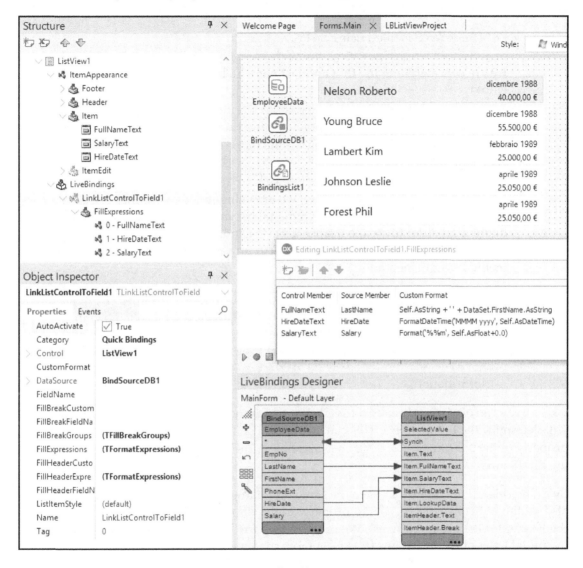

Figure 6.14

The previous screenshot shows three `FillExpressions` components being used to assign values from three different fields to the corresponding appearance objects:

- `FullNameText` is filled using `Self.AsString + ' ' + DataSet.FirstName.AsString`, with `LastName` as the source member. Here, we are concatenating the first and last name to build the full name of the employee.
- `HireDateText` is filled using `FormatDateTime('MMMM yyyy', Self.AsDateTime)`, with `HireDate` as the source member. Here, we are formatting a date value by asking for the name of the month, followed by the four-digit year value.
- `SalaryText` is filled using `Format('%%m', Self.AsFloat + 0.0)`, with `Salary` as a source member. Here, we are using the LiveBindings `Format` method to represent the string as a monetary value (the percent symbol is doubled in order to escape it since it's also captured by the LiveBindings expression evaluator. `+ 0.0` is used to circumvent a subtle bug in the `Format` method's implementation).

This bug has since been addressed due to a bug report I filled in after having a nice technical conversation with another MVP called Stefan Glienke, who helped figure out what was causing the malfunction and found a more general workaround. Please refer to **RSP-23750** on the `https://quality.embarcadero.com/browse/RSP-23750` portal for more information.

`TListView` can also place breaks across items, which means it's easy to provide a value that will determine the break group. This can be done by setting the `FillBreakFieldName` property of the `TLinkListControlToField` object, for example, to the `FirstName` field of the BindSource.

By doing this, all the items that have the same first name will be grouped together (you can also set the `FillHeaderFieldName` property to the same field in order to have its value as the header for the group of items). We can go a step further here and limit the grouping to the initial letter of the first name (to collect more matches in each group). Again, this can be done by specifying the `FillBreakCustomFormat` and `FillHeaderCustomFormat` property values as **SubString(%s, 0, 1)**, as shown in the following screenshot. You can do this by copying the first character of the `FirstName` field and using this single character as grouping criterion:

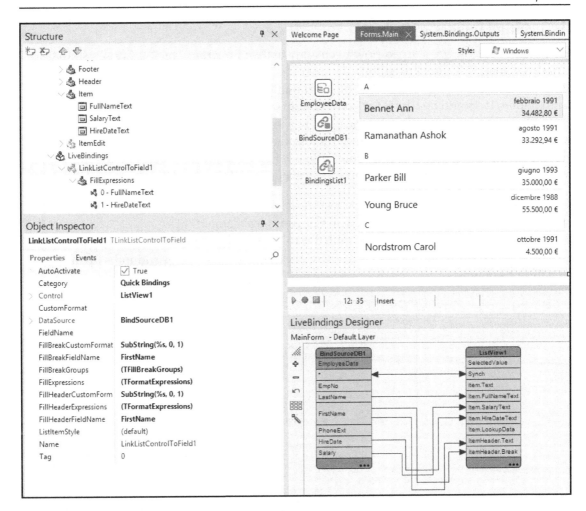

Figure 6.15

The previous screenshot shows the final result. Note the values of the involved properties in the **Object Inspector** window and the visual layout of the list view in the **Form Designer** window. Everything has been achieved with no lines of code. The values of the various formatting properties can be easily loaded from a configuration file or similar.

Associating images with data

Earlier in this book, we learned how to customize the appearance of TListView so that it can show images. There, I used the CustomFormat property to associate a different image with the item according to the value of a certain field. Now that you've reached this part of this chapter, it should be trivial for you to understand that, once TImageList and TListView have a way to specify ImageIndex for each item (you just need to add a TImageList component to your form, set it as the value for the TListView.Images property, and you're halfway set), you can use a LiveBinding expression to determine the value of ImageIndex. This can involve any other field of the record in the expression.

For example, here I have used the IfThen(Self.AsFloat>34000, 0, 1) expression to provide a value for a ThumbsImage item's appearance element (of TImageObjectAppearance). I then added it to the previous layout. This can be seen in the following screenshot (in ImageList1, there are two images – one of a thumbs up and one of a thumbs down):

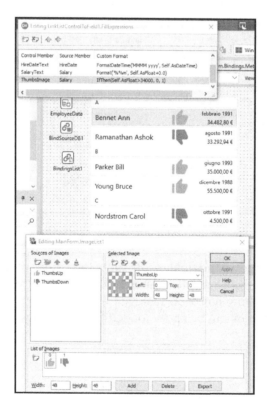

Figure 6.16

This simple behavior (which follows data, meaning that you can change the data in the dataset and see the respective images change automatically), in conjunction with an `OnItemClickEx` event handler (where you can easily discriminate item appearance objects being tapped), can be used to implement button-like images over list view items (you can have more than one per item). This is a common UI pattern on mobile platforms.

LiveBindings events

Most of the examples we've looked at so far involving LiveBindings have been zero-code examples. This is not mandatory and there are situations where you may need to perform some actions (execute some code) tied to data binding.

For example, `TLinkListControlToField` provides some convenient events that you can hook up to apply further customization to your UI. This code will not be executed at design time, only at runtime (this means you are not going to see changes in the **Form Designer** window). A typical example is assigning an `OnFillingListItem` event in order to format some values according to a certain rule. The following code can be used to render the `HireDateText` appearance item with a red font color when the `HireDate` value is less than `1990`:

```
var
  LTextObject: TListItemText;
  LItem: TListViewItem;
begin
  LItem := AEditor.CurrentObject as TListViewItem;
  LTextObject := LItem.Objects.FindDrawable('HireDateText') as
TListItemText;
  if Assigned(LTextObject) then
    if YearOf(EmployeeData.FieldByName('HireDate').AsDateTime) < 1990 then
      LTextObject.TextColor := TAlphaColorRec.Red
    else
      LTextObject.TextColor := TAlphaColorRec.Black;
end;
```

The following is the output you will see at runtime:

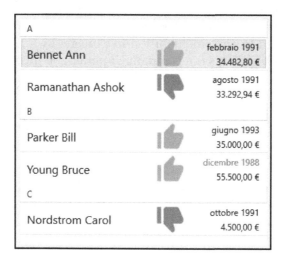

Figure 6.17

The hire date of **Young Bruce** is prior to 1990, so it has been rendered with a red color, making it stand out to the user. We are actually changing the TextColor property of the specific drawable of the current list item here. This means you can customize every aspect of it (Font.Style, Font.Size, and more) except its visibility (eventually, you will be able to set TextColor to Null).

Binding a dataset to a grid control – TLinkGridToDataSource

Even if lists (TListView, TListBox) are the most appropriate controls for rendering data on mobile platforms, FMX also provides grids, as we saw in Chapter 4, *Discovering Lists and Advanced Components*. In that chapter, we provided a brief overview of how to manually provide data to grids, while also describing how to customize some of the UI elements of the grids.

If we have a BindSource (that is, a dataset and TBindSourceDB), then we can populate grids via LiveBindings:

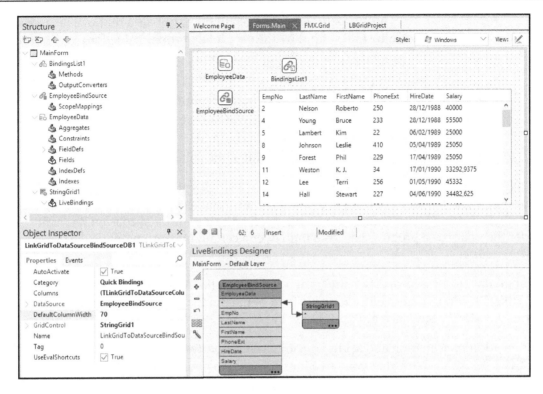

Figure 6.18

As shown in the preceding screenshot, you can simply drag the ⋆ box of EmployeeBindSource (a TBindSourceDB instance) to the ⋆ box of StringGrid1 (a TStringGrid instance) to see data being rendered through the grid. All the columns will be automatically created as TStringColumn instances by default. You can edit the Columns property of the TLinkGridToDataSource object to manually define which columns to render and which kinds of columns to create for each entry.

This will allow you to set a property for the column-specific binding (something equivalent to the FillExpressions expression of the list bindings). Some of these properties are as follows:

- ColumnStyle: By default, the column is created as TStringColumn. However, you may want to select a better value that's related to its content (numbers, date values, and more).
- CustomFormat: This property lets you specify the expression that will be used to render the value in the grid.

- `CustomParse`: This property lets you specify the expression that will be used to transform the value that's input by the user into a proper value for the column.
- `Header`: This property sets the title of the column.
- `MemberName`: This property sets the corresponding field of the column.
- `ReadOnly`: This property defines whether the column can be edited by the user.
- `Visible`: This property sets the visibility of the column (you can create columns and then decide on the visibility of each column).
- `Width`: This property specifies the width of the column.

We'll try to format our grid values so that we have a single column containing the full name of the employee, the date of hiring in a month/year format (enabling editing as well), and a properly formatted salary value. As a bonus, we'll add an additional column that will render the salary as a progress bar (as a ratio over a certain maximum value; that is, `100,000`).

Through the `Columns` property editor, you can click on the **Add All Fields** tool button to have the IDE add a column entry for each field of the BindSource. Then, you can delete the entries you don't need (such as `EmpNo`, `LastName`, and `PhoneExt`).

Add an additional column and set its `MemberName` property to `Salary` and `Header` to `'Salary (100K)'`. Now that you have four columns in your grid, we can set some properties for each:

- `MemberName`: `FirstName`
  `CustomFormat`: `Self.AsString + ' ' + DataSet.LastName.AsString`
  `Header`: `Full Name`
  `ReadOnly`: `True`
  `Width`: `120`

- `MemberName`: `HireDate`
  `CustomFormat`: `FormatDateTime('MMMM yyyy', Self.AsDateTime)`
  `CustomParse`: `'01/'+ToStr(%s)`
  `Header`: `Hiring`
  `ReadOnly`: `False`
  `Width`: `100`

- MemberName: `Salary`
  ColumnStyle: `FloatColumn`
  CustomFormat: `Format('%%m', Self.AsFloat + 0.0)`
  Header: `Salary`
  Width: `80`
- MemberName: `Salary`
  ColumnStyle: `ProgressColumn`
  CustomFormat: `(Self.AsFloat/100000)*100`
  Header: `Salary (100K)`
  Width: `100`

At this point, you should be able to understand most of these settings. However, I do want to point out the use of `CustomParse` on the `HireDate` column. This allows the user to insert a string such as `5/1982`, representing the month of May in 1982, and then change it to `01/05/1982` (May 1, 1982). This is just a simple example of showing how the user can transform the input before looking at field validation (this is the symmetric concept of the `CustomFormat` property, which lets you transform the field's data before hitting the UI).

You should also take note of the last column, which has been set to `ProgressColumn` through the `ColumnStyle` property. It expects values from 0 to 100 to render a corresponding progress bar in the grid cell. The final result can be seen in the following screenshot:

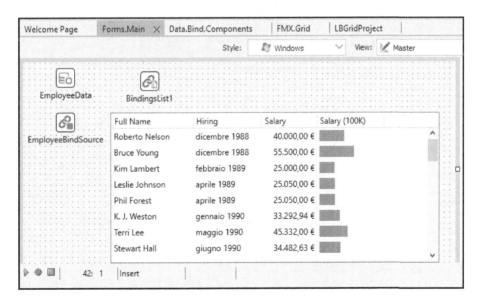

Figure 6.19

Pushing this example a little bit further, let's say we want to have a better **Salary** representation. Instead of having it rendered over a fixed maximum value (**100K**), we may want to find out what the **Max** value in the dataset is and use it.

FireDAC's ability to easily define an aggregate over the dataset will help us here. Simply edit the `Aggregates` property of `EmployeeData` (the `TFDMemTable` instance) and add an entry with `Max(Salary)` set to `Expression` and `Max_Salary` set to `Name`. Then, set its `Active` property to `True`. Also, remember to set the `AggregatesActive` property of the dataset to `True`. Now, you have the dataset maintaining an easy-to-access, always-updated value so that you know the maximum salary in the dataset: `DataSet.Aggregates.AggregateByName('Max_Salary').Value`.

Here, we can add a new column to our grid, bind it to the `Salary` field, and write the following `CustomFormat` expression:

```
100*(
  Self.AsFloat /
  IfThen(
    DataSet.Aggregates.AggregateByName('Max_Salary').Value = 0
  , 100000
  , DataSet.Aggregates.AggregateByName('Max_Salary').Value)
  )
```

As you can see, `IfThen` is being used to avoid a division by zero when `Max_Salary` is zero (that is, the dataset is empty or all the salary values have been zeroed). In that case, the default value (100,000) is used. Obviously, there are alternative solutions to addressing this problem, such as using `IfThen(<Aggregate> = 0, <DefaultValue>, 100*(<CurrentValue>/>Aggregate>))`.

The following screenshot shows the new column rendering the salary, relative to the **Max** approach:

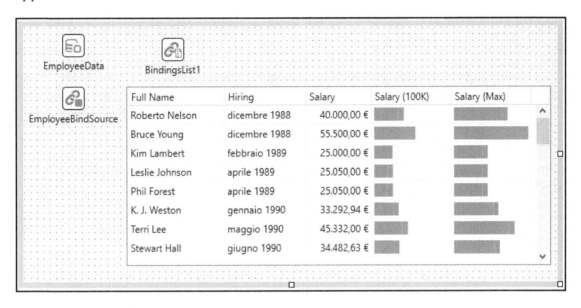

Figure 6.20

This example shows how easy it is to bind a dataset to UI controls (a grid in this case, though the same concept would apply to other controls), even when dealing with aggregate values being calculated over the dataset itself and data being graphically rendered. These capabilities can be a real productivity booster for you as a developer. I hope this chapter has provided you with enough examples of how to deal with LiveBindings in this way.

Even though LiveBindings is supposed to provide data notifications on its own, there are situations where the internal automatisms may fall short and you'll need to manually trigger a refresh of the binding.

One way to do this is to temporarily set the `Active` property of the link component (that is, an instance of `TLinkListControlToField`) to `False` and immediately set it back to `True`. Some specific binding components also provide explicit methods to force a list control to be filled in, according to the nature of the binding.

There are a number of other bindings available, such as `TLinkControlToProperty`, `TLinkFillControlToProperty`, and `TLinkFillControlToField`. The same topics we've covered so far apply to all of them; the only things that change are the Source and Target ends of the binding.

Summary

In this chapter, we covered one of the key elements of all applications: data binding. Even if your application is not heavily data-centric, a lot of situations will involve data being surfaced to the UI and vice versa.

The LiveBindings technology provides great flexibility in this area and allows developers to connect data to controls, as well as properties (even those in non-visual classes) to data or properties to other properties. Mastering this binding mechanism is crucial for your productivity as a developer, and having a good understanding of what's under the hood will save you from a number of issues and hiccups.

In the next chapter, we'll address another key element of the FMX framework known as **Style**. This defines the visual aspect of each FMX control.

Understanding FMX Style Concept

In the previous chapter, we learned about data binding, quite a fundamental piece of knowledge for every developer. Data is provided to the user in order to be consumed or manipulated through the user interface. Specifically, we are talking about the **Graphical User Interface (GUI)** delivering visual interaction for the end user.

In this chapter, we'll learn about a central concept of the FMX framework, that is, **Style**. This is the part of technology that enables the framework to abstract visual aspects from behavioral ones, enabling the styling of applications (including native-platform styling).

This chapter will cover the following topics:

- Learning about multi-platform visual programming
- Introducing the Style concept
- Approaching the TStyleBook component
- Managing styles: the TStyleManager component
- Learning about platform-native controls

At the end of this chapter, you'll be able to understand what Style is, why it is central to the FMX framework, have a general understanding of what's provided by Embarcadero and how it works in order to achieve cross-platform capabilities in Delphi, know how to edit style definitions and how to deal with multiple styles at runtime.

You will also be familiar with the runtime behavior of your applications on multiple platforms, including the concept of platform-native controls, available with some commonly used components.

Technical requirements

Here is the source code used in this chapter: `https://github.com/PacktPublishing/` `Delphi-GUI-Programming-with-FireMonkey/tree/master/Chapter%2007`.

Generally speaking, for the whole book, you need a computer with Delphi set up and a few additional libraries installed (such as **Radiant Shapes** (`https://getitnow.embarcadero.` `com/?q=radiant+shapes`) and **CodeSite Logging** (`https://getitnow.embarcadero.com/?q=` `codesite`)). Having other devices and setting up multiple platforms (iOS, Android, OS X/macOS, and Linux) other than Windows is a plus but not strictly needed to follow the flow of the book.

Learning about multi-platform visual programming

There are a number of peculiarities in the UI that are intrinsic to the specific execution platform. A **Windows** application and an **OS X/macOS** application may have the same functionalities but have a different user interface. They wouldn't necessarily have a completely different UI; just keep in mind that every platform has its own conventions and *look and feel* particularities that you need to respect if you want to provide a UI the user feels is natural in the overall picture of the **operating system** (**OS**) they are acquainted with. This will greatly impact the user-friendliness of the application.

FireMonkey's promise is to let you build a UI application that is cross-platform, meaning the same application will be deployed on several platforms without having the very same aspect on each of them. The application will be *transposed* into the specific *look and feel* of each platform without requiring a complete rewrite of the application's code. *Sounds amazing, doesn't it?*

In the following screenshot, you can see an FMX application running respectively on **(1)** the Windows platform (**Microsoft Windows 10**), **(2)** on the Mac OS X/macOS platform (**macOS 10.14 Mojave**), and **(3)** the Android platform (**Android 8 Oreo**):

Figure 7.1

The point here is the programmer didn't have to adjust the UI to match the underlying OS visuals. It actually is the very same application but different styles have been applied. Note how the switch component differs, as well as buttons, captions, edit boxes, applied fonts, splitters, and scrollbars.

In Chapter 2, *Exploring Similarities and Differences with VCL*, we had our first contact with the Style concept while looking at VCL versus FMX similarities and differences. Visual applications (desktop or mobile) can be seen as a bunch of functionalities (implemented with code) the user is allowed to interact with (more or less actively, depending on the specific case) through a graphical interface. This very basic concept of visual programming acts as a divider across what the application does and how the application looks to the user. This second portion of the software is the one we are going to delve into, expanding the concept of **FMX Style**.

Introducing the Style concept

FMX Style is a definition of the composition (nested structure) and configuration (property values) of FMX objects (visual or not) that are used as elements (building blocks) of a **User Interface (UI)**.

In this section, we are going to learn about how the *whole* style mechanism works, how it is used to achieve cross-platform support for visual Delphi applications, and how to manipulate style definitions in the IDE and compiled applications.

This definition is stored in specific components, namely `TStyleBook` instances, and can be stored in different formats. Most of the time, you will encounter them in either a binary form (compact but requiring an editor) or textual form (bloated but human-readable and editable with a common text editor).

If we have the opportunity to separate what `TButton` does (have a caption, fire a piece of code when pressed, have a state, and deal with focus) from how it looks (that is, a 3D gray rectangle with black text), we gain the ability to change the latter without affecting the former. In other words, we gain the ability to switch onto different platforms (that all have a specific *look and feel*), keeping the same behavioral implementation while providing a different visual asset (a different, platform-specific style).

The following screenshot provides different renderings of the same button on four different platforms, namely, **(1) Microsoft Windows**, **(2) Apple Mac OS X/macOS**, **(3) Apple iOS**, and **(4) Google Android**. The visual differences are tied to the different styles applied:

Figure 7.2

From the preceding screenshot, it should be immediately understandable how central the Style concept is to a multi-platform software development environment. Together with the ability of the compiler toolchain to address a platform, the RTL ability to work against specific OS APIs, it is fundamental for the visual framework to adapt to the specific *look and feel* the application is actually executing.

This is the reason Embarcadero provides FMX with four platform styles, one for each supported platform, that is, Windows, Mac OS X/macOS, Android, and iOS. The visuals of your application will be provided to the target platform by including the corresponding platform style resource at compile time. Every FMX visual component has correspondence in each of the native platform styles meaning that each style contains a specific entry for every standard component in order to provide a visual definition of the component for the specific platform. An additional platform (**Linux**) is supported through the addition of a third-party product (**FMXLinux** by **KSDev**, `https://www.fmxlinux.com/`) that also adds a corresponding platform style to the list.

The following screenshot shows our application running on the Linux platform (**Ubuntu Linux 18.04**):

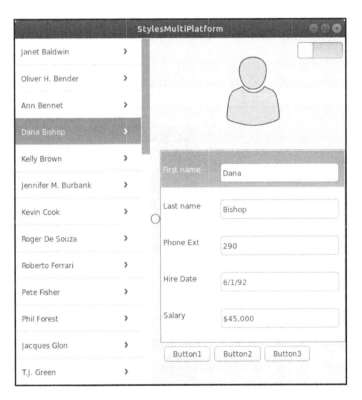

Figure 7.3

Another cool thing about FMX style is that this mechanism, even if it obviously plays a central role in the multi-platform scenario, is a native feature of the framework itself and it is completely general, not tied to the platform target.

Starting from July 2019, Embarcadero ships a license to FMX Linux along with Enterprise and Architect versions of the product, meaning you can add FMXLinux to your product freely through the **GetIt** package manager.

As I've already said, it is an important part of the usability of your applications to be as near as possible to the standard conventions of the actual platform they are being executed on. But theoretically, one may even decide that the application should have specific visuals and a *look and feel* even on different platforms.

This may or may not make sense, depending on several factors (including the aim and kind of the application, company branding requirements, user targeting requirements, and so on), but it can be done by implementing a custom style and using the same style on all platforms. Variations on these topics include having customized styles (for example, embossed company branding or colors) for each platform or for each device scenario (desktop and mobile).

Our application running on the Windows platform would appear as follows:

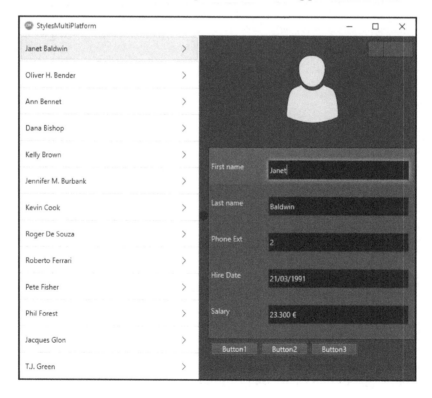

Figure 7.4

The following screenshot shows how our application looks running on the OS X/macOS platform:

Figure 7.5

Here is how our application interface looks on the Android platform:

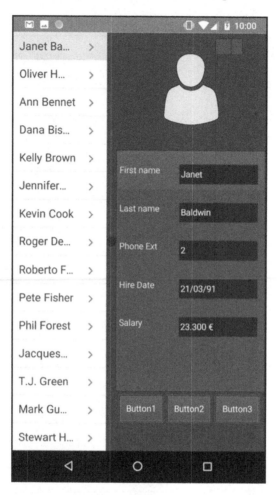

Figure 7.6

From the preceding screenshots, you can see that building a style from scratch can be challenging as you will need to provide a visual definition for all the components used in the application (if a component does not have a matching style definition, it will not be rendered to the user).

You may want to customize a portion of an existing style or clone/customize an entire existing style (let's say changing the color schema). As long as you don't break the link between the style definition and the code implementation (the link that basically relies on a naming convention across code and style elements), you can even delegate style manipulation to a non-developer specialist (that is, a graphic designer).

Embarcadero includes extra styles with Delphi (and some others are available through the GetIt package manager as well) and, as happened with Delphi components, there are third-party vendors of FMX styles out there (one of the most prolific style vendors is DelphiStyles, `https://www.delphistyles.com/fmx/`), as shown in the following screenshot:

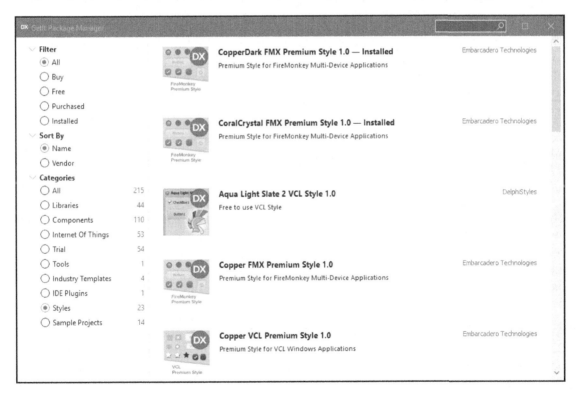

Figure 7.7

As you can see in the preceding screenshot, a number of styles are available in the **GetIt Package Manager**, grouped under the **Styles** category. Let's look a little more into the anatomy of a style in the rest of the chapter.

Understanding the anatomy of a style

So far, we have learned that FMX has the capability to apply different styles to the same application. A style is composed of a list of definitions (one for each UI element, that is, **component**) that are built as a composition of basic elements (like shapes or images) and/or other styled elements, making the whole mechanism really powerful and extensible.

If you are an experienced VCL developer, you can see the style definition as a sort of **DFM file**, where the structure of components is defined together with property values determining specific characteristics of each element. We never addressed the fact it is not trivial to provide a complete definition of the visual asset of a component.

This becomes even harder while keeping in consideration that this definition should be sophisticated enough to deliver a proper version of the component for each supported platform (*up to five different platforms!*) and considering all the surrounding difficulties we covered while talking about mobile development (including different screen sizes, resolutions, and depths).

You may think the style definition of a button object is made of some shapes (TRectangle) where the use of gradients and effects may provide a 3D flavor to the result and some TText component is used to deliver a caption to the button. This is exactly what happens with what I call *Vector styles* and has been supported since the very first versions of FMX.

This approach is very effective while building responsive UIs, meaning you can resize every component without affecting the quality of the rendering as everything would scale consequently through the use of alignments and anchors, as we covered in Chapter 2, *Exploring Similarities and Differences with VCL*, and multi-res images in Chapter 3, *Mastering Basic Components*, but may fall short when dealing with very fine graphic details and has a performance side to consider.

At some point, to address the problem of perfectly mimicking a platform's *look and feel*, **Bitmap** styles were introduced in FMX. They basically rely on a picture where elements (or part of them) are drawn (thus, adding much more flexibility as the limits are the computer graphic skills of the designer) and a precise description of what portion (or portions) of the image are to be used is given according to the component state.

In the next sections, we'll see some more details about these two big families of FMX styles but, before proceeding, we need to learn some basics about style management inside and outside the IDE.

Managing style(s) in the IDE

If you create a new blank FMX application, the IDE will show you an empty form through the **Multi-device Form Designer**. The project is configured to target **Win32** as the compiler target platform and the **Style selector** combobox is set to Windows. Our multi-platform application would be compiled for Win32 and the designer is set to preview the visual aspect of the form on the Windows platform, accordingly. If we drop a TButton instance on the form, we'll see it looking like a standard Windows button, as shown in the following screenshot:

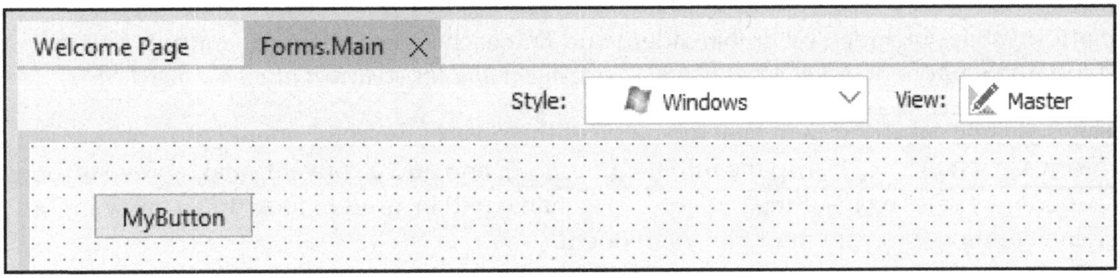

Figure 7.8

The four platform styles provided by Embarcadero to target the four officially supported platforms (Windows, OS X/macOS, Android, and iOS) are listed in the Style selector combobox and you can select a different entry to have the **Multi-device Form Designer** immediately reflect the change and render your form with the new style.

In other words, the IDE (running on the Windows platform) is capable of previewing how your form will look on other platforms. Once compiled, only the style for the target platform is included in the binary resources. To be precise, it's not only one style that gets included. For example, for the Windows platform, **Delphi 10.4 Sydney** includes three styles, namely, win10style, win8style, and win7style.

The same happens for the OS X/macOS platform, where osxstyle and lionstyle are provided. This is needed because even targeting the same platform, you'll need a different *look and feel* to match the actual version of the OS your application is executed in (and this is known only at runtime so all possible styles are included in your app).

Back to the IDE, having a quick way to switch between styles is a big opportunity to save time while designing your UI (targeting multiple platforms, of course) but keep in mind the components on the form are unique, not per-style. So when you switch style (platform), this does not mean you are in a separate designing space where changes are applied to that style (platform).

Every change you make to the component (size, positioning, alignment, and more) will affect its properties' values (you can check them in the **Object Inspector** window). These values are stored in the **FMX file** and are valid for all platforms. The fact you can actually see the component with a different visual aspect when you select one style or another only depends on the different definition the current style contains.

Binding a component to its style

We said we have a TButton instance on our form. We learned there are (at least) four platform styles included by Embarcadero and that each style contains an entry for every standard component. *What about how the component and the style definition are matched?*

The matching algorithm will take the name of the class of the component (TButton), lowercase it (tbutton), strip the initial T (button), and add a conventional style suffix (buttonstyle). The resulting buttonstyle name will be used to look up an entry in the style definition for every TButton component.

A simple override for this selection mechanism is provided through the StyleLookup property (introduced in the TStyledControl class) where a different style name can be specified instead of the conventional default.

Each application has a default style (the matching platform style, by default), but we'll see in the following sections how to include a custom style and select it as default, as well as how to have a different style applied to one or more forms (diverging from the default style).

Exploring the style definition of a component

Now that our `TButton` is on the form and the **Windows** entry is selected in the **Style** selector, we may want to see the actual definition of the `buttonstyle` entry of this platform style. An easy way to achieve this is to right-click on the button instance (in the multi-device Form Designer) and select **Edit Default Style...** from the contextual pop-up menu, as shown in the following screenshot:

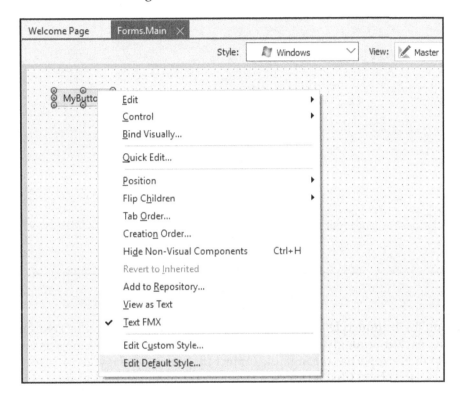

Figure 7.9

This will bring up the **Style Designer** IDE editor window. The IDE **Structure** view will now switch to represent Style elements and you can spot the **Buttonstyle** entry under the **StyleContainer** root node, shown in the following screenshot:

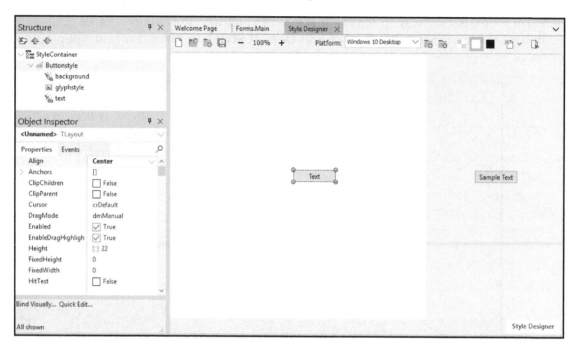

Figure 7.10

If you expand the **Buttonstyle** node, you'll see the actual definition of this style entry, including the **background**, **glyphstyle**, and **text** objects. Selecting these objects will give you access to their properties through the **Object Inspector**, where you can also see the actual class of each object (that is, TButtonStyleObject for the **background** object).

The **Style Designer**, like the **Form Designer**, apart from providing an immediate visual preview, offers the capability to point and click elements of the style. I personally found it easier to use the **Structure** view for this task, though, and it also has an additional right panel where a live preview of the component is available (complete with the style's background dispositions and handy for testing state-related behaviors of the component, such as having or not having the focus or mouse hovering for animations and effects).

A toolbar is provided to host some common operations (such as save/load to/load from file, change the editor's zoom factor, select a different background for the editor). In the same toolbar, a **Platform** selection combobox lets you determine the actual style you are editing (**Windows 10 Desktop**, if you are running Delphi on a **Windows 10** machine, like I do). This matches what we have learned before about platform styles, that is, there may be more than one style available for each platform and the style definitions are separated.

To the immediate right of the **Platform** selection combobox are two buttons that will allow you to switch style and see the actual definition for buttonstyle in each one (the differences are not huge but are still significant across **Windows 7**, **Windows 8**, and Windows 10, for example), shown in the following screenshot:

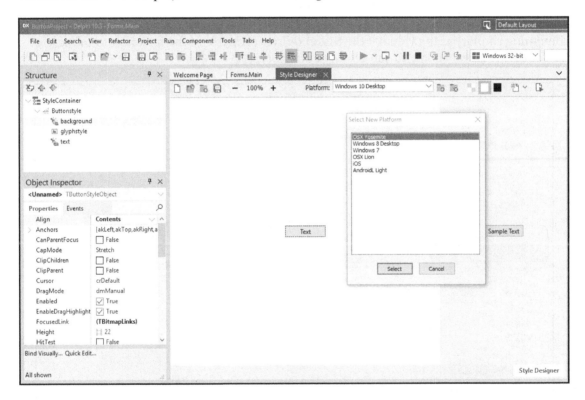

Figure 7.11

Specifically, the **Windows 10 Desktop** style (but the same applies to **Windows 7** and **Windows 8 Desktop**) is a bitmap style, meaning at least part of its definition is based on bitmap images that act as sources. Style objects may refer to a certain image and define the portion of it to be used to render the component (or again, part of it) according to a specific state. We'll cover the bitmap style in more detail later in this chapter.

If you make some changes to the `buttonstyle` entry and you click on the **Apply style** button in the toolbar of the **Style Designer**, the form designer will reflect the changes. If you switch back to your form, you'll see your changes applied to our button; given that you are editing the default style for `TButton`, every other additional `TButton` instance will use the same style definition and so you just managed to determine how all buttons will look in your application.

If you want to edit the style of a specific `TButton` instance (or a set of them), leaving the default untouched, you may want to choose **Edit Custom Style...** from the form designer contextual pop-up menu. The IDE will clone the default style definition (`buttonstyle`) into a new style definition (`Button1Style1`, for example – you can rename it at your will).

To apply this new definition to a **TButton** instance, just write its name (`Button1Style1` or something similar) as the value of the **StyleLookup** property of the instance. In the case of the following screenshot, you can see **MyButtonStyle1**:

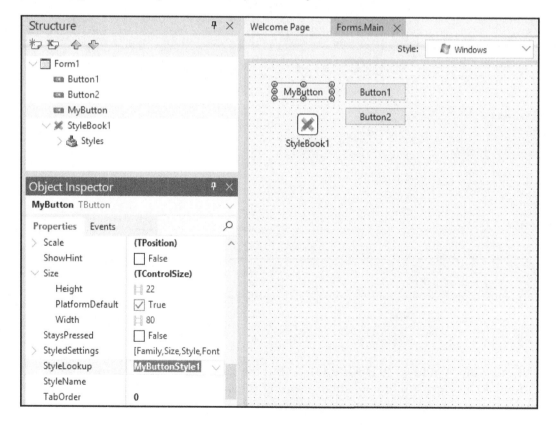

Figure 7.12

These new definitions will be stored in a conveniently created (by the IDE) `TStyleBook` component, which you'll see appearing on your form (**StyleBook1**). Under the hood, the IDE also sets your form's `StyleBook` property to reference the newly created `TStyleBook` instance, that is, from now on, the style definition selection algorithm will first look in the `TStyleBook` instance and then fall back to the application's default style (the platform style).

Now we are familiar with the idea our components will need a style definition in order to build their visual aspect, it is quite straightforward – the mechanism needs a way to deal with collection(s) of these definitions.

In this section, we have learned how a style is defined and how different style definitions are applied in the IDE and at runtime. In the next section, we are going to introduce how style definitions can be stored and edited, with the help of a specific component: `TStyleBook`.

Approaching the TStyleBook component

In this section, we are going to discuss how style definitions can be stored, embedded, and manipulated both at design time and runtime.

The `StyleBook` component has exactly this aim. It is a non-visual component you usually drop onto a form and edit through its component editor (double-click on the component to activate it), that is, the Style Designer we have seen previously. All functionalities related to style persistence (load/save from/to a file) are available at design time and at runtime. If you load one or more styles in `TStyleBook` at design time, data will be stored within the FMX file of the form the component is on. Keep in mind that styles (especially bitmap styles) can be large in size and they actually get compiled into the binaries of your application.

Every FMX form has a `StyleBook` property that you can use to instruct the style selection mechanism to look up in a specific `StyleBook` when looking for style definitions of components on the form. The `StyleBook` component has a `Styles` property that is a collection (dictionary) mapping platform identifiers to the actual style (collection) resource. The actual platform the application is running on is determined through a call to FMX behavior services (refer to the `FMX.BehaviorManager` unit, `TBehaviorServices`, `IDeviceInfo` interface that has a convenient `GetOSPlatform` method).

If no matches are found in the `StyleBook` associated with the form, a second lookup is attempted against the application style. This also means the `StyleBook` can be used as a container for a portion of the style definitions (that is, the one you have customized with respect to the application style or some additional style definitions you may want to use at will as the `TFrameStand` component does, as we will see in `Chapter 8`, *Divide and Conquer with TFrameStand*).

Styles are provided in two different formats:

- **Binary format**: This is more compact (less space utilization), usually saved on disk using files with the `.fsf` extension.
- **Textual format**: This format is more verbose (a bigger size on disk) but probably more portable and editable/inspectable with a common text editor, usually stored with the `.style` extension.

Both formats are handled by the **Style Designer** and keep in mind that binary resources embedded in styles (that is, bitmaps for bitmap styles or multi-res bitmaps for glyph and images) are stored in a textual representation (something similar to **Base64** encoding) in `.style` files, causing an extra overhead in terms of disk occupancy.

 A third format, **Indexed**, is available and supported by the style streaming system. It is basically a binary format with an optimization against duplicated style resources within the same style.

A huge style will need to be loaded in memory to be usable from your application, so keep an eye on trimming the binary resources to the really necessary ones.

In the following sections, we are going to learn about the peculiarities of vector-based styles and bitmap-based styles.

Learning about Vector styles

In your Delphi installation, as said, some FMX styles are included. You can find them in the `C:\Users\Public\Documents\Embarcadero\Studio\21.0\Styles` folder (the actual folder may be different according to the options selected in the installation process). One file in the folder is `Air.style`, containing the textual representation of an FMX style named Air. This style is simple and it is platform-neutral, meaning that it does not include variations of itself to be applied to each specific target platform. It is one style definition for all platforms, delivering the same *look and feel* everywhere.

You may notice some differences still exist in the visuals of the application running on different platforms. Some of these differences depend on the so-called behavioral services FMX implements to keep track of the intrinsic differences across platforms, that is, the default tab position for Android is at the top of a page control while it's at the bottom for iOS. The components may take advantage of such information to fine-tune the user experience according to the actual platform. The following screenshot shows the difference between the position of the default tab in Android and iOS:

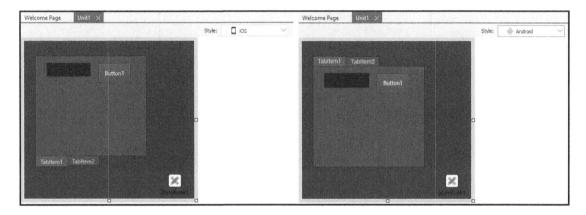

Figure 7.13

We refer to the Air style as a *vector style* because its whole definition does not involve the use of bitmaps (you can open the `Air.style` file with a text editor to check there is no binary data stored in it except for some `TPath` content that refers to SVG graphics). Not using bitmaps means this style uses primitives (`TRectangle`, `TCircle`, and more) and vector graphics (`TPath`) to compose the visuals of the user interface.

Consequently, components are more easily capable of responding to changes in size, delivering a highly optimized experience regardless of the screen resolution or screen density of the actual device. No stretching or lossy interpolation of bitmaps is involved. The use of SVG paths to implement glyphs and other graphical elements completes the picture of a vector style.

The following screenshot shows you the Air style definitions (**buttonstyle**):

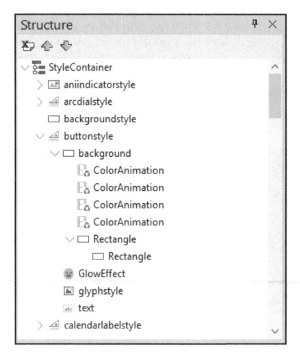

Figure 7.14

Obviously, as you can see, these styles tend to be more suitable in a multi-platform (multi-device) scenario but at the same time, you can immediately spot how the complexity of elements grows as soon as you try to achieve a visually rich user interface. Even though FMX is powerful and natively handles many rendering capabilities (gradients, effects, and animations), a designer may find themselves struggling to implement small details of components.

Understanding Bitmap styles

Historically, drawing bitmaps has been greatly optimized in computer programming. Most operating systems and graphic environments have strong optimization when dealing with bitmaps and graphics elements. This factor, probably in conjunction with the need to accurately replicate visual assets of several target platforms, led to the introduction of bitmap styles in FMX.

Basically, this means the application UI (or part of it) is the result of the combination of different bitmaps or, more often, parts of a large bitmap that acts as a kind of palette. Having a single bitmap is handy in terms of editing (for example, with an external graphic editor) and you have a chance to highly reuse the same parts of the bitmap in several components.

If a vector style is more similar to the composition of FMX objects (primitives, vector graphics, and other sub-compositions of them), a bitmap style usually consists of a composition of style objects describing the portion of some bitmap to be used according to the state of the component or other conditions. The following screenshot shows you the **Style Designer** with a bitmap style loaded, the **buttonstyle** definition:

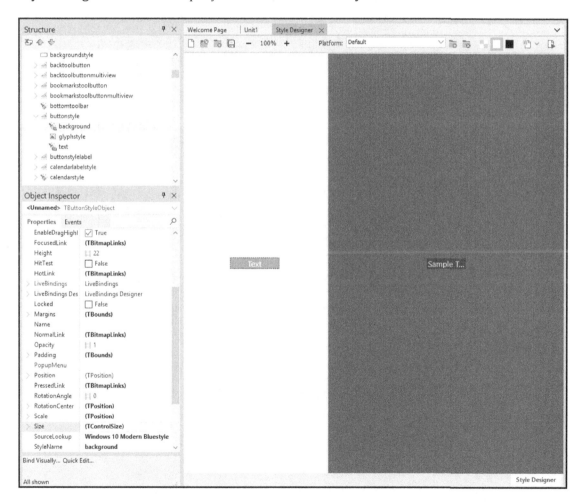

Figure 7.15

A technique named **9-slice scaling** is used to avoid the stretching of images. Basically, if you have a bitmap representing a button, possibly a rounded rectangle-shaped image, it will have a fixed size (let's say 100 x 25). *What if you need to use it and render a button that is 300 x 25?* You surely want to avoid having the image stretched because it would cause unnatural distortion of the corners and, especially near to other different-sized buttons, the user would perceive it as unnatural and messy.

So, you can consider slicing the source bitmap in order to keep the corners at their original size and replicate those parts (like the central one) that are more homogeneous and not affected by distortion when duplicated or truncated. The following diagram shows traditional scaling versus the 9-slice scaling technique:

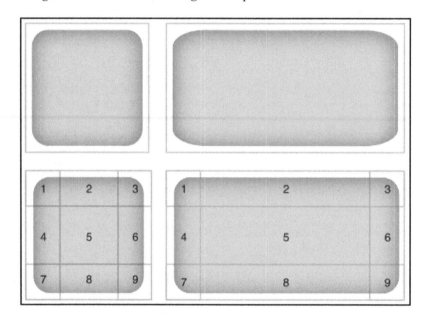

Figure 7.16

Most of the bitmap styles you'll encounter are all based on this concept of defining something more complex than a bare rectangle portion of the source bitmap, through the use of a data structure named TBitmapLinks, which will define all the measures needed for a 9-slice scaling technique (coordinates and the sizing of slices). The supplied component editor will allow you to easily deal with such a data structure through a visual designer.

The following screenshot shows you the **BitmapLinks** editor:

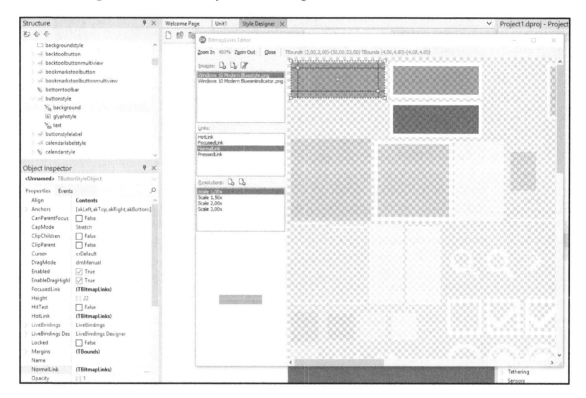

Figure 7.17

The more states a component has to render, the more bitmap links will be available to associate a portion of the bitmap with the component. For example, we can have a look at Win10ModernBlue.Style, again available in your Delphi installation. Considering the **buttonstyle** element, you can see the **background** element implemented with a TButtonStyleObject instance.

Among its properties, you'll spot several TBitmapLinks entries, including FocusedLink, HotLink, NormalLink, and PressedLink. They all refer to the same source image (specified through the SourceLookup property value, set to **Windows 10 Modern Bluestyle.png**) addressing different portions (with different filling and border colors). Respectively, the resulting portions of the bitmap are used in the following instances:

- When the component has the input focus (FocusedLink)
- When the component has the mouse hovering over it (HotLink)
- When the component is in its normal state (NormalLink)
- When the component is pressed (temporarily or permanently if it has this capability) by the user (PressedLink)

 Please note the TBitmapLinks editor supports multi-resolution definitions, meaning you may have several versions of the source bitmap (one per scale factor) and one link definition per scale factor. This greatly simplifies the creation of multi-resolution bitmap styles, assuring the best quality is delivered to end users.

The following screenshot shows you the **Object Inspector** views for **background** and **text** elements, showing the properties [State]**Link**, [State]**Color**, and [State]**Shadow**:

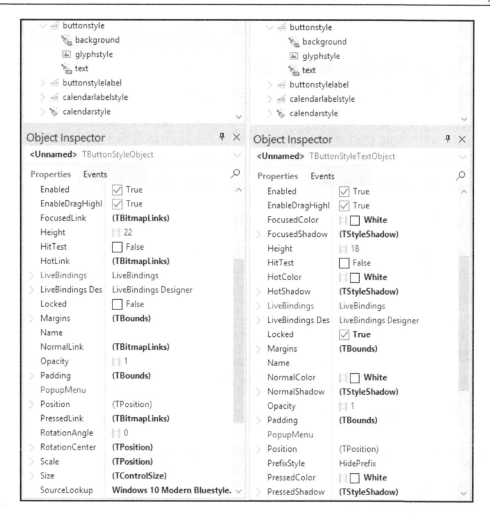

Figure 7.18

A corresponding functionality is available for text objects through TButtonStyleTextObject, which allows the developer to define many visual aspects of a text (color, shadow options, and more) across several states of the component (again, **Focused**, **Hot**, **Normal**, and **Pressed**).

Through the use of bitmap styles, you can achieve complex results by combining the power of computer graphics (surrogated/condensed into a static image) and a kind of layering of several components (including regular FMX objects, used in vector styles), generally granting a performance boost with respect to the vector style approach.

So far, we have discussed static resources and definitions within style definition formats. In the next section, we are going to see that there's also some room for dynamic components.

Adding animation, triggers, and effects

Exploring more advanced FMX styles, you will probably encounter some effects (`TGlowEffect`, to name one) or animations (`TColorAnimation`) that are placed inside style definitions.

We have already said that FMX has powerful graphic capabilities and these elements are actually important to achieve complex visual behaviors for the user. What you may be puzzled about is how such things that obviously need some triggering mechanisms can be stored in style definitions (which lack code or behavior information). FMX has a triggering mechanism that can be used to fire animations responding to some events or state changes in the component itself. The same applies to effects.

The typical triggers you may want to use are `IsFocused`, `IsPressed`, or `IsSelected`. Check the `Trigger` property of `TAnimation` and `TEffect` descendants to see the full list of possibilities. Also, note that animations have a `TriggerInverse` property for your convenience.

In the next section, we are going to discuss how to deal with styles at runtime outside the Delphi IDE.

Managing styles – the TStyleManager component

In this section, we are going to focus on aspects related to style definition while the application is running (at runtime).

We have seen in this chapter that an FMX component is visually rendered through its style definition. This style definition is matched by name following a naming convention (for example, `TButton` has **buttonstyle**, `TEdit` has **editstyle**, and more) and an override mechanism (the `StyleLookup` property). The lookup of the definition is done against the (optional) `TStyleBook` instance referenced by the `StyleBook` property of the component's parent form and against the application style set for the application.

There is a dedicated class in FMX to deal with the application-wide style `TStyleManager` declared and implemented in the `FMX.Styles.pas` unit. This class provides some functionalities you may find handy when dealing with styles:

- It can enumerate style resources embedded within the application, through the `EnumStyleResources` method.
- It can obtain a reference to the corresponding FMX object defined by a style resource (the `GetStyleResource` method).
- It can register a certain style resource to be used with a specific platform (the `RegisterPlatformStyleResource` method).
- It can obtain a reference to `ActiveStyle` (through the `homonym` method).
- It can set the active style (the `SetStyle` method), eventually loading it from an external file (the `SetStyleFromFile` method, supporting the `.style` and `.fsf` file formats) or loading one of the styles you may have embedded in your binary resources (the `SetStyleFromResource` method).

The native platform styles are embedded in your application by default. If you are curious, you can even save them to an external file in order to inspect them. In the `FMX.Styles` unit, there is a `TStyleStreaming` class you can make use of to load and save a style object to and from any stream (including a `TFileStream`, of course) so it should be straightforward enough to save the active style to a file, as shown in the following code snippet:

```
var
  LFileStream: TFileStream;
begin
  LFileStream := TFileStream.Create('C:\temp\Active.style', fmCreate or
  fmOpenReadWrite);
  try
    TStyleStreaming.SaveToStream(
      TStyleManager.ActiveStyle(nil)
    , LFileStream, TStyleformat.Text
    );
  finally
    LFileStream.Free;
  end;
end;
```

As you probably noted, you can specify the `TStyleFormat` desired as the third argument of the `SaveToStream` method.

Understanding the selection algorithm

The native platform style is the obvious default for each FMX application. Once you have built your FMX **Win32** application, you'll probably want one of the Windows 10, Windows 8, or Windows 7 default styles to be applied at runtime in order to make your application look native to the OS.

If you want to set a different style for your application, right from the start, you can add some code to load the desired style directly in the DPR file of the project. You may choose to load your style from an external file (and possibly have some configuration information to select the desired file) or from binary resources of your executable; either way, the style becomes the default application style and every created form will use that style.

If you really want to override the application style in a particular form, you can always add a TStyleBook component to that form and set the StyleBook reference property of the form to that style book. However, this will not completely override the application default style, as the style selection mechanism will try to look up a style definition against TStyleBook on the form (actually, the StyleBook referenced by the homonym property) and, if none is provided, will perform a second attempt against the application style.

These mechanisms allow the developer to keep a default style for the application and customize one or more style definitions (component visual assets) on a specific form (or even multiple forms sharing the same StyleBook component). Using the **Style Designer**, you can easily *copy and paste* style definitions across different StyleBooks, so you can even perform hybridation across different existing styles. Let's follow these steps:

1. Use the GetIt package manager to download a couple of styles. I am going to use CoralCrystal FMX Premium Style 1.0 (https://getitnow.embarcadero. com/CoralCrystalFMXPremuimStyle-1.0/) and CopperDark FMX Premium Style 1.0 (https://getitnow.embarcadero.com/ CopperDarkFMXPremuimStyle-1.0/), but you can choose whatever style you like.

2. Then, create a blank FMX application.

3. Add some button and edit controls to your form.

4. Edit the `DPR` file of the project (this can be found in the IDE's main menu |
   Project | **View source**), adding `FMX.Styles` to the uses list and, as the very first
   line of code, a call to `TStyleManager.SetStyleFromFile`, or from the
   resource, as you prefer:
   ```
   TStyleManager.SetStyleFromFile('<PATH_TO_STYLE>\CoralCrystal.Wi
   n.Style').
   ```
   This will set the `CoralCrystal` style as the application's default style.

5. Run your application and you'll see the `CoralCrystal` style applied to your
   form and controls.

6. Add two `TStyleBook` components (`StyleBook1` and `StyleBook2`) to the form.

7. Open the **Style Designer** for `StyleBook2` (just double-click the component on
   the form and the editor will pop up).

8. Load the `CopperDark` style into `StyleBook2` (click on the **Open** tool button of
   the **Style Designer**).

9. Spot the **buttonstyle** entry among other style definitions. Note that the
   `CopperDark` style is a bitmap style so part of the **buttonstyle** definition relies on
   a bitmap named `CopperDarkstyle.png` (see the `background` object and its
   `SourceLookup` property's value).

10. Select both the `buttonstyle` and `CopperDarkstyle.png` entries in the
    Structure view.

11. Then copy the definitions to the system clipboard (hit *Ctrl* + *C*, or right-click and
    use the context pop-up menu).

12. Close the **Style Designer** for `StyleBook2`.

13. Open the **Style Designer** for `StyleBook1`.

14. Select the **StyleContainer** entry in the **Structure** view and paste the clipboard
    content (hit *Ctrl* + *V*, or right-click and use the context pop-up menu). You should
    see **buttonstyle** and **CopperDarkstyle.png** now listed under the **StyleContainer**
    entry.

15. Close the **Style Designer** for `StyleBook1` and apply the changes.

The following screenshot shows you the resulting page, that is, the Form Designer, Edit and buttons, two stylebooks, and the default **Windows** style:

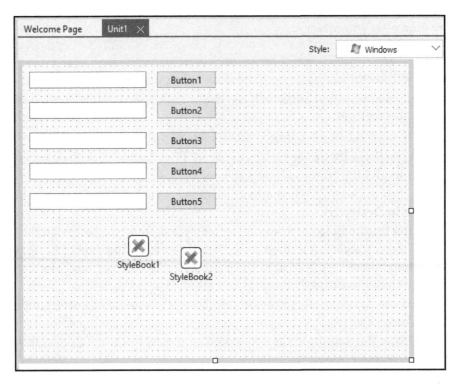

Figure 7.19

You are not going to see changes until you set the form's StyleBook property to StyleBook1. Once done, buttons on your form (at design time) should be rendered using the CopperDark style definition while other controls (that is, Edit) still have the native style applied. The following screenshot shows you the Form Designer after assigning the StyleBook property of the form to StyleBook1:

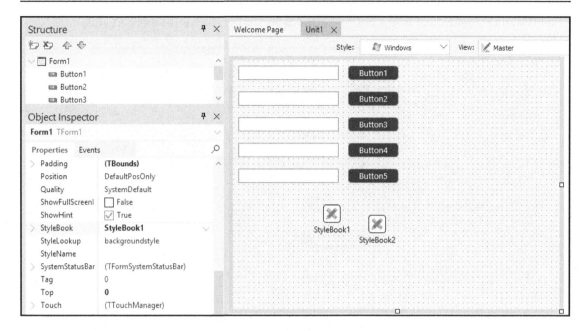

Figure 7.20

Moreover, if you run the application, you'll see the `CoralCrystal` style applied to all elements except buttons, where the `CopperDark` style is used. We actually merged two different styles through the same mechanism FMX provides to perform style customization and overriding.

The following screenshot shows you the application at runtime with merged styles:

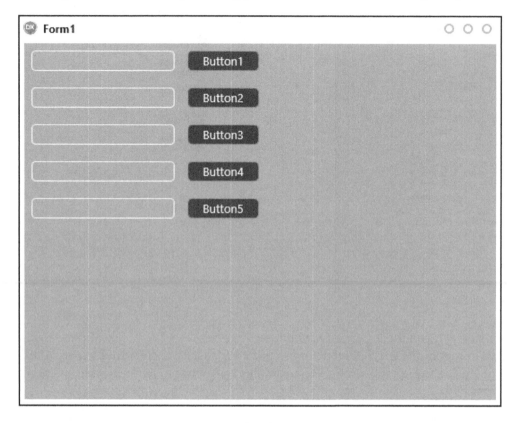

Figure 7.21

We are now familiar with the selection algorithm and the way style definitions get merged. In the next section, we are going to discuss how to load style definitions at runtime without having to rely on external resources.

Loading a style from embedded resources

Loading the style definitions from an external file is quite straightforward, thanks to the `TStyleManager.SetStyleFromFile` method and the `TStyleBook.LoadFromFile/LoadFromStream` methods.

Sometimes you don't want to rely on external files (for a number of reasons, ranging from higher intrinsic security for external modifications to easier deploying operations) and you have a chance to embed one or more styles into your application binary resources. We'll do this by taking the following steps:

1. With your project open in the IDE, open the **Project** | **Resources and Images ...** menu entry. The following screenshot shows you the **Resource and Images** IDE dialog window:

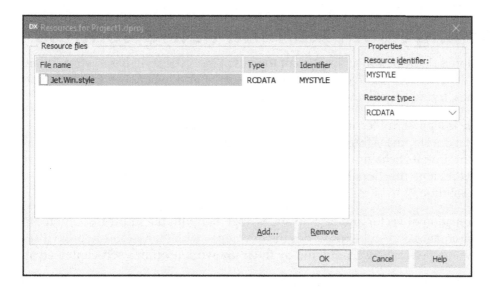

Figure 7.22

2. Add an FMX style file to the list of the resources, keeping **RCDATA** as the resource type but giving a unique name to the embedded resource (that is, **MYSTYLE**). This way, we instruct the IDE to include the file as a binary resource of the final executable.

 Beware that, to actually build your application, you have to use the **Project** | **Build** option from the IDE menu.

3. From now on, you can refer to the embedded resource by name and use the `TStyleManager.TrySetStyleFromResource` method as in the following snippet:

```
TStyleManager.TrySetStyleFromResource('MYSTYLE');
```

If you want to load the style from a resource without actually applying it as a default application style, you may want to call the `TStyleStreaming.LoadFromResource` method.

In this section, we have learned how to deal with style definitions at runtime (apart from the IDE functionalities). In the next section, we are going to discuss another very relevant topic with respect to the application at runtime: platform-native controls.

Learning about platform-native controls

This section is dedicated to an important topic that involves style-based strategy and cross-platform effectiveness. Native controls act as a sort of bridge between two orthogonal approaches, trying to get benefits from a compromise.

FMX Style is a powerful technology, backing important capabilities of this visual application development framework. The idea to separate the visual definition of a component from its behavior is a winning one as it opens up the delivery of different visual assets for the same functionalities, which is a marking point or milestone for every cross-platform solution.

The combination of vector and bitmap styles, together with the multi-resolution capabilities built in for images and styles, provides the developer with many tools to build a stunning, responsive, and effective UI, rendered by the framework itself in a self-contained approach.

However, the real world involves compromises and development is no exception. With respect to a fully self-rendered approach, we may feel some limitations, especially where the OS has strong conventions of important functionalities to offer.

We've already said that making your application look like a first-class citizen of the environment it is running in (platform and OS) is crucial to deliver the best user experience. Modern operating systems have native controls providing some system-wide functionalities to the user (that is, context pop-up menus for edit boxes, including clipboard access, text-to-speech, and voice recognition functionalities, spelling and grammar checkers, and more). It would be natural and immediate for the user to have the same controls in your FMX applications, but obviously, this is in strong opposition to the original approach of self-rendering components built into FMX (support for Style included).

For a few recent product versions (**Delphi XE8**) Embarcadero has added new functionality to FMX components, that is, the ability to decide (for the supported control types) to determine whether to use FMX-native components (built through FMX Style definitions) or to use platform-native components.

The `ControlType` property has been added specifically for this purpose and a page of the Delphi docwiki (`http://docwiki.embarcadero.com/RADStudio/Rio/en/FireMonkey_Native_Controls`) will help you understand which controls are supported on which platforms. Switching a control to its platform-native implementation will improve the user experience in some areas (voice recognition for edit boxes has been crucial for some of my customers in the past), but there are some limitations you have to consider (and that Embarcadero is trying to address from version to version).

For example, it is quite evident that the handling of **Z-Order** (the order in which components are layered in the UI, from bottom to top) is complex, as you can imagine the standard FMX form as a painting surface, where at some point you add an alien component (the platform-native component) that has its own rendering strategies and has no clue about the rest of the application components.

The following screenshot shows you the `Edit` control, FMX-styled, showing the contextual pop-up menu (FMX):

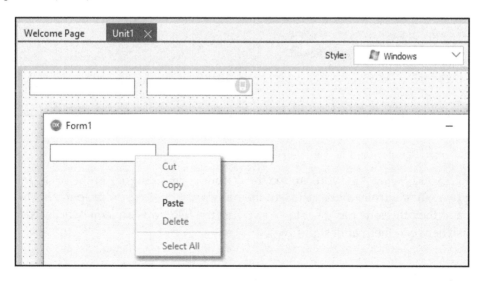

Figure 7.23

The following screenshot shows you the `Edit` control, platform-native, showing the contextual pop-up menu (Windows, Italian localization):

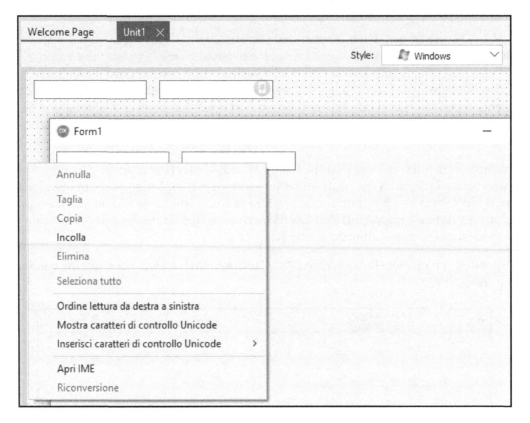

Figure 7.24

In *Figure 7.23* and *Figure 7.24*, you can see the Delphi Form Designer in the background, showing two edit controls, that is, the left one has the `ControlType` property set to `Styled`, and the other one has it set to `Platform` (the IDE adds an icon overlay to let you distinguish between them at design time).

Summary

In this chapter, we learned about FMX Style, a central and fundamental piece of technology for the whole visual application framework. Even though you may simplify styling to the extent of skinning (applying patches to the UI, as was popular in the software of the 1990s, such as **WinAmp**, to name an example), there are some very sophisticated concepts behind it.

Building multi-platform applications is a task where the developer will face problems such as handling a multi-resolution scenario, different visual conventions across platforms and even OS versions, and integration with the underlying OS as well. Through the use of FMX Style, FMX behavioral services, and platform-native controls, you can really build stunning multi-platform applications with a sustainable level of effort.

In the next chapter, we'll continue our journey through technologies and strategies to build user-friendly and responsive multi-platform, multi-device applications. The focus will be on modularizing your UIs to achieve visual continuity and improving the reuse of UI macro-elements through the use of the `TFrameStand` component.

8
Divide and Conquer with TFrameStand

In the previous chapter, we learned what FMX Style is and how it works. As was said in that chapter, **Style** is a very powerful mechanism and is a central part of every FMX application.

In this chapter, we are going to use the concept of Style as part of a general strategy for designing and driving FMX applications based on the TFrameStand component.

Our journey will begin with an overview of some general concepts about UI designing. We'll also learn about TFrameStand fundamentals in this chapter.

In this chapter, we will discuss the following topics:

- Introducing TFrameStand
- Designing UIs for mobile applications
- Exploring TFrameStand – Hello, World!
- Implementing views
- Defining the stand(s)

At the end of the chapter, you will learn how to start a mobile FMX application by using TFrameStand or TFormStand, and even in desktop applications, you will consider using it for some specific tasks.

Technical requirements

Here is the source code used in this book: `https://github.com/PacktPublishing/Delphi-GUI-Programming-with-FireMonkey/tree/master/Chapter%2008/TFrameStand_01`.

Generally speaking, for the whole book, you need a computer with Delphi set up and a few additional libraries installed (such as **Radiant Shapes** (`https://getitnow.embarcadero.com/?q=radiant+shapes`) and **CodeSite Logging** (`https://getitnow.embarcadero.com/?q=codesite`)). Having other devices and setting up multiple platforms (iOS, Android, OS X/macOS, and Linux) other than Windows is a plus but not strictly needed to follow the flow of the book.

Introducing TFrameStand

`TFrameStand` is a non-visual component, which I wrote around September 2015, to simplify mobile view management in FMX applications, promote the reuse of UI elements, add transitions, and gain visual continuity. It is an open source project, hosted at `https://github.com/andrea-magni/TFrameStand` and also available through **GetIt**, **Embarcadero**'s package manager (`https://getitnow.embarcadero.com/?q=tframestand`). Even though it is not actually part of the Delphi product, it is free and the source code is available, so I guess every Delphi developer can benefit from it without worries.

In recent years, I've successfully used this component in several projects and I've showcased it at several international conferences with good feedback every time. It has been trending on **GetIt** for some time and has gotten some nice (and appreciated) mentions from other experts (including Primož Gabrijelčič in his *Hands-On Design Patterns with Delphi* book by Packt Publishing) all around the world.

The following screenshot shows the **TFrameStand** logo as it appears in the GetIt (Embarcadero's official package manager) entry with my name as the author:

Figure 8.1

TFrameStand (and its twin TFormStand) implements a simple but effective mediator that will help developers to lessen the coupling across the views that compose their applications and, at the same time, promotes the **Don't Repeat Yourself** (**DRY**) principle. The DRY principle is a recognized best practice from a code perspective but its effectiveness can be transposed on the UI perspective too. Splitting complexity into UI modules that can interact without being tightly coupled is the key to the success of most applications.

Designing UIs for mobile applications

As we have already discussed in all the previous chapters, building mobile applications is one of the hardest tasks a modern developer has to face. Achieving usability and responsiveness is a challenge to be addressed, considering several factors very specific to the mobile development world, ranging from the computational power of devices to the peculiar form factor of mobile devices and passing by the new usage patterns that are relevant to this specific scenario.

In this section, we will learn about the typical structure of the UI of a (modern) mobile application. There are common conventions and accepted practices that make up the shape of the UI visual experience. Some of them are direct consequences of the nature of the mobile world (touch input, mobile devices, limited screen space, a single user by default, usability-first needs), while some others are probably caused by the quest for the maintainability the software needs.

Just consider how multitasking has evolved over recent decades. In the very early days of computer programming, there was only one program running at a time. Then operating systems came in and computer programming evolved to a point where a single computer could be running hundreds of programs simultaneously.

Some of these programs would even include **User Interface** (**UI**) elements and we all are used to multi-user, multi-window, multi-application graphics environments nowadays (on desktop platforms such as **Microsoft Windows**, **Apple OS X**, and **Linux**). Then came the mobile world, where the user number stepped back to one (it is obviously hard to share a mobile device, at least at the same time) and the same happened for application management.

Usually, a user carrying a mobile device will be using a single application at a time, at least from a UI point of view. There will be other applications/services in the background, but it is unlikely to have more than one visual application in the focus area of the user. This is principally due to the intrinsic characteristics of a mobile device, that is, you are usually standing, possibly walking, looking at a (relatively small) screen to perform a task. Even if it is a bit confusing today, as there's a mobile application for basically everything, with relatively reduced input capabilities (neither mouse nor 100+ keys keyboard available). Even the most recent (and popular) input capabilities (voice recognition) are not particularly effective in a multi-application scenario.

It is quite an accepted fact that a mobile user experience passes through a single application occupying the whole screen of the device, with some secondary artifacts chiming in, such as notification bars or exceptions such as always-on-top elements. This is more on the Android side, at the time I am writing this, such as media players with the ability to keep a canvas on top of other applications or instant messaging systems with the ability to provide you with a shortcut to active conversations on top of the screen.

As a consequence of all these factors together, mobile applications tend to be compact in the UI because of the limited screen space available and because of the touch-driven input method and are often designed as a sequence of *views* (screens) the user is prompted to. Each view will enable the user to accomplish a single task or to navigate a (relevant but not huge) set of application data. These views are usually tied together providing *paths* in the application (think about wizard-like operations) or stacks (delving into a multi-level data structure with one view for each level).

The following diagram shows a graphic representation format very often used with state machines, that is, each circle represents a state of the machine and arcs represent transitions across states:

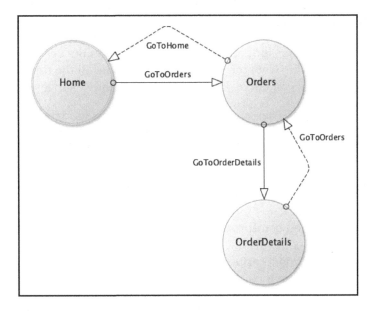

Figure 8.2

As you can see in the preceding screenshot, the **Home** state is bordered and has a different color to state that it is the initial state of the machine. A (finite) state machine, as said, is a very common abstraction used in mobile application design.

If states of the finite state machine represent views of your app, it logically follows that transitions across the states represent an action that the user can initiate in the view, by triggering buttons, through gestures, or as a response to some other external events (notifications or events originated in background executed code).

Now that we have introduced state machines as an abstraction for our application structure, it should be easy to see that views (states) should be unique. Having two similar views in the same app is not forbidden but there must be a valid reason not to collapse them into a single, reusable one. This is known (and has been for decades) as the **Don't Repeat Yourself (DRY) principle**, which we are going to learn about in the following section.

Learning about the DRY principle

One of the most impactful strategies you can set up in your application flow is to provide the user with some common UI elements throughout the application, no matter what state the application is in. Think about some borders or some graphic elements acting as branding for the general look and feel of the app. The actual content may change but the **frame**, that is, around the main spot, may be the same and lets the user stay in a familiar environment all the time. This way, the user will feel at home all the time and will be more prone to focus on the actual content as it is the thing that really changes before their eyes.

The same is true for transitions across views, that is, if you provide the user with a way to go from state A to state B (meaning the transition is allowed), then you implement the transition using an animation (possibly meaningful). It would be very convenient to keep the same convention when going from state B to state C. Obviously, assuming that this makes sense and the transition between A and B is *similar,* that means it has the same meaning or follows the same abstraction as the one from B to C.

Keeping the user familiar and comfortable, a set of conventions is pure gold in terms of overall usability. Doing so could also help the developer to keep the UI minimal. We can eliminate the need for additional captions to make it clear that we got to a certain deeper view, or to inform the user that they are looking at a third-level detail.

We'll drop this (traditional) strategy of labeling everything in favor of using shared conventions conceiving the same understatements, that is, if the transition across the different levels of information delivers a *natural meaning* about going from an element to a sub-element, the user will automatically recognize that they are looking at a third-level detail and probably instantly recognize where they are in the application structure and how they got there.

The following diagram is a state-machine description of the multi-level structure that we are discussing:

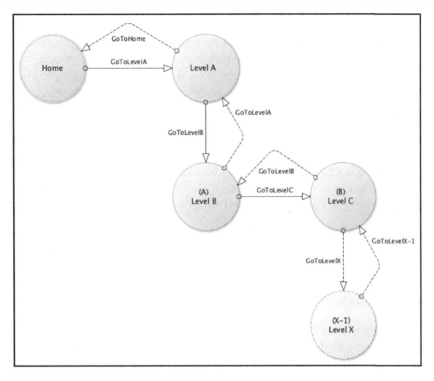

Figure 8.3

A very common scenario found in a mobile application is centered around the functionality of letting the user navigate through hierarchically structured information. Each level will be represented with a separate view, usually containing a list of elements of that level. Selecting an entry will take the user to a deeper level. The typical structure can be described as follows:

1. A view shows a list of items, **Level A**.
2. The user selects one item (**Level A**) from the list.
3. A new view is provided, showing some additional information on the **Level A** item, plus a list of **Level B** sub-items.
4. The user selects an entry of the **Level B** items list.
5. A new view is provided, showing some details about the **Level B** item and a list of **Level C** sub-items.
6. The user selects an entry of the **Level C** items list.
7. A new view is provided with details of the **Level C** item.

You can easily spot a recurrent pattern in this simple example (that is also a quite common use case for a data-centric mobile app) and of course, you may be tempted to build some controls to render this three-level data structure and navigate the user through the set of controls needed at a certain point of the chain. You'll probably end up with some tab control, with a page for each level, switching pages as soon as the user selects an item from one of the lists.

To some extent, there is nothing bad in such an approach but in the long term, it may backfire. First of all, you'll probably have three very similar pages for the tab control with duplicated controls for each level of the data structure. You may even have gotten to the result by composing one and then copying-and-pasting that one to page two and three. This is when your inner *good-programmer* bell should ring.

It is commonly accepted that you should never *copy-and-paste* code, for a number of reasons. Say you are called to refactor the code and reuse that repeated piece of code in a more maintainable flavor (a function call, for example). To some of you, this is so trivial it is not even worth talking about it. But when it comes to the UI, in my experience, developers have to be reminded of this often—even experienced ones.

As it is not a good practice to copy-and-paste code, the same stands for UI elements (complex ones). If you don't follow this simple rule, you could easily find yourself with crowded forms containing hundreds of controls. As we saw in Chapter 2, *Exploring Similarities and Differences with VCL*, these components would be created all together when the form was created. It could probably negatively affect the overall performance and, thus, the user experience.

Also, it is likely that, during the fine-tuning of each page, you'll make some small changes (without actually willing to do so, unintentionally) to components, making them no longer identical. In the long term, you may even experience the need (or temptation) to add another level (thus another semi-identical page), multiplying the situation over and over.

This scenario brings a number of bad practices and pitfalls we need to clearly highlight:

- **All components on a single crowded form**: This is impractical and hard to deal with at design time.
- **Component groups that are supposed to be identical and tend to diverge**: This causes maintainability struggles, making it hard to deal with the project in the long term as it gets worse over time.
- **All components created at form creation time**: This is likely to cause performance issues, with the form taking too long to load (first load/render time is a crucial metric in terms of UX).
- Adding an additional level makes it worse, exponentially.

This is true even when everything is under the control of the same developer. It naturally gets worse when multiple developers are working on the same area of the application, though everyone has their own peculiarities and this often has direct consequences on code/UI changes.

Also, this approach tends to backfire when you need to make some radical changes to your application (that is, substitute data access components). So, you'll be using a lot of components just to replicate the same changes over and over and with the fear that these components that actually should be identical to the previous one you addressed, in fact, are not identical but just a subtle kind of variation.

So, here comes the solution—*don't copy-and-paste; reuse*! Enclose the UI elements that are repeated in a module that you can instantiate multiple times (and then fine-tune them to match the single case).

This way, you are (or should be) already familiar with the code, and it is also available for UI components, in a number of flavors. We can focus on a couple of them:

- **Building your own components**: This is one of the key aspects of development environments such as Delphi and nowadays a number of frameworks/technologies rely on the concept of reusable components. You can start from scratch by inheriting some existing components or build the composition of existing components.

  The downside of this option is that it might be overkill, as it is a general approach, requiring some non-trivial skills to be properly executed, suitable when you are going to reuse the component several times, possibly across multiple projects. In terms of coding, this is nearly equivalent to building your own frameworks and using them to actually build your application logic.

- **Using frames as macro-components**: You should put your components (the ones that would be on each page in our previous example) on a separate frame and then instantiate the frame multiple times, one frame per page of the tab control. This is a very quick approach, where you can take advantage of the **Delphi RAD** side, copy-and-paste your components from where they are to a newly created frame, then substitute them on each page with a single instance of the frame.

The result will be much easier to deal with as you basically end up having a single macro component per page and you have full control over the macro component (you can change the frame definition, have all instances reflect the change, and the other way around). That is, you can make a change to one of the instances without affecting the other instances and with much more control/evidence of the changes. In terms of coding, this is more or less the equivalent of wrapping some code in a function and using the function multiple times, possibly chaining the function with other functions where specific behaviors are needed.

 Since the beginning of this section, we have been discussing which elements of the UI (visual frames around the main content, transitions used to bring up/take away content to/from the user, recurring visual structures/patterns) are important. Most applications tend to use these elements repeatedly and are subjected to the cons we have described previously in this chapter.

Generally speaking, reusing UI elements is really a game-changer in a number of aspects, ranging from developer productivity (especially, in the long term) to user experience (improving it by automatically adding more coherence across the project). To me, this has a direct connection with the **Don't Repeat Yourself** (**DRY**) principle, initially introduced by Andy Hunt and Dave Thomas in the highly recommended book *The Pragmatic Programmer*. The following is what the book states:

> *Every piece of knowledge must have a single, unambiguous, authoritative representation within a system.*

The benefits of following the DRY principle are many but, focusing on our specific UI-related example, we are basically splitting complexity into reusable modules that are easier to master, that is, a *divide et impera* (divide and conquer) approach.

However, although by following this idea, we were able to improve the maintainability of the project and its UI's inner coherence, we still have some issues to solve:

- We addressed only a specific kind of UI coherence, tightly related to the specific content we are delivering to the user (part of a hierarchical data structure that has a recurring pattern, the master-detail relationship, in its own nature).
- We are still in a situation where components will be created all at once, within the creation of the hosting form, affecting the performance of the application at startup (a crucial UX metric in the mobile scenario).

- Once we move from a fine-grained approach (a bunch of components) to a more coarse-grained one (macro-components, that is, frames), we need to find a way to handle and orchestrate these components throughout the application lifespan.

Before addressing these topics from a development point of view, I'd like to spend some words on the first entry of the list, that is, UI coherence. There is a more specific term for the general underlying topic—**visual continuity**.

Until now, we have been stressing how important, in terms of user experience, it is to leave the user inside his/her comfort zone. From a UI perspective, this comfort zone is amenable to a pervasive familiar look and feel for the application (the concept can be spawned across multiple applications or even across the whole set of UI-provided software running on the device, including the OS).

Let's learn about visual continuity in the next section.

Understanding visual continuity

If you are a long-time computer user, there surely are conventions you feel familiar with. The more conventions of a system you are familiar with, the better your overall experience using that system is. After a while, you may not even notice you are so acquainted with a number of these conventions but it becomes immediately evident when some of these conventions are set apart; for example, it happens when a long-time Windows user tries a Linux or OS X/macOS system.

Most of the time, you'll find yourself disoriented because of something you were expecting to be somewhere in the UI, but it is now in another place or hidden somewhere waiting for you to find it. Being a professional developer, I have been in this painful situation many times, as I often work with **Windows** virtual machines inside a **MacBook Pro** environment (**OS X**), sometimes also interacting with **Linux** virtual machines. This results in different conventions for the same user, making the user struggle to accomplish even the simplest tasks just because an extra amount of attention is needed to recognize and adjust every step for the current platform.

One of the simplest examples that comes to my mind is about the system icons in each window (usually minimize, maximize, close), that is, by default, a **Windows** user will immediately look for an **X** (close) button in the top-right corner of the caption bar of the window they want to close. The very same button, on **OS X**, is in the top-left corner of the caption bar. If you put a user that is acquainted with **Microsoft Windows** in front of a Mac OS X system (or the other way around), you can easily spot them looking for the button in the wrong place.

This is not going to happen once; it will happen several times. It will take a while for the user to get acquainted with the new convention (and they'll possibly need to pay attention to this forever).

The following screenshot is a composition (from top to bottom) of the file explorer on three different desktop systems, that is, **Windows 10**, **Ubuntu**, and **Mac OS X 10**:

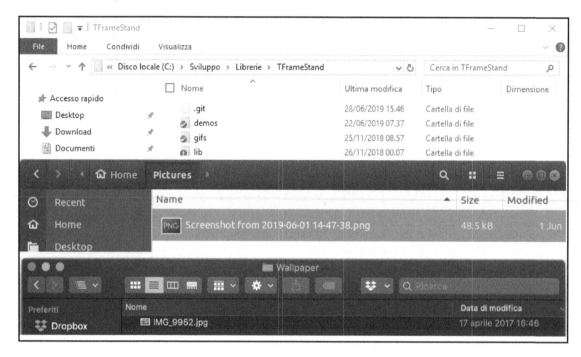

Figure 8.4

The preceding basic example visualizes how the same concepts may visually differ and proves two things:

- Conventions may differ across systems and users are so acquainted with them that they might only notice them when they are taken away for some reason (that is, after switching to a different OS/platform).
- Conventions actually drive user experience and make the user more efficient in everyday tasks.

Especially regarding the second point, we should make it clear that providing the user with a set of consistent, ubiquitous, immediate conventions will greatly improve the usability of your application.

Opening a detail view through a specific transition (that is, sliding the detail view from right to left), possibly providing the detail view of some shared elements (such as a border with a **Close** button) means the user will learn every time this kind of animation happens and that border is available that they can use these items the same way, disregarding the specific content/detail they are looking at.

Distinguishing between *what* we are presenting to the user through the UI and *how* this content is delivered is the key point for reusability. Finding a way to decouple the content from its container will enable reusing the same container (including some dynamic characteristics about the way it is taken or removed from the user's attention) with several pieces of content and this also stands the other way around, that is, using the same content passing through the experience of different containers.

If the first option (reuse container, change content) is clearly a proper way to reuse the modality we are using to present different content to the user (imagine a slide or fade effect), the second scenario (reuse content, change container), for example, may be adopted to stress some specific conditions of the actual visualization of the content. Keeping some rules aside, for example, imagine some kind of data validation rules to mark whether the current data is valid or not by changing the background color accordingly.

Both presentation strategies will add some visual continuity to your application by keeping a familiar context (whether the content or the container) in the current view the user is facing. It is not mandatory that each view of your application has to be composed of these two elements. Often, the content alone is enough, while it is harder, yet not impossible, to imagine situations where you would want to show the *usual* container with no content. Imagine, for example, situations where data needs to be fetched from a remote service and it is temporarily not available when the user asks for it.

The TFrameStand component addresses exactly the scenario described so far, that is, how to decouple yet easily manage *content* and *containers* of UI elements. From an implementation point of view, *content* can be implemented using TFrame descendants (a native concept of the Delphi development environment since version 7 at least) while *containers* (which have a slightly more *visual-only* nature) are implemented using Style objects. For the following portion of the chapter, we'll adopt this terminology:

- The *content* will be named **Frame** (as it is implemented through a Delphi TFrame instance).
- The *container* will be named **Stand** (as it is something *supporting* the Frame).
- The combination of Frame and Stand is **FrameStand** and all the information related to this joint is represented in a specific data structure named TFrameInfo<T> where T is a TFrame descendant.

The developer will create FrameStands through the TFrameStand component by doing the following:

- Providing the Stand definition through a TStyleBook component
- Explicitly stating the actual TFrame descendant class they built for the content (which will then be easily accessible in a type-safe manner thanks to the use of generics in the TFrameInfo<T> type)
- Selecting a parent component where the FrameStand should be placed (by default, if none is provided, the owner of the TFrameStand component, generally a TForm descendant, is used)

 TFormStand is a twin component of TFrameStand so almost everything that is written here for TFrameStand also applies to TFormStand with the only thing that needs to be done is to substitute every reference to TFrame with TForm.

In this section, we learned about some concepts related to designing UIs for mobile apps. We also learned how the DRY principle fits in a visual context and understood how important the concept of visual continuity is. We also understood how it affects the ease of use of the app. We should now share a common background of the available approaches and their pros and cons.

So let's move on to the next section about the TFrameStand component, related to the DRY approach.

Exploring TFrameStand – Hello, World!

Keeping as a background what we have discussed so far in this chapter, we'll now explore some functionalities built into the TFrameStand component. As you may have noticed, the problem we are addressing (finding an efficient strategy for building a usable application) is very general and the mechanisms provided by TFrameStand are also quite general. So, there are multiple uses of the component each developer may consider from time to time.

In this section, we'll cover some standard use cases, showcasing how TFrameStand functionalities and related mechanisms help in dividing the whole program into modules that are easier to design and maintain. The proposed approach also makes use of data modules, which is a very native concept in the Delphi development environment, around for decades.

Typically, you'll drop a `TFrameStand` component on a `TForm` descendant. Following our model of the mobile app based on the finite state machine approach, we'll definitely put the `TFrameStand` instance on the main form of the application.

A `TDataModule` instance (or even a simple class) can be used to hold the current state of the application and the definition of the allowed transition across states.

A set of `TFrame` can be used to implement the views corresponding to each state of the application. Other support classes (I'd suggest `TDataModule` instances) may be added to the application to cover specific areas (one for remote communication, one for local data access, maybe some others to deal with sensors aboard the device, such as the camera or GPS).

Try to imagine everything under the *divide and conquer* mantra, that is, pushing the single responsibility principle as much as possible will make your application easy to extend and maintain over time. *Need to change the communication layer?* Ideally, changes will only impact the data module taking care of remote communications. The same would apply to local storage technologies and sensors.

There is a very important point that most developers will object to at this point, that is, *if everything is separated, how can the application work as a whole?* A good messaging system may be used to implement the internal communication of all these elements. Delphi RTL provides the `System.Messaging` unit where you can find a simple, effective, and extensible observer pattern implementation.

We'll cover the messaging system in detail in `Chapter 12`, *Exploring Cross-Platform Services*. At the moment, it is enough to be aware that such a system exists and is structured with messages that can be sent from a subject to a dispatcher that will deliver them to all the subscribers for that specific message type. The message (and the dispatcher of course) is the only dependency linking the two ends of the communication (meaning this is a good way to keep your system loosely coupled, again to favor maintainability).

The following diagram provides a general overview of the application structure we are discussing:

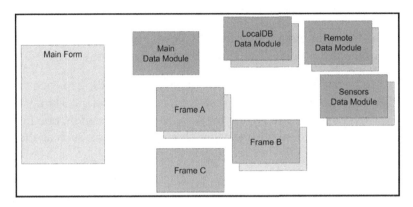

Figure 8.5

For instance, let's step back to our empty FMX application with a single form (the main form) hosting a TFrameStand component on itself and a data module that is capable of keeping track of the application state. The creation order will be first the form and then the data module (you can control this in the **Project Options** | **Forms** entry of the IDE).

For the sake of simplicity, we'll use a simple enumerated type to represent the application state; the data module will have a property exposing the current state of the application and some methods to perform transitions across different states. Each time the state changes, a message will be sent to the dispatcher in order to notify listeners.

The form will subscribe to the state-changed message in its OnCreate event handler, and when the data module gets created, it will initialize the application state to a certain value (Home). This will cause a message to be added to the dispatcher, which will notify the (only) listener (the form) by calling the provided message handler, an anonymous method defined in the form's unit to respond to the application state change.

What should the form do when it gets notified that the current application state is Home*?* It should build and present the corresponding view to the user, of course. This is done by calling the GetFrameInfo method of the TFrameStand instance, which will retrieve any previously created instance of the FrameStand data structure (TFrameInfo<THomeFrame>) embedding THomeFrame, or create a new FrameStand for this purpose. THomeFrame is a simple frame implementing a basic menu with a graphic background. It is easy to imagine this frame with a list of icons, each one corresponding to a different state of the application, so clicking on the icon will cause a call to some method of the data module trying to change the application state.

Key points of the use case described so far are as follows:

- The application behavior is driven by the data module (the state control triggers UI changes).
- The data module knows nothing about the form or the frames.
- Communication is done through a messaging system.
- The form has a dependency on the THomeFrame class.
- The THomeFrame class knows nothing about the form.
- The THomeFrame class has a dependency on the data module.

In the next section, we'll see how views are built. To stress this example, we'll keep the main form of the application empty from a visual point of view. It will only host the TFrameStand instance along with a TStyleBook instance containing stands.

The main data module (holding the app state) will expose a method for each possible state, such as GoToHome, GoToOrders, GoToOrderDetails, and others. Better said, it will have a method for each allowed transition (from state A to state B), having a chance to control what should happen before or after the triggering of each transition.

 The example discussed in this chapter is TFrameStand_01 with the full source code provided on GitHub.

In this basic example, we'll assume the initial state is not relevant so methods are to be considered as a shortcut to put the application in a certain state.

Implementing views

We are modeling our application as a finite state machine where states are tied with corresponding views. The main form will be responsible for orchestrating the views in front of the user and will make use of TFrameStand to manage this task.

Views are built using TFrame descendants, one for each view (in more complex scenarios, you may want to have hierarchies of TFrame descendants or compose them as needed).

As a general note, you can create a new frame in the IDE by selecting the **File** | **New** | **Other** | **Individual files** | **FireMonkey** frame.

You may want to customize the rapid entries in the **File** | **New** menu, through the available **Customize** entry, in order to shorten the operation.

The following screenshot shows the IDE **New Items** dialog with the **FireMonkey Frame** entry selected:

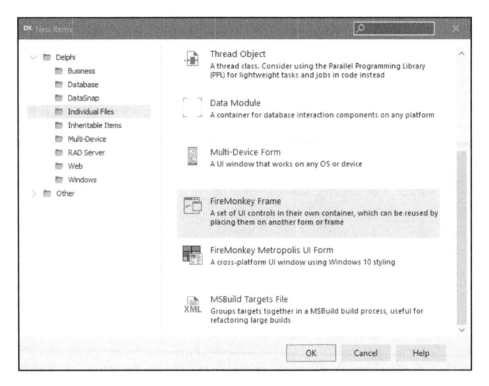

Figure 8.6

I tend to follow this naming convention for frames/forms, such that each frame has its own unit with a uniform name, that is, TFooFrame | Frames.Foo.pas. Remember to set the Align property of the newly created frames to Client as we want the frame to completely fill the available space in the FrameStand that will host it.

Let's proceed further by exploring the views of the application, their structure, and how they have been built.

Understanding the THomeFrame frame

Every application has a **Home** page and, usually, it is the first view presented to the user. Our Home view provides the user with a set of icons to access further functionalities of the app. A toolbar and a background image will complete the UI structure opening for eventual buttons or titles to be added.

We'll use `TFlowLayout` as a container for the function icons and `TImage` components as icons themselves. A glow effect is added to be triggered when the user taps on one of the items.

`TFlowLayout` will take up most of the view's space and ideally will be able to host a bunch of function entries, properly arranging them according to the actual screen size of the current device.

`TToolbar` will automatically align with the top of the frame and we can add an extra `TImage` instance (named `OverlayImage`), setting its `Align` property to `Contents`. In order to cover the full area of the frame (without considering other components on the frame), set its `Opacity` value to some very low value (`0.1` should be fine). Also, check its `HitTest` property is set to `False` (making it a pure visual asset and disabling any input being handled by it) and bring it on top of all other components. This will make the image act as a watermark over the content. This is demonstrated in the following screenshot:

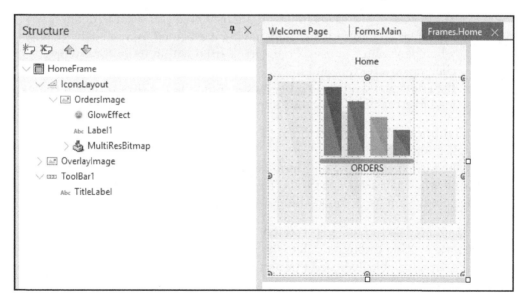

Figure 8.7

There's only a small portion of code in this view, that is, when a function icon is clicked/tapped, we are going to ask the main data module to change state to the corresponding one. Around this call to `TMainData.GoTo[State]`, we'll enable/disable the glow effect for an amount of time sufficient for the user to see it (100 milliseconds should be fine to make it visible to the user). Here, you can see the actual implementation for the `OrdersImage.OnClick` event handler:

```
procedure THomeFrame.OrdersImageClick(Sender: TObject);
begin
  GlowEffect.Enabled := True;
  TDelayedAction.Execute(100
  , procedure
    begin
      MainData.GoToOrders;
      GlowEffect.Enabled := False;
    end
  );
end;
```

`TDelayedAction` is a small class implemented in the `SubjectStand` unit (which contains the common ancestor of `TFrameStand`/`TFormStand`). It will help you to execute some code after a certain amount of time (without blocking the execution flow but keeping the code in the main thread context so that you can manipulate UI elements in the deferred code).

> `TDelayedAction` is useful in situations where you want to defer operation execution rather than having it executed immediately (that is, when you want to close a FrameStand from within itself, for example, clicking on a button, and this would cause the immediate destruction of the FrameStand, including the button initiating the closing, and this may lead to errors because some animations or tasks would be still ongoing).

It is quite straightforward to consider the `Home` state as the initial state of our state machine. Our FMX application containing `TForm` (`MainForm`) and `TDataModule` (`MainData`) will run, creating the form first and the data module right after that. The form will subscribe itself to respond whenever a `TAppStateChanged` message is available. We talked about a messaging system we can use to make different parts of the application communicate.

When the `MainData` data module gets created, at the `OnCreate` event handler, it will initialize the state to `Home` through a call to the `SetAppState` method. This will update the internal `FAppState` variable (exposed through the `AppState` property) and will deliver a `TAppStateChanged` message to the dispatcher. The (so far) only subscriber, `MainForm`, will respond, updating the UI to create and show the `THomeFrame` view, with the aid of the `TFrameStand` component.

This is how our Home view gets to the user as we start the application:

1. The app starts (**DPR file** code gets executed).
2. Then `TMainForm` gets created.
3. Then, `MainForm` subscribes for `TAppStateChanged` messages.
4. After that `TMainData` also gets created.
5. The `OnCreate` handler gets fired, that is, its code sets the initial state to `Home` and sends a `TAppStateChanged` message.
6. Then, `MainForm` receives the `TAppStateChanged` message and, through `TFrameStand`, composes a FrameStand with `THomeFrame` as the view.

Once the Home view is in front of the user, we expect the user to select one of the available entries from the function icon list.

Learning about the TOrdersFrame frame

One of the functionalities of our basic app is to provide the user with a list of orders (this could be any other kind of dataset). This is what `TOrdersFrame` is there for and it is tied to the `Orders` state of our application.

When the user selects (taps) the **Orders** function icon in the Home view, a call to the `MainData.GoToOrders` method is performed, the app state changes to `Orders`, and a `TAppStateChanged` message is delivered to the message dispatcher. `MainForm` will handle the message, trying to have a `TOrdersFrame` instance inside a FrameStand presented to the user, as shown in the following screenshot:

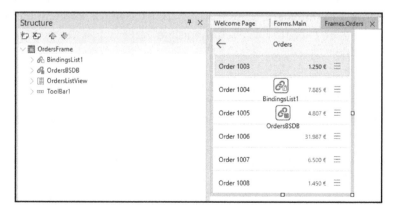

Figure 8.8

`TOrdersFrame` is essentially composed of a `TToolbar` and a `TListView` component. The toolbar will be at the top of the frame and will host a button to go back to the Home view (please note this is done by asking the `MainData` data module to update the application state and not by simply closing the view). The `Listview` will be linked, through LiveBindings technology, to a dataset containing data.

A proper data module (`TOrdersData` in the `Data.Orders.pas` unit) has been set up to hold datasets with related data, and bindings have been set up (at design time!) between `TListView` and the datasets contained in the `TOrdersData` data module (note, `TOrdersData` has no dependencies on other parts of the application).

An *application-wide lazy-loaded singleton* `TOrdersData` instance will be accessed by `TOrdersFrame` itself when it is shown to the user, delaying as much as possible access to data. In our simple scenario, a data module gets created when the frame is shown as it is the first use of the global instance in the app. This lazy-loading approach saves time at application startup and gives the developer a chance to deal with possible longer loading times for data, that is, when dealing with remote data.

TFrame does not provide an `OnShow` event to hook up to perform tasks in correspondence with the moment the frame becomes visible. However, this is quite a common need and I have decided to give `TFrameStand` the ability to mimic an `OnShow` event for the hosted frames.

Indeed, given that `TFrameStand` has full control over the creation, showing, hiding, and destruction of the frame, the component knows the exact moment all these events happen. To continue to support every pure `TFrame` descendant out there (with no inheritance constraints or interface implementation requirements), I introduced `BeforeShowAttribute` (defined in the `SubjectStand.pas` unit) to mark some methods of the frame to be executed as event handlers. `AfterShowAttribute` is also available.

In a simple scenario, you could also set up data access in the constructor of the `TOrdersFrame` class as we are dynamically creating the `TOrdersFrame` instance only when needed, but generally speaking, having a chance to perform such initialization at the final moment when the frame is shown to the user can be a significant advantage.

Once a data module is available, the `TBindSourceDB` component needs to reference the right dataset to fill the `TListView` component with data contained in the `OrdersTable` dataset (hosted on the `TOrdersData` data module global instance), as demonstrated in the following code:

```
uses (...), SubjectStand (...);

  TOrdersFrame = class(TFrame)
  (...)
  public
    [BeforeShow]
    procedure OnBeforeShow;
  end;

procedure TOrdersFrame.OnBeforeShow;
begin
  OrdersBSDB.DataSet := TOrdersData.Instance.OrdersTable;
end;
```

We can expect the user to click/tap on the orders list to trigger a transition toward a different application state, that is, `OrderDetails` with a very similar path to what we did when passing from the Home view to the Orders view: app state changes, a message is dispatched to `MainForm`, and a new `OrderDetails` view being created and shown to the user.

Understanding the TOrderDetailsFrame frame

The last frame of our basic demo is `TOrderDetailsFrame`. It will be used to expose more detailed data about a single order.

The structure is minimal but flexible—a `TToolBar` component with a title to state which specific order is being shown and a `TListBox` instance. Multiple items can be added to the list, allowing a lot of order-related data to be available through a single component and each item can be customized to properly handle the specific nature of each piece of information (text, graphic, and more). Using a list component means having the opportunity to take advantage of its intrinsic vertical scrolling capabilities (a must, especially on phone devices).

The following screenshot shows the **OrderDetailsFrame** structure and appearance in the form designer:

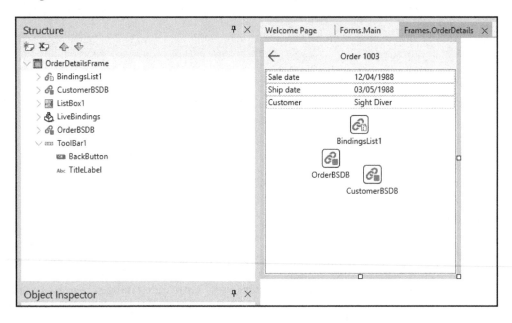

Figure 8.9

LiveBindings technology is used to fill UI elements in the listbox with data from the `OrdersTable` dataset. As was done for the `TOrdersFrame` case, the `BeforeShow` mechanism offered by `TFrameStand` is used to set up data access against the `TOrdersData` global instance, as shown in the following code:

```
uses (...), SubjectStand (...);

TOrderDetailsFrame = class(TFrame)
(...)
public
  [BeforeShow]
  procedure OnBeforeShow;
end;

procedure TOrderDetailsFrame.BeforeShow;
begin
  OrderBSDB.DataSet := TOrdersData.Instance.OrdersTable;
end;
```

One of the items in the details listbox is actually a lookup, implemented through LiveBindings technology, to a customer table. The order data contains a **CustNo** field, which is a key to access the corresponding customer in the `TOrdersData.CustomerTable` dataset. This is shown in the following screenshot:

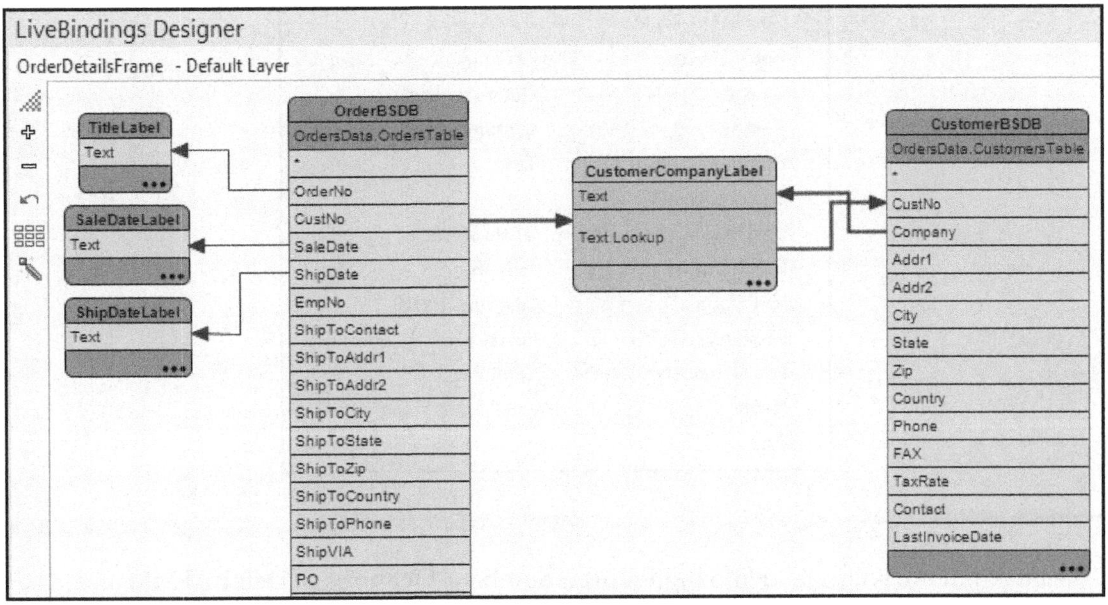

Figure 8.10

As you can see in the preceding schema diagram, the LiveBinding link is between the `OrderBSDB.CustNo` field and the `CustomerCompanyLabel.Text` property. Without further configuration, this would show the customer's ID in the text of the label.

You'll need to set the **LookupDataSource**, **LookupKeyFieldName**, and **LookupValueFieldName** properties of the LiveBindings link component in order to obtain more human-readable information. To represent the customer in the UI, the company name will be better than its ID.

The company name will show up in the label instead of a (possibly opaque) ID value:

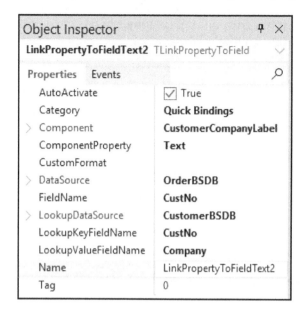

Figure 8.11

This basic but not so trivial demo highlights a number of features of Delphi, FMX, and TFrameStand. There's obviously more to be added to the application for it to be functional (search data, edit data, and more), and some mechanisms may need a power-up, but the aim of this example is to showcase the skeleton of the application structure, with the proper separation of involved elements from the UI level (forms and frames) to app state control (MainData) and data access (OrdersData). The last note is about the messaging system that is used as a low-dependency glue within all these elements.

The application is now working and we may want to add some UI effects to it. This is where TFrameStand stands can chime in to ease the process.

Defining the stand(s)

Our MainForm hosts the TFrameStand component and, through it, handles the management of the views (including the creation, destruction, and showing/hiding them). As previously said, a TStyleBook component has been added to the form as well, to host stand definitions (note the FrameStand1.StandBook property references the StandsBook component).

The actual code that the form uses to build the FrameStands is as follows:

```
procedure TMainForm.UpdateViewToState;
begin
  case MainData.AppState of
    Home:
      begin
        FrameStand1.CloseAllExcept(THomeFrame);
        FrameStand1
          .GetFrameInfo<THomeFrame>
            .Show;
      end;
    Orders:
      begin
        FrameStand1.CloseAll(TOrderDetailsFrame);
        FrameStand1
          .GetFrameInfo<TOrdersFrame>(True, nil, 'fader')
            .Show;
      end;
    OrderDetail:
      begin
        FrameStand1
          .GetFrameInfo<TOrderDetailsFrame>(True, nil, 'slider')
            .Show;
      end;
  end;
end;
```

We have seen that the TFrameStand.GetFrameInfo method is capable of retrieving a reference to a previously created FrameStand for the specified frame class or creating a new one on the fly. Arguments to this method are optional (meaning default values would be used when they are not explicitly defined) and include ANewIfNotFound, AParent, and AStandStyleName:

- ANewIfNotFound simply defines whether the GetFrameInfo method should create a new FrameStand instance for the specified frame class if none is available yet. If this is the case and the argument is set to False, the method will return nil.

- AParent is the parent object to be used for the newly created FrameStand (if a pre-existing FrameStand instance is returned, no changes are made to reflect the specified parent). The parent object of a FrameStand is where the visual structure composed by the stand and the frame as a whole will be parented.

If none is specified, the TFrameStand instance will determine a default one through the TFrameStand.DefaultParent property's value or, if this is not set, will default to the form owner of the TFrameStand instance itself (a good case, when you are using frames as views and the main form as a container for the views, as in our example).

- AStandStyleName is the name of the stand definition to be used to build the FrameStand for the specified frame class. If this argument is not provided, TFrameStand will use its DefaultStandName property's value (that is, framestand) instead to look up the stand definition in the TStyleBook component referenced by the TFrameStand.StandBook property.

If the stand definition is not provided or the StandBook property is not set, a basic transparent stand is internally built by TFrameStand (using a simple TLayout instance, with the Align property set to the Contents value). So, keep in mind that a Stand component is always available, whether a custom, a default, or a minimal one.

 Remember the Name property does not have meaning in a style definition; only the StyleName property should be used.

As we saw in Chapter 7, *Understanding FMX Style Concept*, the TStyleBook component is capable of storing multiple style definitions and these definitions are a composition of FMX objects (visual or non-visual components) to construct the visual asset of a certain element.

Following a driven-by-convention approach, the definition of a TFrameStand's stand should be as follows:

- An outer element acting as a sort of root node for the definition and providing the definition's name through its StyleName property's value. I tend to use TLayout as it is powerful for alignments, margins, and paddings settings, and at the same time, it is transparent though non-obtrusive.

- An inner element (nested at whatever level) acting as a container for the frame instance the stand will be used in conjunction with; this element (which could be whatever type) is identified through a simple naming convention mechanism, that is, its `StyleName` property should be set to **container** to instruct `TFrameStand`. This element must contain the frame instance. If no **container** object is provided, the `Stand` itself will be used as a container.

This should provide clarification for the notice I gave, earlier in this chapter, to set the `Align` property of frames in order to determine their aligning behavior inside their container.

The following screenshot shows the **Structure** view IDE window for our `StandsBook` component (when the **Style Designer** is activated). You can spot the two stand definitions (**fader** and **slider**) and the **container** element for the **slider** stand (the **fader** stand has no inner container and the frame will be parented to the stand itself):

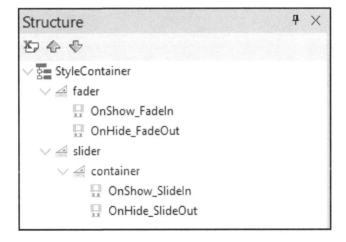

Figure 8.12

The `TFrameStand` component also comes with a component editor, which you can activate by double-clicking on it. The component editor, shown in the following screenshot, provides you with a list of available stands and a dummy frame to test them at design-time:

Figure 8.13

You can tweak properties for the frame and parent object to test achieving the desired behavior. Two buttons, **Show** and **Hide**, will let you trigger the creation of the FrameStand (using the dummy test frame) to test animations also.

Learning about animations

An easy way to add animations to stands is to add them while editing the stand in the Style Designer and follow the `TFrameStand` naming convention:

- All animations with a name starting with **OnShow** will be automatically fired by `TFrameStand` when the FrameStand is shown to the user.
- Symmetrically, all animations with a name starting with **OnHide** will be fired at the hiding of the FrameStand.

This applies to all animations—those contained in the *Stand* definition as well as those contained in the *Frame* definition—at whatever nesting level.

We also have a whole chapter dedicated to animations, `Chapter 10`, *Orchestrating Transitions and Animations*. In this section, we are talking about the support for animations in `TFrameStand` and not delving too much into animation details.

You can have multiple animations for both events (show/hide) and they will all be fired simultaneously (according to the corresponding event of course). If you want to concatenate subsequent animations, you can use the `Delay` property of `TAnimation` to defer some of them.

If you need to, the naming convention used by default can be changed through the values of the `TFrameStand.AnimationShow` and `TFrameStand.AnimationHide` properties.

`TFrameStand` will consider the time needed to complete all these animations before actually hiding the FrameStand (so, if you call the `Hide` or `HideAndClose` methods on a `TFrameInfo<T>` instance, you don't have to deal with the time needed for animations to complete).

Next, we'll now learn about the fader stand and slider stand definitions, which were mentioned in the *Defining the stand(s)* section.

Defining the fader stand

Back to our example: the fader stand is very basic but will add a nice fade in/out transition when showing/hiding the FrameStand to the user.

It is implemented using a TLayout component whose Align property has been set to the Contents value, filling the Parent object it will be associated with. No children with a StyleName container have been added so, as we have seen, we can expect the frame to be parented to the stand itself, using the aligning strategy of the frame (considering its Align, Anchors, and Margins properties and the like).

Two animations (TFloatAnimation instances, precisely) have been added to the TLayout component:

- OnShow_FadeIn: This transitions the Opacity property of its parent (TLayout) from value 0 to value 1 with a duration of 400 milliseconds and a Quadratic interpolation. TLayout implementing the stand is basically the most outer element of the framestand composition and, due to the behavior of the Opacity property of FMX objects, the variation of the opacity will apply also to its content (the frame).
- OnHide_FadeOut: This transitions the Opacity property of its parent (TLayout) from value 1 to value 0 with a duration of 400 milliseconds and a Quadratic interpolation (it is basically the same animation as the OnShow_FadeIn component but with the Inverse property set to True).

That's it! No code needed. There is no impact on the contained frame(s), and there is a possibility to load stands from an external file with a single line of code (through TStyleBook.LoadFromFile/LoadFromStream methods). In our demo project, we use this stand with the TOrdersFrame view.

Defining the slider stand

Another common transition (always remember you should keep an eye on the meaning delivered by the transition to the user, possibly using them to make evident some implied reason a new view is being shown) is the one sliding the new content in front of the user, from right to left when entering the view and the other way around when leaving the view (there's no specific dictation about direction—again, you should fit the meaning of it within the context of your app).

We can start again from a simple TLayout container as the outer component, with its Align property initially set to None. Give TLayout a StyleName (**slider**) and a size (that is, Width: 400, Height: 400) so you should see it centered in the **Style Designer** as the following screenshot shows:

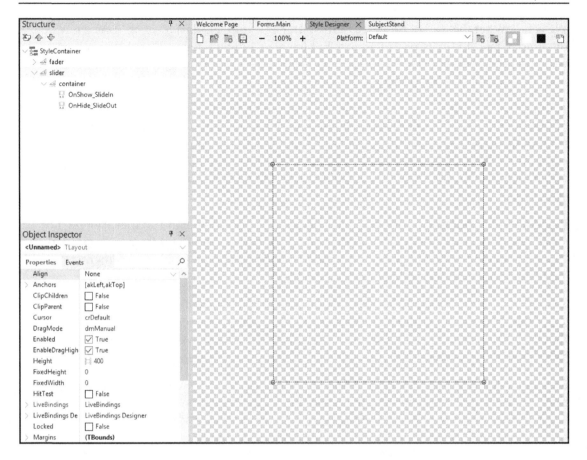

Figure 8.14

Now add another TLayout and name it **container**, position it at (0,0) coordinates and
give it the same size as its parent (**slider** TLayout). Set its Align property to the Scale
value so that it will keep the same aspect ratio as its parent (this will also cause all
its Anchors properties to be set).

If you change the size of the outer TLayout (**slider**), you'll see the inner TLayout
(**container**) following the change. This is different with respect to setting the Align
property to Client as you may think that we are tying the size of the two instances
of TLayout but not their position (this will be important, as we'll see in a second).

We can now set the Align property of the outer TLayout (**slider**) to Client as we want the FrameStand to fill its parent area. What we have now is a kind of double-layered structure, the outer one tied to the parent object of the FrameStand and the inner one free to move independently but retaining the same size as the first one.

Adding two TFloatAnimation instances, changing the value of the Position.X property of the inner TLayout (**container**), will implement the transition of sliding our content in front of the user. The idea is to set the horizontal position to a high value so that the **container** will be offscreen (actually, out of the visible portion of the FrameStand's parent) and then transition the Position.X value to zero to have it completely visible on the screen again.

Remember the **container** will retain the same size as the **slider** stand so there will be no stretching of the **container** (as would happen if we had chosen to set the Align property to Client and play with Margins; that would be a different effect as the container would *roll out* from right to left but stretching its content).

You may argue about what *high value* should be chosen to be sure the **container** is out of sight, that is, the outer **slider** layout has a specific width in the Style Designer but, given that its Align property is set to Client, at runtime, it will get a different sizing according to the parent object ones.

Possibly a different one each time is shown to the user. If we provide a value that is too high, the transition won't be smooth (as the time of the transition is fixed, so if you set the value to 2,000 instead of 500, assuming Duration is 1 second and Interpolation is set to Linear, you'll see nothing for 0.75 seconds and then a quick slide of the container in the remaining 0.25 seconds). On the other hand, if we provide a low value, you might risk seeing the **container** sliding only a small portion of the **slider** layout, giving the feeling of popping out the **slider** and subsequently (possibly slowly) sliding to the left.

To correctly tune the animation at runtime, we can make use of an event provided by TFrameStand, that is, OnBeforeStartAnimation will be fired each time an FMX TAnimation is triggered by the TFrameStand, just before calling its Execute method. You have there a chance to fine-tune the animation as the Stand, Container, and parent object will all be accessible at that time through the TSubjectInfo object (TSubjectInfo is an ancestor of TFrameInfo<T>).

In the following code block, you can see how I am changing the values of the start and stop values of our animations for the slider stand:

```
procedure TMainForm.FrameStand1BeforeStartAnimation(
  const ASender: TSubjectStand; const ASubjectInfo: TSubjectInfo;
  const AAnimation: TAnimation);
var
  LAni: TFloatAnimation;
begin
  if (ASubjectInfo.StandStyleName = 'slider') then
    if (AAnimation is TFloatAnimation) then
    begin
      LAni := TFloatAnimation(AAnimation);
      if LAni.StyleName = 'OnShow_SlideIn' then
        LAni.StartValue := ASubjectInfo.Stand.Width
      else if LAni.StyleName = 'OnHide_SlideOut' then
        LAni.StopValue := ASubjectInfo.Stand.Width;
    end;
end;
```

This is a very useful mechanism to deal with dimensions you are prevented from knowing until runtime. The same concept applies to some sizing you may want to apply to the Frame or the Stand, apart from the animations. This is a good use case for the `TFrameStand.OnBeforeShow` event where, again, you'll be passed the `TSubjectInfo` object just before making it visible to the user, with a chance to make the same last-call modifications to all of its parts.

Our `'slider'` stand is quite easy to understand once you have good background knowledge of how the `Align` property works (we covered this in Chapter 2, *Exploring Similarities and Differences with VCL*) and with some knowledge about animations. `TFrameStand` will greatly simplify some tasks, such as triggering animations automatically and waiting for them to complete before hiding/destroying the FrameStand, keeping you in full control of most aspects to perform tuning of all the involved elements at runtime.

Stands can be much more complex than this (with multiple animations and effects) but in the end, they all rely on the concepts listed in this chapter. From an architectural point of view, it is a very good point that stands are completely separated from frames (views) so that you may even deploy different stands according to the final device characteristics (or even make it an in-app configuration thing, letting the user choose among a minimalistic versus choreographic set of transitions).

Learning about TFormStand

This section is dedicated to `TFrameStand`, historically the first UI coordinator component I built, back in 2015. I've been showcasing `TFrameStand` at a number of in-person events, including conferences all around Europe (**EKON** and **Delphi Code Camp** in Germany,

ITDevCon in Italy, **PasCon** and **SDN** events in the Netherlands, the **DAPUG** event in Denmark, and **ZlotDelphi** in Poland) and online webinars. I always get very good feedback from developers but also a recurring question: *why support frames and not forms?*

When I initially designed TFrameStand, I looked at frames for performance reasons, that is, on a mobile app having secondary forms had a performance hit (especially at creation time). Also, frames represent a smaller portion, suitable for UI reuse at a level way lower than whole-view size (think about floating panels, action buttons, and other common UI elements).

However, Embarcadero fixed the performance issues with secondary forms on mobile (somewhere around **10.1 Berlin**, I guess) and introduced **FireUI technology**, a very powerful feature to deal with the UI adaptation of the same app for multiple platforms.

In 2019, also with the aim of including it in this book, I announced TFormStand, that is, the same concepts explained in this chapter but supporting forms instead of frames.

It has been less trivial than you might think, though, as TFrame and TForm are quite different and the first common ancestor is TFmxObject, which is a bit too abstract to be handy. Also, FMX forms do not have a native way to be parented to other controls.

I really wanted TFrameStand and TFormStand to keep the ease of use TFrameStand had so I heavily refactored TFrameStand, introducing an ancestor TSubjectStand (and TSubjectInfo as an ancestor for TFrameInfo<T> and TFormInfo<T>) and inheriting the two new components from it. You can now enjoy TFormStand and TFrameStand the same way, taking advantage of generic use in data structures and of some inner features that my components provide to let you thread forms with TFormStand like frames with TFrameStand.

You can obviously also mix the use of TFormStand and TFrameStand wherever you need in the app.

Summary

In this chapter, we learned how to modularize your FMX applications using TFrameStand. The capabilities of this little component are very effective at splitting the application into more manageable units. At the same time, it promotes the reuse of UI elements and visual conventions with a positive impact on the overall user experience and maintainability of the project. So it is a good addition both from the user and the developer/project manager point of view.

We have learned how to split our application into views, following the natural flow of the user experience. On mobile platforms, applications work very close to state machines where each state is a different view and transitions are driven by actions accessible in the current view. With TFrameStand, it is easy to implement loosely coupled views and bind them together to build up the application as a whole. Add-ons such as animations and visual continuity elements are also at hand. Therefore, the developer will be able to focus on application-specific development and, at the same time and with little effort, deliver a high-quality user interface.

In the next chapter, we are going to mix what we have learned so far in order to achieve responsiveness of the UI, in the sense of building UIs capable to properly adapting to different screen sizes and densities. TFormStand (TFrameStand's twin) will come to the rescue, adding FireUI capabilities to the approach we have seen used in this chapter with frames.

Building Responsive UIs 9

In the previous chapter, we learned how to effectively use the `TFrameStand` component to structure our applications. The focus has been about achieving modularization, visual continuity, and a good code/UI reuse rate across the whole application.

In this chapter, we'll particularly focus on the capability of an application to be responsive. This quality has been important for every application for many years, but it surely represents a crucial point when referring to cross-platform applications. We are going to start from the definition of responsiveness itself and then continue exploring some of the peculiar aspects related to it. We'll also go through an overview of the many factors involved.

In this chapter, we will cover the following topics:

- Understanding responsiveness—visual meaning
- Building visual layouts
- Introducing FireUI technology
- Exploring TFormStand

At the end of this chapter, you will have acquired an understanding of various technologies, including layout components, FireUI capabilities, and `TFormStand` components to achieve responsiveness in your applications.

Technical requirements

Here is the source code used in this chapter: `https://github.com/PacktPublishing/Delphi-GUI-Programming-with-FireMonkey/tree/master/Chapter%2009`

Generally speaking, for the book as a whole, you need a computer with Delphi set up and a few additional libraries installed (such as **Radiant Shapes** (`https://getitnow.embarcadero.com/?q=radiant+shapes`) and **CodeSite Logging** (`https://getitnow.embarcadero.com/?q=codesite`)).

Having other devices and setting up multiple platforms (iOS, Android, OS X/macOS, and Linux) other than Windows is a plus but not strictly necessary in order to follow the flow of the book.

Understanding responsiveness—visual meaning

In this section, we will briefly review the meaning of responsiveness along with its relevant factors. We will also look at Bootstrap's (`https://getbootstrap.com/`) grid system.

A visual application is software provided with a **Graphical User Interface** (**GUI**). The interface is there to let the user interact with the application functionalities. Common tasks are related to reading rendered data, monitoring the progress of tasks running in the background, changing the application state through the available controls, and so on. The actual scenario of the application that will be executed within can be very variegated. Nowadays, the same application can be running against several systems (different devices, different platforms) and driven by users with diverse habits (some may want to let the application be displayed in fullscreen mode, while others may want to use it side by side with other applications).

Of course, this is a general argument that can't be applied every time everywhere and there surely are edge cases where this heterogeneity is simply non-existent. However, the average application will need to face the challenge to be run against a significant number of different scenarios. The ability to retain its usability and to properly adapt across all these scenarios is what we call **responsiveness** from a visual point of view.

Over time, the term *responsiveness* has been attributed with a number of different meanings. I wish to emphasize that this chapter is about the visual meaning of the term and not, for example, about the ability to promptly respond to user interactions regardless of the application being busy doing some heavy processing (this will be the topic for `Chapter 11`, *Building Responsive Applications*).

Exploring Bootstrap's grid system

Bootstrap (`https://getbootstrap.com/`) is a very popular toolkit for building websites and applications. One of the key factors of its success has always been the ability to produce responsive web pages (usable both from desktop and mobile devices) with a single code base.

The most common example when talking about visual responsiveness is the Bootstrap's grid system (`https://getbootstrap.com/docs/4.5/layout/grid/`). It is based on a kind of abstraction of size metrics that relate every sizing to a twelve-column system. Element sizes are expressed using a number between 1 and 12 and this number is used to size the element in relative terms with respect to its container (so, 6 means half of the container). Many elements can be used as containers and nested, but the root container is (generally) the browser window (on mobile devices, basically the same size as the screen). So far, it simply sounds like a relative sizing system, but another dimension has been added to the mechanism: the size of the container is ranked according to five classes (extra-small, small, medium, large, and extra-large).

The ability to define a different size for each element and class adds great flexibility to the UI composition. Sizing generally happens when assigning classes to HTML elements, choosing among pre-built ones from the Bootstrap framework.

For example, the same column may set a width of 3 units (3/12, 25%) when the current class of the container is large (adding the `col-lg-3` class to the element definition) and, at the same time, also be set a width of 12 units (12/12, 100%) when the class is extra-small (adding the `col-sm-12` class). This would mean that the column would be occupying a quarter of the width of the container when this is large enough to show the column's content (and possibly other columns). The same column will take the full width of the container on very small devices (that is, an old mobile phone held in portrait orientation where 25% of the screen would probably be too small to render the content). Subsequent columns will eventually run over to the next row (moving from a column-based layout to a row-based layout). This will ensure that the content of the column is readable in both cases (large and small device screen) as a double definition of the UI layout is provided to properly match both cases.

The following HTML code snippet exemplifies the situation we've just discussed:

```
<div class="container">
  <div class="row">
    <div class="col col-lg-3 col-sm-12">
      1 of 2
    </div>
    <div class="col col-lg-9 col-sm-12">
      2 of 2
    </div>
  </div>
</div>
```

The following screenshot shows the rendering of this HTML fragment when the container is large enough to match the *large* class (more than 992 pixels for Bootstrap 4):

1 of 2	2 of 2

Figure 9.1

Whenever the container changes size (for example, because it is being rendered on a smaller device or because the user resized the browser window to a smaller width), Bootstrap will recognize the change, assign a new class to the container, and switch to the *small* sizing for all elements.

The result in rendering is shown in the following screenshot, where you can observe that the first element is taking the whole row (12/12) instead of a quarter of the width (3/12):

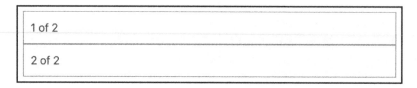

Figure 9.2

The example may look trivial, but this kind of automation will greatly improve general usability of the layout (as it fits both large screens, for instance, a desktop, and small ones, say mobile devices) without requiring too much effort on the part of the developer (there was a time where two different websites had to be implemented, one to serve desktop users, and a second one to serve mobile users). Also, this is very dynamic: you can grab a desktop browser rendering this example and resize the window back and forth to see the layout immediately adapt to the current size class. This is generally the concept used to showcase what visual responsiveness means to a developer encountering the issue for the first time.

Obviously, there are many cases that fall in between very large screens and very small ones and that's why Bootstrap provides five classes ranging from *extra-small* to *extra-large*. There is a distinct probability that your final user will fall into one of these five cases or not too far from one of them (the best match will be applied). Once again, this is an effective trade-off between providing a myriad of different sizes to match every possible situation and having a one-size-fits-all approach that would only match the same case where the developer tested the layout.

Moreover, you may think of it as only being a matter of how large (in pixels) the container is and applying a different sizing to all children elements, but there's more. The general concept of responsiveness applies with respect to a number of different factors that, as a whole, basically determine the actual scenario the application is run within.

Understanding the relevant factors of responsiveness

As have already been introduced, a number of factors need to be considered when talking about responsiveness.

Here is a list of some of the most significant ones:

- Device type (desktop, mobile, and so on)
- Screen resolution
- Screen form factor (3:4, 16:9, 16:10, and more)
- Screen density (depending on screen size and resolution), aka pixel ratio
- The ability to change orientation during the lifetime of the application (generally true for mobile devices)

Let's have a quick glance at all of the aforementioned factors and how they relate to one another. In a perfect world, our application should be capable of seamlessly adapting to deliver a fully functional, effective, eye candy **user interface** (UI) in every possible case. This is really hard to achieve and developers all around the world are struggling every day to improve their applications and technologies to shorten the distance to this goal.

Leveraging device and application peculiarities

Devices running our application can be classified by type: desktop or mobile is probably the most common split for GUI-enabled applications. It is not only a matter of screen size (although that can surely make a difference), but also of other aspects such as the input type of the device (keyboard and mouse rather than touch sensors), the probability of a change in the orientation of the screen during operation, the probability the device will be operating in an indoor or outdoor environment, and other similar aspects.

If some of these aspects have a straightforward link to the main topic of the chapter (responsiveness as the UI's ability to adapt to the actual use case), others may sound somewhat unrelated.

It is easy to agree that using a keyboard and a mouse means using a high-precision, fine-grained, input system. We can have UIs crowded with many small buttons lined up in multi-row toolbars and still be sure the user will have no trouble selecting the desired one (using the mouse or the keyboard). *But what happens if we transpose the very same UI to a smartphone, where the only available input method is the touch-enabled display? Are we really asking the user to aim for a particular button, with this probably being smaller than the tip of the user's finger?* We may ask the user to have a capacitive pen (or other similar devices) in order to use our application, but this would result in a significant (*unacceptable?*) physical requirement in terms of using our application. No doubt this would qualify as an evident failure in our quest for the ability to adapt.

To properly address the differences between input types, we may consider adequately adjusting the size of certain elements (that is, buttons, edit boxes, and list items) in order to be bigger and possibly better spaced. So we'll need to properly recognize which case (desktop/mobile) our application is running within and find a way to deliver a conveniently adjusted UI in each situation.

For sure, arguments can arise regarding the opportunity to deduce the input type (keyboard and mouse versus touch system) from the device family (desktop/mobile). A better approach would be to specifically identify the input type and discriminate accordingly. Once again, in order to keep complexity reasonably low, there are some simplifications applied (and it is up to the developer to understand whether this simplification stands up or not).

Handling changes in device orientation

Similar arguments can be applied to the next aspect I've listed: changes in screen orientation (within the lifetime of the application).

I am making the base assumption that we are talking about screens with an aspect ratio that isn't one (squared screen). This is an easy assumption to make regarding *classic* devices (desktop and mobile), but less certain if we also consider IoT or wearables devices. Having an aspect ratio of one, however, may greatly simplify the problem (but other peculiar aspects may arise as well).

Even if it's not an absolute truth, you are unlikely to find a desktop device where the orientation of the screen can be easily changed by the user during normal operation. On the other hand, the opposite generally applies to most mobile devices. Therefore, we can safely use the device family again to determine whether our UI will need to adapt to match a change in orientation of the screen.

In practical terms, this may mean we are switching from a width/height ratio of 0.5 to the reverse value of 2 (this would be the actual case for my **Google Pixel 3a device**, having a resolution of 2220 x 1080 pixels).

The following screenshot clearly summarizes how important the impact of a change in orientation is with respect to available space in order to lay out the UI controls correctly:

Figure 9.3

Even if it may seem a very mobile-specific topic, this is actually a very similar situation to what happens on desktop applications when the user resizes the application window. The content should be able to rearrange itself in order to properly make use of the available space, irrespective of whether the width/height ratio changes more or less drastically.

Considering the field of application

So far, we have seen how we can reasonably deduce typical input type and orientation capabilities by device type. This also applies to the last entry on my list of aspects: indoor/outdoor use. Even if it is not strictly tied to device type, I think we can agree that it is generally hard to see a desktop machine being used outdoors.

There are a number of topics relating to the fact that our device will be used indoors or outdoors and some of them have an impact on the UI as well.

Let's think about a mobile application being used outdoors: we may need to design our user interface in order to positively adapt to changes in the environment luminosity, so as to keep the user comfortable throughout the day and depending on all weather and light conditions. This may be accomplished by switching from a dark theme to (one or more) lighter ones, or the other way around, depending on the actual need.

Some operating systems already have some support in this area (and we may decide to rely on this), but I've seen specific cases where additional explicit support has become a requirement for the application's usability. This may seem a very tenuous argument, but there are a number of situations when such an adjustment may draw a line between delivering an application that can actually be used and one that cannot.

And, just to prove this, in the same way as the other aspects can also overcome the boundaries of device-type discrimination, you may find yourself with the very same requirement even on desktop applications; for example, with industrial applications operating in environments where light control is a business requirement (that is, laboratories or industrial processing involving light-sensitive materials). Obviously, having to deal with environmental luminosity is a more likely scenario when dealing with mobile apps.

I think it should be clear by now that many not-so-evident aspects may actually have an impact on the usability of your applications (desktop or mobile). Obviously, the list of actual topics that makes sense to address is strongly specific to the application domain. Just keep in mind that you have to address them by making a number of assumptions (it is worth checking these, too, before proceeding with implementation).

Generally speaking, I would say it is safe to use the device type to deduce some characteristics of the device itself (such as the main input type and the ability to change orientation easily) or of the surrounding operating environment (such as indoor/outdoor primary use considerations).

Understanding screen resolution and density

The screen resolution and density factors are universal. They are not tied to a specific type of device or a specific platform. The problem of how to handle different resolutions has been around for decades. More recently, screen density also has become a common topic.

 Screen density has become a common topic probably from the time when Apple introduced its **Apple Retina** display.

We need to familiarize ourselves with some basic terminology (the numerical examples in the following paragraph will refer to my **Google Pixel 3a** smartphone, featuring a 5.6" display with 2220 x 1080 resolution and a 441 ppi screen density):

- The **screen size** is the measure of the diagonal of the screen in physical units (inches generally), that is, pixel 3a has a 5.6 inch display (14.22 centimeters).
- The **screen resolution** is generally stated as a pair of numbers, *A x B*, where *A* is the number of graphical units on the width side, and B has the same meaning for the height side. By graphical units, we mean pixels for digital displays and dots for print. The aspect ratio can be determined directly from the screen resolution (dividing 2220 by 1080 gives you the Pixel 3a ratio of 2.056, which, when conventionally expressed as a fraction of 9, is known as 18.5:9. Other common ratio examples are 3:4, 16:9, and 16:10).
- The **screen density** is the number of pixels in a single physical length unit of the screen. PPI stands for **pixels-per-inch** and identifies the number of distinct pixels on the side of a square inch area of the physical screen (note: counter-intuitively, the term *density* may lead you to think that this value refers to the number of distinguishable pixels in the area unit, as when talking about the population density of a country, which is measured by the number of people per square kilometer).

The ppi value is to be intended as the length in pixels of the side of the square of the single area unit, so if you say *n* ppi, you mean *n* rows and *n* columns of pixels, resulting in *n*n* total pixels per square inch area. In our context, ppi and dpi are often used interchangeably (there is no need to explicitly state the eventual distinction across displayed and printed resolution).

The pixel 3a screen, according to specifications, has a 441 ppi screen density, so you can easily get this number by dividing the diagonal length in pixels (obtained by applying **Pythagoras'** theorem) by the diagonal length in inches, as shown in the following formula:

$$\frac{\sqrt{1080^2 + 2220^2}}{5.6\text{ ''}} = 440.85 \simeq 441\ ppi$$

Figure 9.4

Another, more sophisticated way to achieve the same result is to calculate the screen area both in squared pixels (logical) and squared inches (physical). The ratio between the two values will give the actual number of distinct pixels per square inch. The square root of that number is the length in pixels of the side of the square, which is, once again, the screen density as described before. The following diagram shows you the screen of the smartphone with the diagonal, width, height, and diagonal angle quoted:

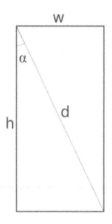

Figure 9.5

The following mathematical formulas will show you how to perform the calculations:

$$d_{inches} = 5.6, \ w_{px} = 1080, \ h_{px} = 2220$$

$$\alpha = \tan^{-1} \frac{w_{px}}{h_{px}} = 0.45278 \ rad$$

$$w_{inches} = d \sin \alpha = 2.45$$

$$h_{inches} = d \cos \alpha = 5.036$$

$$A_{px^2} = w_{px} h_{px} = 2397600$$

$$A_{inches^2} = w_{inches} h_{inches} = 12.3382$$

$$\frac{A_{px^2}}{A_{inches^2}} = \frac{2397600}{12.3382} = 194323.32$$

$$density_{\frac{px}{inch}} = \sqrt{\frac{A_{px^2}}{A_{inches^2}}} = 440.82 \simeq 441 \ ppi$$

Figure 9.6

There is also another conventional way to refer to screen densities: keeping a 160 dpi base, you can easily classify screen densities as a factor of the baseline. The following diagram (taken from Android's official documentation at `https://developer.android.com/training/multiscreen/screendensities`) clarifies the concept:

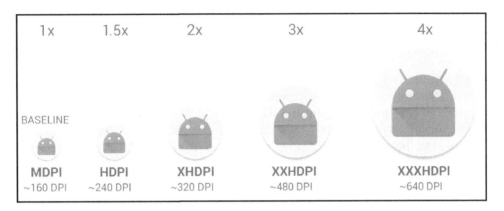

Figure 9.7
(Image credit: Android open source project, and used according to the terms described in the Creative Commons 2.5 Attribution License)

It is not unusual to also consider very low resolution devices (0.75x, 120 dpi), but there is a trend showing that dpi values are growing over time (the newer the device, the higher the resolution).

The higher the resolution, the more room for control over the screen is available. The higher the density, the more detailed graphics and images can be (keeping the same screen physical size, a higher resolution means a higher density). The background concept of having to support multiple densities is to provide a coherent and efficient graphic resource according to the actual screen capabilities and keep the UI consistent across the differences (the preceding diagram is showing five versions of the same icon which, seen on screen with the labeled density, should appear to be the same physical size without stretching or blurring).

Now that we have introduced what screen density and resolutions are, we can proceed to discuss how this affects our applications from a visual point of view. In Chapter 3, *Mastering Basic Components*, we already discussed the need for multi-resolution bitmaps in order to deliver the best graphic experience to the user, without overly affecting performance (especially on low-end devices, where serving hi-res images can negatively impact the overall usability of the application). Multi-resolution bitmaps, a built-in functionality of the FMX framework, will allow the developer/graphic designer to deliver the best compromise each time, at the cost of resource occupancy (bigger application bundles, for example).

FMX bitmap styles, as we have seen in Chapter 7, *Understanding FMX Style Concept*, also take advantage of the multi-res bitmap support as the bitmaps used can be provided in different resolutions to match the actual scale the application needs.

Other techniques, such as the **9-slice-scaling** we saw in Chapter 7, *Understanding FMX Style Concept*, may help to deal with the need for several variations of graphic resources and to use them with unpredictable dimensions all over the application while retaining good quality (possibly, a pixel-perfect quality).

Last but not least, **vector graphics** (we'll discuss them in Chapter 7, *Understanding FMX Style Concept*, are another way to overcome the problem. As we have seen, not only are there a number of (eventually drastically) different screen resolutions, form factors, and densities to support, but also the need to deal with dynamic factors (such as a change in orientation during the application lifespan or other environmental factors occurring and mining the final usability of our UI). Our goal of developing a single multi-platform, possibly multi-device, application cannot avoid addressing some, if not all, of the most common scenarios described.

So far we have covered a number of strategies/techniques to deal with responsiveness:

- Apply different positioning/sizing sets to our controls in order to match the primary input type or the orientation of the device.
- Apply different styles in order to react to changes in environmental luminosity.
- Take advantage of the built-in multi-resolution support for graphics (and multi-res-enabled FMX styles) to properly deliver the best available resource to the user.
- Take advantage of the built-in support for the 9-slice-scaling with FMX styles.
- Make use of vector graphics where possible (remember FMX vector styles, as discussed in Chapter 7, *Understanding FMX Style Concept*).

In the following sections, we'll learn how to implement the first two points in the list, including how to master some FMX components and peculiarities that will greatly simplify our efforts to deliver a responsive application.

The key to success in this area is to master relative positioning and take advantage of technologies such as FireUI that are included in the FMX framework. FireUI will help you differentiate the positioning and sizing of the controls for different scenarios (device type, screen sizes). Before delving into FireUI (and its combined use with TFormStand), we are going to cover some basic capabilities that FMX offers in order to achieve the relative positioning of visual components.

Building visual layouts

In this section, we will learn about the various visual layouts/components.

UI is made of visual components (eventually with the aid of some other non-visible ones). By *layout*, we are usually referring to the strategy used to place these visual components in front of the user.

The placement of components always follows a particular model, for example, the **box model** where components can be regarded as rectangular-shaped boxes, hence, with a width and a height, and positioned using a set of coordinates (relative to a conventional origin). In our case, the origin is set to be the upper-left corner of the parent container of the component and, by convention again, the placement is expressed in coordinates of the upper-left corner of the component.

Delphi historically has adopted this model for placement of visual components in conjunction with the concept of parenthood. In the VCL framework, every component needs to have a Parent object: a visual component will be contained in its parent, its positioning will be relative to it, and some other characteristics may be inferred from the Parent object (the background color or font settings are common examples). By design, in VCL, a component will never exceed the boundaries of its Parent object (it is hard for a child component to draw something outside the boundaries of its Parent). Sizing is driven by the Width and Height properties, defining the boundaries of the box where the component lives. Another dimension is represented by the Z-Order of components: if you pile up several components in the same area, you will be able to determine which one should be on top, which one should be at the bottom, and so on.

The term **Z-Order** refers to the order of visual components in a pseudo-3D organization. If positioning on a (flat) screen is naturally made using a set of two coordinates (X and Y), you require a third coordinate (Z) to determine what happens when two components share the same XY position (or they overlap). Conventionally, the Z axis grows toward the user (so a higher positive value generally means **top** or **front**, and a negative value means **bottom** or **behind**).

The following diagram summarizes the basics of the box model (shared across VCL and FMX frameworks, even if with some differences, such as the fact that X and Y are integer values in VCL and floating-point values in FMX):

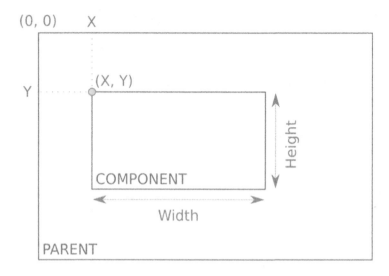

Figure 9.8

In addition to the initial static, positioning, and sizing, other features concur in the behavior of the component during its lifetime and especially drive the relationship with its parent: the Align and Anchors properties (we already encountered them in Chapter 2, *Exploring Similarities and Differences with VCL*).

Starting with the Align and Anchors settings, the behavior of the component becomes more dynamic than completely static. To some extent, a component can be set to adjust itself to react to changes occurring in the parent component. Other properties, such as Margins and Paddings, can be useful to get more control over the final result.

Margins will let you control some space to be added to the outside boundaries of the component (so if you align a component to the right, you can also state that you want some spacing added on the right margin rather than seeing your component to be exactly adjacent to the right boundary of its container). Paddings are a similar concept, but within a component's boundaries, and are useful for defining the spacing to be preserved inside a container object.

Using these capabilities, it is already possible to reach a good level of responsiveness in our UIs as we can move from a completely static model (position and size, generally set at design time) to a set of rules driving a relative positioning and sizing of the components.

Moreover, components can be nested and, if you remember what we have seen in `Chapter 2`, *Exploring Similarities and Differences with VCL*, a big difference of FMX with respect to the VCL framework is that every component can host children components (whereas in the VCL, only some components, such as `TPanel`, are capable of being a container for others). This basically means you can nest components one inside the other, for example, to make their positioning relative or to ensure they will share the same visibility, combining their opacity or rotation angle.

I've often seen this technique applied while working with VCL applications too, using nested `TPanel` components, so as to obtain a relative positioning and sizing of a group of components. The side-effect here is that in doing so, we are also adding complexity, as `TPanel` is actually a solid component from a visual point of view and, from a resource usage point of view, not completely zero-cost to use (each `TPanel` component allocates a window handle, for instance).

In the FMX framework, things are different given the following:

- Components can be nested with no restrictions (you can put a `TEdit` inside a `TButton` and the other way around).
- The `Align` property has much more available options than VCL (that is, the `Center`, `Content`, or `Scale` entries just to name a few).
- Being contained in a component does not imply that the component fits its boundaries (you can have a small component containing a larger one).
- A set of components is there to help you, acting as effective containers: `TLayout` and its siblings will provide you with a container without being bulky (they are, in fact, very lightweight, transparent components).
- The advanced features (such as rotation or opacity management) that are incorporated in the FMX framework for all visual components significantly increase the opportunities related to the ability to nest/compose components at will.
- The layouts component can even be used to easily implement (or simplify) layers in your UI (Z-Order).
- Alignment and layouts can be used to scale content or to keep some aspect ratio throughout the resizing of components and their composition.

Putting all the aforementioned capabilities together opens up the way to achieve full responsiveness in your UI, building a composition of components that are elastic and scalable instead of static and fixed.

Arranging components with TLayout

The TLayout component is a simple container for FMX visual components. It is rendered as a dashed rectangle at design time, but at runtime, it is completely invisible (transparent).

One of the most straightforward uses of TLayout is to group components together: all components inside the same container share the same positioning system, relative to the upper-left corner of the container. When you move the container, all the contained components move as well. If you change visibility in relation to the container, for example, setting the Visible property to False, the container and all its content will no longer be rendered to the user. Contained objects will retain the ability to have their own visibility that will be combined with that of the parents. This combination also applies to other properties such as Opacity and rotations applied to the components.

For example, if we put a TButton instance inside TLayout and we set the Opacity property of the button to a value of 0.5, we'll see the button rendered semi-transparent (alpha 50%). If we also set the Opacity property of the containing layout to 0.5, we'll notice a further fading out of the TButton down to 25% absolute transparency. The following screenshot shows this behavior both at design time and runtime. Notice how the button on the right has an absolute opacity of 0.25 even if its Opacity property is set to **0.5**:

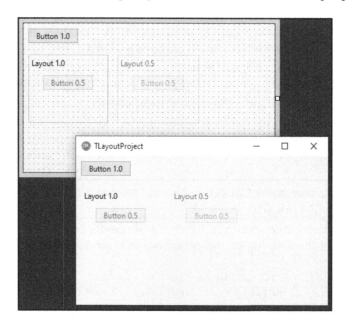

Figure 9.9

The components are also grouped in a sort of a single Z-order layer and this may come in handy when organizing components in different layers using different layouts. A local Z-order setting is set inside the same layer so you still have full control (between components in a layer and between different layers). I have seen a number of situations where this approach has been used to implement wizard-like functionalities or to handle different application states requiring different component sets to be available/visible during the lifetime of the application.

When working with the FMX framework, the IDE behaves so that changing visibility to `TLayout` also has an impact at design time (this does not happen, for example, when using `TPanel` in a VCL application). This means that even at design time, you can use this approach to simplify the design operations of a complex form (relatively soon, however, I would suggest switching to a `TFrame`-based approach, using `TFrameStand` as described in `Chapter 8`, *Divide and Conquer with TFrameStand*). Also using them to implement dialog-like functionalities can be easy and effective (again, in low-complexity cases).

The following screenshot exemplifies the use of layouts as containers in a *layer-oriented approach*. Of course you can even *group* these layers by putting more layouts inside one, possibly setting the `Align` property of the inner layouts to `Contents` to fill the outer layout boundaries:

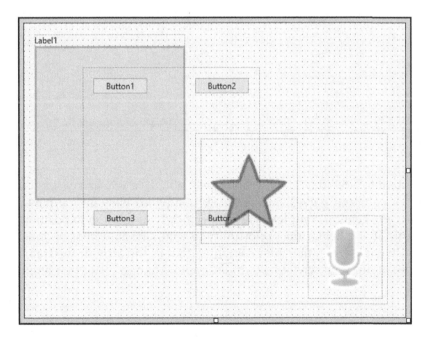

Figure 9.10

Effects and animations may be applied to `TLayout`, resulting in them being applied to all children as well. So you may want to grayscale a number of components to reflect an application state or highlight them for some purpose.

The following screenshot shows the same form with two effects (a `TGlowEffect` instance on the middle layout and a `TMonochromeEffect` instance on the right layout) applied:

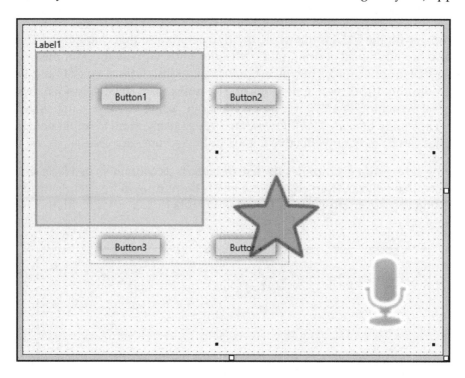

Figure 9.11

It is also important to note that `TLayout` is align-enabled, so you can easily use it to implement rows, columns, panels, and so on. Splitting your view into different parts will help you reduce the general complexity and, specifically in relation to positioning and the sizing of controls, it also brings the opportunity to relativize a number of dimensions and achieve responsiveness when the outer container (that is, the form or the frame) gets resized (because of different screen resolutions applied or as a result of manual user intervention).

For example, you can put some layouts onto a form and set the `Align` and `Margin` properties to achieve a common visual layout. The following screenshot of a `TLayoutProject` example (`Form3`) exemplifies this:

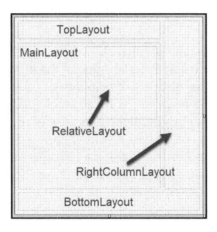

Figure 9.12

As shown in the previous screenshot, we can add five layouts to a form (the `Paddings` property of the form has been set to `10` to also make the layout boundaries more evident in the screenshot):

- `TopLayout`: This could be used to host a title or a toolbar for our view. The `Align` property has been set to the `Top` value, `Margins.Right` has been set to `10`, and `Height` has a value of `50`.
- `BottomLayout`: This could be hosting some summarized information or action buttons. The `Align` property has been set to `MostBottom` in order to ensure that it would occupy a portion of the parent container (the form) covering the whole width. `Height` has been set to a value of `50` (to pair the `TopLayout`'s one).
- `RightColumnLayout`: This could be hosting some quick action buttons or some tips for the user. The `Align` property has been set to `MostRight` in order to overcome `TopLayout` (while being overcome by `BottomLayout`), `Width` has been set to `100`, and `Margins.Bottom` to `10`.
- `MainLayout`: This could be hosting the main content of this view (some text or list control for instance). Its `Align` property has been set to `Client` and `Margins.Top/Right/Bottom` has been set to `10`. Both the width and height of this layout will be calculated according to the size of the outer container (the form) and the size of other sibling layouts. `RelativeLayout` has been added as a child of `MainLayout` and its `Align` property has been set to `Scale`.

It has been manually positioned (10 pixels from the upper-right corner of its container, MainLayout) and sized (200 x 200) to occupy a fraction of its container area. It could be used to show some details related to the main content (for example, if MainLayout hosts a list control, some details pertaining to the selected item).

The resulting composition has some peculiarities worth noticing. For instance, the form has been designed with a size of 530 x 540 pixels. Some of the dimensions are fixed: TopLayout.Height, BottomLayout.Height, and RightColumnLayout.Width. Some others are relative: Position.X and Height of RightColumnLayout will be automatically changed (as it will always be kept right-aligned because of the Align property), and the same will happen for BottomLayout.Position.Y, BottomLayout.Width, TopLayout.Width, MainLayout.Width, MainLayout.Height, RelativeLayout.Position.X, RelativeLayout.Position.Y, RelativeLayout.Width, and RelativeLayout.Height.

What we achieved here is to retain the same layout regardless of the dimensions of the outer container (the form that also generally means the screen resolution on mobile devices).

The following screenshot shows how the layout responds to changes in the outer container (the form) when it is rendered (1) half of the original width, (2) half of the original height, and (3) half of the original dimensions (of both, width and height):

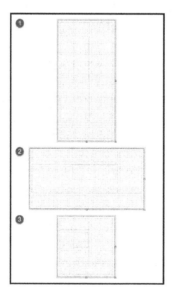

Figure 9.13

The behavior shown in the previous screenshot is a first achievement in terms of responsiveness. In simple terms, we have a layout always making use of the available space, regardless of how drastically this has been changed with respect to the original design. Of course, there are still aspects that could be improved, but for a **no-code approach**, it is already a satisfactory result.

There is no limit to what you can achieve by proceeding with this approach since, as we have already discussed, you can nest layouts without restrictions and, if needed, overlay different layers (if the by-containment approach is too strict for your needs).

List controls and scroll boxes may finally help you to deal with content that is hard to actually fit into the layouts, providing scrolling capabilities that may be reasonably accepted by the user or seen as a last resort to access the content on small-sized devices (or in crowded UIs that are generally something to avoid).

TLayout is a very central and commonly used component, but there are also some other components (siblings, even if not actually sharing a common ancestor other than TControl) that are also providing effective capabilities when dealing with component placement and sizing. In the next section, we'll provide an overview of their peculiarities too.

Letting components flow as text with TFlowLayout

As we said, talking about responsiveness often means you need to rearrange components differently than originally designed and according to the actual characteristics of the device. While always keeping in mind that you can actually combine and nest FMX visual components as you wish, we are now going to introduce the TFlowLayout component.

As the name suggests, this will allow the developer to arrange a set of components, letting them flow in a very similar manner to how text runs in a **Word** processor. Elements will be running in a row, one beside the other, until the boundary of TFlowLayout is reached. Then the next element (the one not fitting the remaining space between the prior element and the layout boundary) is allowed to run over a new row.

The following screenshot shows you a `TFlowLayout` component with 15 children components (buttons):

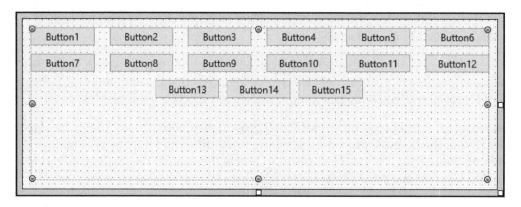

Figure 9.14

As you can see, there is a vertical and horizontal gap of 10 pixels between elements that has been defined. Elements are arranged with full justification, but the last row is set to be centered instead of justified.

Some `TFlowLayout` properties will help tune how the placement is set up:

- `FlowDirection`: This property determines how children components should flow. Available values are `LeftToRight`, the default, and `RightToLeft`.
- `HorizontalGap` and `VerticalGap`: These integer values determine the eventual spacing to be retained among elements. `HorizontalGap` is applied to elements in the same row (on the left and right side of each element), while `VerticalGap` is applied across rows, vertically. The spacing is automatically managed so as to keep in consideration element wrapping, thereby avoiding unnecessary spaces being applied to the first and last elements of a row.
- `Justify`: This property is used to determine how to arrange elements inside the same row. Available values are `Center`, `Justify`, `Left`, and `Right`. The behavior is very similar to what happens dealing with text in a Word processor. The additional property `JustifyLastLine` comes to differentiate the arrangement for the last row (given you may want to apply a different value for the final, eventually spared, elements of the list).

No restrictions are set vis-à-vis the size of contained elements (they can retain their original width and height and if they change, the flow layout will be updated immediately, rearranging all elements to fit the new dimensions). The `Align` property of the contained elements will be ineffective until the component is parented to the flow layout.

Rows will be automatically sized in height to match the maximum height value of elements in that row, as you can see in the following screenshot (notice **Button3** and **Button4** have a greater `Height` value than other buttons, causing the second row to slide downwards):

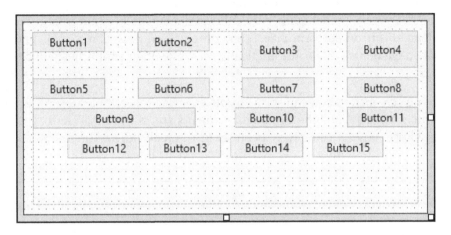

Figure 9.15

Another component available in FMX to be used in conjunction with `TFlowLayout` is `TFlowLayoutBreak`. This component can be added as an element to `TFlowLayout` and will act as a new line/carriage return (to get back to our text flow analogy). It will also provide you with the opportunity to change the flowing rules (justification, gaps, and more) from that point on.

To correctly set the position of `TFlowLayoutBreak` between two regular elements of `TFlowLayout`, I have found no other way than to edit the FMX file manually (in text mode).

The use of `TFlowLayout` can greatly simplify UI views where a number of blocks may need to run over on multiple lines according to the available space. Remember that elements in the flow layout may have different sizes and may be resized (by code) when needed.

Building grid layouts with TGridLayout

Another typical situation when dealing with component placement is having a number of equally sized entries to be arranged in a grid model. The TGridLayout component will enforce the sizing of all contained objects to be equal to its ItemHeight and ItemWidth property values.

Items will be placed one beside the other, filling rows (or columns, depending on the actual value of the Orientation property) within the boundaries of this container component. Similar to the TFlowLayout behavior, row/column management is automatic, but contained elements are all the same size. Some properties (Position, Width, and Height) of the contained elements will be automatically set while other properties will be explicitly ignored (Align).

In the following screenshot, you can see a simple example where ItemHeight and ItemWidth are set to 100, and the contained elements are TRectangle and TCircle components whose Margin value have been set to 10 on all sides. TGridLayout has been set to Align = Client with a Margin value of 10 on all sides:

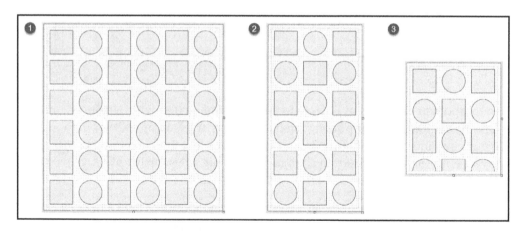

Figure 9.16

As you can see, the screenshots of three variations are provided, with different outer form sizes to show how the grid layout gets arranged accordingly. In the first screenshot, the size of the form has been set to 620 x 620 and you can see that exactly 36 elements fit the view. In the second screenshot, the form's width has been reduced to half, so there are 18 elements in the view. The final screenshot shows a 320 x 370 form (9 full elements shown and only half of the last row visible). Notice that the ClipChildren property of TGridLayout has been set to True.

There is no such concept of vertical and horizontal gaps in `TGridLayout`. Nonetheless, you may individually set `Margins` for contained elements to achieve some spacing where needed. Once again, consider you can use other layout components (`TLayout`, `TFlowLayout`) as elements of `TGridLayout`, building a composition that may be very effective in a number of situations.

Advanced arrangements with TGridPanelLayout

`TGridPanelLayout` is a special container where components can be organized in rows and columns. With respect to the other containers we have just seen, this time, every contained component is assigned to an existing cell. Cells are elements of a row and column system that can be defined at design time or at runtime and they can be sized according to an absolute model; a relative one, based on the percentage of the total available space (`Width` or `Height`, depending on whether we are talking about a row or a column item); or automatically sized according to the content size (at the point when the content is added to the container).

Columns and rows are managed through two collection properties—`ColumnCollection` and `RowCollection`. Each element of this collection has two properties—`SizeStyle` and `Value`. As already mentioned, the sizing style can be chosen from among the `Absolute`, `Percentage`, and `Auto` values.

The component will arrange a new child in the next available cell and, if none are left available, it may grow the rows or column collections to add more room. The `ExpandStyle` property will determine how this happens. Three possible values can be assigned to the `ExpandStyle` property: `AddRows`, `AddColumns`, and `FixedSize`. A new row or column, respectively, will be added if one of the first two options is selected. Otherwise, when `ExpandStyle = FixedSize`, you'll get a runtime exception when trying to add new components to the container (at design time, the component will be added in any case, but not assigned to a cell, of course).

Having a percentage-based sizing system is quite a novelty in the Delphi environment and this has been clearly taken by many web development technologies. This makes `TGridPanelLayout` handy in a number of situations where you wish to retain the relative sizing of elements (or groups of them as, once again, you can nest layouts as elements of `TGridPanelLayout`) while resizing the outer container (where the size of the frame/form or screen of the device changes).

A number of extended functionalities are incorporated in the **grid model** offered by this component, including the ability to increase the spanning over the row/column of each item. Once a component has been added as a child of the TGridPanelLayout component, a corresponding entry in the ControlCollection collection is added. This is an instance of the TControlItem class exposing some properties:

- Control is a reference to the contained component.
- The Column and Row properties represent the coordinates of the cell hosting the control.
- The ColumnSpan and RowSpan properties, respectively, determine how many adjacent cells can be considered as adjoined to the cell hosting the control (the one identified by the Column and Row property values). This is a handy shortcut to have exceptions in the grid model where you need a single element to fit more than a single cell (a common functionality in most spreadsheet software also).

As the following screenshot shows, you can easily compose non-straightforward layouts using TGridPanelLayout. Here you can find a 2 x 2 grid, the cell dimensions are set to be 50% of the total available space (both the width and height are set to 50 percent), three elements have been added to the container, and the third one has been spanned over two columns (notice the ColumnSpan value of **2** in **Object Inspector**):

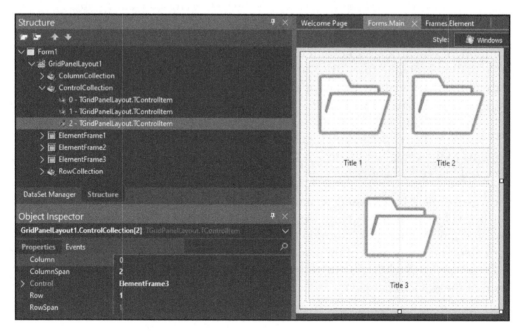

Figure 9.17

`TGridPanelLayout` represents a good opportunity to lay out components dynamically, taking advantage of relative sizing and the automatic growth of the layout itself (at runtime). A common use of this component is to implement touch-enabled home screens for mobile applications (launchers).

In this section, we learned about visual components, along with the `TLayout`, `TFlowLayout`, `TGridLayout`, and `TGridPanelLayout` components.

In the next section, we'll dive into the FireUI technology.

Introducing FireUI technology

Mastering techniques related to the positioning and sizing of components, including the smart use of layout components, is a vital requirement for developers striving to keep their applications responsive.

However, even if an impressive level of flexibility can be achieved this way, there are some situations where something more effective is needed to achieve the goal.

The FireUI name includes a number of technologies. Embarcadero has been included in Delphi since version **XE7**. One of the most significant capabilities that has been added is the view specialization of the UI according to a platform/form factor combination.

In other words, we have so far tried to design our UI according to a one-size-fits-all strategy, trying to add sufficient flexibility to our positioning and sizing strategies in order to achieve a satisfactory result in most situations. As we said at the beginning of this chapter, we may need to adjust significantly some dimensions or UI-related settings so as to best fit our UI on a specific device family or type. A good general design for mobile applications, for example, may need special tuning to properly address edge cases (very small phones and/or high-resolution tablets). The sizing or placement of some elements may need tuning in particular cases and so on. We are not talking about providing very different UIs, but having the ability to change an alignment setting, margins, sizes, or visibility.

If you are an experienced Delphi developer, you may know about **Visual Form Inheritance (VFI)**: the ability to inherit a visual form from another one. Delphi forms are implemented by **Object Pascal** classes united with **Delphi Form** (**DFM**) file information (we talked about the component streaming system in `Chapter 2`, *Exploring Similarities and Differences with VCL*), so technically it is possible to inherit a second class from a base one.

The IDE and the component streaming system have full support for merging DFM information and let you edit an inherited form (or the ancestor one) and see changes immediately applied from a visual point of view. The FireUI view specification is a similar (yet not coincidental) concept with respect to VFI.

The idea is to have a master visual definition where components are added and configured, exactly as we have discussed so far throughout this book. All the settings applied to the visual components at design time are registered in the **FMX** file (DFM equivalent in the FireMonkey framework). Then, once we have a functioning UI, we can define an inherited view to be used in a particular context.

The inherited view definition will entail a separate **FMX** file where differences with the master view will be recorded. The component streaming system will be able to load and merge at runtime the correct view according to the actual context the application will be running. Be aware that the code portion (the `.pas` file or, more specifically, the class implementation) of the form definition will be shared across different views. This is, in my opinion, a good compromise in terms of keeping the code base single and, at the same time, introducing the ability to better tailor the UI definition for every necessary platform/device combination (or just for some of them, of course).

We can now use a minimalistic example to explain how the code works at a practical level and what the final effects are.

Creating a new view

Create a new empty FMX application, then add a `TToolbar` component, and, inside it, add a `TText` instance (set the `Align` property to `Contents` to fill the toolbar and act as a title).

The following screenshot shows what the IDE looks like with our form in the designer:

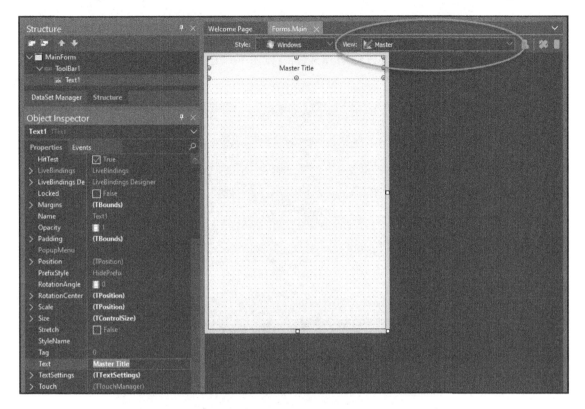

Figure 9.18

In the previous screenshot, I've circled a combo box, part of the IDE, that is the view selector. The dropdown lists all the available combinations a view can be created for. The IDE holds a list of available devices (and their characteristics, such as screen resolution) that you can even edit to add your custom devices (select **IDE menu | Tools | Options | User Interface | Form Designer | Device Manager**). The following screenshot shows the default entries that are available for views:

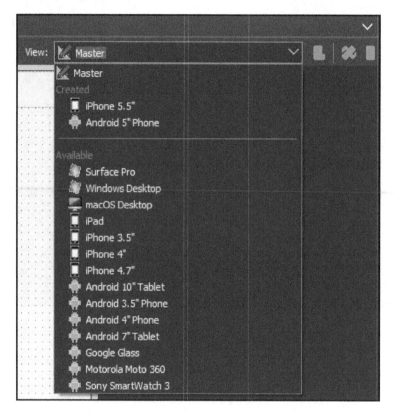

Figure 9.19

As you can see in the previous screenshot, the list is divided into three parts: the **Master** view entry, the **Created** section, listing all the specific views that have already been created, and the **Available** section, listing the other devices for which you can create a specific view. To create a new view for a desired device, just select the corresponding entry in the list. I've created views for an **iPhone** device (**iOS**, 5.5 inch display) and another one for an **Android** phone (5 inch display).

Once you select a specific view, **Form Designer** will reflect the change, generally providing a background picture (form frame) to match the device and adapting the form dimensions to fit the display of the current device. The following screenshot shows the view generated for an iOS iPhone:

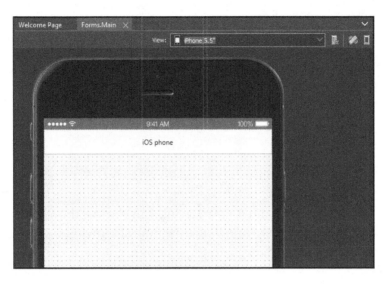

Figure 9.20

Also, under the hood, a separate FMX file is created to host any changes applied to the visual components. Keep in mind that components will always be added to the Master view **FMX** file (even if you drop them on the **Form Designer** while a specific view is shown). This is due to the fact that we are talking about the same class implementing the form (so each component is actually a field of the corresponding TForm descendant Object Pascal class). More philosophically, FireUI is not intended to derive different views (meaning visuals and code together) for different devices. The aim is to have a single view (single code base) with some visual differences applied to specific devices.

The mechanism used to implement the FMX separation across master and specific views is called differential streaming. We can have a look at the FMX generated for the **Master** view and for a secondary view. Here's the master view of the previous example. Please consider that the **Windows** style (the default option for a newly created FMX application) is selected:

```
object MainForm: TMainForm
  Left = 0
  Top = 0
  Caption = 'MainForm'
  ClientHeight = 480
  ClientWidth = 320
```

```
      FormFactor.Width = 320
      FormFactor.Height = 480
      FormFactor.Devices = [Desktop]
      DesignerMasterStyle = 0
      object ToolBar1: TToolBar
        Size.Width = 320.000000000000000000
        Size.Height = 40.000000000000000000
        Size.PlatformDefault = False
        TabOrder = 1
        object Text1: TText
          Align = Contents
          Size.Width = 320.000000000000000000
          Size.Height = 40.000000000000000000
          Size.PlatformDefault = False
          Text = 'Master Title'
        end
      end
    end
```

In the `.pas` file corresponding to our `MainForm`, we can observe the addition of a `{$R}` compiler directive for each created view, as shown in the following code snippet:

```
{$R *.fmx}
{$R *.LgXhdpiPh.fmx ANDROID}
{$R *.iPhone55in.fmx IOS}
```

In the previous snippet, the first line is the customary one, while the second and third lines have been added to include the additional **FMX** files in the resources of the final executable (the streaming system will need it to properly load the form at runtime, as we discussed in Chapter 2, *Exploring Similarities and Differences with VCL*).

The generated FMX file for the iPhone 5.5" device is given as follows:

```
inherited MainForm_iPhone55in: TMainForm_iPhone55in
  ClientHeight = 716
  ClientWidth = 414
  DesignerMasterStyle = 0
  inherited ToolBar1: TToolBar
    Size.Width = 414.000000000000000000
    Size.Height = 44.000000000000000000
    inherited Text1: TText
      Size.Width = 414.000000000000000000
      Size.Height = 44.000000000000000000
      Text = 'iOS phone'
    end
  end
end
```

You can easily spot that the iPhone55in string is appended to the name of the form (and the form's class name in the **FMX** file) in order to distinguish the fragments of visual definitions across different views. The iPhone view automatically applies the iOS style to the form so, for example, the ToolBar1 height has changed accordingly (from being set to 40 in the Master view to a value of 44 in the iPhone view). The Width value of the toolbar also changed because of the different screen resolution set for the iPhone 5.5" view (notice the ClientHeight and ClientWidth property values in the preceding FMX file snippet).

As you can observe from the FMX file of the iPhone view, object definitions are not introduced with the object keyword, but through an *inherited* one. This basically means that all properties set in the Master view still stand and this local definition is going to override some property values or specify a number of new property settings.

The single, manually entered, change you can also observe in the **FMX** file (and looking at the previous pictures) is that I changed the Text property of the Text1 component from Master title to iOS phone in the iPhone-specific view.

Following the same process, I've also created an Android 5" device-specific view, where the Text1.Text property has been set to Android phone to differentiate it. In the following code snippet, you can find the content of the corresponding **FMX** file:

```
inherited MainForm_LgXhdpiPh: TMainForm_LgXhdpiPh
  ClientHeight = 695
  ClientWidth = 450
  DesignerMasterStyle = 0
  inherited ToolBar1: TToolBar
    Size.Width = 450.000000000000000000
    Size.Height = 48.000000000000000000
    inherited Text1: TText
      Size.Width = 450.000000000000000000
      Size.Height = 48.000000000000000000
      Text = 'Android phone'
    end
  end
end
```

The same differences we noted in relation to the iPhone are now tailored for the Android 5" device. It is easy to run this application against three different platforms (Windows, iOS, and Android) and notice the differences. I've said Windows platform even if I have not created a specific view for the Windows Desktop entry: it is not mandatory to have a specific view for each supported platform. Where a specific view is not available, the Master view will be used. Please note also that there is a matching algorithm to select the best view for the actual use case, so the Android phone view will also be used for an Android tablet (if a superior match, such as a tablet-specific view, is not provided).

Another functionality delivered through the use of device-specific views is the ability to easily mimic orientation changes for mobile devices (that otherwise could have been simulated by manually resizing the form, swapping the Width and Height values).

The Multi-Device Preview window

Given that FMX and the Delphi IDE allow us to design views with device-specific variations, it may be challenging to keep everything under control. A very significant aid for this is provided by the **Multi-Device Preview IDE** tool window, located in the same tab control of **Project Manager** in the IDE window.

In a single spot, you can have a rendering of the current form against a number of selected devices (against the fact that you can design only one view at the time).

The following screenshot shows the **Multi-Device Preview** window with the example seen in the previous section:

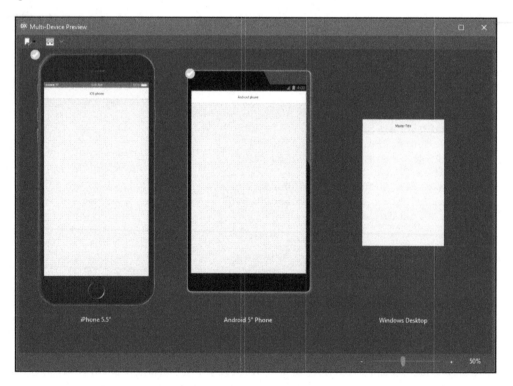

Figure 9.21

The preceding screenshot, where the **Multi-Device Preview** window has been undocked from its original position, shows how the IDE is capable, in real time at design time, of previewing how the specific views will look like at runtime (the *yellow-white checkmark* on the upper-left corner of the first two previews is there to indicate that those are actually created views while the third one, **Windows Desktop**, shows how the Master view would fit the device). The two buttons available in the toolbar at the top of the window will let you determine which views to include in the rendering and how to visually arrange them.

I've often said that design-time support is an important advantage in terms of the effectiveness of the developer and Delphi shines in this regard in a number of ways. **Multi-Device Preview** is clearly part of the RAD nature of Delphi in a multi-platform context.

Using the FireUI Live Preview app

In the previous section, we learned about the Multi-Device Preview IDE functionality. However, there is another element of FireUI that will let you have a preview of your under-design forms on multiple devices at the same time.

The FireUI Live app is a multi-platform application that Embarcadero ships together with Delphi both in compiled form for desktop platforms (through installers located in the `C:\Program Files (x86)\Embarcadero\Studio\21.0\LivePreview` folder) and with full source code (located in the `C:\Program Files (x86)\Embarcadero\Studio\21.0\source\Tools\FireUIAppPreview` folder).

Being a regular FMX application, having the source code means you can immediately build and deploy it for every platform your Delphi version supports. The application's aim is to render, in real time, while you are designing your form and UI in the IDE, the same UI over other multiple devices (especially possible target devices such as smartphones, mobile devices, desktop workstations running Windows, **Mac OS X/macOS**, or **Linux** operating systems).

The following screenshot shows the Delphi IDE in the background with a running instance of the **LivePreview** application (Windows version) showing a preview of the same form visible in **Form Designer**:

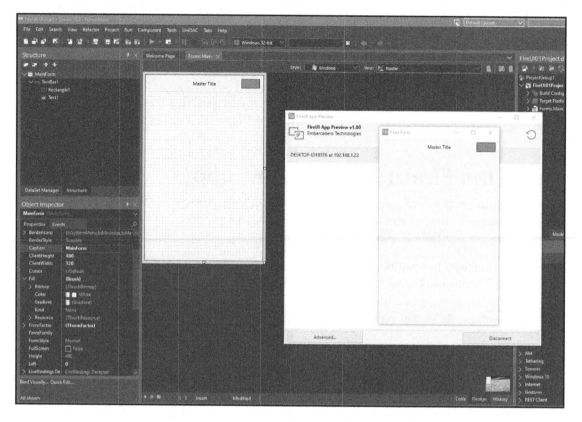

Figure 9.22

The Delphi IDE basically acts like a server broadcasting the **FMX** file (component definitions, plus possibly other design-time information) of the current file, to client applications (**FireUI App Preview** instances). The client applications will be able to render all standard components (obviously, no code will be executed or transferred; we are talking about UI definition information that's stored in the **FMX** file, and not the **PAS** file).

The following screenshot shows the same **FireUI App Preview** application but in its macOS X/macOS version, previewing the very same form as *Figure 9.22*:

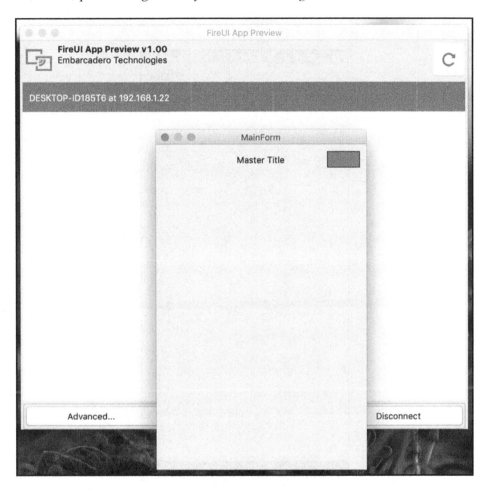

Figure 9.23

As has been said previously, you can deploy **Fire UI App Preview** to mobile platforms as well, and the following screenshot shows the preview of our form on the Android platform, through the **LivePreview** app that I built and deployed to my Pixel 3a device using Delphi itself:

Figure 9.24

A number of reasons make this functionality really important for FMX multi-platform development. For example, it would be impossible for **Multi-Device Preview** (the functionality we discussed earlier) to render a native control (we introduced this in Chapter 7, *Understanding FMX Style Concept*). The IDE runs on the Windows platform, so it would only be able to represent Windows-native controls. Think about UIs, including components where the ControlType property has been set to Native. *How would it be possible to render them on a different platform?*

The following screenshot shows **FireUI App Preview**, previewing a form with `TEdit` set to use the native controls (notice the Windows 10 localized full pop-up menu instead of the FMX standard one):

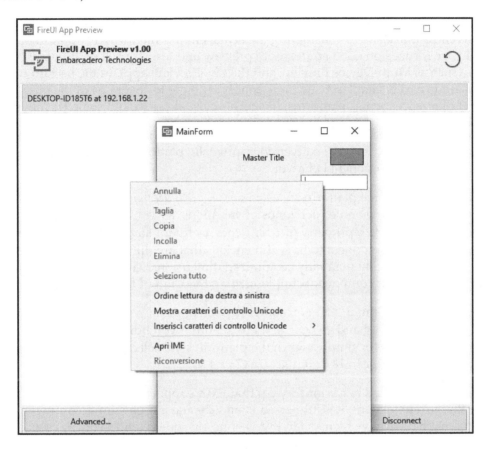

Figure 9.25

Other physical characteristics of the device may actually be needed to test your UI. *Remember, in the first part of the chapter, when I was talking about environmental luminosity and similar situations? How would you replicate those factors in the IDE?*

Having the possibility to stream (*in real time!*) your UI design to a physical device (or even multiple ones at the same time) can be a game changer for the whole team (developer, designer, graphic designer, tester) striving to achieve responsiveness.

This tool can also be very effective in the prototyping phase, where many subjects (including even the final user) may be at some stage.

Considering other FireUI capabilities

Earlier in this chapter, we discussed some of the many factors that responsiveness can be related to. One of the central arguments is the positioning and sizing of elements (that's why we spent some time on multi-res bitmaps, alignment strategies, anchors, and layouts). **Responsiveness** is also about considering the actual environment where applications live. That's why we focused on good strategies to preview and test your UI on different scenarios (such as Multi-Device Preview and the LivePreview app). In the background (as we discussed in earlier chapters), the **Style** concept is there to cover one of the most significant differences across platforms: the general visual aspect and some UI conventions.

There are, however, aspects that are hard to catch even when using all these technologies altogether. For example, some UI conventions are really platform-specific and need to be cooked down inside component behavior.

For example, even if native platform styles (Chapter 7, *Understanding FMX Style Concept*) may be able to internally handle such kinds of variations, a PlatformDefault property has been added to the Size property of TControl, useful for stating that the developer wants that particular component to have dimensions that are different from one platform to another, rather than having manually customized dimensions. This may be handy for buttons, edits, and other components implementing this kind of functionality.

For example, when you put a TButton component on a Master view, you can read (and see) that Width is set to 80 and Height is set to 22. But if you build and run your application on Android (or simply switch the platform style selector in the IDE), you'll see your button with a significantly different size (73 x 44).

This is due to the so called behavior services that FMX supports. A component can be aware of the current scenario it is immersed in and change its behavior accordingly. Differently to what we have seen so far, this is done via code (I tend to always separate behavior from presentation, drawing a line between code and visual definitions).

The TControl.GetDefaultSize method, for instance, is implemented by several visual components and some of them, such as TCustomButton descendants, make use of the behavior services in their implementation. One of the most elementary strategies is to provide different values for the default size according to the actual running platform.

A component may access the default behavior manager using the singleton `TBehaviorServices.Current` (in the `FMX.BehaviorService.pas` file) and query for a specific service implementation. The list of available services to query includes `IStyleBehavior`, `IDeviceBehavior`, and `IFontBehavior`. `IDeviceBehavior`, for instance, may be used to determine the current platform (Windows, OS X/macOS, iOS, Android, Linux, and more), the class of the device (phone, tablet, watch, and more) or specific display metrics of the current device (screen resolution, density, scale, font scale, form factor, and so on).

Another obvious example regarding the use of behavior services is the implementation FMX provides to properly handle a significant difference in the interpretation of a common component such as `TTabControl` by the two most popular mobile platforms (iOS and Android). On an iPhone, the user will expect tabs of a `TTabControl` component to be on the bottom side of the control, while an Android user will expect the exact contrary, looking for tabs at the top side of the control.

FMX solves this inherent difference between the behavior of this ubiquitous component by adding a `TabPosition` property to the component, but also having an entry for the available values that is `PlatformDefault`. This means that the developer can willingly determine the tab's position (and possibly differentiate it using FireUI device-specific views), but also that there's a built-in implementation that, being aware of the actual execution context, can determine the correct value to use as the default for the `TabPosition` property.

The following diagram shows how the very same UI changes just switch the native platform style selector in the IDE Form Designer (that also affects the behavior services, of course):

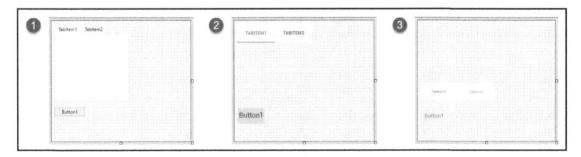

Figure 9.26

As you can see, the changes in the UI are due to switching the native style selector in the IDE, selecting Windows (**1**), Android (**2**), and iOS (**3**), respectively.

Another component that we already encountered in Chapter 4, *Discovering Lists and Advanced Components*, and that is taking advantage of behavior services is TMultiView. A single component (panel) is then able to deal with some significant variations in conventions across device types (phones versus tablets) or orientations (portrait versus landscape with a tablet).

These may appear to be trivial examples, but they add up to the whole set of capabilities the FMX framework has for supporting cross-platform development. The final application gains much in quality and usability thanks to the built-in capabilities (and so is applied everywhere in the application, effortlessly) and the developer still has full control over every aspect of the application (eventually being able to tune things differently where needed).

In this section, we learned about the FireUI technology. We also created a new view and learned how to use the Multi-Device Preview window along with the FireUI Live Preview app.

In the next section, we will explore the TFormStand component.

Exploring TFormStand

Chapter 8, *Divide and Conquer with TFrameStand*, was dedicated to TFrameStand. There are mechanisms in TFrameStand that are useful for gaining visual responsiveness in your applications (such as the TFrameStand.OnGetFrameClass event, to name just one, that allows you to replace at runtime the actual frame class used, for example, with a more appropriate descendant one).

However, Embarcadero's FireUI technology is targeting forms and there is no support for frames in FireUI at the time I am writing this. This pushed me to implement a twin component, TFormStand, aiming at using forms instead of frames mostly because this would have enabled FireUI technology.

This actually happened and you can now mix all the benefits of TFrameStand with those of FireUI. For instance, you can check the TFormStand_HelloWorld demo, where SecondForm is coming with a specific view for Android devices.

The following screenshot shows the same application (`FormStandHelloWorld.dproj`) running on two different platforms:

Figure 9.27

As you can see, the **TFormStandHelloWorld** application is running on two different platforms, Windows (**1**) and Android (**2**), taking advantage of the FireUI technology.

As has already been stated while discussing `TFrameStand`, by using `TFormStand`, you will be able to do the following:

- Take advantage of FireUI technology to achieve responsiveness for your applications (does not apply to `TFrameStand`)
- Keep resource usage low at runtime as views can be dynamically created on demand (and manage their lifespan through `TFormStand`)
- Promote the reusability of your UI views, thereby achieving visual continuity
- Properly master the complexity and maintainability of your projects
- Add animations and transitions across your mobile applications (a crucial point regarding mobile usability and the general appeal of your mobile applications).

TFormStand will also add the ability to mimic the missing Align property, a form inside another container. Through the use of a custom attribute, you can drive the alignment of a form in its new parent (that is the base mechanism of TFormStand, as TFrameStand does for frames). Similar support has been provided for another missing property in TForm: ClipChildren.

TFormStand is part of the TFrameStand project, free to use (even in commercial projects) and open source. The project is currently hosted on GitHub at https://github.com/andrea-magni/TFrameStand. It is also available through Embarcadero GetIt (https://getitnow.embarcadero.com/?q=tframestand), the official package manager for Delphi.

Summary

In this chapter, we have addressed one of the most important success factors in terms of a multi-platform, multi-device application, that is, responsiveness, from a visual point of view. We have defined and reviewed the possible factors involved. We have learned how to leverage some of them in order to provide a better UI in terms of responsiveness.

Lastly, we have acquired confidence in a number of technologies (including layout components, FireUI capabilities, and the TFormStand component) to properly address the issues associated with achieving responsiveness in visual applications.

In the next chapter, we'll focus on a topic that is somehow related, as it has something to do with a very natural aspect of mobile applications (although desktop applications are also increasingly evolving this way): animations and transitions. Your multi-platform, multi-device application will have to fulfill the expectations of final users in terms of usability, and part of this comes through the use of meaningful transitions. At the same time, the aesthetic argument about them is also a factor when it comes to making your application successful and appreciated.

10
Orchestrating Transitions and Animations

In the previous chapter, we learned how to build responsive **User Interfaces (UIs)** in order to deliver the best possible user experience in every scenario.

In this chapter, we will provide a full overview of **FireMonkey's** capabilities so that you can add animations and transitions to your multi-platform applications.

We have already mentioned a number of success factors for multi-platform applications, ranging from coherent stylization (with respect to the target platform or company requirements) to responsiveness (from a visual point of view). Another very important aspect is the presence of meaningful transitions in our applications. It has been quite some time since graphics animations were introduced in computer programming, even for business applications. However, recently, given that UIs are becoming minimalistic, especially on mobile platforms, this aspect has become more and more important.

The term *meaningful transition* stresses that this is not a mere aesthetic concern. Instead, we are aiming to deliver some meaning through the proper use of animations in our UI.

This may have something to do with the visual continuity concept we discussed in `Chapter 7`, *Understanding the FMX Style Concept*, as well as the fact that reducing UIs so that they fit small displays and touch-enabled devices sometimes requires we take advantage of the visual path we use in our apps to go from view A to view B. Regardless, this is related to differences in content or to the feedback that's gathered from actions being performed.

In this chapter, we will cover the following topics:

- Introducing animations and transitions
- Learning about interpolation
- Learning about the TAnimation class

Once you've read this chapter, you will have a good understanding of how animations are integrated within the FMX framework. You'll also be able to use them and tune them as per your needs in order to deliver modern UIs.

It will be quite challenging to explain animations in a printed book, but with the help of some pictures and code examples that you can run on your computer, you should be fine.

Let's get started!

Technical requirements

The following link will take you to the source code that will be used throughout this chapter: `https://github.com/PacktPublishing/Delphi-GUI-Programming-with-FireMonkey/tree/master/Chapter%2010`.

Generally speaking, for the entirety of this book, you'll need a computer with Delphi set up and ready to go, as well as a few additional libraries installed (such as **Radiant Shapes** (`https://getitnow.embarcadero.com/?q=radiant+shapes`) and **CodeSite Logging** (`https://getitnow.embarcadero.com/?q=codesite`)). Having other devices and setting up multiple platforms (iOS, Android, macOS/OS X, and Linux) other than Windows is a plus, but not strictly needed to follow the flow of this book.

Introducing animations and transitions

Modern UIs have plenty of animations. Today, many visual elements are enriched due to transitions, which means that lateral panels, menus, and more are now closed and opened through fancy, smooth visual transitions. It has not always been like that, though.

Basically, if we reduce our programming world to the iterative and discrete model, we can understand what it would mean to change the size of a panel from 300 pixels down to 80 pixels. Most programmers would come up with some kind of loop code instead of a single step to change the value, as the following snippet of (pseudo) code tries to exemplify:

```
// one step change:
MyPanel.Width := 80;

// multi-step change:
while MyPanel.Width > 80 do
  MyPanel.Width := MyPanel.Width -1;
```

From the preceding code, you can see that a number of under-the-hood aspects are involved here. For example, it may not be granted that assigning a new value to the `Width` property will cause the component to redraw itself (so that the user will see the change step by step in the second scenario).

Also, in contrast to the VCL framework, we have seen that FMX uses floating-point values for properties such as `Width`. *So, is how many steps that are performed an arbitrary choice of the developer? Why 220 (300 to 80 pixels) steps rather than 2,200 steps of 0.1 pixels in size?*

Moreover, if the UI framework is designed to use a single-threaded message loop-based system to keep the UI updated, we may never see the intermediate steps being rendered as the code detailing them is the current code being executed (preventing the code in charge of repaint from stepping in). I am pretty sure that the experienced VCL developers reading this are thinking about calling `MyPanel.Update` to force the component to repaint itself, possibly in conjunction with `Application.ProcessMessages` to let the application respond to repainting messages.

What if painting the step is time-consuming? Let's say the duration of each repaint depends on the specific step or similar factors. What if it is not even constant in terms of duration? Our transition will suffer a lot from these factors as it won't be as smooth as we want it to be. Ideally, we want to define a transition that has a constant duration that's independent of the environment (the computational power of the actual machine, the status of the system load, and other concurrent code executions taking place in our own application) and is smooth. To be smooth, a visual transition needs to have a good frame rate. The human eye can perceive 10 to 12 images per second as distinct still frames. Higher frame rates are perceived as motion.

In the next section, we'll learn about **interpolation**, which is a technique that's used to build intermediate values across two values (begin and end values, for instance). Being able to properly build intermediate values is a key concept when it comes to implementing animations in software.

Learning about interpolation

In this section, we will learn about interpolation. We will also have a look at non-linear interpolations so that we gain an in-depth understanding of the topic. We will then build a demo project to demonstrate what we have learned.

To define animations using a constant duration, we need to move from our *number of steps* concept to a time-framed concept. We want to change the value of our **Width** property from **300** to **80** within a certain time period (1 second).

The other change we need to acknowledge is the one from iterative or imperative programming to a more event-driven approach; that is, in a time period starting from a certain point in time and within a defined duration, each X milliseconds, we want to use some code. This code will calculate the current value our **Width** property should have at this moment in time. This process is called **interpolation**.

The following graph shows this interpolation process:

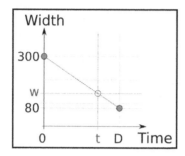

Figure 10.1

As you can see, we have two values at the extremes of an interval (**300, 80**). Here, we want to infer (one or more) values in-between (*w*). By following this model, we can understand how FMX animations work. The most elementary way to interpolate between two values is by using linear interpolation, which is equivalent to making the assumption that the change is evenly distributed. The following formula interpolates a single value between two extremes:

$$w = 300 + (80 - 300) * N(t)$$
$$N(t) = \frac{t}{D}$$

Figure 10.2

From the preceding equation, we can see that *N(t)* is a normalized time over the duration (so, *N(t)* is 0 at the beginning of the animation and 1 at the end).

This formula gives us the ability to determine the correct value for **Width** at any time during the animation period. What we need now is some mechanism to trigger the calculation with proper timing so that we can achieve a sufficient frame rate. FMX uses a timer based on `FMX.Types.TTimer`, except when it comes to the **Android** platform. In the case of Android, a special inherited class called `FMX.Ani.TThreadTimer` is used that relies on a background thread instead of the messaging mechanism.

So, in the FMX framework, there is a global timer that's used for all animations that periodically notifies all running animations that it is time to execute the next step in the process. As we've already mentioned, FMX and most UI frameworks out there, including VCL, are designed around the concept of a single thread running the UI.

Due to this, if you have many animations or their steps are time-consuming – or even because of other factors including the general system load – the statistical distribution representing the *event animation's turn to implement the next step* will not be uniform. What actually happens is that, after a certain amount of (normalized) time has passed, the animation is notified it is time to update. Take a look at the following graph and see if you can spot the time frames tagged **a**, **b**, **c**, **d**, and **e**:

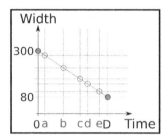

Figure 10.3

You can think of the spotted letters as the real moment, given that they are not equally distributed. This is because they are fired by a timer with a defined interval, so the animation should perform a step. The timer will know of the actual values for the time frames (such as the moment the animation starts), so along with the interpolation formula we discussed previously, it will be easy to find the actual values for **Width** at each time.

Now that we've covered basic interpolation, we will go a little further and consider that linear interpolation is just one (and the simplest) of the interpolation functions that's out there. In the next section, we will learn about non-linear interpolations.

Understanding non-linear interpolations

Given that interpolation occurs when you want to move from value A to value B, there are infinite ways to cover the path from A to B. In fact, some visual effects are implemented through non-linear animations. A number of real-world experiences are tied to quadratic equations – think about gravity or acceleration in general. Another huge set of cases are based on trigonometric functions such as *sine* and *cosine* – think about oscillations or springs.

A simple way to apply a modifier function to our interpolation is to transform its argument – time. We've already introduced the concept of normalized time over a duration period – N(t) – ranging from 0 to 1.

Now, think about what would happen if, instead of using a linearized interpolation of time, you substituted it with a non-linear one. The values of the interpolation will vary accordingly, without changing the interpolation formula itself. Following our example, I've prepared the following table with values of **Width** over a time period of 1 second, with 10 frames applied. So, ideally, the timer interval will be set to 0.1 seconds here:

Width	N(t)	I(N(t))	Quad(N(t))	I(Quad(N(t)))
300	0,000	300,00	0,000	300,00
	0,100	278,00	0,010	297,80
	0,200	256,00	0,040	291,20
	0,300	234,00	0,090	280,20
	0,400	212,00	0,160	264,80
	0,500	190,00	0,250	245,00
	0,600	168,00	0,360	220,80
	0,700	146,00	0,490	192,20
	0,800	124,00	0,640	159,20
	0,900	102,00	0,810	121,80
80	1,000	80,00	1,000	80,00

Table 10.1

As you can see, the interpolation function, I(), that was applied to the third and fifth columns gives us the same result. What changes here are the time values since they're passed through a quadratic function (check the fourth column for values) before being used for interpolation (the last column shows the interpolated values).

For formal completeness, here is the formula for I():

$$I(t) = A + (B - A) * t$$
$$A = initial\ value, B = final\ value$$

Figure 10.4

The following formula is for *Quad()*:

$$Quad(x) = C * x^2 + B$$
$$C = 1, B = 0$$

Figure 10.5

This is the formula for *N()*:

$$N(t) = t/D$$
$$D = duration$$

Figure 10.6

The effect of applying the quadratic function to time can be visually represented with the following graph:

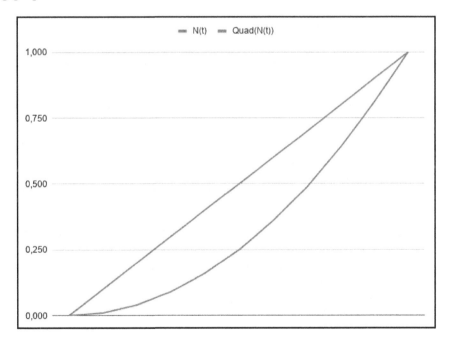

Figure 10.7

As you can see, the initial and final points are actually the same, even though we followed a different path to go from 0 to 1. To get a good idea of what we are doing here, take a look at the points where the two lines reach the value **0,500** and consider how late the **Quad(N(t))** function is with respect to **N(t)**. Of course, the X-axis is time (from 0 to the duration).

On the other hand, the following graph shows the effect of the interpolated data on the graph (once again, remember that the interpolation function, *I()*, is the same):

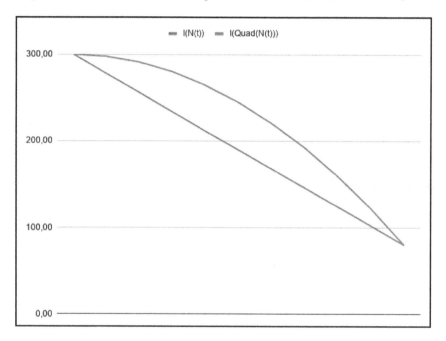

Figure 10.8

It is really important that the initial and final points are the same (thus fulfilling our wish to resize our panel from 300 pixels in width down to 80). However, the actual values that are used to implement the transition from the initial value to the final one are significantly different and will deliver a different feeling to the user. In the *Understanding interpolation modifier functions* section, we'll learn that FMX provides a number of interpolation modifier functions that are ready to use.

In order to explore the concepts we've covered so far, I've built a simple demo application called FMXAni. We'll look at it in the next section.

Working with the FMXAni demo project

The main form hosts two `TTrackBar` components, a rectangle with a red circle at the bottom-left corner, and some controls, as shown in the following screenshot:

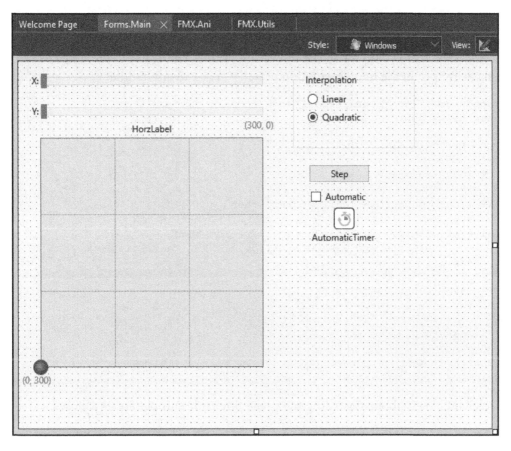

Figure 10.9

As you can see, the idea is to manually variate the **X** value (the `XTrackBar` control) and look at the resulting interpolated value on the `YTrackBar` value. At the same time, the **X** and **Y** values will be used to set the position of our red circle (over a rectangle that acts as a raw plot grid). The **X** value can range from **0** to **300** and two interpolation functions are available; that is, **Linear** and **Quadratic**. A **Step** button is available so that you can change the **X** value and add 1 to it, as well as an automated mechanism that is implemented using a checkbox and a `TTimer` component. This will range **X** from **0** to **300** with a 20-millisecond interval.

Every time the **X** value changes, we are going to calculate a new **Y** value via code (while considering the selected interpolation). We are also going to update some UI elements (such as the `PinLayout` component's position and the `HorzLabel.Text` property) to make all the internals evident to the watching user.

The following code snippet shows the `OnChange` event handler of the `XTrackBar` control. It is fired every time the user slides the handle of the `XTrackBar` component, when the user presses the **Step** button, and when the trackbar's value is changed by `AutomaticTimer` (as you can easily spot in the implementation of its `OnTimer` event handler):

```
procedure TMainForm.XTrackBarChange(Sender: TObject);
const MAX = 300;
var
  LX, LY: Single;
begin
  LX := XTrackBar.Value;

  if LinearIntRadioButton.IsChecked then
    LY := MAX - InterpolateLinear(LX, 0, 1, MAX) * MAX
  else if QuadraticIntRadioButton.IsChecked then
    LY := MAX - InterpolateQuad(LX, 0, 1, MAX, TAnimationType.&In) *
    MAX;

  PinLayout.Position.X := LX-1;
  PinLayout.Position.Y := LY-1;

  YTrackBar.Value := MAX - LY;

  HorzLabel.Text := Format('X: %.3f, Y: %.3f', [LX, MAX - LY]);
end;
```

Some relevant observations regarding the preceding code snippet are as follows:

- `PinLayout`: This is the name of a 2 x 2 `TLayout`. I've interposed between the rectangle and the red circle; this allows us to align the circle to the center of it and, at the same time, not have to deal with the actual size of the circle when positioning it. Those –1 subtractions are there to center `PinLayout` over the desired X and Y coordinates.
- `InterpolateLinear` and `InterpolateQuad`: These are part of the FMX framework (`FMX.Ani.pas`) and many others are available, as we'll see later in this chapter.

- `InterpolateQuad`: With respect to the previous function, this has an additional parameter, which is the animation type we want to apply; animation types are concerned with the interpolation modifier function. For the quadratic function, switching from `TAnimationType.In` to `TAnimationType.Out` basically rotates the curve so that it still passes from the origin and the point via (D, 1) coordinates.
- I've reversed the Y-axis (you should be able to see some *MAX - Y* expressions) to make the application more consistent with the graphs we implemented previously in this chapter, as well as with the general behavior of having the Y-axis growing upward. Computer graphics conventionally set the origin in the upper-left corner of the rectangle. Here, X grows to the right while Y grows to the bottom.
- Some of the functionalities that have been built into this demo actually overlap what we'll see in the remainder of this chapter (such as using the `TFloatAnimation` component). This has been done for educational purposes.

While trying out the demo, follow the red circle's trajectory (you can even switch the interpolation while automatic mode is running) and try using a different representation of the Y value with respect to the X value on the trackbars.

 As a simple exercise, add all the available interpolation modifier functions to this demo.

It will be evident how late the Y value follows the X one when the quadratic interpolation modifier is selected.

In this section, we learned about general interpolation. Then, we looked at non-linear interpolation. We also looked at a demo project so that we know how to implement and understand what's been covered so far.

Now that we've learned about the base concepts surrounding animations, we'll look at a very central class in the FMX framework when it comes to animations: `TAnimation` (*nomen est omen*).

Learning about the TAnimation class

The TAnimation class, which is contained in the FMX.Ani.pas source file, is a TFMXObject descendant and is the ancestor of TCustomPropertyAnimation (it is the ancestor of most animation components in FMX). This class also holds an instance of the global timer FMX uses to notify the running animations that time has passed.

In this section, we will learn about the TAnimation class, along with its inherited classes, in detail. We'll also learn about the global animation functions and interpolation modifier functions associated with it.

The TCustomPropertyAnimation descendant class uses **Run Time Type Information (RTTI)** functionalities to attach the animation to a specific property of the Parent component. This way, you can add a TCustomPropertyAnimation (descendant) to any FMX object and address one of the properties with the animation's execution. The ability to refer to the property by name (string) means you can configure the animation without needing to know the (low dependency) target component's internals.

Essentially, the TCustomPropertyAnimation class only adds a PropertyName property to TAnimation and implements the lookup of the target property by name (to support dotted syntax, as well to reference subfields of objects and components). If the defined name is not valid or cannot be resolved, calling the Start method on TAnimation will be ineffective. Further descendant classes (such as TFloatAnimation) will use the referenced property to set its value (via RTTI) while the animation runs.

In practical terms, to add an animation to an FMX object, simply choose a TCustomPropertyAnimation descendant from the component palette in the **integrated development environment** (**IDE**) and add it to your project. Be sure to parent it to the target component (I usually do this through the **Structure View** IDE window). By doing this, you'll be able to list all the compatible properties through the component editor that's provided for the PropertyName property of your animation. The following screenshot shows this behavior through the use of a **TButton** and the **TFloatAnimation** component:

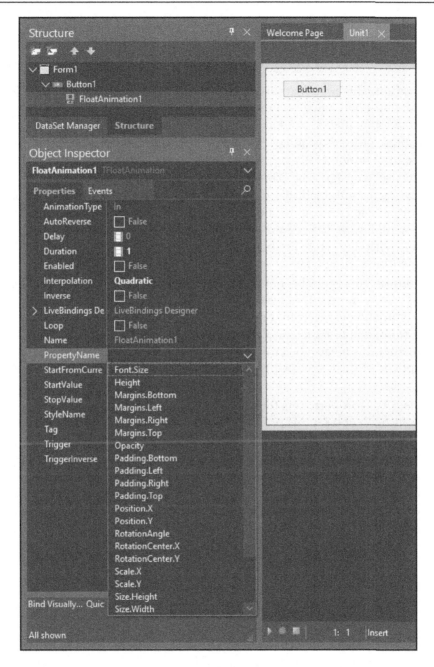

Figure 10.10

The responsibility of the `TAnimation` class is to provide some general infrastructure that's used by all descendant components (such as the `TFloatAnimation` component shown in the preceding screenshot). Let's take a look at its properties and events:

- **Duration**: This property expresses the duration, in seconds, of the animation. It is a floating-point value, so you can specify whatever amount of time you wish the animation to play for, not just integer values.
- **Enabled**: Strictly speaking, this property determines whether an animation can be started or not. However, the general understanding of this property is related to its use at design time. You can set **Enabled** to `True` if you want the animation to be started automatically once it's been loaded; if you turn this property from `True` to `False` at runtime, this will also cause the animation to start at that moment. Please don't confuse **Enabled** with the **Running** property (which has public visibility while **Enabled** is a published property) and think of **Enabled** as something stating whether this animation has to be started.
- **Running**: This is public, not published, and is why it's not listed in the **Object Inspector** window. This read-only property can be used to determine whether the animation is currently ongoing. The value of this property will be `True` when the animation is started and will hold this value until the end of the animation (whether this means the entire duration or if, for some reason, the animation is stopped before it can finish). A finished animation will have **Running** set to `False`.
- **Delay**: This property sets the time, in seconds, the animation will wait before executing. If you set this property to `1` (second) and call the `Start` method, the animation will do nothing until 1 second has passed.
- **Interpolation**: We've already discussed what interpolation means in terms of FMX animation support. This property will let you choose which interpolation modifier function will be applied to this specific animation. The available values are listed as follows. We are going to provide a more detailed explanation in the *Understanding interpolation modifier functions* section:
  - `Linear`
  - `Quadratic`
  - `Cubic`
  - `Quartic`
  - `Quintic`
  - `Sinusoidal`
  - `Exponential`
  - `Circular`

- Elastic
- Back
- Bounce

- **AnimationType**: This property is concerned with interpolation, and you can think of it as its modifier. In most cases, you can think of it as a choice of where to stress the interpolation between the starting and final value. The available values for this property are `In`, `Out`, and `InOut`. A more visual explanation of this property will be provided shortly.

- **Inverse**: You can set this property to `True` to invert the animation direction; specifically, what you are actually inverting is the time flow through the animation (you can easily prove this by printing the `NormalizedTime` value within the `OnProcess` event handler of an animation). This also implies that all animations are reversible.

- **Loop**: This boolean property determines whether the animation should be repeated in a loop once it's been started. Setting this property to `True` will cause the animation not to finish once the transition from the initial value to the final one has completed (or when `Duration` has expired). Usually, setting this property also has some implications on the next one in the list – that is, `AutoReverse` – as you may not want to blindly repeat the same transition from the same initial point to the target. This is exactly what happens by default when setting `Loop` to `True`.

- **AutoReverse**: As we have already seen, all animations can be inverted and can be configured to loop. The `AutoReverse` property sets the animation to automatically invert itself (by toggling the `Inverse` property) once the first run has finished. So, if you are transitioning a value from A to B, once B has been reached, the same animation (this time with `Inverse` set to `True`) will run the other way around; that is, from B to A. The resulting duration will follow the (eventual) `Delay` + `Duration` (A to B) + `Duration` (B to A) schema. Please note that no `Delay` will be applied before the second iteration; this functionality is generally tied to setting `Loop` to `True` (though it is not strictly related to it and will work independently nonetheless).

- **CurrentTime**: This read-only property will provide the current execution time of the animation; it will be 0 if the animation is not running. You can think of it as a stopwatch that's started when the actual transition begins (so `Delay` is never included). You will see this value grow when `Inverse` is `False` and shrink if it is `True` (this also happens when this is caused by the value of the `AutoReverse` property).

- **NormalizedTime**: As we've already discussed, applying interpolation functions to your animation is actually you applying a function to time through the animation. The `NormalizedTime` property gives you access to the current value of time, including the interpolation. If you compare `CurrentTime` and `NormalizedTime` while the animation is running, you will see differences (if any) between the actual time and the time that's used for interpolation (by using linear interpolation, you'll see coinciding values).
- **Pause**: The `Pause` property lets you hold the animation's execution while its value is `True`; you can set this property while the animation is running (or before).
- **OnProcess**: You can set a handler for the `OnProcess` event so that you're notified each time the animation is going to calculate a new step; in normal situations, this will happen often. The default frame rate for the animation is 60 and the interval for the global animation timer is set accordingly, so you can expect this event to be called 60 times per second. This is a good place to monitor the animation's `CurrentTime` or `NormalizedTime` property values and use them for some additional purpose (synchronization, logging, and so on).
- **OnFinish**: When the animation has gone through all the intermediate steps and the current value of our transition coincides with the final desired value set for the animation (we'll cover this later in the *Learning about specialized animation components* section), that's the time the `OnFinish` event gets fired.

This event can come in handy when you're dealing with asynchronous animations – those you start but are not waiting to finish before you do something else in the application – as you have to delegate the execution of your code once the animation has completed. Keep in mind that only the `OnFinish` event occurs once. This means that if you pause the animation – even multiple times – during the same execution, the `OnFinish` event won't be fired. The same applies to the use of the `AutoInverse` property, which, when set to `True`, basically causes the animation to run twice but will not cause the `OnFinish` event to fire twice.

Now that we know what `TAnimation` represents and have learned about its properties, let's take a closer look at the global animation timer and the global frame rate setting.

Understanding global animation management

As we've already discussed, the model for FMX animations relies on the presence of a global timer that periodically pings active animations to solicit each to perform the next step (providing a delta amount of time to cover in the animation).

This timer is usually created using the `IFMXTimerService` provider, which is platform-specific and built into the FMX framework. You can query an `IFMXTimerService` reference through `TPlatformServices.Current` in the `FMX.Platform` unit. For the Android platform, a different, more thread-oriented, path has been chosen for implementing the timer. Apart from this small detail, animations will be consistent across all supported platforms (a huge advantage for the developer) and will follow the model we've described so far.

A reference to the global timer is available through the `TAnimation.AniThread` property (an instance is created on-demand, generally at the start of the first animation). Its interval property value will be set according to the `AniFrameRate` value (see the `TAnimation.AniFrameRate` property and its default value, `TAnimation.DefaultAniFrameRate`, which is typically set to `60`).

You can set this property to a different value if you like. If you do, take note of the differences between animation executions. Keep in mind that there are some forced limits regarding the value of the property; for example, the minimum value is 5 (regardless of what lower value you set in your code), while the maximum value is 100. Generally speaking, if you want a timer event to be fired X times per second, a good strategy is to set the interval so that there is room for it to be fired at least X times per second. For example, if you want a frame rate of 60, you may want to follow this pseudocode:

```
var LFrameRate := 60;
var LInterval := 1000 / LFrameRate; // numeric value = 16.667
LInterval := LInterval / 10; // numeric value = 1.667
LInterval := Trunc(LInterval); // numeric value = 1
LInterval := LInterval * 10; // numeric value = 10
```

Setting the `Interval` property to `10` milliseconds would theoretically mean having a frame rate of 100. This is perfectly fine if we're following the general background assumption that FMX animations are designed to be time-consistent (with respect to their duration), and this can be achieved without strictly enforcing the desired frame rate.

In the next section, we'll delve into interpolation modifier functions. These determine how the transition from the initial value to the final one is made. We introduced this in the *Learning about interpolation* section, so now, we are going to learn how to tune the animation using different kinds of interpolation.

Understanding interpolation modifier functions

Earlier, we discussed how interpolation works and how it's implemented in the FMX framework. As you may have experienced, these topics can be hard to follow without some visual examples (possibly live), but at the same time, a more mathematical approach can be more precise. This section intends to look at both sides of the coin by using images to explain the mathematical concepts behind interpolations.

The following screenshots show the different behaviors of all the interpolation modifier functions. The large red circle is positioned at the final spot, while the smaller red dots are used to represent the trajectory that was followed during the animation.

 Please note that the `Opacity` property of these dots has been set incrementally (reflecting the normalized time) so that you can follow the dynamic while looking at the point's opacity value. For each function, three screenshots have been provided. The left one is for when `AnimationType = In`, the central one is for when `AnimationType = Out`, and the last one is for when `AnimationType = InOut`. These screenshots were individually generated using the `PlaygroundProject` application (the source code for this has been included in this book's GitHub repository).

In the following image, you can see the rendering for **Linear** interpolation:

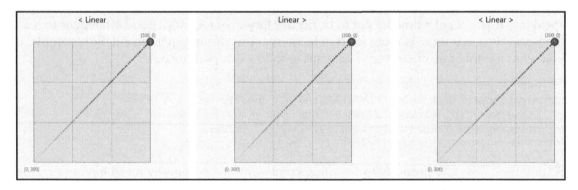

Figure 10.11

Linear interpolation is very straightforward to understand. Here, you can see how proportionally distributed the red dots are throughout the transition. The shape of the graph suggests that each segment of the animation follows the same behavior and that a certain gap on the X-axis corresponds to the same gap on the Y-axis.

The following image shows **Quadratic** interpolation:

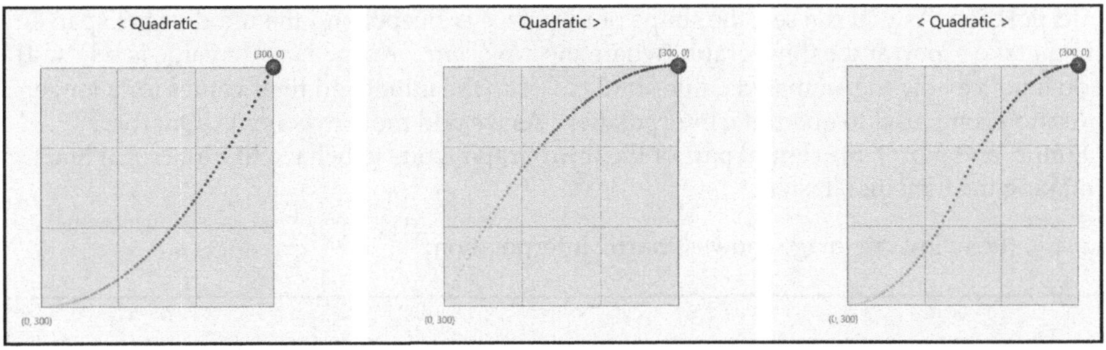

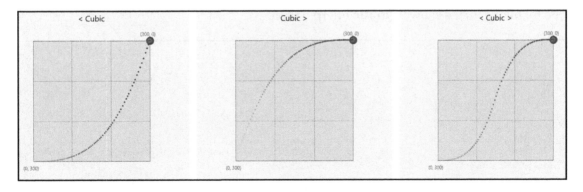

Figure 10.12

In real life, a number of situations involve quadratic equations (gravity above all and the motion/acceleration laws of physics in general). The graphs shown in the preceding image shows the typical parabolic behavior. Here, you can see how the distribution of the red dots differs at the beginning/end of the transition in all three cases (changing the `TAnimationType` argument).

There are many real-life examples of such behavior, and many users feel that this kind of transition is natural. A very common scenario is using a quadratic-shaped transition to change the opacity of UI elements to make them pop in/out of the user's view. Another very common example is to apply it to sliding UI elements, such as the pages of a tab control.

The following screenshot shows **Cubic** interpolation:

Figure 10.13

Cubic interpolation ($y=x^3$) is also very common and, together with other higher grade functions such as **Quartic** and **Quintic**, can be seen as a variation (*boostening*) of quadratic interpolation. As you can see, the shape of the curve is steeper and the red dots get sparser. If you take a look at the third graph (where the `TAnimationType.InOut` value is selected), you'll notice how the animated value stays closer to the initial and final values for a longer duration compared to quadratic interpolation. As we add more exponents (Quartic, Quintic, and more), the central part of the third graph tends to behave like a vertical line (making the transition faster).

Lastly, the following image shows **Quartic** interpolation:

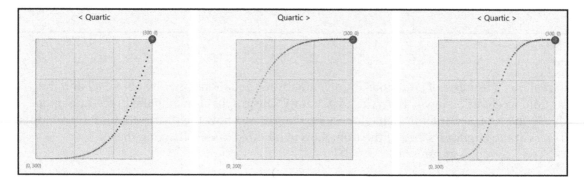

Figure 10.14

Similar to the cubic and quadratic interpolation functions, you can see the behavior of the **Quartic** ($y=x^4$) function. The same considerations that were made for cubic interpolation also apply here. As you can see, the curve is steeper with respect to lower-grade functions.

The following image shows **Quintic** interpolation:

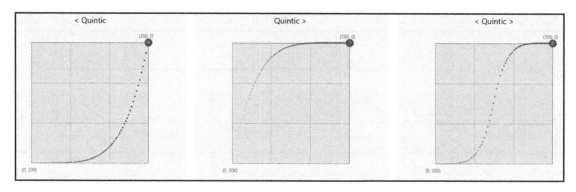

Figure 10.15

The last available interpolation related to polynomial equations is known as **Quintic** interpolation. Take a look at the first graph to understand how the behavior shown here is different with respect to the quadratic one; that is, at the first vertical divider (one third of the whole graph and thus the animation time), the animated value still seems to have the same value as the initial moment, though just a fraction greater. After the second divider, we are lower than one-sixth of the final value, but the function is growing faster and faster. In the third graph, more than 80% of the whole graph changes and becomes closer to the final value.

The following image shows **Sinusoidal** interpolation:

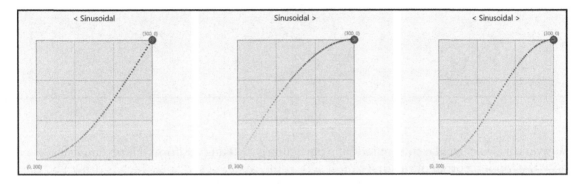

Figure 10.16

Trigonometric functions are very important and well-related to real-world situations. Using **Sinusoidal** interpolation means you can have variations in value, along with a null derivative at the endpoints (initial and final). This provides smooth effects where you can make a smooth transition and gently depart from the initial value to land at the final value.

The following image shows **Exponential** interpolation:

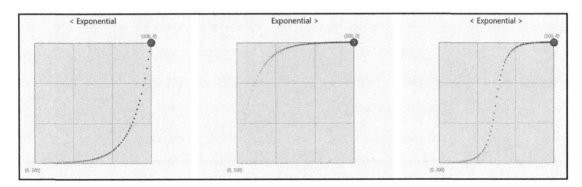

Figure 10.17

The **Exponential (y=1ˣ)** function is generally faster than other polynomial functions (as you can see by comparing the preceding image with the one for the Quintic function). It is a very common function and if useful when you're performing quick transitions.

The following image shows **Circular** interpolation:

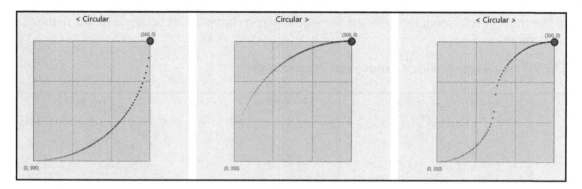

Figure 10.18

As you can see, **Circular** interpolation is particularly soft and uniform. Here, you can see how the top-left corner of the first graph acts as the center of the arc, which is drawn by the red dots marking the animation path. The same applies to the second graph but while considering the bottom-right corner. In the third graph, even though the dots are very sparse, you can think of the line connecting the dots as perfectly vertical in the middle of the range.

The following image shows **Elastic** interpolation:

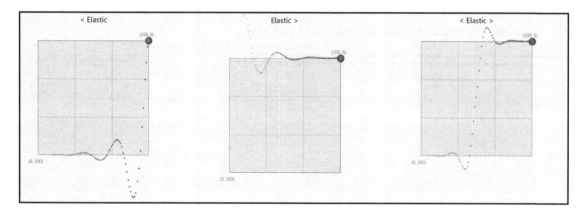

Figure 10.19

Apart from the classic mathematical functions, we also have other functions, such as the **Elastic** one. Its shape immediately recalls the movements of something non-rigid. As you can see, the animated value can reach values lower than the initial value or higher than the final one. This may deliver some meaning to the user or add a nice effect to your transitions.

The following image shows **Back** interpolation:

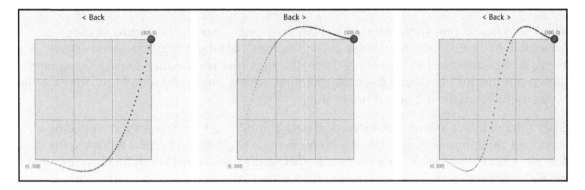

Figure 10.20

The **Back** interpolation function can be used to mimic the behavior of something being pulled back to some extent and then released. Many real-life mechanisms act this way, so you can find this interpolation function useful if you wish to mimic something similar in your UI elements.

The following image shows **Bounce** interpolation:

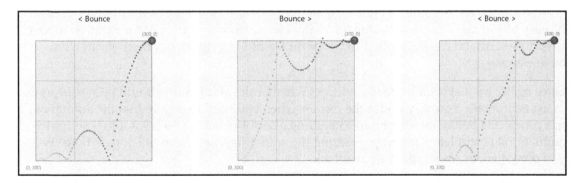

Figure 10.21

The final interpolation function we'll be looking at here is known as the **Bounce** function. As you can see, it immediately recalls how a golf or tennis ball bounces on a hard surface. This can be used to achieve effects where the initial (or final) value is reached multiple times before the animation is completed.

It is easy to take linear interpolation as a reference and measure the others accordingly. You can always image/visualize the diagonal line of the square to see if the current interpolation is faster (stays over the diagonal) or slower (stays under the diagonal) at a specific point.

The X-axis here is time (not distorted and covers a range from the beginning of the animation to the end, which makes it `Duration` long). Most of the interpolations never break the boundaries of the linear one (visually, all points are included in the gray square). This is not true for Elastic and Back interpolation, where, during the animation, the current value may slip off the initial and final value.

Even though I have a strong mathematical background due to my education and being a computer programmer means I deal with math regularly, I find it helpful to look at these kinds of visual diagrams so that it's easy to choose the best interpolation function for what I need.

Now that we have learned about the various interpolation functions we can use to fine-tune the behavior of the transition we want to implement, we'll learn about trigger animations. In the next section, we are going to understand how the FMX framework allows developers to animate whatever property they want programmatically.

Learning about TAnimator shortcuts

Now that we have introduced all the capabilities of `TAnimation`, you may think it should be easy to animate a property value for FMX objects. However, the FMX animation model is very generic and can be applied to whatever Delphi objects are out there (from UI to business classes).

Once again, we just need to clearly address whether the animations should be synchronous or asynchronous. You may prefer the former when you need to ensure that the animation has completed before moving on to something else. Obviously, you'll want to wait for the animation to complete without preventing the animation itself from finishing; otherwise, you'd be stuck in an infinite wait deadlock.

The second kind of execution (asynchronous) also has some tricky aspects that we need to deal with. *If you launch (one or more) animations and you want to continue doing other things without waiting for them to complete, who will take care of them once they've finished? If you dynamically create them, who'll be responsible for their life management (destruction)?*

The TAnimator class (in the FMX.Ani unit) is there to help you handle most simple cases. Apart from some helper methods such as StartAnimation and StopAnimation, which will begin or stop a named preexisting animation in a certain target component, there are a number of helper methods that may come in handy to help you perform one-shot animations via code. Some of these helper methods are as follows:

- The AnimateFloat method animates the value of a floating-point numerical property over time and through a specific interpolation.
- The AnimateFloatDelay method is similar to the AnimateFloat method, except it also adds an initial delay before starting the process.
- The AnimateInt method animates the value of an integer's numerical property over time and through a specific interpolation.
- The AnimateColor method animates the value of a color property over time and through a specific interpolation.
- The AnimateFloatWait method is similar to the AnimateFloat method, except it performs the operation synchronously (the method call will only return after the animation process has come to an end).
- The AnimateIntWait method is similar to the AnimateInt method, except it performs the operation synchronously (the method call will only return after the animation process has come to an end).

The method names that have *Wait* as a suffix indicate that the method will synchronously wait for the animation to complete. You should avoid them, especially on mobile platforms, as Wait is basically a while loop calling Application.ProcessMessages and a Sleep(0) to promote context switching. My suggestion is to go async as much as possible and take advantage of TAnimator, which will take care of TAnimation instances that are created under the hood to accomplish your needs.

The following code snippet exemplifies how to grow the width of a button by adding 25% of its current width. I've chosen Back interpolation here, set the AnimationType argument to Out, and defined a duration of 1 second:

```
TAnimator.AnimateFloat(
  Button1, 'Width'
, Button1.Width * 1.25
, 1
, TAnimationType.&Out
, TInterpolationType.Back
);
```

The preceding one-liner will cause the `Width` property of `Button1` to transition from its actual value to 125% of it, asynchronously. If you add a second call for addressing `Height`, you'll notice that both animations take place at the same time:

```
TAnimator.AnimateFloat(
  Button1, 'Height'
, Button1.Height * 1.25
, 1
, TAnimationType.&Out
, TInterpolationType.Back
);
```

The final effect is a joint growth of the `Width` and `Height` properties of the button, along with a nice effect and a smooth run.

So far, we have discussed animations by following mathematical abstraction, which leads us to consider values as real numbers (floating-point values). This comes in handy in a number of situations since many of the properties in the FMX framework are implemented through real numbers (think of `Width`, `Height`, `Position.X`, `Position.Y`, `RotationAngle`, `Opacity`, and so on).

There are a number of other data types we might want to involve in transitions across time. Obviously, different data types means that there will be different intrinsic characteristics (possibly even different interpolation strategies), which means this topic can become more complicated.

We'll learn about specialized animation components in the next section.

Learning about specialized animation components

Let's take color transitions as an example. *How does a color shift from red to blue?* If you have a basic understanding of color representation in computer graphics, you can relate the transition to a **Red Green Blue (RGB)** representation, where the red, blue, and green components are represented by 8-bit values (ranging from 0 to 255).

This means that transitioning from red (255, 0, 0) to blue (0, 0, 255) can be seen as a double transition; that is, moving a red channel from 255 to 0 and the blue channel from 0 to 255, respectively. This is just one of the possible paths we can take, and this becomes evident if you imagine the RGB space as a cube where each point inside the cube is a color point (a different set of R, G, and B channel values); that is, between two points, there are infinite connecting paths.

This brings us back to the beginning of this chapter, where we defined animations as the process of moving from a starting *point* to a final one. This starting *point* can be a single numeric value (this is easy to explain with simple math, as we did in the previous section) or a more complex data structure (such as RGB triplets, a more complex matrix, bitmaps, data lists, and more).

FMX provides some components that specifically cover some common data structures that are used in visual programming. We are going to cover them briefly here before explaining them in more detail. They are all (but one!) descendants of the TCustomPropertyAnimation class, so they all intend to target the property of another component.

The property's type obviously matters and should match the specific component for the animation to be executed. The current (interpolated) value is generally not directly available by inspecting the TAnimation descendant instance alone, but you can generally access the value of the target property during the animation's execution if you need intermediate values.

> The IDE has integrated support for animations in FMX. Sometimes, you may see a film wheel icon near some values in the **Object Inspector** window. This means that a specialized animation is available for that value. The associate component editor, which is usually a picklist for available values, will also show additional entries to shortcut the creation of a new TAnimation descendant that addresses that property. You can see this icon near the Duration property in *Figure 10.10*.

As a side note, please remember that you can always instantiate these components dynamically in your code and that you are not necessarily forced to use them while using visual programming. A common case where I've seen animation in action is in simulation models where some parameters need to be changed dynamically. This had little to do with visual programming but it worked pretty well as a simple engine for simulation calculus.

The TAnimation inherited classes that are available in FMX are as follows:

- TFloatAnimation
- TFloatKeyAnimation
- TColorAnimation
- TColorKeyAnimation
- TGradientAnimation
- TRectAnimation
- TBitmapAnimation
- TBitmapListAnimation
- TPathAnimation

In the following sections, we are going to have a closer look at all the aforementioned TAnimation inherited classes.

TFloatAnimation

This animation targets floating-point values. It is commonly used since many FMX properties are floating-point values (the Single type specifically). We have already seen some simple examples of the Width, Height, and Position (X and Y) properties throughout this chapter. Opacity, RotationAngle, and Scale (X and Y) can also be used with this kind of animation.

We've already discussed that TCustomPropertyAnimation can address a sub-property (regardless of the nesting level) of the target component and that that's what you are actually doing by setting PropertyName to Position.X rather than Scale.Y. Even if more specific animation types are available (TRectAnimation), you can do this with respect to the Margins and Paddings properties of a TFMXObject. The difference is that you'll be handling sub-properties individually rather than addressing them as part of a larger data structure (TBounds).

TFloatAnimation has two Single type properties representing StartValue and StopValue. An additional StartFromCurrent Boolean property will instruct the animation as to whether it should read the value of the targeted property before starting the animation (and use it as StartValue) or use StartValue, as defined as design time (or set before calling the Start method).

TFloatKeyAnimation

TFloatAnimation implements animations going from A to B values. Sometimes, you need to cycle through a number of intermediate steps between the starting and final points. The TFloatKeyAnimation class implements this kind of animation, allowing you to define a list of pairs (key-value pairs).

If you set up *N* entries, they will be split up into a sequence of animations from A to B, B to C, C to D, and so on, up to *N-1* to *N* entries. The interpolation function will be applied globally but not to each segment of the animation. The key value is used to define at what point of the duration interval (using normalized time, in the 0 to 1 range) the value should be positioned.

In other words, you are not simply providing a list of values (that would be equally distributed across the 0 to Duration interval), but rather defining a segmentation of the duration period with a value associated with each section.

Let's consider the following TFloatKeyAnimation definition:

```
object FloatKeyAnimation1: TFloatKeyAnimation
  Enabled = True
  Duration = 3.000000000000000000
  Interpolation = Quadratic
  Keys = <
    item
      Value = 1.000000000000000000
    end
    item
      Key = 0.333299994468689000
      Value = 0.899999976158142100
    end
    item
      Key = 0.500000000000000000
      Value = 0.250000000000000000
    end
    item
      Key = 1.000000000000000000
      Value = 1.000000000000000000
    end>
  OnProcess = FloatKeyAnimation1Process
  PropertyName = 'Opacity'
  StartFromCurrent = False
end
```

As you can see, `TFloatKeyAnimation` has been attached to an FMX component (let's say a button) in order to set its `Opacity` property over a 3-second duration. Four keys have been defined – 0.0, 0.33, 0.5, and 1.0– basically adding two intermediate points between the initial and final values.

The `Quadratic` interpolation has been selected for this. Here, you can see the graph rendering the values that were assumed during the transition. Looking at the following graph, you may be a little puzzled as you might expect to see a correspondence between the key values (0, 0.33, 0.5, and 1) and the X-axis points where the line has singularities (0, 1.73, 2.14, and 3):

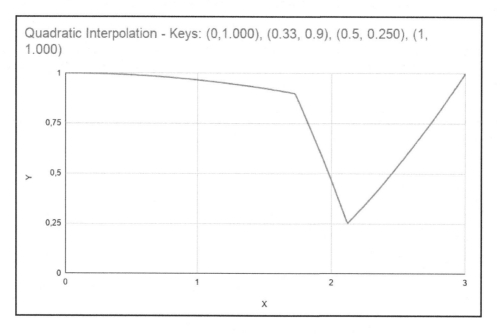

Figure 10.22

Remember, we applied interpolation (**Quadratic**) to the animation, so the X-axis (time) has been distorted accordingly. The following graph shows the same animation running with **Linear Interpolation** selected:

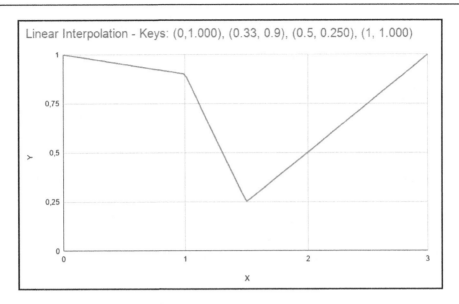

Figure 10.23

As you can see, this time, the key values (0, 0.33, 0.5, and 1) match the X-axis values (considering the `Duration` aspect of the animation has been set to 3 seconds), which are 0, 1.0, 1.5, and 3.

Remember that a sequence of *N* animations with the non-linear interpolation function applied is different from a single `TFloatKeyAnimation` with the same non-linear interpolation function applied. In the first case, interpolation would be applied to each animation, while in the second case, it would be applied globally.

TColorAnimation

The colors in FMX pass by some data types, namely `TAlphaColor`, `TAlphaColorRec`, and `TAlphaColorF`. They are all numerical representations of an **RGB + Alpha** interpretation of colors (this is a typical choice in visual programming).

The `TColorAnimation` component helps you implement color transitions between two colors. The interpolation is linear and is applied over the four color components (R, G, B and alpha channels) independently. I am not going to talk about color theory here; I just want you to understand that this is an arbitrary choice and that other interpretations exist **(Cyan, Magenta, Yellow, and Black (CMYK); Hue, Saturation, and Lightness (HSL); and Hue, Saturation, and Value (HSV)** are other such options).

If you set up a color animation going from red to blue, for instance, you can track the steps through the usual `OnProcess` event handler, as we did previously. The following table briefly shows the kind of result you may expect:

R	G	B
255	0	0
254	0	1
253	0	2
...	...	...
129	0	126
128	0	127
126	0	129
...	0	...
0	0	255

Table 10.2

As we've already discussed, different interpolation modifier functions can be applied to the animations (acting on the `time` component). The following graph renders the values of the RGB components while assuming the use of linear interpolation:

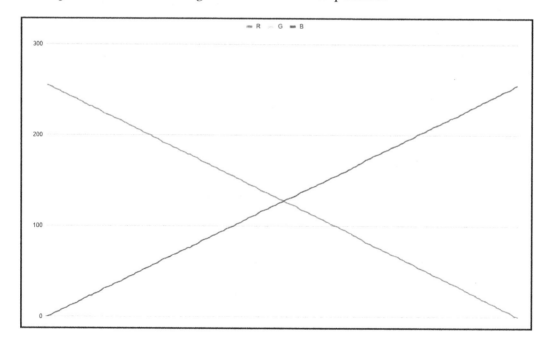

Figure 10.24

As you can see, the values of the blue channel are linearly growing with time, from 0 to the maximum value (255). On the other hand, the red channel is going in the opposite direction, while the green channel is constant, at 0.

Now, let's say you apply a quadratic interpolation to the graphic changes, as shown in the following graph:

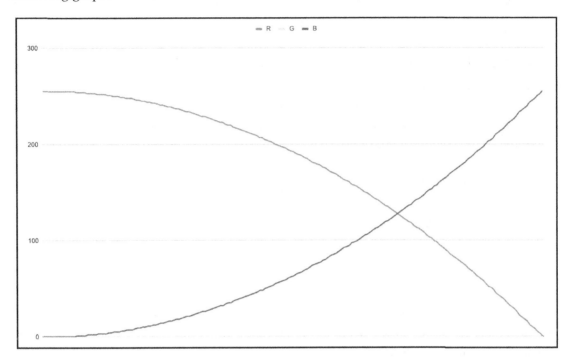

Figure 10.25

As you can see, by extension, you should be able to imagine another kind of interpolation being applied to this animation. However, it is very straightforward to drop a TRectangle on an FMX form, add a TColorAnimation targeting its Fill.Color property, and play with it to see it running.

TColorKeyAnimation

TColorKeyAnimation is related to TColorAnimation, in the same way TFloatKeyAnimation is related to TFloatAnimation. It can hold a sequence of key-value pairs in order to perform a multi-step animation through the values provided, using the key as a driver for distribution. The same considerations about interpolation we made for TFloatKeyAnimation are valid for TColorKeyAnimation too.

TGradientAnimation

We encountered gradients in Chapter 3, *Mastering Basic Components*, since FMX supports filling implemented through gradients natively. A dedicated data structure, TGradient, is defined in the FMX.Graphics unit. Design-time support has also been added to the IDE to deal with gradients in the Object Inspector window (using a dedicated property editor).

You can think of TGradientAnimation as something that naturally applies the animation concept to two different gradients. Unfortunately, even though FMX supports multi-step gradients, animations don't seem to deal with them properly, so at the moment, it's best to keep the initial and final gradients at the same number of steps.

TRectAnimation

TRectAnimation was introduced due to the very common situation of dealing with the Padding and Margins properties of FMX's visual objects. The data structure being addressed here is TBounds (defined in the FMX.Types unit), which is the actual type for margins and paddings in FMX.

TBitmapAnimation

We discussed color animations in the *TColorAnimation* and *TColorKeyAnimation* sections earlier. Bitmaps, in their very raw form, are large arrays of color values (one per point of the bitmap) and can potentially include alpha channel information.

At this point, you may be thinking that bitmap animation takes place by animating every single pixel color from the initial value to the corresponding one in the final bitmap. But this is not what happens.

Here, FMX takes advantage of its built-in graphics capabilities and adopts a more efficient strategy. Each step of the animation from a source image toward a target image will consist of the drawing of the source image, along with a certain opacity (alpha) value, immediately followed by a drawing of the target image, along with a complementary opacity.

The following image exemplifies this process:

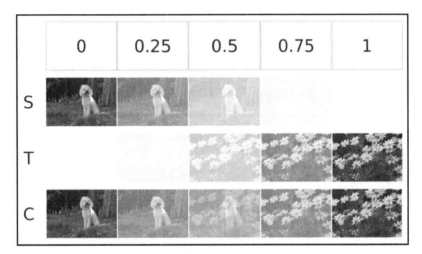

Figure 10.26

As you can see, `NormalizedTime` is labeled on top of each step (ranging from 0 to 1); that is, the frame obtained by progressively fading out the source image (**S**), the frame obtained by progressively fading in the target image (**T**), and the composition (**C**) of both frames. The composition is what needs to be considered as the step value of our animation, and it will be the bitmap value that's applied to the target property of the `TBitmapAnimation` instance.

Once again, setting `Interpolation` will work as it usually does, affecting the time component of the transition.

TBitmapListAnimation

*Ever seen those **sprites** that were used to implement the first electronic games out there?* `TBitmapListAnimation` will help you provide exactly the same functionality inside your applications. Think of a graphic animation as a sequence of frames to be displayed in a certain amount of time – that's the definition of what the `TBitmapListAnimation` component offers.

Once you or your graphic artists have a picture showing all the key frames beside each other, you just need to instruct `TBitmapListAnimation` to create a copy of this bitmap and specify the number of frames contained within (possibly arranged on multiple rows). After that, you are all set. Targeting a `TBitmap` property (that is, `TRectangle.Fill.Bitmap.Bitmap`) and starting the animation will result in a burst of frames being used to set the target bitmap.

The following image shows the bitmap that I prepared using a Delphi logo (the logo was rotated 30 degrees each frame until it reached the initial position once more):

Figure 10.27

In the following code snippet, you can see how I set up `TBitmapListAnimation` so that it rendered my little spinning Delphi logo inside a `TRectangle` instance:

```
object BitmapListAnimation2: TBitmapListAnimation
  AnimationBitmap.PNG = {
    89504E470D0A1A0A0000000D494844520000008000000009E0806000000A624EA
    // ...
    426082}
  AnimationCount = 13
  Enabled = True
  Delay = 1.000000000000000000
  Duration = 1.000000000000000000
  Interpolation = Quadratic
  Loop = True
  PropertyName = 'Fill.Bitmap.Bitmap'
end
```

Note that the `AnimationCount` property has been set to reflect the actual number of key frames in the bitmap and that I've chosen `Quadratic` interpolation here.

 I've omitted the large bitmap showing raw data from the preceding code snippet as it wouldn't have been very informative.

Here, the interpolations are applied to time and there is no transition across one single frame and another. What we are animating here is the index of the currently displayed frame.

TPathAnimation

The last kind of animation we are going to cover is `TPathAnimation`. Vector graphic definition is a large topic and it's way beyond the purpose of this book. For now, we'll focus on the fact that we may want to animate a visual object so that it follows a certain path.

Specifically, we are going to talk about animating the position (and possibly the rotation) of the object; we won't be addressing any other properties, as we have done for the other animations we've covered. `TPathAnimation` does not inherit from `TCustomPropertyAnimation`, even though it addresses some of the properties of the target object. The addressed properties (`Position` and `RotationAngle`) are simply hard-wired into the animation object.

First of all, we need some SVG data defining the path. There are a number of SVG editors out there, but one of the most popular ones is **InkScape** (`https://inkscape.org`). We can use one of the available tools in the editor to draw a line (I've used the freehand tool through my **Wacom** pen tablet), as shown in the following screenshot:

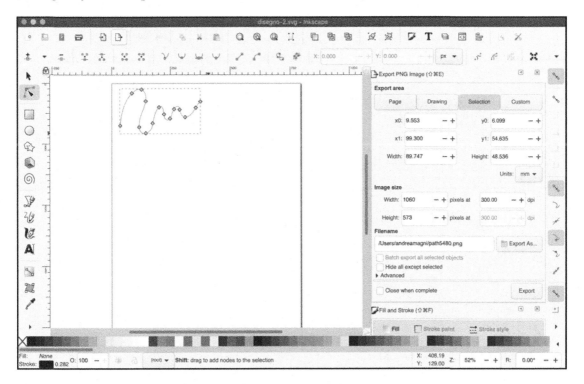

Figure 10.28

Note that I used the **Simplify** function to smooth the line a bit before saving the file by selecting the **Optimized SVG output format** option. The result is a `.xml` file that you can take a look at in a text editor of your choice, as shown in the following screenshot:

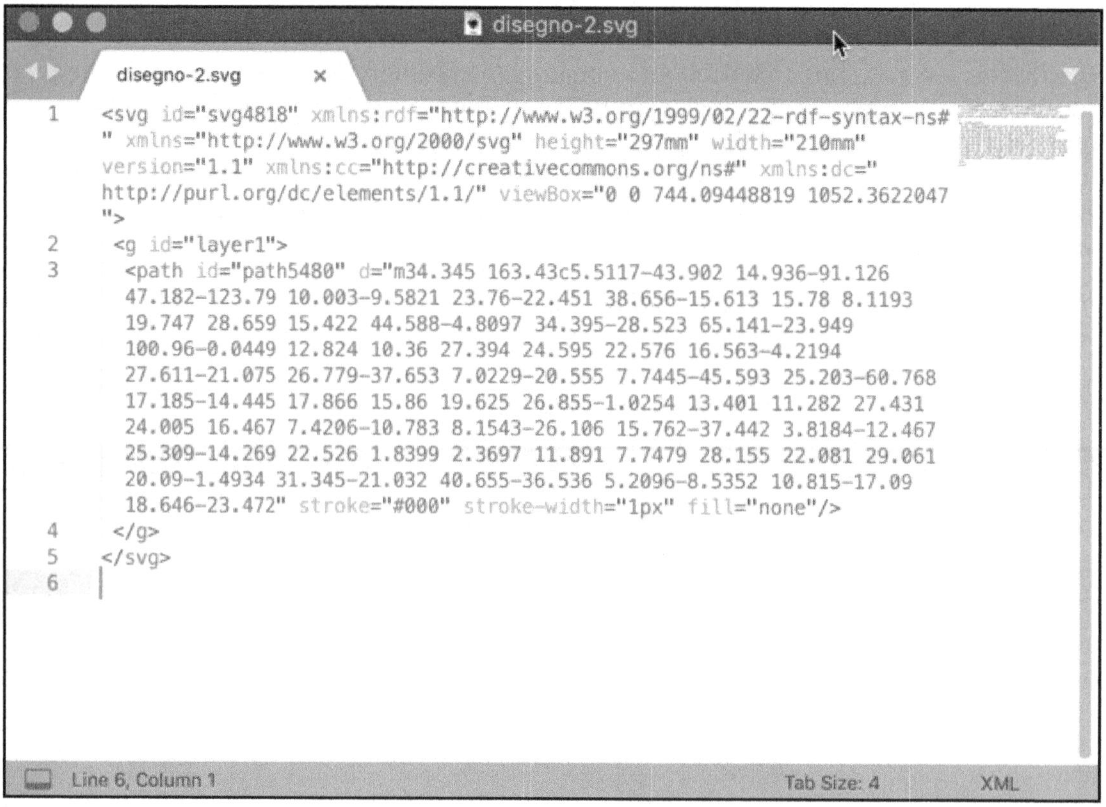

```
1    <svg id="svg4818" xmlns:rdf="http://www.w3.org/1999/02/22-rdf-syntax-ns#
     " xmlns="http://www.w3.org/2000/svg" height="297mm" width="210mm"
     version="1.1" xmlns:cc="http://creativecommons.org/ns#" xmlns:dc="
     http://purl.org/dc/elements/1.1/" viewBox="0 0 744.09448819 1052.3622047
     ">
2      <g id="layer1">
3      <path id="path5480" d="m34.345 163.43c5.5117-43.902 14.936-91.126
       47.182-123.79 10.003-9.5821 23.76-22.451 38.656-15.613 15.78 8.1193
       19.747 28.659 15.422 44.588-4.8097 34.395-28.523 65.141-23.949
       100.96-0.0449 12.824 10.36 27.394 24.595 22.576 16.563-4.2194
       27.611-21.075 26.779-37.653 7.0229-20.555 7.7445-45.593 25.203-60.768
       17.185-14.445 17.866 15.86 19.625 26.855-1.0254 13.401 11.282 27.431
       24.005 16.467 7.4206-10.783 8.1543-26.106 15.762-37.442 3.8184-12.467
       25.309-14.269 22.526 1.8399 2.3697 11.891 7.7479 28.155 22.081 29.061
       20.09-1.4934 31.345-21.032 40.655-36.536 5.2096-8.5352 10.815-17.09
       18.646-23.472" stroke="#000" stroke-width="1px" fill="none"/>
4      </g>
5    </svg>
6    |
```

Line 6, Column 1   Tab Size: 4   XML

Figure 10.29

As you can see, FMX supports **Scalable Vector Graphics** (**SVG**) being used through a number of components (such as TPath, TPath3D, and TLabelPath), all of which use an internal data structure (TPathData, defined in FMX.Graphics) that can parse and use data from SVG definitions. In the preceding screenshot, you can spot the d attribute of the path element, which is what we are talking about here.

In the IDE, a property editor will help you set (and preview) the value of the Path property of a TPathAnimation instance, as shown in the following screenshot:

Figure 10.30

As you can see, once again, interpolation gets applied to time and can be used to achieve impressive results. I suggest that you try out the available demo, set Interpolation to Bounce, and see what happens.

I've included some code in the demo project that will help you visualize the path as soon as the target component (a button) covers it. Here is the code snippet I used as a handler for the `TPathAnimation.OnProcess` event:

```
procedure TMainForm.PathAnimation1Process(Sender: TObject);
const CircleSize = 5;
begin
  if FDotPosition.Distance(Button1.Position.Point) > CircleSize then
  begin
    FDotPosition := Button1.Position.Point;
    var LDot := TCircle.Create(Self);
    try
      LDot.Parent := MainForm;
      LDot.Height := CircleSize;
      LDot.Width := CircleSize;
      LDot.Position.Point := FDotPosition;
      LDot.Position.Point.Offset(-CircleSize/2,-CircleSize/2);
    except
      LDOt.Free;
    end;
  end;
end;
```

The preceding code creates a new `TCircle` instance every time the current position is far enough from the previously marked point. While running the demo, you'll see the small circles that show up alongside the ongoing animation. This has only been done for demonstrative purposes and to provide a significant screenshot for this book.

The result (linear interpolation applied) of executing the demo application can be seen in the following screenshot:

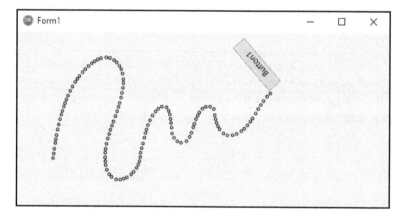

Figure 10.31

From the preceding screenshot, we can see that the animation has a duration of 5 seconds, with a 1-second delay at the start of the application. You can also set the usual properties here, such as `Loop`, `Inverse`, and `AutoReverse`. An extra property is available for this animation; that is, `Rotate`.

Setting this to `True` will imply that each animation step will also set the `RotationAngle` property of the target component. The angle will be determined using a simple algorithm (basic trigonometry) that will consider the current and previous points that were used to set the `Position` property of the target. This will emphasize the effect of the target *following* the path; this is also visible in the preceding screenshot. I've set the `RotationCenter` property of the button to (0,0) so that it coincides with the same point that was used to set its position (top-left corner).

The capability provided by `TPathAnimation` is very powerful and useful while you're building special animations in your visual applications or components.

In this section, we learned about the `TAnimation` class and its properties. We also learned about interpolation modifier functions. Finally, we looked at `TAnimator` shortcuts, along with specialized animation components. Now, let's summarize this chapter.

Summary

In this chapter, we learned about FMX animations. We covered various background concepts, including the event-oriented approach and the mechanics of time interpolations. A complete overview of the built-in capabilities of the FMX framework in terms of animations has been addressed, including the various specialized animations that target some common use cases.

By now, you should have the confidence and skills needed to add various animations and transitions to your own applications (or components). This is a good skill to acquire as a modern developer. As we discussed in this chapter and earlier in this book, part of usability nowadays is conceived through the use of meaningful transitions.

In the next chapter, we are going to discuss another technique that is crucial when building mobile applications: responsiveness in terms of the ability to readily respond to user interactions. We'll learn how Delphi and the included parallel programming library will help you, as a developer, achieve such a result in your apps.

Section 3: Pushing to The Top: Advanced Topics

This section contains advanced topics that you'll need to make your applications soar. We are building real-world applications, and we need to master the implementation details of the core functionalities of these applications. If delivering neat, modern, and effective UIs is crucial for the success of your application, then correctly and effectively implementing core functionalities is equally important.

We are going to learn how to implement complex behaviors without affecting the application's responsiveness, how to take advantage of FMX services to implement application features in a cross-platform flavor (with a single code base), and, last but not least, how to deal with the 3D functionality in FMX.

This section contains the following chapters:

- Chapter 11, *Building Responsive Applications*
- Chapter 12, *Exploring Cross-Platform Services*
- Chapter 13, *Learning about FMX 3D Capabilities*

11
Building Responsive Applications

In the previous chapters, we learned how to build visually responsive applications and how to add transitions and animations to them. **Responsiveness** also has another meaning—being capable, as an application, to promptly respond to user interactions throughout its lifespan, even when some heavy tasks are ongoing.

In this chapter, we are going to discuss how to achieve such a capability. Delivering a truly responsive application automatically implies the overall user experience is great. The user will never be staring at the screen, uninformed of what's happening, waiting to understand whether something is going on or the application is stuck.

The topics that we will be covering in this chapter are the following:

- Understanding multithreading
- Understanding the thread safety of UI frameworks
- Exploring threads and tasks
- Introducing the Parallel Programming Library

At the end of the chapter, you should be able to understand what responsiveness means in this context, why it is crucial, and how to recognize and deal with the most common pitfalls. Many features of the Delphi built-in Parallel Programming Library will ease your work as a developer.

Please remember that it is way beyond the purpose of this book to cover parallel programming in depth. **Parallel programming** is a very wide topic ranging from synchronization strategies to performance considerations. Many other collateral yet non-trivial arguments would pop up (exception handling to name one). The purpose of this chapter is to teach you the most relevant aspects of parallel programming in terms of UI interaction.

Technical requirements

Here is the source code used throughout the chapter: `https://github.com/PacktPublishing/Delphi-GUI-Programming-with-FireMonkey/tree/master/Chapter%2011`.

Understanding multithreading

In `Chapter 9`, *Building Responsive UIs*, we talked about achieving responsiveness with visual meaning. In this chapter, we are going to discuss the particular ability of an application to look responsive to the user even when some time-consuming or computationally heavy operation is ongoing.

In this section, we will learn about the thread safety of UI frameworks. We will also learn how to distinguish between synchronous and asynchronous code execution. This will also need a discussion about synchronization techniques to mix and merge the two approaches.

If you are an experienced programmer, you will surely have been in situations where the UI of your applications seemed to freeze because of some heavy computation (long loops, network calls, or other I/O operations). The general behavior is to have a blank window or a frozen one, and the user has no choice other than killing the application or patiently waiting for the operation to complete, even if the application seems stuck. I clearly remember this situation used to be the standard with reporting functionalities on desktop platforms in the last 20 years or so.

Generally, the (lazy) developer expects (or explicitly asks) the user to simply wait for the operation to finish rather than terminating the process just because it seems unresponsive. More recently, operating systems have started to stigmatize this behavior by explicitly asking the user to terminate the process—*this process is not responding, would you like to kill it?*

In this situation, where the UI is not responding to user input, moving the mouse over controls results in no change and clicking on buttons seems to have no effect. We are also going to learn how to avoid glitches, or repaint of controls, and so on, is what we are going to learn to avoid.

This is universally recognized as a non-user-friendly experience and, moreover, this may also actually lead to issues with your software as you may have unexpected behaviors as users may decide to brutally terminate your applications, leading to malfunctioning or unrecoverable situations. Moreover, mobile operating systems have stricter policies about general device responsiveness and may even autonomously determine to kill your app when it is not responding for too long (think in terms of fraction of a second).

Mobile platforms particularly stress developers to avoid the **application not responding** (**ANR**) situation also because this has been identified as one of the most important factors in user evaluations of applications (and, by extension, of the whole mobile platform). The final user of the device (that is, the real customer of **Apple**, **Google**, and device manufacturers) is not always able to properly ascribe responsibilities of an unresponsive device among app developers, the system environment, or even hardware capabilities.

So, Apple (or Google) stress developers to produce more responsive apps in order to improve the overall user experience of their device (the **iPhone** or **Android** phone). This basically can be observed when asking non-technical people why they prefer iOS over Android or the other way around. They tend not to distinguish between the device and the running OS.

Generally speaking, the user will perceive the UI as responsive when the average response to an action is within 100-200 ms. Clicking on a button and having no immediate feedback (a change in button visuals or something similar) will be perceived as *does not work* almost immediately. I would say 500 ms is the maximum allowed.

The general problem is that the UI needs to accomplish its own tasks in order to properly render all the typical visual effects that the user is familiar with. Think about clicking on a button and seeing it changing color (or inflating) to visually represent the fact the button is pressed. Then, once the user releases the button, it should change back the other way around to how it was.

This is done by actual code running at some level (generally at the component level) and obviously takes its time to run. The more effects (or components) are involved, the more processing time is consumed to keep the UI up to date. Obviously, processing time is also consumed to run the application-specific tasks so there is an evident competition between the UI and the core business of the app.

Normally, the UI update is driven by a large number of shortcode executions. This code takes less time to execute, while the core tasks may be fewer but take longer to complete. As a consequence, while a long core task is being executed, a number of UI-related small tasks will be neglected or delayed, resulting in missing or delayed UI updates.

You may think that this scenario with many small tasks that are to be executed to keep the UI responsive would be a perfect fit for parallel (multithreaded) programming. On the contrary, there are very few UI frameworks using parallel programming this way. In the next section, we are going to explore the reason for this.

Understanding the thread safety of UI frameworks

The most popular UI frameworks out there (including VCL and FMX) are not thread-safe.

 Thread safety is the ability something (like a piece of code, a library, a framework, or something else) has to properly work in a context where multiple concurrent threads are involved. *Properly work* here means having no runtime errors, memory leaks, memory overwriting, and so on. It does not mean it is the most efficient way to accomplish the task.

Everything is run in a single thread that will be the owner of all UI objects and the executor of all UI-related tasks. The reason is that a thread-safe UI environment would likely require a lot of synchronization. **Synchronization** is what is needed to avoid collisions while dealing with the same object and multiple threads. There are a number of techniques related to synchronization but, to get the concept, we can consider one of the simplest forms of synchronization.

When a resource is (or has to be) shared across multiple threads, we can use a singleton object to protect access to it. Think about a **Capture the flag** game where the access to the resource is granted to (and only to) the carrier of the flag. All the other contenders will have to wait until the flag returns before attempting to get it and have their turn. Obviously, to implement such a mechanism, some code needs to be run and this would negatively affect performance up to a point where the benefit of having multiple threads would be wasted.

Delphi applications, by default, are single-threaded (this is a simplification—we'll delve into this later in this chapter), meaning we have a UI thread that also is the thread where event handlers are executed. This is obviously made for the sake of simplicity as, most of the time, event-handlers of UI elements (controls) would interact with other UI elements—for example, clicking on a checkbox in order to cause an edit box to be read-only, clicking on a button in order to add a new row in a grid, and so on.

We have this single-threaded application executing both UI and core application code and both are in a race for resources (CPU, memory, exclusive access resources). We already stated we can't spread UI code across multiple threads (as the UI framework is not thread-safe) so we are left with the only option to move the core code (or relevant parts of it) in one or more secondary threads.

Synchronous versus asynchronous execution

Generally speaking, multithreaded programming is one of the most difficult topics to master as a developer. As human beings, we are intrinsically used to thinking sequentially and many programming languages (like **Pascal**) have been designed to be used in an imperative, synchronous, deterministic paradigm. We usually design our code thinking in terms of a sequence and making the assumption that steps are not overlapping (and that they follow the **first-in-first-out approach**, for example).

Let's try to use a real-world example of a sequential operation that we feel is naturally sequential and where the need for synchronization is completely transparent (as we are used to automatically managing underlying complexity as human beings). Think about serving yourself a glass of water. The sequence seems pretty straightforward:

1. Put the glass on the table.
2. Open the bottle.
3. Pour water into the glass.
4. Close the bottle.
5. Get the glass.
6. Drink the glass of water.

After reading the preceding steps, it may sound obvious that each step is non-overlapping and the sequence is fulfilled even if there is no sign of explicit synchronization.

What if step 1 were to finish after step 3? We would probably pour water on the table. A better representation of the task (algorithm) should have taken into account that some steps might overlap (like *steps 4* and *5*, or *6*) while other steps will not (*steps 1* and *3*, or *steps 2* and *3*). You need to wait for the glass to be positioned before pouring water in. It is obviously something that would be automatic for a human being but actually, it is implemented through a number of assumptions and coordination mechanisms that are put in place, even if they're made unconsciously.

Another approach would be to think of our sequence in terms of *proceed to the next step once the current one has completed*, which can be read as *do nothing until the current step is finished*. Instead of doing nothing, we may think to perform non-core stuff while waiting for the step to complete. In the glass of water example, you are doing a number of things while going through the steps, such as breathing or looking—non-core stuff in this context. In terms of software applications, you can translate it to *freely perform your UI (non-core) stuff and take care of core things only once they are ready*.

The underlying fact is each step would naturally become asynchronous—you start it but you are not going to wait for the completion before moving to the next step. You are immediately free to execute (initiate) the next step. Whether this is a good idea or not is up to you (and, of course, the nature of the steps). Overlapping may be a feature or a bug. Over many years of consulting, I can surely say this switch from a completely synchronous paradigm to an asynchronous (or mixed) one is by far the most challenging task for developers.

There are a number of situations where an async task will be useful. Think about downloading a file from the web—you may want to continue surfing the web while a download is ongoing. If you are building a mobile app, there's a good chance you'll need to interact with a remote data source and this implies making network calls. Mobile networks may have limited bandwidth or be affected by severe variations of connection quality.

Moreover, you may start a request to a remote data source without knowing the size of the response. All these factors suggest that you perform the action in a separate, dedicated thread of execution and deal with the response only once it is locally available.

To further improve the user experience, it is important that, even if the long operation takes place in a secondary thread, the UI provides some feedback to the user. For example, the user should be notified of the start of the operation, possibly get some progress updates, and lastly, be notified that the operation has come to an end (successfully or not). A very common pattern is to use some sort of animated indicator (spinner) to advise the user that something is ongoing and the application is not stuck.

Obviously, we'll need some sort of synchronization mechanism to match the activities of the two (possibly more) threads involved—the UI thread and the secondary one(s). Before delving into technical details, we can briefly discuss two options we have—**Synchronize** and **Queue**.

The following screenshot gives you a (simplified) representation of the two synchronization strategies, both aimed at determining the execution context of a certain bit of code, generally to make it execute in the main or UI thread:

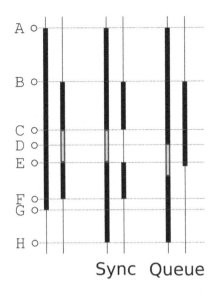

Figure 11.1

As you can see in the preceding screenshot, time is to be read from top to bottom, and threads are represented with vertical lines that are thin (when the thread is idle) and bold (when it is executing some code). A special portion of code has been marked in gray and it is the portion we would like to be executed in the main or UI thread (the leftmost of each couple). I've marked some specific time frames with capital letters (**A-H**) to make it easy to reference.

The very first observation you can make from the screenshot is that the synchronization (no matter if through **Synchronize** or **Queue**) has a cost. Out of the three cases represented (no sync, **Sync**, **Queue**), the first one (no synchronization, with the gray task executed in the secondary thread) terminates at time **G**. The other two cases (**Sync** and **Queue**) terminate at time **H**. The gap (**H-G**) is about the same as the duration of the gray task (**E-C**). Obviously, there is an assumption made here: for some reason, you need to execute the gray task in the context of the first (UI) thread. A simple (and very common) reason may be that code needs to manipulate some UI elements or non-UI elements, such as datasets, which will cause the UI to change indirectly.

Such a requirement of manipulating the UI elements from a secondary thread is very common and in the next section, we'll learn how to do it properly. Moreover, we'll consider how to choose between synchronization and queueing, considering the underlying implications. So, we'll learn about `Synchronize` and `Queue` in the following sections.

Utilizing the Synchronize method

The first option we have in order to execute a piece of code (no matter how complex) in the context of the UI thread is to call the `TThread.Synchronize` method. We'll have a closer look at the `TThread` class later in this chapter.

The method has two overloaded versions, both with two arguments:

- For both versions, the first argument is a reference to the `TThread` instance we want to be the executor of code.
- The second argument represents the code portion to be executed; that is, one version accepts a reference to a regular method, while the second version of the method accepts an anonymous method.

We can imagine, as you have seen in *Figure 11.1*, the worker (secondary) thread will process some code and, at some point (**C**), reach the need to synchronize with the UI (main) thread. That is the moment that the call to `Synchronize` has to take place. Without delving too deeply into the internals, we can think/imagine that the UI thread stops its activities to get in charge of the execution of the gray portion of the code. Everything the UI thread was about to execute will be postponed to moment **E** and, in the time slot between **C** and **E**, the gray code will be executed in the context of the UI thread.

Let's consider some (more or less obvious) implications:

- The UI thread, while executing the gray code, will not be able to process normal UI events. This basically means the UI will freeze from time **C** to time **E**. If there are some loop-based mechanisms involved (like with **Windows** applications), events will be queued for the time between **C** and **E**. They might get processed only after time **E**—at the first chance the UI thread has to check the message loop.
- The execution of the gray code will take place in the context of the UI thread, meaning every control will be safely manipulatable by the gray code. Feel free to resize controls, create new ones, or destroy some others. The application will be back in a single-threaded manner, avoiding all the difficulties multithreaded programming brings.
- The worker thread will hold on until the gray code execution has completed. In other words, the call to `Synchronize` is synchronous—it does not return to the caller (the worker), until it has completed and it completes only after the gray code execution (in the main/UI thread context) has come to an end.

The following code exemplifies the situation by setting up a worker thread, launched by the UI thread to handle the task of incrementing the LCounter variable from 1 to 5. With the help of a thread-safe logging framework (**Raize CodeSite**: https://raize.com/codesite/), we'll have the exact trace of what's happening under the hood.

 The **CodeSite Express** edition is freely included in **RAD Studio** (in Delphi though) and it is a one-click install process through **GetIt** (Embarcadero's package manager).

The following code also implements the OnClick event handler for the SynchronizeButton instance (the SynchronizeAndQueue demo project included with this book):

```
CodeSite.SendMsg('SYNCHRONIZE example');
CodeSite.SendMsg('UI: Launching Worker...');

TThread.CreateAnonymousThread(
  procedure
  var
    LCounter: Integer;
  begin
    CodeSite.SendMsg('Worker: starting...');
    LCounter := 0;

    Sleep(1000);
    Inc(LCounter);
    CodeSite.SendMsg('Counter: ' + LCounter.ToString);

    Sleep(1000);
    Inc(LCounter);
    CodeSite.SendMsg('Counter: ' + LCounter.ToString);

    Sleep(1000);
    Inc(LCounter);
    CodeSite.SendMsg('Counter: ' + LCounter.ToString);

    TThread.Synchronize(nil
    , procedure
      begin
        CodeSite.SendMsg('Gray code: starting...');
        Sleep(1500);
        CodeSite.SendMsg('Gray code: completed');
      end
    );
```

```
    Sleep(1000);
    Inc(LCounter);
    CodeSite.SendMsg('Counter: ' + LCounter.ToString);

    Sleep(1000);
    Inc(LCounter);
    CodeSite.SendMsg('Counter: ' + LCounter.ToString);

    CodeSite.SendMsg('Worker: completed');
  end
).Start;

CodeSite.SendMsg('UI: Worker launched');
end;
```

In the preceding code, `Sleep` calls are used to dilute a bit of time and make things more observable from a human being's perspective. `Sleep` is a system call, is synchronous, and will hold the caller thread for the specified amount of time. The `TThread` class is used to define and start a secondary (worker) thread and to provide synchronization facilities (like the `Synchronize` method, in fact).

Among other functionalities, `CodeSite` provides useful information such as the calling thread's ID and a customizable representation of log entries' timestamps (I've selected the **Offset** option). The following screenshot shows the **CodeSite Live Viewer** after clicking the `SynchronizeButton` button. I've highlighted the two lines bordering the gray code execution:

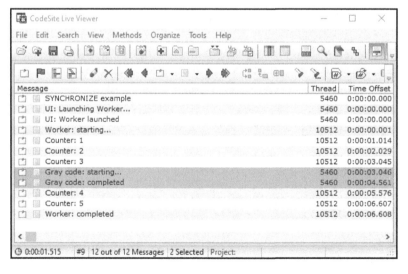

Figure 11.2

As you can see from the previous screenshot (and also according to *Figure 11.1* in this chapter), the gray code execution takes place in the UI thread (ID: **5460**) and the worker thread (ID: **10512**) is on hold until the gray code execution has come to an end. You can see this by looking at **Time Offset** for the **Counter: 4** entry; it happens more than 2.5 seconds after the **Counter: 3** entry.

Thread context switching isn't free and away from trivial examples like this, you can actually experience its cost. The more switching happens, the more this hidden cost will show up, growing to a significant amount of time in the worst cases. When too much coordination is needed across the threads of your application, it may fire back as a performance issue and it is usually a symptom of a far from perfect design.

We'll now move on to learning about the **Queue** approach.

Learning about the Queue approach

The other option we have in order for a piece of code to be executed within the context of a specific thread (the main/UI thread specifically) is the **Queue** approach. Basically, it relies on the capability of the threads to maintain a queue of pieces of code to be executed.

This capability has some pitfalls; for example, event in the queue of a thread that gets destroyed, either because it has come to its end or has been terminated from outside, or maybe it has been disposed of and never been executed. But again, I am not going to discuss corner cases here. In most UI-related situations, you most likely want to queue code executions within the main/UI thread, which are extremely unlikely to be terminated before you need that code to be actually executed.

Look at the **Queue** part in *Figure 11.1*. From the diagram of code execution in the three situations (no sync, **Sync**, and **Queue**), you can notice how the gray code gets executed in the context of the UI thread while the worker thread continues (almost) immediately on its way. Also, you can notice the gray execution does not take place immediately in the main thread but, in fact, after a while.

This happens because the code execution has been queued and, if the main thread is busy doing something else, it may be delayed. In many situations, this delay will not cause any issue as, from the UI thread point of view, it is basically the same as if the worker thread had taken longer to execute.

Things may get trickier if you have many queueing events and several threads involved but, generally speaking, if your gray code does not have dependencies/interactions with the execution of other threads, you are safe.

A typical situation where I'd use **Queue** instead of **Synchronize** is to update a hypothetical progress bar while downloading a file in a worker thread.

It is better to avoid slowing down the UI just to update a progress bar immediately rather than a few milliseconds later when the UI thread would probably be sitting idle.

If we take the code listing we used for `Synchronize` and substitute that call with `TThread.Queue`, we will see different behavior. That is exactly what I've done in the `OnClick` event handler of the `SynchronizeAndQueue` demo project that has been included.

The following screenshot shows the different output in the **CodeSite** log viewer:

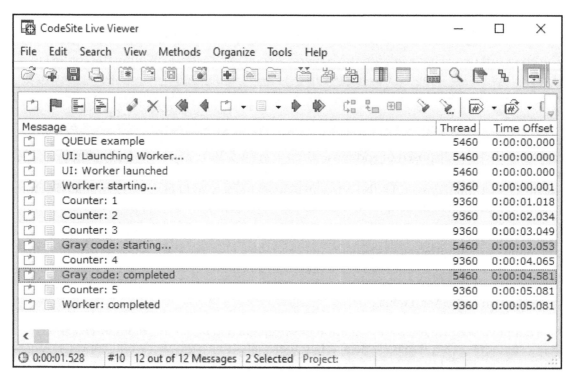

Figure 11.3

You can see from the preceding screenshot, as done before, I've highlighted the start and finish entries of the gray code execution. Let's look at some considerations about it:

- You can clearly see how the worker thread pays no cost by queuing the execution of the gray code. Check the **Time Offset** column for the **Counters 1**, **2**, **3**, **4**, and **5** entries and you'll see they are all about 1 second (1,000 ms) distant from one another (no delays due to the gray code execution).

- In this particular run, the gray code gets executed almost immediately (by the main thread, ID: **5460**) after being queued (by the worker thread, ID: **9360**). This is not mandatory and results may differ if you stress the main thread a bit.

- The total execution time is **5.081** seconds against the **6.608** seconds of the run with `Synchronize`. This does not mean the diagram in *Figure 11.1* of the chapter is wrong (there, **Sync** and **Queue** end at the same time, **H**) but simply that we are not logging much from the main thread. The **Worker: completed** entries are, on the diagram, respectively happening at time **F** and **E** for `Synchronize` and `Queue` versions; in fact, the difference is about 1,500 ms, which is comparable with the gray code execution time.

> To be accurate, *Figure 11.1* should show a burst of occupancy usages for the first (UI) thread. The continuous line I've used is for the sake of simplicity but it would mean the UI thread is 100% busy, and this is a situation you want to avoid and that would lead the UI to freeze. You should really think of the UI thread as an executor of event-driven segments of code, being executed as soon as possible after when they are scheduled.

These two strategies, through `Synchronize` and `Queue`, are very important in your quest for responsiveness. Parallel programming can be very difficult to properly get without these fundamental concepts.

In this section, we learned about how most popular UIs are not thread-safe. We also learned the difference between sync and async multithreading. We also learned about the `Synchronize` and `Queue` approaches.

Given this, we need to learn how to set the execution context of some code to a secondary thread. There are some options available and we need to learn the peculiarities of each in order to make the right choices. So, in the next section, we will learn about threads and tasks.

Exploring threads and tasks

Threads are a first-class citizen concept of modern operating systems and their model has been used for decades to implement the concurrent execution of different sets of instructions. In a very simplistic way, you can think of threads as independently executed lists of instructions—there is a sequence in each list but they are independent of each other.

In this section, we will learn about the `TThread` class. We will also understand the thread's lifespan. We are going to familiarize ourselves a bit with the Parallel Programming Library, along with synchronization.

Other conceptualizations may render threads as independent agents executing their own program within the main program. In the end, they represent a way to organize code execution in order to do the following:

- Take advantage of full hardware resources (modern CPUs have multiple processors/cores)
- Deal with UI responsiveness
- Deal with asynchronous operations (those operations have a non-predictable duration)—you don't want to busy-wait for completion as this would freeze your application in the meantime
- Handle multiple communication channels simultaneously, for example, when you are building server-side software like an HTTP or REST server

Basically, when a thread gets started, it performs some instructions and then terminates. Two very common patterns while using threads are the following:

- Performing some long task in the thread and, when it terminates or while it's ongoing, notify the caller thread of some result or updates about the task being executed in the secondary thread

- Launching a persistent background thread to let it periodically do some work or check some condition; the main thread might be notified from time to time about some condition that occurred or was recognized in the background thread

The first pattern can be seen as a one-shot operation being executed in the background of the application. It can be either a one-way operation with no implications for the UI once it has finished or something we need to collect the result/outcome of at the end of the operation. The user might be willing to wait for the operation to finish but, from a code point of view, this waiting will be a non-busy wait (letting the UI thread freely run in the meanwhile).

The second pattern is more like having a secondary thread existing in your application (not necessarily from the beginning to end of its life) that, from time to time, may have the need to interact with the user or the UI. Real-world examples of the two patterns, respectively, are as follows:

- Downloading a file from a remote server
- Polling for some update against a remote data source

Delphi introduced support for threading a long time ago (back in **Delphi 2**, 1996). In those days, terms like preemptive multitasking, multi-core, and multi-threading had started to become popular. Operating systems (like **Microsoft Windows 95**) were trying to get the advantage of multitasking in order to enable users to perform multiple operations at the same time. Historically, Delphi followed the Windows approach to multithreading, relying upon the Windows APIs for the purpose.

In the following section, we'll learn about the TThread class, the classical way to handle threads in Delphi. Later in this chapter, we'll introduce the **Parallel Programming Library** and its classes (the TTask class to name one).

Introducing the TThread class

The TThread class (unit System.Classes) is a wrapper around the concept of the thread object. The idea is you can inherit your own class using the TThread class as a parent and then provide a custom implementation of the Execute method. The code you put in the Execute method will be executed in a separate thread. You only need to create an instance of your new class and start it by using the TThread.Start method.

Shared resources are always problematic when it comes to parallel (multi-threaded) programming. A common scenario is to define your TThread inherited class, onboarding all necessary data as class members (fields or properties). Before starting the thread (yet after creating the instance), you need a chance to provide values for these fields or properties.

The running thread will make use of these values without worrying about concurrency issues or synchronization requirements. Obviously, this is easy to do for primitive data types (strings, numbers, records, and so on), but may need more attention with object instances or other shared data.

In fact, making a copy of a reference to an object does not mean that you are providing your thread with a copy of the whole object. Eventual interactions due to others sharing the same reference may occur. This makes the object a shared resource and you generally need to pay attention in this situation. You will probably need to implement some synchronization or a locking strategy to ensure the object gets safely manipulated by different concurrent threads.

You can select **File** | **New** | **Delphi** | **Individual files** | **Thread Object**, and have the IDE produce a new file with a template structure. The following screenshot shows the IDE dialog with the **Thread Object** entry selected:

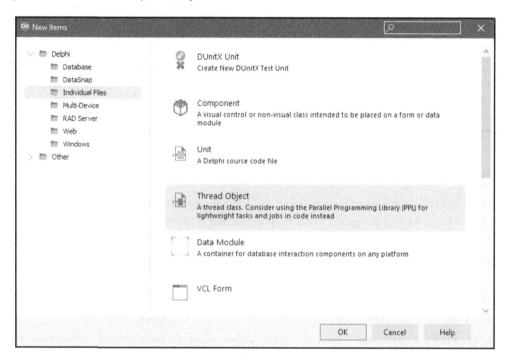

Figure 11.4

The IDE will bootstrap a new file that should be similar to the following code:

```
unit Threads.Simple;

interface

uses
  System.Classes, System.SysUtils;
```

```
type
  TSimpleThread = class(TThread)
  private
  protected
    procedure Execute; override;
  end;

implementation

{ TSimpleThread }

procedure TSimpleThread.Execute;
begin
  { Place thread code here }
end;

end.
```

To create and start a new `TSimpleThread` instance, you simply need to call its parameterless `Create` constructor. This will create a new instance and immediately start the execution. If you need to set up your instance (for example, to set a value to some of its properties), you may want to perform either one of the following:

- Provide a custom constructor for your `TSimpleThread` class, passing data as an argument and storing it for use during the thread execution.
- Create the thread in a suspended state using another version of the `Create` constructor, having a `CreateSuspended` Boolean argument, set up your instance, and then call the `Start` method to actually let the thread execution begin.

 Keep in mind the constructor of the thread will be executed in the calling thread context (that is, probably the main/UI thread) so it is a safe place to manipulate shared objects or data.

Along with the `Start` method, the `TThread` class provides the implementation for some useful features that we'll briefly discuss in the following sections.

Understanding a thread's lifespan

Each thread instance has a Boolean field, namely `Terminated`, that can be set through a call of the public `Terminate` method. You may think to call `Terminate`, which will have some immediate effect, like stopping the thread or brutally killing it, but this is not the case.

Calling `Terminate` will simply set the `Terminated` field to `True` and call
the `TerminatedSet` protected procedure as a consequence.

 Beware, the `Terminate` method will execute in the context of the caller
thread (that is, the main/UI thread) and so will happen for the consequent
`TThread.TerminatedSet` method execution.

It is the thread code's responsibility to periodically check whether somebody (from outside)
asked for premature termination of the thread. This might be done between steps of a
multi-step operation, for example, or if the thread has a control loop, at the end of each
iteration of the loop. A simple way to handle such a situation would be exiting from the
`Execute` method, causing its termination. The following code block exemplifies two
common patterns of handling `Terminated` in thread code:

```
// multistep operation, checking between steps
procedure TSimpleThread.Execute;
begin
  DoSomething1;
  if Terminated then
    Exit;
  DoSomething2;
  if Terminated then
    Exit;
  DoSomething3;
end;

// loop control, checking before each iteration
procedure TSimpleThread.Execute;
begin
  while not Terminated do
    DoSomething;
end;
```

In the preceding code, the pattern obviously gives great control (and responsibility) to the
thread's implementor, granting the opportunity to properly deal with thread-specific
internals, that is, to clean up intermediate data on termination.

If the thread gets stuck in some infinite loop (or never checks for the `Terminated` value)
there will be no easy way to stop it from the outside gracefully. This means that the thread
will be isolated. The only contact point with the outside is the `Terminated` property. As
you would do with a non-responding process, there are brutal ways (available through API
calls) to terminate a thread, but this may lead to resource losses.

Another significant feature `TThread` provides is an `OnTerminate` event, which is fired once the `Execute` method has completed. Given that threads are generally used to implement asynchronous operations (shoot-and-forget or shoot-and-report), you may need to perform something once the thread has come to an end. Providing an `OnTerminate` event handler will do the trick.

For your convenience, the execution of the event handler is synchronized with the main thread of the application (so, it is a safe place to interact with the UI). Properly handling the lifecycle of your thread instances is mandatory in order to avoid memory leaks or inconsistent behaviors.

You need to pay attention to the thread that has its own state (created, running, terminated, or destroyed) and you need to take this into account while using a reference to a thread object. The `SimpleThreadProject` demo should be of help in understanding the chain of events occurring during a thread's lifetime.

Some considerations about the thread (and, in general, every Delphi object) should be made considering the actual memory model you are using. For desktop platforms, we have manual object lifecycle management so you are responsible for each created object.

For mobile platforms (and the Linux platform) the compiler (LLVM-based) has **automatic reference counting** (**ARC**) enabled.
A good reference to understand memory management is *Delphi Memory Management: For Classic and ARC Compilers,* from Dalija Prasnikar and Neven Prasnikar Jr.

Let's discuss some aspects of the demo (the full source code is provided with the book).

An `FThread: TSimpleThread` field has been added to our main form. This will act as a reference to our secondary thread for all the form's event handlers. To start the thread, we are using the following code:

```
FThread := TSimpleThread.Create(True);
FThread.FreeOnTerminate := True;
FThread.OnTerminate := TerminateThreadHandler;
FThread.OnProgress :=
  procedure
  begin
    StatusLabel.Text := 'Running, counter = '
      + FThread.Counter.ToString;
  end;
FThread.Start;
```

As discussed, we are creating the thread in a suspended state so we can set some properties of the actual instance before starting it.

The `TThread.FreeOnTerminate` property allows you to set the instance for auto-destruction after it has completed its execution. This is obviously a very handy feature in shoot-and-forget situations, but also for shoot-and-report ones, as it allows the developer to find a proper timing for the thread's destruction. Destroying the thread in the `OnTerminate` handler may lead to problems as it is generally a bad practice to destroy an object within an event handler of the object itself.

The `TSimpleThread.OnProgress` property is something added on purpose to let `TSimpleThread` notify some progress updates during its operations. It is an event implemented through an anonymous method. It is a very handy modern language feature—you really need to learn it if you are not already familiar with it.

> To improve your Delphi language skills, I strongly suggest looking for all of Marco Cantù's books and material available online.

If you are new to anonymous methods, just think about it as a piece of code you can pass as a value. `TSimpleThread` will have the opportunity to execute it when needed. We are delegating a portion of the `TSimpleThread` implementation to the caller thread, with the ability to write a piece of code in the scope of the main/UI thread that will be called from within the code of `TSimpleThread`.

> Beware not to confuse the concepts of code definition, scope, caller, and execution context. A piece of code has to be defined somewhere (in OOP, that is within a class method, for example) and gets executed by "someone" (a thread) because of a call to it. In our case, we have a class (`TSimpleThread`) wrapping a thread object (executor).

We also have a form (a `TMainForm` instance, that is living in the main/UI thread) providing the definition of some code (through the anonymous method). The anonymous method is defined within the form (so it has access to UI elements, living in the main/UI thread), it gets passed to `TSimpleThread` through the `OnProgress` property assignment, and finally, it gets executed because of a call to it made by some code (that is, code placed in the `Execute` method—it may be arbitrary code) in the `TSimpleThread` implementation.

In other words, it is defined in the `TMainForm` class and called by `TSimpleThread`. The caller has a chance to determine the executor. If the call is made directly, the caller and the anonymous method will share the executor (the `TSimpleThread` worker thread).

Otherwise (through synchronization mechanisms), the caller may put the anonymous method execution in the context of another thread (that is the main/UI thread). Parallel programming can be tricky to get at first.

Finally, the thread gets started through a call of its `Start` method. The thread (system) object gets actually allocated. The execution will begin and will include the provided implementation of the thread, that is, its `Execute` method.

In the following code, there is a control loop that checks at each iteration whether `Terminated` is still false:

```
begin
  (...)
  FCounter := 0;
  while not Terminated do
    DoSomething;
  (...)
end;
```

The following code shows if the condition stands (meaning the thread has not yet received a termination request), then `DoSomething` gets executed:

```
procedure TSimpleThread.DoSomething;
begin
  (...)
  Sleep(1000);
  Inc(FCounter);

  if Assigned(OnProgress) then
    Synchronize(FOnProgress);
end;
```

Once again, the `Sleep` function is used to mimic some intensive processing that is being done. A counter gets updated at each execution of `DoSomething`. The `OnProgress` event (if any handler is provided) occurs and its handler gets triggered through a call to `Synchronize`. This implies the executor is the main/UI thread. This turns out to be handy as it is very common for the typical `OnProgress` event handler to have something to do with the UI. By being executed in the context of the main UI thread, all visual components will be accessible in a thread-safe manner.

The following code shows the other event handler, that is, `TerminateThreadHandler`:

```
procedure TMainForm.TerminateThreadHandler(Sender: TObject);
begin
  StatusLabel.Text := 'Completed, counter = '
    + FThread.Counter.ToString;
  FThread := nil;
end;
```

As you can see from the previous code, it does nothing else than updating `StatusLabel` with the final value of the counter. It also sets the `FThread` variable to `nil`. This is different from actually destroying the object—we are just cleaning our reference to the thread instance because we know the thread is going to be destroyed (thanks to the `FreeOnTerminate` mechanism) and we don't want to accidentally reference it anymore.

> The actual demo, provided with the book, also has a number of CodeSite calls to log all events. CodeSite also retains the information about the thread that it is logging so it will help you properly follow what is happening and which thread is responsible for a different log line.

Last, but not least, since we have a loop in our thread that is not going to finish until the thread gets terminated from outside of the same `TThread` class, we need a button to stop the running thread. The following code shows its `OnClick` event handler:

```
procedure TMainForm.TerminateButtonClick(Sender: TObject);
begin
  if Assigned(FThread) and FThread.Started then
  begin
    FThread.Terminate;
    StatusLabel.Text := 'Terminated, waiting completion...';
  end;
end;
```

In the previous code example, we can see that a thread gets created, configured with some event handlers (`OnTerminate` and `OnProgress`), set for auto-destruction through the `FreeOnTerminate` property, and then launched. The thread will enter in a loop, periodically executing some code and it will notify progress at each iteration (executing the provided `OnProgress` event handler). Once requested to terminate, some code (that is, the `OnTerminate` event handler) will collect the final result of the thread. Then, it will self-destruct and we'll be ready to start over again (with a new instance, of course).

The aim of this small example is to highlight all the aspects you'll need to consider while doing parallel programming—for example:

- *How is the code organized?*
- *How is it being executed?*
- *From which thread is it being executed?*
- *Which synchronization technique is being used and when?*

The **CodeSite** output should help you check what's actually happening under the hood. The following screenshot shows a typical output of the program:

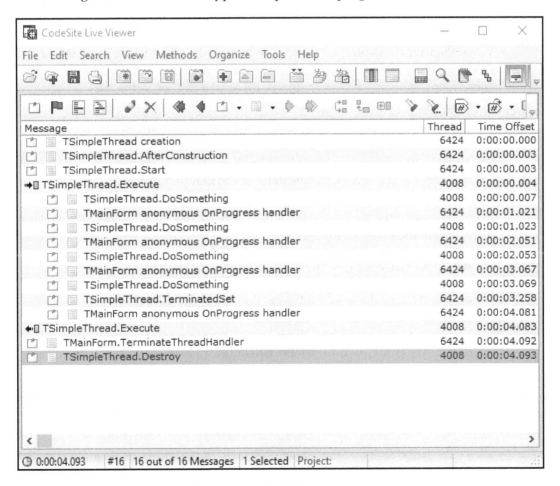

Figure 11.5

The following are some considerations about the previous screenshot:

- The main/UI thread has an ID of **6424**; you can see how the creation of the thread takes place in the main thread as well as `AfterConstruction` and the call to the `Start` method.
- Once the threads begin its execution, you can see a new thread ID for the log entries: **4008**.

 Note that the `TSimpleThread.DoSomething` method is being executed in the secondary thread (**4008**) while the `OnProgress` event handler takes place in the context of the main thread (**6424**) because of the use of `Synchronize`.

- When the user clicks on the `Terminate` button, the termination request takes place; it is the main/UI thread to execute the `Terminate` method (and the subsequent `TerminatedSet` method call) as you can see in the logs (**Thread: 6424**).
- Once the `Terminated` property is set to true, the loop stops iterating (completing the current iteration, of course) and this explains why you can read the last execution of the `OnProgress` event handler after `TerminatedSet`.
- `TerminateThreadHandler` takes place in the main/UI thread.
- The last log line is for the `TSimpleThread` destructor, as the thread destroys itself (because of the `FreeOnTerminate` property being `True`); note the executor thread is not the main/UI thread.

 A common mistake is to think every method of the `TThread` inherited class will be executed in the context of the secondary thread. In other words, the mistake is to think code definition has something to do with code execution, which is not the case.
You have to follow the call chain and keep an eye on synchronization functions in order to understand which thread is executing which piece of code.

I suggest, if you are not already familiar with multi-threading programming, you carefully examine this example until every aspect becomes clear. Multi-threaded programming is usually seen as very complex but can be mastered with some effort and diligence.

If you are really interested in parallel programming, I would strongly suggest you properly delve into this matter with the help of a specialist like Primož Gabrijelčič.

As I said, the initial multi-threading support was added to Delphi a long time ago. Modern language features, such as anonymous methods, have been added to the language in the meantime, and they can help in making things easier. In the next section, we'll have a closer look at some alternatives provided.

Exploring alternative solutions

With the advent of modern language features such as anonymous methods, a new opportunity has become available for Delphi developers. Instead of inheriting a new class for each task to be executed in a separate thread, a delegation mechanism has been implemented in the `TThread` base class. The concept is the same—I've used it to add the `OnProgress` event to my `TSimpleThread` class.

Actually, this behavior has been implemented in another class—TAnonymousThread (the `System.Classes` unit) and a shortcut class function have been added to `TThread` for convenience. TAnonymousThread inherits from `TThread` and basically holds a reference to the anonymous method to be executed and executes it in its `Execute` method.

The `TThread.CreateAnonymousThread` class function (available since **Delphi XE**) provides you with a handy way to define an anonymous method that will be executed within the `TThread.Execute` method.

This means the `TThread` class is now able to have a different (delegated) behavior without the need to inherit a specific class from `TThread` every time. This is extremely useful and greatly simplifies the writing of multithreaded software (especially when the tasks to be executed are not complex).

The following code shows how to mimic the same behavior when we have the
`SimpleThreadProject` demo while using the anonymous thread:

```
procedure TMainForm.StartButtonClick(Sender: TObject);
begin
  if Assigned(FThread) then
    Exit;
  (...)
  FTerminated := False;
  FThread := TThread.CreateAnonymousThread(
    procedure
    var
      LCounter: Integer;
    begin
      (...)
      LCounter := 0;
      while not FTerminated do
      begin
        (...)
        Sleep(1000);
        Inc(LCounter);

        TThread.Synchronize(nil
          , procedure
            begin
              (...)
              StatusLabel.Text := 'Running, counter = '
                + LCounter.ToString;
            end
        );
      end;

      FFinalCounter := LCounter; // Sync needed
      (...)
    end
  );

  FThread.OnTerminate := TerminateThreadHandler;
  (...)
  FThread.Start;
  StatusLabel.Text := 'Started';
end;
```

As you can see from the previous code, this approach implies that there is no need to define
a specific class type (`TSimpleThread`) to accomplish the task. Being short of the type
definition, we also lose a place to define variables or private data for the thread instance
execution.

On the other hand, using an anonymous method, we gain access to the scope where the anonymous method itself has been defined. So, we can take advantage of the form's fields and properties to access UI components, or to store values calculated in the thread (that is, the `FFinalCounter` field). We also need some replacement for `TThread.Terminated`, which is not publicly visible thus it can't be used in the same manner as we did within the `TSimpleThread` code. A simple Boolean variable (`FTerminated`) suffices.

Sometimes, inheriting a `TThread` class is still the right thing to do. Having a type definition also means more options to implement proper information hiding and code isolation. On the other hand, a **Keep It Simple Stupid** (**KISS**) approach kicks in sometimes and an anonymous method can greatly simplify common cases.

The following screenshot shows the **CodeSite** log for the typical run of the `AnonymousThreadProject` demo (full source included):

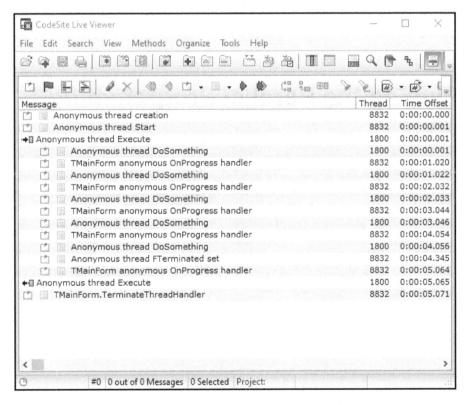

Figure 11.6

The preceding screenshot shows you the execution flow of this version of the program. This is evidently a more compact solution. Less *boilerplate* code means the overall readability improves, as the task definition is in a single place and you can focus on it instead of code being needed to simply implement the internals of multi-threaded programming. It makes a huge difference, especially when the task definition is small.

 For the sake of simplicity, I deliberately avoided synchronizing the passing of the final value of LCounter to the FFinalCounter variable. This is evidently an operation that would, in theory, need some synchronization as we have a different (background) thread manipulating an object (the form) living in the main/UI thread. Moreover, I made up this demo in order not to have multiple threads and this greatly simplifies the general scenario.

Now that we are confident with classical concepts of multi-threaded programming, we can take another step forward and learn about Delphi's Parallel Programming Library. It was introduced a few years ago and it is part of the RTL (and so is, available on all supported platforms).

Introducing the Parallel Programming Library

In the previous section, we saw how handy it is to take advantage of modern language features such as anonymous methods. This kind of feature may, at first sight, leave the developer with the idea they have no practical implications on existing code. But the TThread case obviously proves that making use of an anonymous method provides a concise, functional, effective, and simple-to-use alternative to address the same problem.

With **Delphi XE7** (September 2014), a new library has been added to the Delphi RTL (and so is, available both from VCL and FMX)—the **Parallel Programming Library (PPL)**, mostly centered on the System.Threading unit.

Modern computers (including mobile devices) have multi-core CPUs. Modern software applications have a growing demand for multi-threaded code (for a number of reasons, some of which we have discussed earlier in this chapter). Modern language features (introduced with **Delphi 2010**, August 2009) offer a modern approach to the old issue of multi-threaded programming.

We will cover some basic information about the Parallel Programming Library and how it can greatly impact your approach to multi-threading.

First of all, we are going one step further in terms of abstraction—we'll focus on tasks to be executed, no longer on threads executing code. As said, especially when dealing with the UI, you need to execute some code in the background and, possibly, interact back with the main/UI thread to deliver results. A task is the portion of code to be executed in the background. You can enclose in a task whatever instructions you would put in the Execute method of a TThread inherited class.

The parallel programming library provides some data structures (classes) to implement this new model, for example, the TTask, TParallel, and TFuture classes.

Another crucial point you need to understand about PPL is the concept of thread pooling. Imagine having a hundred tasks being defined and executed in a short period of time. It is not an impossible number, especially as we just stated the perfect scenario involves small tasks to be defined and scheduled for execution as needed. In theory, using the classic TThread approach, we would end up with a hundred threads being created, executed, synchronized from time to time against the main/UI thread and then destroyed. All this just to execute some small tasks in the background of our application.

A more effective way to handle such a situation involves a concept very well known to database experienced developers—**pooling**. Instead of spending resources (time, CPU, memory) on repeatedly creating and destroying threads, just to use them for a brief amount of time, we can think about maintaining a pool of threads and using them to execute tasks.

In our example, we will have 100 tasks defined (in what you can think of as a queue) and a number of executors (threads) consuming the tasks queue. Basically, we are reusing thread instances instead of continuously setting them up and tearing them down. In the database world, this has been proven to have a great positive impact on performance as, by reusing connections, we skip all latency times and connection setup times (greatly improving performance in high throughput scenarios).

The Parallel Programming Library is used by other parts of the RTL, FMX, and VCL. Generally speaking, the ability to easily implement parallel programming results in the improvement of performance in many areas (non-UI).

This approach adds the capability to properly size the pool, also according to the actual hardware (CPU cores) available. Also, this prevents the starvation of the CPU with too many threads being created. Obviously, this all makes sense if it is acceptable to queue tasks, in other words, you don't need tasks defined simultaneously to be also executed simultaneously. Sometimes this is far from trivial to determine but, in the general case we are addressing (UI interactions), it is generally an easy assumption to make.

From now on, you are no longer *starting threads*; instead, you are asking the **Parallel Programming Library** (**PPL**) to run a task on a secondary thread (no matter which one but belonging to the pool).

Let's have a closer look at the TTask class, a first-class citizen in the PPL. In the next section, we'll learn how to use its capabilities.

Introducing the TTask class

It should sound natural at this point that task definition passes through anonymous methods. The following snippet shows how easy it is to define a new task through the PPL:

```
uses System.Threading;

TTask.Run(
  procedure
  begin
    // Do something
  end
);
```

We should recall the TThread.CreateAnonymousThread class function but a bit more abstracted. The anonymous method will be executed as soon as this task gets assigned to a thread of the PPL pool.

There is no magic—the underlying elements are all still there (threads, synchronization needs, and so on). In other words, this is the typical case of *syntax sugar* added over a classic problem.

Our example can be translated using PPL elements as shown in the `PPLProject` demo (full source code included). The following excerpt is from the `OnClick` event handler of `StartButton`:

```
procedure TMainForm.StartButtonClick(Sender: TObject);
begin
  if Assigned(FTask) then
    Exit;

  FTask := TTask.Run(
    procedure
    var
      LCounter: Integer;
    begin
      (...)
      LCounter := 0;
      while FTask.Status = TTaskStatus.Running do
      begin
        (...)
        Sleep(1000);
        Inc(LCounter);

        // OnProgress equivalent
        TThread.Synchronize(nil
          , procedure
            begin
              (...)
              StatusLabel.Text := 'Running, counter = '
                + LCounter.ToString;
            end
        );
      end;

      // OnTerminate equivalent
      TThread.Synchronize(nil
        , procedure
          begin
            FFinalCounter := LCounter;
            StatusLabel.Text := 'Completed, counter = '
              + FFinalCounter.ToString;
            FTask := nil;
          end
      );
    end
  );
  (...)
  StatusLabel.Text := 'Started';
end;
```

In the previous code, please note `TTask.Run` returns a reference (type `ITask`) to the defined task. You may, for example, query the task status (through the homonymous property) or take some actions against it (that is, cancel the task, wait for completion, and so on).

This example is equivalent to the original program (the `SimpleThreadProject` demo) but it is a clear translation of the original approach using new tools (the PPL). You can streamline this demo to be more *task* oriented and less *thread* structured. Moreover, PPL gives its best (in terms of code readability) in shoot-and-forget and shoot-and-report situations. Control loop situations are less appropriate to match the PPL approach.

As said, the PPL acts a bit like syntax sugar over multithreading programming problems. Under the hood, many topics are the same as seen before, including the synchronization needs. In the next section, we'll learn how to address synchronization using PPL.

Dealing with synchronization

Once you start using tasks (or threads as we have seen) you'll probably be facing the need for synchronization. The ability to spread code execution simultaneously across multiple cores does not eliminate the occasional need for some kind of synchronization. You may parallelize some code execution but, subsequently, you may need to wait for some of the tasks to be accomplished before proceeding further. Or, as already said, you may need to find some mechanism to properly access some shared resources that would get ruined if accessed indiscriminately.

A number of functionalities to deal with tasks are built into the PPL. Let's have a brief overview of the most significant ones.

Waiting for a task to complete

Assume that we have a task reference (`ITask`) and we want to wait (synchronously) for its completion before proceeding further.

The `ITask.Wait` method is provided exactly for this purpose. It also accepts an argument for the desired timeout, making it very easy to fine-tune the operation. The following code shows the `ITask.Wait` method:

```
var
  LTask: ITask;
begin
  LTask := TTask.Run(
    procedure
```

```
    begin
      Sleep(5000); // Do something...
    end
  );

  LTask.Wait();
  // Completed
end;
```

In the previous code, assuming that we are running this code in the main/UI thread, the expected behavior here is that the task will run in the background, and the main/UI thread will synchronously wait for the task completion. Obviously, especially if the task is not immediate, this will block the main/UI thread so this is not a good practice to achieve responsiveness.

The following code shows how we can try to avoid blocking the main/UI thread for the whole execution time of the task by using the Timeout argument of the Wait method, so we can split the waiting time into multiple segments, having a chance to execute some code in between:

```
var
  LTask: ITask;
  LCompleted: Boolean;
begin
  LTask := TTask.Run(
    procedure
    begin
      Sleep(5000); // Do something...
    end
  );

  LCompleted := LTask.Wait(10);
  while not LCompleted do
  begin
    Log('Waiting, task status: '
      + TRttiEnumerationType.GetName<TTaskStatus>(LTask.Status));
    LCompleted := LTask.Wait(500);
  end;
  Log('Completed');
end;
```

In the previous code, we are waiting for a very short amount of time (10 ms) and then, if the task has not finished, we enter a loop of wait calls having 500 ms as the timeout. If the task (that is running in the background) completes while a Wait call is on, the call will immediately return true, otherwise, it will hold the wait till the timeout (500 ms) elapses (and return false).

This second implementation version gives you some control during the waiting but it is still very synchronous (thus, blocking). The main/UI thread will not be able to keep the UI alive and responsive because it is busy waiting for the task to complete. This is obviously far from what we are looking to achieve.

We introduced tasks to avoid blocking the UI while doing some lengthy operations. Blocking the UI that is waiting for the background operations to complete is definitely the opposite of our goal, that is, we want the UI thread to be free to flow while the lengthy operation is performed in the background.

The most experienced Delphi developers here may argue about adding an `Application.ProcessMessage` instruction in the `while` loop. This, especially on message-queue-based systems, would let the UI handle messages (including paint related messages), giving the impression that the application is not frozen. However, this is only a placebo instead of being an actual solution to achieve responsiveness.

The following code shows the third wait implementation provided in the `PPLWaitProject` demo:

```
var
  LTask: ITask;
begin
  Log('Button clicked');

  LTask := TTask.Run(
    procedure
    begin
      Log('Task start');
      Sleep(5000);
      Log('Task end');
    end
  );

  TTask.Run(
    procedure
    var
      LCompleted: Boolean;
    begin
      LCompleted := LTask.Wait(10);
      while not LCompleted do
      begin
        Log('Waiting, task status: '
          + TRttiEnumerationType.GetName<TTaskStatus>
          (LTask.Status));
        LCompleted := LTask.Wait(500);
```

```
      end;
      Log('Completed');
    end
  );
end;
```

From the previous code, you can spot that the same code is used in the second version but this time it is wrapped in a `TTask.Run` call. We are moving the synchronous wait into another task, so we'll have a task performing some long operation and a second task waiting for the first to complete.

The execution of this piece of code will return immediately, meaning the caller (the main/UI thread) will not be blocked either by the launch (and execution) of the working task or by the launch (and execution) of the waiting task.

> In the demo, I've used CodeSite to log and you can immediately notice the differences by looking at the log viewer and checking the **Thread** column. In the last example, you'll notice three different thread IDs involved—the main/UI thread, the thread executing the working task, and the one executing the waiting task.

As a final note, please consider that waiting for a task should not be your first option. Most of the time, you can simply have a piece of code (properly synchronized if it needs to be) as the last portion of the task definition in order to signal that the task has been completed. The following code implements a typical shoot-and-report task:

```
TTask.Run(
  procedure
  begin
    Sleep(5000); // Do something ...

    TThread.Synchronize(nil
      , procedure
      begin
        ShowMessage('Completed');
      end
    );
  end
);
```

As you can see in the preceding code, the code we want to be run after the task has completed is written as the tail of the task itself. This way, we are delegating the execution of that code to the task itself, at the proper moment, and with the opportunity to choose whether or not to synchronize with the main thread.

Waiting strategies, however, may be very handy, especially in a situation involving multiple (possibly nested) tasks. In the next section, we'll see how to deal with multiple tasks at a time.

Waiting for tasks to finish

Consider a scenario where you have defined and started multiple tasks. For instance, imagine you are downloading multiple items from the web in order to process them and build some UI elements for the user.

Assume you started a task for each item and you stored the references in an array (the `TArray<ITask>` type). You may decide to wait for the completion of all items before proceeding to process them or start processing items as soon as one of them is available.

Two methods are available to handle both cases:

- The `TTask.WaitForAll` method: It will accept the array of `ITask` references as an argument and will synchronously wait until all of them have been completed. A second optional argument is available to set a timeout for the wait, and all considerations are made in the previous section about waiting synchronously or asynchronously standing.
- The `TTask.WaitForAny` method: It has identical arguments but will return as soon as one of the items has been completed.

The preceding two methods once again greatly simplify the writing of multi-task code, letting you focus on the application code instead of dealing with details of task synchronization.

 Another option to run multiple tasks and have a chance to check the global status of the operations is to use the `TParallel.Join` function. It is an asynchronous call but it returns an `ITask` reference that you can use to check its `Status` property.

Now we have acquired some confidence with tasks and their synchronization mechanisms, we can introduce another feature, built with these building blocks. *If we have the ability to define a task, have it running in the background, and possibly wait for its completion, how about using these capabilities to parallelize the calculation of some values we already know we'll need at some point in the future?*

The key point here is that we know we'll need the value and we know how to calculate it. We just want a simplification where, if we can calculate it in advance, that's good; otherwise, we need the code to wait until the value is actually available. The next section will show us how to achieve this easily thanks to the PPL's capabilities.

Learning about futures

Last but not least, we can find goodies in the PPL, which are futures. A future can be defined as a value that we already know we'll need in the future. The key point is getting (calculating, building, retrieving, and so on) a value that is expensive in terms of computation resources (CPU, time, network, and so on), and that we don't want to affect the main/UI thread with this burden.

The following code shows the implementation of a future:

```
var
  LFuture: IFuture<Integer>;
begin
  LFuture := TTask.Future<Integer>(
    function : Integer
    begin
      Sleep(5000); // Do something...
      Result := 42;
    end
  );

  ShowMessage(LFuture.Value.ToString);
end;
```

The previous code example shows how a future is defined. Basically, we provide a builder function that is capable of returning our value and we wrap this function in a task.

The future implementation relies on another modern language feature—**generics**. We are trying to handle a value of a certain type (for example, X) and so we'll need to provide a function returning a value (the X type). In the same way, we'll need to hold the value (once available) in a variable of type X and so on. I suggest you make yourself familiar, at least, with basic concepts about generics (refer to Marco Cantù's books).

If you put the previous code in an OnClick handler of a button, you'll notice the application will freeze (for 5 seconds). This happens because we define the future (and this is immediate), then we ask for the future value. At this point, the future will try to retrieve the value and will not return the value until it is available.

To make sense, we need to define the future way before we need its value. This way, once defined, the future will run in the background (in a dedicated task) and will build the value (that we are going to need in the future) way before we ask for it.

Keep in mind that a future will try to build its value as soon it has been defined (a task is started for the purpose). When its value is used in some expression or instruction, if it is already available, you will have no wait time, otherwise, your execution flow will be on hold until the value becomes available.

This is a great simplification as you, at this point, can ignore all synchronization issues and just use the value (returning to a sequential execution model—so natural for human beings) with two assurances:

- If it has been possible to pre-build the value before the point we are trying to use it, no wait will occur.
- If the value is still building, the wait will step in automatically.

It is hard to get the advantage of when looking at a single future scenario but if you have multiple futures (defined in a single or multiple points), you'll see that the code will be parallelized automatically. Defining three futures will cause three tasks to be set up in order to build the three values, simultaneously.

Imagine, for example, a business application starting up—the loading of some remote resources may be of great advantage when it's done with futures. Even on single functionalities, you may write your code in order to be able to *get ahead* of some needs and have the related code running in the background while the user is doing some data entry or browsing some preliminary data.

In terms of responsiveness, please remember you still may fall into blocking waits so consider boxing the futures into tasks in order to keep the whole thing smooth from the perspective of the main/UI thread.

In this section, we learned why responsiveness is important and the techniques used to achieve it. We paid attention to the most common pitfalls, such as freezing the **User Interface** (**UI**) while performing long tasks in the UI thread and missing proper synchronization between the UI thread and secondary threads. It is important not to miss the advantages of the built-in Parallel Programming Library while dealing with common tasks in modern application development.

Summary

In this chapter, we have learned what we mean by the term responsive applications and how to achieve responsiveness in your applications. Even if our coverage of them was far from exhaustive, the key concepts of multi-threaded programming should now be clear. As stated, multi-threaded programming can be challenging to understand and needs some proper attention to be mastered.

You now have an understanding of how multi-threaded programming has been supported in Delphi for a long time, following the classical approach around the `TThread` object. We have introduced some background concepts tied to the synchronization needs that are intrinsic to this kind of scenario. You also have learned about the Parallel Programming Library (introduced with Delphi XE7) and its main elements, such as tasks and futures. You are now able to apply synchronization concepts to these elements for your usage.

In the next chapter, we are going to discuss some cross-platform services the FMX framework conveniently wraps for the cross-platform developer in order to make them available over for all supported platforms.

Further reading

- *Delphi High Performance*, Packt, 2018, Primož Gabrijelčič (`https://www.thedelphigeek.com/`); see also his parallel programming library (OmniThreadLibrary)
- *Delphi Memory Management: For Classic and ARC Compilers*, Dalija Prasnikar, Neven Prasnikar Jr, CreateSpace Independent Publishing Platform (24 June 2018)
- Marco Cantù books and his material about Delphi language (*Object Pascal Handbook*, to name one)

12
Exploring Cross-Platform Services

In the previous chapter, we learned about the use of parallel programming to achieve responsiveness in our applications. This is indeed a very desirable characteristic to gain, regardless of the target platform you are addressing. From a certain perspective, `System.Threading` capabilities are abstractions over the parallel programming mechanisms of each platform and will let you implement your applications with a single code base even when the internals of each of the platforms are different.

From the same perspective, a number of capabilities are available in FMX in order to wrap underlying implementations of each platform, at least where a corresponding implementation is available for the specific platform.

In order to take advantage of the powerful abstraction layer FMX provides, we are going to cover the following topics in this chapter:

- Accessing the clipboard service
- Managing dialog forms
- Leveraging touch capabilities
- Understanding messaging support
- Using native HTTP client implementations
- Getting familiar with Bluetooth support

Without FMX wrapping support for these capabilities, you would need to learn and acquire familiarity with all the different approaches/libraries needed to create a multi-platform application featuring modern capabilities such as those in the list.

Let's begin our journey exploring the goodies that are available out of the box. The full list of available platform services is available in the official **RAD Studio** documentation at the following link: `http://docwiki.embarcadero.com/RADStudio/en/FireMonkey_Platform_ Services`.

At the end of this chapter, you should be able to build complex applications, using many modern features such as HTTP connections or Bluetooth services. Also, you will be confident with how touch-enabled applications can take advantage of gestures and other peculiarities of this input method (which is crucial nowadays). If you are an experienced developer, you'll understand how differently dialogs behave in mobile (responsive) applications with respect to the desktop scenario.

Technical requirements

Here is the full source code used throughout this chapter: `https://github.com/PacktPublishing/Delphi-GUI-Programming-with-FireMonkey/tree/master/Chapter%2012`.

Accessing the clipboard service

In this section, we will encounter our first (simple) example of a platform service wrapped by the FMX framework. Clipboard support may be taken for granted but actually is an integration with the underlying OS (and has more platform-specific behaviors than you may notice at first glance). This will serve you in two different ways, that is, to understand and properly use the clipboard in your applications, and as an introduction to the FMX approach to wrapping platform services.

The **clipboard** is a very widely used feature of most operating systems out there. Basically, it provides the user with the capability to share a piece of content (text, graphics, custom content) across different parts of the application; for example, to copy some text from an edit box and paste it in another one. It can even be across different applications, such as copying some text from a browser to a text editor (*you're brave!*).

Even though it is a very popular feature and it has been around a long time, this doesn't mean it is actually implemented in the same way against all supported platforms. For instance, on each platform, the application needs to deal with different **operating system (OS) Application Programming Interfaces (APIs)**. Another point to consider is that these different, OS-specific APIs do not share the same functionalities.

For example, **Android** does not support the copying or pasting of images while **Windows**, **Linux**, **OS X/macOS**, and **iOS** do.

I've prepared a simple demo for you, showcasing an FMX application accessing the clipboard. There are four buttons to respectively copy and paste some text or some graphic content. The following screenshot shows the main form of the `ClipboardProject` application in the Form Designer window of the Delphi IDE:

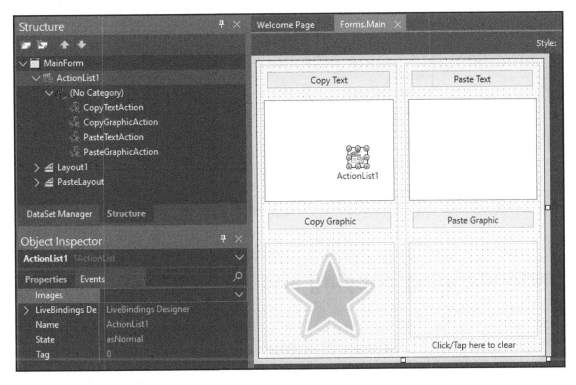

Figure 12.1

From the preceding screenshot, we can have a look at how the clipboard service is discovered and referenced. There are two different services wrapping the clipboard; they are `IFMXClipboardService` (defined in the `FMX.Platform` unit) and `IFMXExtendedClipboardService` (defined in the `FMX.Clipboard` unit).

We are going to use the latter as the first one, which is very basic. The RAD Studio documentation (`http://docwiki.embarcadero.com/Libraries/en/FMX.Clipboard. IFMXExtendedClipboardService`) states availability for the service as you can see in the following screenshot:

Platform Support			
Platform	**Text Format**	**Image Format**	**Custom Format**
Windows	✔	✔	✔
OS X	✔	✔	✔
iOS	✔	✔	✔
Android	✔		3.0+

Figure 12.2

We should note, as you can see in the preceding screenshot, the documentation suggests a workaround to deal with images on Android using a clipboard custom format, supported by **Android 3.0** and later.

In the following sections, we will learn about copying and pasting text as well as graphic content.

Understanding copying and pasting text

In the demo application, I am using actions (TAction instances) in order to take advantage of OnUpdate or OnExecute events and provide a nice user experience to the user. If something is written in the leftmost memo component, the **Copy Text** button becomes enabled and the user can use it to set the clipboard content as text.

As the clipboard is no longer empty, the **Paste Text** button becomes enabled (only if the clipboard content is textual, of course). The same considerations apply to the second row of components, for graphic content. An additional click or touch-enabled label has been added to give the user a chance to clear the PasteImage component. At application startup (the main form's OnCreate event handler), we look up the platform service we desire, that is, the clipboard. The following code snippet shows how:

```
procedure TMainForm.FormCreate(Sender: TObject);
begin
  if not TPlatformServices.Current.SupportsPlatformService(
    IFMXExtendedClipboardService, FClipboardService)
  then
    raise ENotSupportedException.Create('Clipboard not supported on this
platform!');
end;
```

From the preceding code, the `FClipboardService` field has been added to the form declaration (the private section) so as to be available to all code in the form's methods, including actions' event handlers. The reference to `IFMXExtendedClipboardService` is retrieved through the `Current` singleton instance of `TPlatformServices` in the `FMX.Platform` unit. If the service is not available on the current platform, an exception is raised.

> In real-world situations, you may want to let your application behave differently. If the service you are looking up is mandatory for the application to run, raising the exception is probably fine. Otherwise, you may want to adapt your application, possibly switching off those functionalities requiring the availability of that specific service.

Now that we have a reference to the `IFMXExtendedClipboardService` instance, we can use it to implement our actions. For instance, the following snippet shows the code to copy the text content of the `CopyMemo` component to the clipboard and to update the `Enabled` property of the corresponding action:

```
procedure TMainForm.CopyTextActionExecute(Sender: TObject);
begin
  FClipboardService.SetText(CopyMemo.Text);
end;

procedure TMainForm.CopyTextActionUpdate(Sender: TObject);
begin
  CopyTextAction.Enabled := not CopyMemo.Text.IsEmpty;
end;
```

The corresponding code to handle paste from the clipboard is shown in the following code block:

```
procedure TMainForm.PasteTextActionExecute(Sender: TObject);
begin
  PasteMemo.Text := FClipboardService.GetText;
end;

procedure TMainForm.PasteTextActionUpdate(Sender: TObject);
begin
  PasteTextAction.Enabled := FClipboardService.HasText;
end;
```

The preceding code is very simple and easy to read. The convenient `SetText`, `GetText`, and `HasText` methods of the `IFMXExtendedClipboardService` instance make it really straightforward to implement copy and paste functionalities of text content in your FMX app, and in a fully cross-platform way (Windows, OS X/macOS, Linux, Android, and iOS).

We'll now move on to the next section, about copying and pasting graphic content.

Learning about copying and pasting graphic content

As we have said, our service supports text and images (and custom formats you may want to register), even though the functionality is wrapped for all platforms but available only on some of them (all but Android, in fact).

This means we can still query for a reference to this service on the Android platform but functionalities will be limited and calling some methods of the interface may result in exceptions or ineffective behavior.

The following code block shows how the `CopyGraphic` action has been implemented (`OnExecute`/`OnUpdate` event handlers):

```
procedure TMainForm.CopyGraphicActionExecute(Sender: TObject);
var
  LBS: TBitmapSurface;
begin
  LBS := TBitmapSurface.Create();
  try
    LBS.Assign(CopyImage.Bitmap);
    FClipboardService.SetImage(LBS);
  finally
    LBS.Free;
  end;
end;


procedure TMainForm.CopyGraphicActionUpdate(Sender: TObject);
begin
  {$IFDEF ANDROID} // clipboard does not support images
  CopyGraphicAction.Enabled := False;
  {$ELSE}
  CopyGraphicAction.Enabled := Assigned(CopyImage.Bitmap);
  {$IFEND}
end;
```

From the preceding code, the `SetImage` method of the service interface accepts a `TBitmapSurface` argument we can build and fill using the `CopyImage` content. The code will compile on every platform but will raise an exception on Android. I've decided to handle this situation by disabling the action for the Android platform (check the `CopyGraphicActionUpdate` implementation).

I could have avoided the use of the **IFDEF compiler directive** and checked `TOSVersion.Platform` to determine when the application is running on Android. These are different techniques with the same result. The best option would have been to have a separate service for copying/pasting images and check whether it is supported or not on the actual execution platform.

On the other hand, to deal with the pasting of graphic content, we can stick to some code very similar to the one we used for text in the previous section. Relying on the documentation statement of `HasImage` always returning `False` on Android (http://docwiki.embarcadero.com/Libraries/en/FMX.Clipboard.IFMXExtendedClipboardService.HasImage), we can skip checking the actual platform and simply use it. The action will never be enabled on Android, so eventual calls to the `GetImage` method are prevented, as shown in the following code:

```
procedure TMainForm.PasteGraphicActionExecute(Sender: TObject);
begin
  PasteImage.Bitmap.Assign(FClipboardService.GetImage);
end;

procedure TMainForm.PasteGraphicActionUpdate(Sender: TObject);
begin
  PasteGraphicAction.Enabled := FClipboardService.HasImage;
end;
```

Now that we have discussed all the relevant code in our application, we can run it on different platforms and have a look at the results. The following screenshot shows the application running on Windows (left) and OS X/macOS (right):

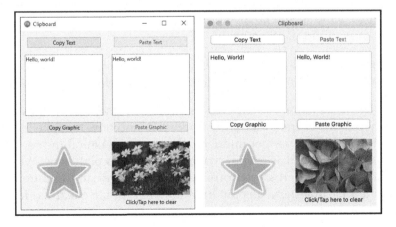

Figure 12.3

As you can see, in the previous screenshot the **Copy Graphic** and **Paste Graphic** buttons are enabled (and have been used). The following screenshot instead shows a screenshot from an Android phone running the same application:

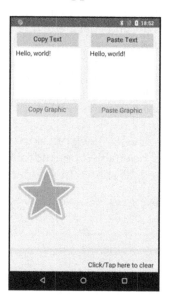

Figure 12.4

As you can see, the components related to graphic content are disabled (one hardcoded by us with IFDEF and the other one because the HasImage function always returns false, disabling the action consequently). This application's UI has been tuned using the **FireUI** technology (an Android 5" view exists, featuring better sizing of the buttons), so a good improvement to this demo would be to simply hide (set Visible to False) the disabled components for the Android platform.

Having built-in support for the system's clipboard is a basic but nice-to-have feature and, as we have seen, not immune from pitfalls related to the cross-platform support.

In this section, we learned about the clipboard service. We also learned how to access it, how to detect whether the current platform supports it, and how to make use of it calling the methods of the provided wrapper interface. We also understood the copying and pasting scenarios of text as well as graphic content on various platforms. We have also seen in detail the first example of a cross-platform service. Now we can continue through the others and note their peculiarities, keeping in mind what we have learned from the ClipboardProject demo.

In the next section, we will look at dialog functionality and how to manage it.

Managing dialog forms

Dialogs are very popular functionality. Many applications rely on dialogs to present the user with some content.

In this section, we will look at dialogs and how to properly use them in modern applications. One of the biggest differences is about their *modality*, that is, an experienced developer may expect their code to hold until a dialog is on the screen while in a modern application (on a mobile platform, for example), dialogs follow an async pattern, by default.

There are many different dialog types, ranging from the simplest ones that are used to provide a simple text message, to more complex dialogs such as selecting a file from the filesystem. Many functionalities pass through dialogs as they are a natural way to interact with the user to inform them or to fetch some value needed by the current operation.

Nonetheless, dialogs in a multi-platform context can be tricky to handle. First of all, some of the dialogs are actually provided by the underlying OS and you really want them to be the original ones. We don't want some dialogs mimicking the native ones, for example, because of some built-in functionalities and, generally speaking, to keep the user *at home* instead of using a custom dialog they aren't familiar with.

Another major distinction comes with the fact that some operating systems adopted a different paradigm with respect to dialogs, that is, most desktop operating systems follow a synchronous approach while mobile operating systems tend to avoid blocking calls and embrace an asynchronous approach. Also, mobile operating systems (iOS specifically) drifted by desktop's trend to be file-oriented.

The world of mobile phones is made of apps, where each one should be considered standalone and with its own data (and storage capabilities). You don't usually navigate through files on a mobile device; you are more likely to use an app and, from time to time, you may want to share some content with other apps.

This is the reason some dialogs are not available on mobile, such as the **file open** dialog, wrapped by the `TOpenDialog` non-visual component, which you can use in desktop applications. On the other hand, mobile has *share sheet* functionalities, being very familiar to the user as (especially on the iOS side up to **iOS 12** version) they represent the only way to share app-specific content to another app or other OS facilities (that is, the clipboard to name one).

The `FMX.DialogService` unit (part of the FMX framework) provides the `TDialogService` class. Using the methods of this class, you can easily manage basic dialogs in your applications, abstracting from the platform.

There are three types of dialog, each one wrapped in a different method (actually, methods as overloaded versions are provided), namely, `ShowMessage`, `InputQuery`, and `MessageDialog` (if you are familiar with the VCL world, these names will certainly be recognizable).

The first one delivers a text message to the user, the second one prompts the user for some input (one or more values), and the last one is a sophistication of the first as it lets the developer set an accent for the message (informative, error, warning, and so on) and a number of buttons the user can choose among to respond to the message.

Those of you who are long-time developers will immediately notice a significant difference between the mobile and desktop world, that is, dialogs (starting with the simplest, yet ubiquitous `ShowMessage`) are asynchronous. So let's learn about synchronous and asynchronous modes in the next section.

Understanding differences between synchronous versus asynchronous modes

As stated before, dialogs are asynchronous (async), this practically means the execution flow will not wait for the user to handle the dialog (close the message, respond to a question, prompt some values) before proceeding to the next instruction.

This simple yet very significant difference across the mobile and desktop worlds can be difficult to get, especially by experienced developers. You may be really acquainted with the synchronous (sync) model for dialogs. I've seen developers using dialogs for decades to pause the execution flow (`ShowMessage` *debugging, anyone?*), and relying on such behavior has a significant impact on your application design.

In very simple terms, on desktop platforms, the call to `ShowMessage` doesn't return control until the user closes the dialog, that is, you are assured that the next line of code you wrote after the `ShowMessage` call isn't executed until the user has closed the dialog.

On the mobile platform, you have a call to `ShowMessage` that will return immediately after the dialog begins to be visible to the user (way before the user closes it) and the next instruction is executed immediately.

Although the `ShowMessage` scenario may not lead to problems, you'll probably find your application piling up dialog boxes instead of having one dialog at a time in front of the user.

Things may get more complicated with questions to the user such as *would you confirm deletion of the current record?* The answer should be *Yes* or *No* because the next line of code (very likely to be some *if user_response = Yes then Delete Record*) will be executed before the user actually has a chance to respond. Actually, you'll have no chance to collect the user response to the question. The same problem arises when you need to prompt the user for some input values (*Please input a quantity for the item:*).

 This very same situation happens with forms shown through the `Show` and `ShowModal` methods, that is, on desktop, you'll see a different behavior while on mobile you'll get the same (non-modal) behavior.

Let's consider the following code snippet:

```
procedure TMainForm.ShowMessageButtonClick(Sender: TObject);
begin
  TDialogService.ShowMessage('Hello, world!');
  ShowMessageButton.Text := TimeToStr(Now);
end;
```

We can see two instructions: the first one will show a dialog to the user and the second one will update the `Text` instance of a `ShowMessageButton` component. The snippet actually represents the `OnClick` event handler for the button itself. It gets executed when the button is clicked. The first instruction will behave differently when the application is run on a desktop platform (Windows, OS X/macOS, or Linux) than on a mobile one (iOS and Android).

 `TDialogService` also provides a `PreferredMode` class property to let you determine the actual behavior without relying on the per-platform defaults provided by FMX. However, you have to consider that some combinations (mode/platform) may not be available or suitable.

Specifically, on an Android phone, the second instruction will be executed immediately after the first one (so the dialog will be shown to the user and, without waiting for the user to close the dialog, the `Text` instance of the button will be updated). On the other hand, let's say on the Windows platform, the opposite will take place, that is, the second instruction will not be executed until the user has closed the dialog (being `ShowMessage`, this means either clicking on the **OK** button or the eventually available **Close** button).

As already said, such a difference in the control flow of the program can be very significant, especially when the actual intention of the developer is to use a dialog to hold the program execution from proceeding further.

The following diagram summarizes the difference between synchronous and asynchronous behavior:

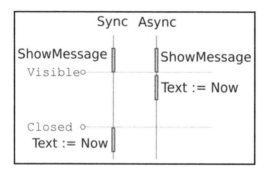

Figure 12.5

The lapse of time between the **Closed** and **Visible** labels is in the hands of the user, of course. The **Async** scenario (the default on mobile platforms) can be ineffective in some situations. There are two other overloaded versions of TDialogService.ShowMessage to properly sync code execution to the user response, as shown in the following code snippet (taken from the interface section of the FMX.DialogService.pas source file):

```
class procedure ShowMessage(const AMessage: string;
  const ACloseDialogProc: TInputCloseDialogProc); overload;

class procedure ShowMessage(const AMessage: string;
  const ACloseDialogEvent: TInputCloseDialogEvent;
  const AContext: TObject = nil); overload;
```

Basically, we can pass (using an anonymous or regular object method reference) some code to be executed after the user has responded to the dialog. The exact term for this is **delegation**, that is, we are passing a portion of code (either literally through an anonymous method or by referencing the second overloaded version), delegating its execution to the ShowMessage implementation. This gives the developer a chance to defer code execution in response to the event "*the dialog has been closed*." This is perfect in all cases in which you need to subordinate in time the execution of some code to the behavior of the user with the dialog.

Please note that, nonetheless, the general behavior is still asynchronous. Let's have a look at the following code snippet, showing the implementation of the OnClick event for the ShowMessageCloseButton component:

```
procedure TMainForm.ShowMessageCloseButtonClick(Sender: TObject);
begin
  TDialogService.ShowMessage(
    'Opens at ' + TimeToStr(Now)
  , procedure (const AModalResult: TModalResult)
    begin
      TDialogService.ShowMessage('Closes at ' + TimeToStr(Now));
    end
  );
  ShowMessageCloseButton.Text := TimeToStr(Now);
end;
```

From the preceding code, we are now using the second version of the ShowMessage method, passing an anonymous method as an argument of the call. Using this functionality, we can set the execution of the anonymous method after the moment the user actually responded to the dialog. But the outer call (that is, the TDialogService.ShowMessage call) is still asynchronous so the next instruction (the assignment of the current time to the Text property of the button) will take place immediately after the dialog shows up to the user (probably way before they have had a chance to respond to the dialog itself).

I've used the TimeToStr(Now) instruction to provide a textual representation of the current time of each step. If you go through the provided demo (without hurrying up too much as the resolution of TimeToStr is generally 1 second), you should be able to verify the exact temporal sequence events take place.

The following diagram visualizes the sequence of events that takes place in this scenario:

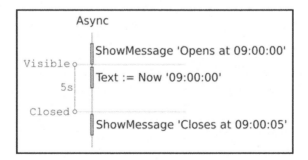

Figure 12.6

If you are new to async programming, you may find it confusing that the sequence of the instructions (as written in code) can differ from their execution sequence. Nonetheless, this is not different from event handling implementation where you provide a piece of code to respond to an event (whenever it occurs). Just beware here, as we are mixing sync and async instructions so you really need to have the point clear to avoid confusion or undesired side effects taking place.

The provided (available on GitHub) demo project (`DialogProject.dproj`) also showcases some other functionalities provided by the `FMX.Dialogs` and `FMX.DialogService` units. For example, you may find it useful to learn how to respond to a message dialog asking the user to choose among different actions, as shown in the following code snippet:

```
procedure TMainForm.MsgDialogWarnButtonClick(Sender: TObject);
begin
  TDialogService.MessageDialog(
    'This is a warning message'
  , TMsgDlgType.mtWarning
  , [TMsgDlgBtn.mbOK, TMsgDlgBtn.mbRetry], TMsgDlgBtn.mbOK, 0
  , procedure (const AResult: TModalResult)
    begin
      case AResult of
          mrOk: TDialogService.ShowMessage('OK: ' + TimeToStr(Now));
        mrRetry: TDialogService.ShowMessage('Retry: ' + TimeToStr(Now));
      end;
    end
  );
  MsgDialogWarnButton.Text := TimeToStr(Now) + ' Warn';
end;
```

As you may notice from the preceding code, the anonymous method passed (working as a completion handler) now has a different signature with respect to the one we used with the `ShowMessage` method. The caller will provide a `TModalResult` value to let the developer discriminate what to do according to the actual user response.

Once again this seems trivial but you still need to cope with the async behavior, that is, you can't suppose the execution will hold until the user has actually responded. You'll have to rethink your logic following an event-based pattern where the user making a choice is one of the involved events.

In this section, we have learned about dialogs. We also learned about the asynchronous and synchronous behavior of dialogs by using a demo project.

In the next section, we are going to learn how a crucial aspect of mobile (but not only mobile) applications is generalized and abstracted in the FMX framework, that is, touch capabilities. Even if this may not be evident at first glance, Android and iOS implement touch capabilities with very different approaches, and having a common abstraction layer in FMX is a very powerful feature.

Leveraging touch capabilities

Modern devices often include touchscreen capabilities. In this section, we are going to learn about touch capabilities and we'll use the different types of events to understand the available related functionalities.

Obviously, every platform has its own set of APIs to deal with touch capabilities and, building a cross-platform application, you would end up dealing with an API set for each supported platform. FMX wraps many touch capabilities for you in a convenient set of functionalities you can easily take advantage of in your applications.

Many abstractions are already built into the FireMonkey framework, that is, you can build a cross-platform application with a button that can be clicked (using the mouse or trackpad) on the desktop platform and, at the same time (with no additional effort), tapped on mobile platforms.

Many components implement touch capabilities enabling the user to scroll the content or interact with the component naturally. The TListView class, for example, also provides a pull-to-refresh built-in implementation.

Apart from these standard and built-in functionalities, as a developer, you may want to add some custom functionalities to your applications. There are three ways to easily implement touch-enabled capabilities in FMX, let's have a look at them in the next section.

Playing with the form's OnTouch event

Especially on mobile platforms, devices have multi-touch support. Basically, the user can interact with the screen of the device using one or more fingers. FMX provides a simple way to handle touches on the screen, that is, the OnTouch event exposed by TForm descendants.

The event handler you can provide has the following signature:

```
procedure TMainForm.FormTouch(Sender: TObject; const Touches: TTouches;
  const Action: TTouchAction);
```

Arguments include `Touches` and `Action` parameters. The first is an array of `TTouch` structures (records) basically representing the point the touch has happened at. Given the multi-touch support, you'll have an entry in the array for each finger actually detected on the device. The `Action` argument will help you discriminate which kind of event is happening among the `None`, `Up`, `Down`, `Move`, and `Cancel` possibilities.

You can easily keep track of the number of fingers currently on the active surface by tracking the `Up` and `Down` actions, as shown in the following code snippet:

```
case Action of
  TTouchAction.None: ;
  TTouchAction.Up: Dec(FDownCounter);
  TTouchAction.Down: Inc(FDownCounter);
  TTouchAction.Move: ;
  TTouchAction.Cancel: FDownCounter := 0;
end;

DownCounterLabel.Text := 'Down: ' + FDownCounter.ToString;
```

The preceding code is extracted from the `TouchProject` demo (available on GitHub) that you can run on Android and iOS devices. You can touch the screen of the device with one or more fingers and see up to 10 circles tracking your touches.

There are some underlying differences about the multitouch support and you can notice them easily running the `TouchProject` demo. One of the differences is that on Android it is easy to handle up to 10 touches simultaneously, while on the iOS side, it seems 5 is the maximum. Also, there is some different handling of `Up` and `Down` events causing some slight differences across the two platforms. However, these differences are built into Android and iOS so there's no chance of FMX getting around them.

The following screenshot shows the `TouchProject` application running on an Android device. The user touched the screen with four fingers and so the first four circles are now placed where the fingers were. The **Down** counter shows zero as, at the time the screenshot was taken, fingers were no longer touching the screen:

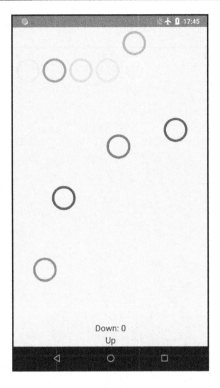

Figure 12.7

If you look at the preceding screenshot, you can also see the Text value of ActionLabel is **Up**, as the last action triggered was the one detecting the finger of the user leaving the device's screen.

Now that we are familiar with the OnTouch event, we will look at another event available to handle touch-related events, namely, the TForm.OnTap event in the next section.

Considering the form's OnTap event

The TForm.OnTap event will fire each time the user taps (using fingers, not clicking with a mouse) on the form. Beware that, if there is a component under the finger of the user, the form's event handler will not fire and the handling will pass to the component.

The TapProject demo shows you how easy it is to handle taps on the main form and clone a TCircle instance in the touched position. This time, with respect to the OnTouch event, the event is single and the only argument passed to the event handler is the tap position (coordinates).

The following screenshot shows the `TapProject` demo running on an iOS device (iPhone):

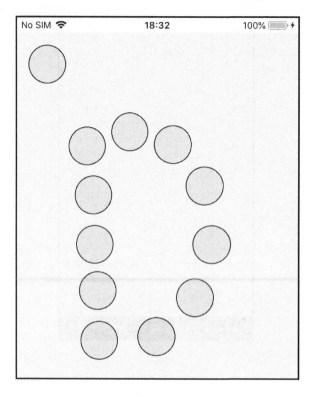

Figure 12.8

In the previous screenshot, you can see the circles dynamically created each time the user (that is, you) touched the **iPhone's** screen surface.

The following snippet shows the `OnTap` event handler implementation:

```
procedure TMainForm.FormTap(Sender: TObject; const Point: TPointF);
var
  LNewCircle: TCircle;
  LNewPos: TPointF;
begin
  LNewCircle := Circle1.Clone(Self) as TCircle;
  AddObject(LNewCircle);

  LNewPos := Point;
  LNewPos.Offset(-LNewCircle.Width / 2, -LNewCircle.Height / 2);
  LNewCircle.Position.Point := LNewPos;
end;
```

You can see in the preceding code how the actual position of the circle is determined so that the center of the circle will be at the touch position. The key point of these examples is to show how the underlying touch handling is wrapped and surfaced in FMX, for your convenience.

Apart from custom handling of touch-screen related events, FMX also provides convenient wrappers for many standard gestures. We will learn about that in the following section.

Exploring standard gestures

To enable gesture recognition and the subsequent firing of corresponding events, you just need to drop a TGestureManager component on your forms. The list of available gestures includes a number of **Standard** gestures (*you can see this list of gestures easily in the IDE*) you can easily bind to actions (TAction instances) in order to have the action executed when the gesture is recognized, as shown in the following screenshot:

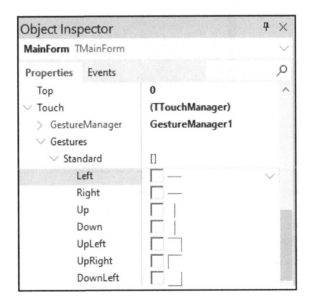

Figure 12.9

It is very immediate to add gesture support to your existing applications, especially if you have already implemented your functionalities using actions (something I would strongly recommend most of the time). The StandardGesturesProject demo showcases how to enable touch support in a simple application.

As you can see in the following screenshot, the main form of the application features a `TGlyph` component showing an image to the user. The image is taken from a `TImageList` instance and the user can change the current picture by clicking on two `TButton` instances on the toolbar:

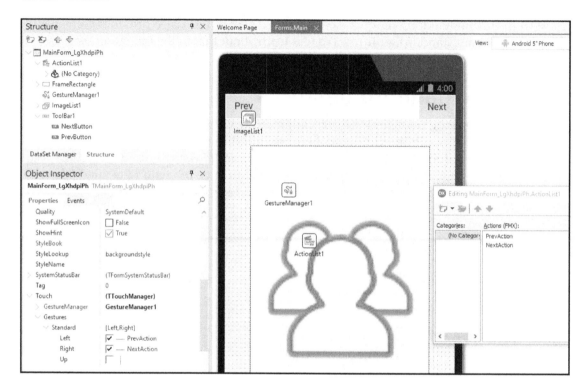

Figure 12.10

As you can see in the preceding screenshot, there is a `TActionList` component with a couple of actions available, namely, **PrevAction** and **NextAction**. The action implementation is trivial as it simply consists of changing the `ImageIndex` property of the `FrameGlyph` component one step forward (or backward).

The following code snippet shows the `OnExecute` and `OnUpdate` code for the `NextAction` action (you can guess, or check in the included sources, the `PrevAction` corresponding implementations):

```
procedure TMainForm.NextActionExecute(Sender: TObject);
begin
  FrameGlyph.ImageIndex := FrameGlyph.ImageIndex + 1;
end;

procedure TMainForm.NextActionUpdate(Sender: TObject);
begin
  NextAction.Enabled := FrameGlyph.ImageIndex < FrameGlyph.Images.Count -
1;
end;
```

So far, as you can see in the preceding code, it seems like a very normal application using controls (buttons) to let the user interact with the contents. Given that we added a `TGestureManager` component to the form (and selected it as a value for the `GestureManager` property of the form itself), we can also enable touch recognition by clicking on the checkbox beside the `Left` and `Right` actions. We can also set (using the component editor lookup) the action we'd like to be triggered when the gesture is recognized. Check *Figure 12.10* and the **Object Inspector** values to see the full configuration required.

That's it – from this moment, on touch-enabled devices, you can swipe your finger from left to right (triggering the `Right` gesture) or the other way around (triggering the `Left` gesture), and get the corresponding action executed. You can run the demo application on Android and iOS and see it working.

Over the years, touch support has evolved following several conventions (not always coherent with each other); for example, you may want to invert the swiping direction (swiping from right to left in order to see the next image). The choice is up to you and can be easily implemented by simply switching an action assignment in the **Touch** property of the form.

In the next section, we are going to learn about interactive gestures. Touch support has evolved into the recognition of complex gestures and users expect to use them in your app in specific situations (that is, zooming in on an image).

Implementing interactive gestures

If standard actions are immediate to enable and use (binding them to `TAction` instances), different behavior is often expected by the user. Instead of waiting for the full gesture to be completed (and recognized), some touch-driven features imply the execution of some code during the life of the gesture itself.

Typical examples are the following:

- **Zoom**: This gesture is about two fingers getting closer to or further from each other, in a pinch movement.
- **Pan**: This gesture is about a single finger sliding on the touch screen (not necessarily in a straight direction).
- **Rotate**: This gesture is about two fingers mimicking the act of rotating an object.
- **Long tap**: This gesture is about pressing and keeping a single finger on the touch screen.

Other variations include the double tap, press, and tap. You can check the `InteractiveGesture` property of the `Touch` node of the form for a complete list.

For instance, you may want to implement a way for the user to swipe through all the image collection in a single gesture. To implement such a behavior, we may take advantage of the pan gesture and take into consideration the position of the finger and the corresponding image index to select.

Of course, interactive gesture implementations generally are more custom than the mere use of a standard gesture trigger. Some code will be needed to implement the desired behavior in your application. Once you've enabled the gesture in the `InteractiveGesture` property of the component (or form) where you dare want the gesture to be recognized, you'll need to provide a handler for the `OnGesture` event.

The `InteractiveGestureProject` demo is a slight variation of the `StandardGestureProject` one where, instead of having the two standard gestures (`Right` or `Left`), we can swipe the finger over the `FrameRectangle` component and see the current image change according to the relative position of the finger within the rectangle (no assumptions made about vertical movements).

The following code snippet shows the `OnGesture` event handler implementation:

```
procedure TMainForm.FrameGlyphGesture(Sender: TObject;
  const EventInfo: TGestureEventInfo; var Handled: Boolean);
var
  LHorzPos: Single;
  LNormPos: Single;
  LImageIndex: Integer;
  LMaxIndex: Integer;
begin
  if EventInfo.GestureID = igiPan then
  begin
    LMaxIndex := FrameGlyph.Images.Count-1;
    LHorzPos := EventInfo.Location.X - FrameRectangle.Margins.Left;
    LNormPos := LHorzPos / FrameRectangle.Width;
    LImageIndex := Round(LNormPos * LMaxIndex);

    if LImageIndex < 0 then LImageIndex := 0
    else if LImageIndex > LMaxIndex then
      LImageIndex := LMaxIndex;
    FrameGlyph.ImageIndex := LImageIndex;
  end;
end;
```

The preceding code has been oversimplified for the sake of clarity, so you can see how the position of the finger is translated into the corresponding image index to be selected. Keep in mind the `OnGesture` event will be fired very often during the gesture, so you need to keep its implementation lightweight and consider possible performance implications when dealing with UI changes or heavy operations triggered in the event handler.

 A number of implementation examples for interactive gestures are available in the official documentation (`http://docwiki.embarcadero.com/CodeExamples/en/FMXInteractiveGestures_(Delphi)`).

A nice experiment you can try yourself is to add some consideration for the y axis, for example, to restrict gesture activation only when the user slides the finger in a specific portion of the rectangle, that is, the top or the bottom.

The correct implementation of interactive gestures can greatly improve the usability of your application and make them seem more modern (obviously, where a touchscreen is available). The touchscreen is actually the primary input method for mobile apps and, when it makes sense, you should use it as much as you can.

In this section, we have learned about touch and gesture capabilities, which are so ubiquitous in today's modern devices. We also learned about the OnTouch event, along with the OnTap event. We also looked at standard gestures and how to deal with more advanced interactive gestures.

Moving a bit away from user interaction, the next section introduces a Delphi capability that is built into the RTL. **Messaging support** is crucial to serve as a glue in many situations that involve touch, gestures, dialogs, and other topics we've covered so far.

Understanding messaging support

A very nice functionality that is built into the **Delphi RTL** (not only FMX) is contained in the System.Messaging unit. In this section, we are going to learn about this feature and how to take advantage of it in many situations where communication across different code parts is crucial. This also includes async events related to touch, gesture recognition, dialogs, and more.

Basically, it provides a customizable, pluggable, publish-subscribe mechanism that can be used by application developers to bend toward an event-driven approach. This is especially useful while dealing with asynchronous interactions and, generally speaking, it is a good way to keep dependencies low (resulting in loosely coupled code).

This mechanism is used inside the FMX framework to provide some functionalities (that is, some OS-to-application interactions such as requesting an image from the system's image library or camera). We have seen it in action in Chapter 8, *Divide and Conquer with TFrameStand*, (I tend to use messaging as a part of the state-machine based approach you can adopt with TFrameStand). The immediate outcome is that the message subsystem acts as the glue between otherwise highly isolated modules. You actually want to split complexity into separated modules but then you still need ways to let these modules interact and provide functionalities to the final user.

In the next few sections, we'll provide a simple overview of the messaging system. You can refer to the official documentation to find out some other samples (http://docwiki. embarcadero.com/RADStudio/en/Using_the_RTL_Cross-Platform_Messaging_Solution).

The core functionality of this messaging system consists of defining message types in order to let subscribers watch for them (specifically, type by type). A dispatcher entity will be responsible for notifying each subscriber about the new message (and then disposing of the message itself). The notification mechanisms consist of the execution of a provided message handler (either a method reference to be called or an anonymous method).

In the next section, we are going to introduce some basic elements and data structures related to the messaging subsystem. Specifically, we need to understand how to deliver specific content messages over a general message dispatching facility.

Introducing message definitions as data types

In the `System.Messaging` unit, you can find some base definitions such as `TMessageBase`, `TMessage<T>`, and `TObjectMessage<T>`. The type of the message is a crucial point of this mechanism as you can send a message of a certain type X, you will subscribe to a message by its type X, and the message handler will probably need to know details of the message content (tied to its type X, or T if you are using `TMessage<T>`).

If you simply need to define a new kind of *event*, you may want to define a type and inherit your type, `TEventX`, from `TMessageBase`:

```
TEventX = class(TMessageBase);
```

The type definition is unique in the type system so it can be used as a key to bind a listener to that specific type.

Moreover, if you need to carry some values within the message, you may want to make your type more complex, adding properties and/or constructors to initialize them.

 Beware that memory management follows the standard rules for object instances, that is, somebody will be responsible for freeing the message after all the subscribers have been notified.

A handy shortcut to define message types that only differ in the content they carry is the use of the `TMessage<T>` facility. Thanks to the generic definition, it's easy to define a message that has a value of type T without having to repeat the fact that it has a `Value` property and a `Create` constructor allowing value initialization. The following code snippet shows how to define messages with different content types easily:

```
TWarningMessage = class(TMessage<string>);
TErrorMessage = class(TMessage<string>);
TCounterMessage = class(TMessage<Integer>);
TRandomMessage = class(TMessage<Integer>);
```

The `TMessage<T>` class is a holder for a value of type T. You can pass the value to hold as an argument of the constructor and then access it through the `Value` read-only property. Please consider that defining two different classes with the same signature, that is, `TMessage<Integer>`, means that they have the exact same layout (until you don't add something to them) but can be actually distinguished by the *messaging-matching* mechanism.

I mean that having two different types will allow you to subscribe distinctly for each one of them instead of, hypothetically, subscribing for a *message holding an integer*, which would result in receiving a notification for both types of messages. This happens, for example, if you go for the following declaration variation that actually defines aliases for the `TMessage<Integer>` type:

```
TFirstMessage = TMessage<Integer>;
TSecondMessage = TMessage<Integer>;
```

Subscribing a handler for `TFirstMessage` will actually mean subscribing to `TMessage<System.Integer>`, the very same signature `TFirstMessage` and `TSecondMessage` share (thus, the handler will be triggered for both messages, regardless of the type alias name).

Please consider that `T` (in `TMessage<T>`) can be of any type, that is, primitives, objects, records, or interfaces. This means you can have messages as complex as needed for your purpose with no effort.

Sending messages through the message manager

Once you have defined your message types, you'll need to create messages and give them to an entity that will take care of passing them to the current subscribers. This entity is called `TMessageManager` and the RTL has a singleton instance acting as the default manager. Most of the time, I tend to use the default manager to drive my custom messages too; however, you are free to define and instantiate your own `TMessageManager` instance (or instance of a descendant class you may want to define).

`TMessageManager` exposes two relevant methods—`SendMessage` and `SubscribeToMessage`.

In this section, we'll focus on the `SendMessage` method and, in the next section, we'll have a close look at the latter.

The SendMessage method will add a new message to the dispatching system. Actually there is not a queue of messages, that is, the mechanism is synchronous. So when you send a message, what you are actually doing is asking the dispatching system to iterate over all subscribers for that message (that specific ClassType, as already discussed) and fire the listener provided. Once done, the message gets disposed (a call to the Free method of the message will happen before leaving the SendMessage method).

The second version of the SendMessage method allows you, through the convenient ADispose argument, to specify whether the disposal of the message should take place or not.

It is important for you to understand that by not having a queue of messages, only subscribers who provided a listener before the call to SendMessage will get notified. Moreover, the notification process being synchronous, you can make assumptions about the handling of the message. That is, when the SendMessage function returns, all subscribers will have already finished with the processing of the message, such that, if not otherwise specified by the sender, they will already have been destroyed at that point.

Another implication is that the handling of the message happens in the same threading context of the caller of the SendMessage method. This messaging system is not intended to be thread-safe. If you find yourself in a multi-threaded situation, you need to take care of proper synchronization and thread-safety.

On this matter, I would suggest you keep listeners and calls to SendMessage in the same thread (the main thread if you are not doing parallel programming) and keep the effort for your thread-safety at that level. If you really need to do parallel programming, consider taking a more drastic approach, that is, have your own TMessageManager instance (thus avoiding using the RTL singleton instance), properly decide the threading context, and keep it consistent.

For example, you may want to synchronize the thread to send a message with a specific thread handling your custom message manager instance. The same synchronization should happen to subscribe or unsubscribe listeners to/from the message manager. Keep in mind instance life cycle management for messages, as discussed before, in order to avoid premature (or never-happening) message destruction with respect to subscribers' notifications.

You can build your own queueing mechanisms, if you need them, using this part of the RTL as a building block. Using generic collections, System.Threading and System.Messaging facilities, it is easy to build up even sophisticated solutions.

A companion argument of the `SendMessage` method is the `ASender` parameter. You can use this argument (which will also be available to the message listeners) to provide some additional context to the handlers of the message.

As previously given information, if you just need to send a message, here is the code you need:

```
TMessageManager.DefaultManager.SendMessage(
    Self
  , TEventX.Create
);
```

We are using the RTL-provided `TMessageManager` singleton to send a `TEventX` message (whose life cycle management will be delegated to `MessageManager`) and we are using `Self` as the sender.

When dealing with messages having some content, you will also have to provide the value of the message. Following our previous example, here is how you can send a new `TRandomMessage` component to the system:

```
TMessageManager.DefaultManager.SendMessage(
    Self
  , TRandomMessage.Create(Random(100))
);
```

Of course, you may try to shorten the scripture by providing accessory functionalities. In this simple example of a message containing a random number (suitable for consumption by listeners), you may add a new constructor to `TRandomMessage` and have the number generated internally:

```
const DEFAULT_RANGE = 100;
constructor CreateNewRandom(const ARange: Integer = DEFAULT_RANGE);

{...}

constructor TRandomMessage.CreateNewRandom(const ARange: Integer);
begin
  inherited Create(Random(ARange));
end;
```

Using the newly introduced `CreateNewRandom` constructor, your line of code to send a new message becomes shorter:

```
TMessageManager.DefaultManager.SendMessage(
    Self
  , TRandomMessage.CreateNewRandom
);
```

You can go further and let the message determine the message manager to use. Keeping in mind the basic principle stating dependencies should be injected rather than hardcoded, you can provide a class function having convenient default behavior to cover the most common case of using the default message manager:

```
TRandomMessage = class(TMessage<Integer>)
public
{...}
class procedure GenerateAndSend(
  const ARange: Integer = DEFAULT_RANGE;
  const ASender: TObject = nil;
  const AManager: TMessageManager = nil);
end;
```

I think I've already stated that I am against striving to reduce lines of code just for the purpose of doing it, but I really think improving readability has something to do with writing less verbose (yet, immediate to understand in purpose) code. The final version of our call to send a new `TRandomMessage` component will look like this:

```
TRandomMessage.GenerateAndSend();
```

The implementation of the `GenerateAndSend` procedure is trivial and basically plays around with the arguments and their default values. The code is provided in the following snippet:

```
class procedure TRandomMessage.GenerateAndSend(
  const ARange: Integer; const ASender: TObject;
  const AManager: TMessageManager);
var
  LManager: TMessageManager;
  LMessage: TRandomMessage;
begin
  LMessage := TRandomMessage.CreateNewRandom(ARange);
  LManager := AManager;
  if not Assigned(LManager) then
    LManager := TMessageManager.DefaultManager;
  if Assigned(LManager) then
    LManager.SendMessage(ASender, LMessage);
end;
```

Again, you may argue that GenerateAndSend violates the single responsibility principle (this method creates and sends the message) but as we are not retaining the two actions to be executed separately and you generally create a message with the main purpose of sending it, I think we can accept the trade. I like to think I am a pragmatic programmer and so principles are important but not to be blindly followed every time and everywhere.

In the next section, we'll gain an understanding of the SubscribeToMessage method.

Subscribing and responding to messages

A messaging system is basically a mechanism to notify some observers about the firing of some event. The event may have some attached information that we call message content but the notification of the event is the crucial point of the whole thing.

We have seen so far how messages are defined and sent through the message manager. Now it is time to learn how to subscribe for notifications. Multiple observers may register themselves to be notified when the event occurs (that is, a matching message passes through the message manager).

The TMessageManager class offers a SubscribeToMessage method you can use to provide an event handler (once again, with two main options, that is, implementing the handler through an anonymous method, or using a standard method reference).

The following snippet shows how to subscribe for the TEventX message we have used in previous paragraphs:

```
TMessageManager.DefaultManager.SubscribeToMessage(
  TEventX
, procedure(const Sender: TObject; const M: TMessage)
  begin
    Log('EventX happened');
  end
);
```

As you can see in the preceding code, we, as the caller of SubscribeToMessage, are adding our event handler to the DefaultManager instance in order to get it triggered when the same DefaultManager is responsible for delivering a TEventX message.

The SubscribeToMessage return value is a numerical ID that we can use to later unsubscribe from the manager. As you can see from the preceding code snippet, the anonymous methods get called with two arguments, that is, the Sender reference and the M reference.

The signature of the anonymous method is standard so M is a generic TMessage type. Actually, M will be an instance of the type of message we are subscribing to (TEventX in our example). If the message has some content, you'll need to typecast M to the actual type to access its properties or fields. The following snippet shows how a listener for TRandomMessage can access the random value aboard the message:

```
TMessageManager.DefaultManager.SubscribeToMessage(
  TRandomMessage
, procedure(const Sender: TObject; const M: TMessage)
  begin
    Log(M.ClassName + ' received: ' + (M as
TRandomMessage).Value.ToString);
  end
);
```

So, it is pretty straightforward that we are tying the anonymous method execution to the arrival (at the message manager instance) of a message of type X.

 Please beware that no inheritance relationships are taken into account for the match. That is, you can have a hierarchy of message types (for example, to share some common implementations or infrastructure) but the match at the message manager is an exact type match.

As we did before, we can try to shorten our code a bit, introducing some utility functions (at the type level, using a separate utility class, or even using type helpers).

For example, we can reach shorter (and simpler yet equivalent) code to add an anonymous method as a listener for TRandomMessage:

```
TRandomMessage.SubscribeTo(
  procedure(const Sender: TObject; const M: TRandomMessage)
  begin
    Log(M.ClassName + ' received: ' + M.Value.ToString);
  end
);
```

From the preceding code, this new way of coding is easier to read, doesn't clash with the **Law of Demeter**, and lets the developer avoid the (pretty useless) typecast of M to the actual type. The targeted message manager instance can be explicitly stated using the second (optional) argument of the SubscribeTo method, as we previously did for the GenerateAndSend method.

The following snippet shows an implementation for the `SubscribeTo` method:

```
class function TRandomMessage.SubscribeTo(
  const AListener: TRandomMessageListener;
  const AManager: TMessageManager = nil): Integer;
var
  LManager: TMessageManager;
begin
  LManager := AManager;
  if not Assigned(LManager) then
    LManager := TMessageManager.DefaultManager;

  Result := -1;
  if Assigned(LManager) then
    Result := LManager.SubscribeToMessage(TRandomMessage
      , procedure (const ASender: TObject; const AMsg: TMessageBase)
      begin
        if Assigned(AListener) then
          AListener(ASender, AMsg as TRandomMessage);
      end
    );
end;
```

Messaging infrastructure can be a significant help for the developer aiming to keep their modules loosely coupled. Having `System.Messaging` built in with the Delphi RTL makes it easy to implement your own message facilities with no effort. A number of programming problems can be solved using messaging, starting from event-oriented mechanisms, multicast events, inter-application communication, and so on.

In this section, we learned about the built-in messaging capabilities Delphi provides for the FMX and VCL frameworks. This is a powerful general-purpose feature that can be very handy in many situations.

Modern applications are not islands. That means they are often connected to some remote data or service provider. The next section is dedicated to HTTP client implementations, the default communication method especially for mobile platforms where the connection is generally unstable.

Using native HTTP client implementations

Network interaction is becoming more and more common in most applications. Delphi developers have had the opportunity to deal with networking using **Indy** (https://www.indyproject.org/). It is an open source client/server communication library supporting low-level (**TCP**, **UDP**, and more) and high-level (**FTP**, **HTTP**, and more) protocols.

In this section, we'll understand the use of HTTP client implementations. These are native to each platform and conveniently wrapped by the Delphi RTL to provide developers with a common, handy way to develop single code base applications featuring HTTP client capabilities.

With the stress of multi-platform applications and distributed applications, the HTTP protocol has become more and more important among others (the world is now dominated by **REST services**). The need for security has also pushed most services to shift toward HTTPS (now an industry standard even for basic things).

Indy relies on **OpenSSL** implementation, which means you need to deploy OpenSSL together with your applications, opening up a number of things to consider. For example, you need to keep OpenSSL up to date, or you'll risk being targeted by anti-virus software (or mobile store scanners) as a security flaw. Also, you'll need to deal with the compatibilities (and availabilities) of the library with the final target platform. Moreover, there are a number of topics around networking that are more and more managed by the operating systems (**proxy settings**, **VPNs**, and more).

At some point, (**Delphi XE8**) Embarcadero introduced two components to wrap the operating system's HTTP libraries. This component will allow you to make HTTP calls without worrying about details such as encryption algorithms or the like, and taking advantage of the intrinsic capabilities of the underlying device/platform. All this with a common source code base, of course!

The two components that Embarcadero introduced are as follows:

- `TNetHTTPClient` wraps most of the HTTP(S) functionalities through convenient methods and properties, given as follows:
    - `GET`, `POST`, `PUT`, `OPTIONS`, `DELETE`, `TRACE`, `HEAD`, `MERGE`, and `PATCH` commands are available (each one through a convenient **Pascal** method, sometimes with additional overloads to cover common use cases).
    - Cookies are managed through a `CookieManager` instance.
    - A `CustomHeaders` property lets you provide extra header values for your calls.
    - A `ProxySettings` property allows custom configuration where needed.
    - Functionalities such as the handling of redirections and authentication strategies are easy to tune and implement using properties and events exposed by `TNetHTTPClient`.

Another very important thing to consider is that you can easily set your commands to be asynchronous (non-blocking) by simply turning the `TNetHTTPClient.Asynchronous` property to `True`. The library is designed to support async executions, a very common practice in modern applications, as already discussed throughout this book.

- The `TNetHTTPRequest` class represents an HTTP request (and holds its response too). It is built upon the `TNetHTTPClient` functionalities in a complementary manner, as shown in the following screenshot:

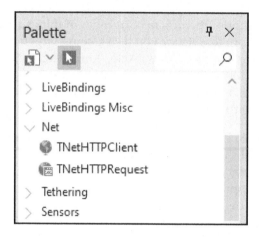

Figure 12.11

It is important for you to note that this significant abstraction over HTTP implementation is a key point for cross-platform development. Being part of the Delphi RTL, it is available on all supported platforms (ranging from Windows to OS X/macOS, Android to iOS, and Linux).

These functionalities actually represent the building blocks for many other higher-level functionalities such as, most notably, the **REST Client** library, as shown in the following screenshot:

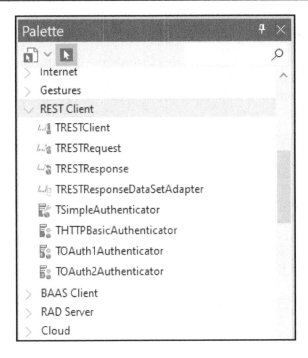

Figure 12.12

As you can see in the preceding screenshot, the **REST Client** library is a high-level, feature-rich library to implement client applications targeting REST servers by being modern (that is, with built-in support for async execution) and well-integrated with other Delphi technologies (including **LiveBindings**). It represents a significant helper for the cross-platform developer. It comes with many examples you can study to understand how it works and its capabilities.

As you can see from the preceding screenshot, once again, Delphi is helping you as a developer by providing easy-to-use components to deal with common programming tasks (think about **OAuth** authentication). Having it done for all the supported platforms makes the difference in terms of development productivity and the maintainability of products.

Similar to what we have seen with HTTP functionalities, we can discuss the **Bluetooth** capabilities of modern devices. So let's move to the next section about Bluetooth support.

Getting familiar with Bluetooth support

More and more functionalities of real devices include the need for interactions with other smart devices or sensors. Bluetooth technology is the connectivity standard for these kinds of interactions: it implements a local networking facility connecting different nearby devices.

In this section, we'll learn about Bluetooth technology and the support built into the FMX framework. For example, we'll learn how to scan for other Bluetooth-enabled devices, along with how to connect to or interact with them.

Bluetooth is a wide-ranging technology that has been around for a few years now. The original Bluetooth has been widely adopted and can be used in a multitude of applications (desktop and mobile). To provide coverage of Bluetooth specifications is way beyond the scope of this book, but I want to show you how Delphi can be used to target a specific slice of the Bluetooth family, that is, **Bluetooth Low Energy (BLE)** devices.

The Delphi RTL provides two components wrapping around Bluetooth and Bluetooth LE functionalities—**TBluetooth** and **TBluetoothLE**—from the **System** category of the **Palette** component, as shown in the following screenshot:

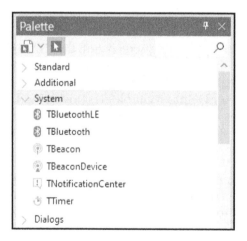

Figure 12.13

Bluetooth Low Energy (BLE) is a specific portion of Bluetooth specification targeting devices that have a small amount of data to exchange and low power consumption. Typical examples are smart devices such as wearables (that is, heart rate sensors) or real-life devices with some sort of smart interface (to configure them or to get some feedback about their state, such as a scale, or a lock).

With the arising of the so-called **IoT (Internet of Things)**, BLE is becoming more and more important as it is often the interface used to interact with smart devices (using a smartphone, for instance). Another important topic around IoT, BLE, and mobile apps is the so-called **proximity**. Being able to build cross-platform applications making use of BLE can be a considerable success factor for modern industry.

The basic functionalities a BLE-enabled application needs to fulfill are the following:

- Discovering nearby BLE devices
- Exploring and filtering them by exposed services or characteristics (**GATT**)
- Connecting to read or write characteristics
- Subscribing to notifications

With Delphi, you can achieve all the preceding four capabilities with a single code base. The `TBluetoothLE` component is a non-visual component that conveniently wraps BLE functionalities (implemented at the OS level) in a single common interface. The following screenshot shows you Bluetooth LE support against the operating systems:

Platform Support

Platform	Bluetooth Low Energy	
	Client	Server
Windows(*)	10+	10+ (**)
OS X	10.7+	10.9+
iOS	5+	6+
Android	4.3+	5+

Figure 12.14

The preceding screenshot is taken from Delphi's official documentation (`http://docwiki.embarcadero.com/RADStudio/en/Using_Bluetooth_Low_Energy`) and states the supported versions of BLE across different platforms. Implementations of the BLE specification are different from OS to OS and the added value of having a single interface is very significant in this area.

Let's now move on to the next section, about scanning for nearby devices.

Scanning for devices

To scan for devices in the BLE range, you can call the `DiscoverDevices` method of the **TBluetoothLE** component:

```
BLE1.DiscoverDevices(3000, [SERVICE_UUID]);
```

From the preceding code, the first argument represents the timeout for the discovery, in milliseconds. The second (optional) argument is a list of UUID identifiers. When the second argument is provided, it acts as a filter over devices in the range. **GATT** specification states each service and characteristic exposed through BLE has a **unique identifier** (UUID) so it is easy to discover all devices matching at least one of the listed service UUIDs. The following screenshot shows the **Object Inspector** pane listing **TBluetoothLE** events:

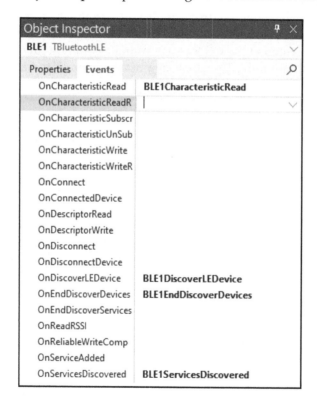

Figure 12.15

Most of the functionalities around BLE are asynchronous so there are a number of events exposed by the component you'll need to handle. For example, once the device discovery has been started (using the previous line of code), you may want to wait for the **OnEndDiscoverDevices** event to fire.

Then, you can access the list of discovered devices (already filtered if you have specified service UUIDs in the discover call). The list of devices is available as an argument of the event handler or through the `DiscoveredDevices` property of **TBluetoothLE**. The items in this list are instances of the `TBluetoothLEDevice` class, providing a convenient wrapper around the concept of the BLE device.

You may also consider having an event handler for the `OnDiscoverLEDevice` event, fired each time (during discovery) a device is added to the list of discovered devices. If you are providing a UI where devices are listed, you may want to refresh the list accordingly.

Next, we'll look at a section about connecting to a BLE device.

Connecting to a BLE device

Once you have a reference to a `TBluetoothLEDevice` instance, you can discover the services exposed by the device in order to get access to a `TBluetoothGattService` instance. This instance represents the service you are looking for and will get you access to the underlying characteristics.

Once again, the model is asynchronous so you will call `Connect` on the `TBluetoothLEDevice` instance and then start the discovery of its services with a call to the `DiscoverServices` method. Then the `TBlutoothLE.OnServicesDiscovered` event will fire when the operation completes. A convenient argument of the `AServiceList` event handler, `TBluetoothGattServiceList` will let you iterate through the discovered services and, for each service, you can enumerate its characteristics (through the homonym property).

A reference to the characteristic is needed to read and write data, using the `TBluetoothLEDevice.ReadCharacteristic` and `WriteCharacteristic` methods, as shown in the following code snippet:

```
    SelectedDevice: TBluetoothLEDevice;
    FCharacteristic: TBluetoothGattCharacteristic;
{...}
    SelectedDevice.ReadCharacteristic(FCharacteristic);
```

The read and write process is, once again, asynchronous so you should not try to read the characteristics' value after a read. You should implement an `OnCharacteristicRead` event handler that will fire after the requested read operation has been completed. The following code snippet shows a typical event handler implementation:

```
procedure TBLEData.BLE1CharacteristicRead(const Sender: TObject;
  const ACharacteristic: TBluetoothGattCharacteristic;
  AGattStatus: TBluetoothGattStatus);
begin
  if AGattStatus = TBluetoothGattStatus.Success then
  begin
    FValue := TEncoding.UTF8.GetString(ACharacteristic.Value);
    TBLEReadSuccessfulMessage.Send(FValue);
  end;
end;
```

The convenient `AGattStatus` argument will let you determine a successful operation. At that point, it will be safe to read the characteristic `Value` property (a `TBytes` value, with raw binary data). The preceding code example assumes `Value` represents a **UTF8 string** value, so the code will retrieve a string representation using `TEncoding` functionalities.

With the aid of a messaging mechanism, discussed in the previous part of this chapter, we can notify subscribers when a new value is available for consumption.

Subscribing for notifications

If the BLE device exposes a characteristic with notification capabilities, our application can subscribe to adequately handle them. Basically, you simply need to state notifications from those characteristics are enabled using the following code:

```
    FSubscribed :=
  SelectedDevice.SetCharacteristicNotification(FCharacteristic, True);
```

Please note, `SelectedDevice` is a `TBluetoothLEDevice` instance you already connected to and explored services/characteristics of. `FCharacteristic` must be a valid reference to a `TBluetoothGattCharacteristic` instance of the selected device.

When the notification is received, the characteristic is read again and the `OnCharacteristicRead` event will be fired consequently, allowing you to properly react in your application code.

BLE is really on the rise for modern application development and the Delphi cross-platform support is very convenient as it enables writing applications in a wide range of use cases, especially around the IoT world.

In this section, we learned about Bluetooth (Low Energy) support in Delphi and FMX. Apart from discovering nearby devices, we learned how to connect with them and explore their services and exposed characteristics.

Summary

In this chapter, we have seen a number of examples where FMX actually enables the developer to focus on an application's core functionalities and take advantage of built-in cross-platform capabilities.

Features provided by the underlying platform (with native implementations) are conveniently wrapped by Delphi and the FMX framework. This lets the developer of cross-platform applications have a single code base (a big advantage as stated before, and throughout the whole book) while addressing multiple platforms. Services such as the clipboard, Bluetooth LE capabilities, dialogs, and HTTP client functionalities are crucial to most modern applications (mobile or desktop). The beauty of FMX abstractions is one of the key aspects of this multi-platform application framework.

This immediately represents a boost factor in development productivity as there is theoretically no need for the application developer to delve into platform-specific details, relying instead on the common abstraction provided by FMX.

You now have the skills to build complex applications, using features such as HTTP connections or Bluetooth services. The opportunity to use a single approach and code base even while addressing complex tasks (such as HTTP/BLE interactions) is a great productivity booster for the developer.

In the next chapter, we'll delve into another interesting topic where this ability to abstract from platform-specific details is crucial, that is, **3D programming**. FMX lets the developer implement 3D graphics and effects without having to worry about the specific hardware or software underlying layers of different platforms and devices.

13
Learning about FMX 3D Capabilities

In the previous chapter, we saw how to take advantage of FMX as an application framework and gain access to cross-platform services while retaining the single-code-base approach. Some of the topics covered represented clear examples of how FMX is a high-level abstraction of underlying platform/device capabilities. Just remember what we have seen about touch capabilities.

This chapter is dedicated to **FMX 3D** related capabilities. 3D graphics can be very effective for a certain slice of applications and provide a chance to deliver some extra visuals or effects to the end user.

Generally speaking, **3D programming** is surely one of the most challenging areas for the developer. To properly master this topic over all available platforms would require years of learning. The cross-platform approach that FMX represents is a huge opportunity for the developer to make an application stand out. Nonetheless, comprehensive coverage of the topic is way beyond the scope of this book. We'll cover the following topics enough to provide you with all the elements required to understand and explore the available opportunities:

- Introducing 3D with FMX
- Building a 3D application
- Merging 3D and 2D visual objects

After reading the chapter, you will be able to use 3D objects in your applications as part of a standard (2D) **User Interface** (**UI**), or within a virtual environment filled with lights, cameras, and other goodies.

Technical requirements

FMX is a general-purpose framework so the aim is to provide 3D support across multiple platforms. You can benefit from 3D functionalities across Windows, iOS, Android, OS X/macOS, and Linux platforms. A modern graphics card is required. The Neon libraries for Android are also required (though they are the same as for the FMX framework in general).

Here is the source code used in this chapter: `https://github.com/PacktPublishing/Delphi-GUI-Programming-with-FireMonkey/tree/master/Chapter%2013`

Introducing 3D programming with FMX

3D programming is one of the most difficult areas to master as a developer. It involves a specific understanding of the geometric rules applied and also of the many techniques used to conveniently implement 3D graphics in computer software.

In this section, we will consider the main approaches to the 3D programming of applications and how FMX supports the typical use cases.

Adding a third dimension means to step outside of the classic and comfy computer programming environment. It generally also means having to deal with an augmented number of objects to render, easily paving the way to performance issues.

Over the years, computer graphics have evolved a lot toward 3D capabilities. Nowadays 3D-enabled GPUs and video hardware are almost ubiquitous and not only found in top-level expensive equipment. At the same time, many different approaches to 3D graphics programming have arisen.

Once again, the problem we are trying to address is not how to build the perfect 3D application but more how to build a single 3D-enabled application that runs on several different platforms (featuring different software and hardware layers).

There are several types of 3D application you may want to build. From in-person simulations of virtual 3D spaces you may want to move in, to 3D representations of objects, or aggregates somehow driven by the application. Think about modeling software or producing a customized rendering of some item based on data the user provides or selects. But you can also use 3D to enrich the user experience of your user within a regular 2D application. For instance, you may want to implement some 3D animation, just to level up the visual appeal of your mobile (or even desktop) app.

There are two things I want to stress before proceeding:

- **Rendering of complex 3D graphics can be computationally intensive**:
  Hardware is evolving each day to provide more and more graphics processing
  power to new devices and this is also due to the continuous growth of 3D
  graphics use in modern applications. This is a natural effect since we, as human
  beings, live in a 3D world.

  That is, many aspects of our life are now enriched or mediated through the use of
  digital devices. Matching the number of dimensions is required in many
  circumstances and is a big plus in the quest for the ideal user experience. The
  closer to being natural a digital experience is, the easier it is for the final user.
  Even though hardware is evolving fast, a professional 3D programmer needs to
  master a number of optimization tricks and techniques to actually unleash the
  potential of the running device. Be aware that this includes deep knowledge of
  the underlying internals of the chosen 3D environment and APIs, down to the
  metal (hardware layer) sometimes.

- **A 3D-enabled graphics application is not necessarily provided with a real-
  world-rules engine**: The fact you are drawing 3D objects on the screen does not
  mean these objects will automatically fit any real-world physics laws (including
  gravity, elasticity, or the impenetrability of matter). If you want to add a physics
  engine to your application in order to impose real-world physics laws on your
  virtual world, that's up to you and this will add another complexity level to the
  scenario.

  You'll obviously need to track every object in your world and find an efficient
  way to apply those laws (do some calculations, including the transformation from
  a continuous model to a discrete one). This will generally include a need for the
  fourth dimension, that is, *time*. A lot of synchronization and efforts will be needed
  to achieve coherence. I would suggest picking one of the available physics
  engines available out there if you are going down this road.

The **FireMonkey** framework provides you with a convenient, cross-platform, 3D-rendering
capability that enables developers to run their applications on several different platforms.
When running on mobile devices, the underlying technology is the **OpenGL ES library**. On
Windows, **Direct3D** (part of **DirectX**) is used, while **OpenGL** is the choice when running
on **Apple Mac OS X/ macOS** and using **Delphi** up to **version 10.3**.

Recently, **Delphi 10.4 Sydney** added support to run your FMX applications against the
Apple Metal framework, which is a GPU rendering framework highly optimized for the
Apple platform (https://developer.apple.com/documentation/metal/).

Proving that FMX is a very high-level abstraction, it is very easy to enable Metal support in your FMX applications. As explained in detail in the **Grijjy blog** post (`https://blog.` `grijjy.com/2020/05/25/boost-mac-performance-with-metal-and-delphi-10-4/`) by Erik van Bilsen (an Embarcadero MVP), you can instruct the FMX framework to use a Metal canvas implementation by adding the following instruction (after including the `FMX.Types` unit in the uses list contained in the DPR file of your project):

```
GlobalUseMetal := True;
```

Enabling the Metal framework in your FMX apps will result in immediate and significant performance enhancements. You can easily experience the difference by setting the `GlobalUseMetal` variable to false/true for the same app and checking it out. Consider that the Metal framework may optimize rendering not to exceed 60 FPS (or matching the video settings on your machine). You should be able to see a very different CPU/GPU usage in either case.

In the next section, we are going to learn how to build 3D-enabled applications with the FMX framework. We'll go through all the basic elements we are going to use to build a 3D scene with lights, objects, and cameras. We are also going to learn about the positioning and sizing system.

Building a 3D application

In this section, you will learn how to build your first 3D application. We need to learn how to set up a 3D viewport and to deal with lights and materials.

There are basically two ways to enable 3D capabilities in your applications:

- Build a 3D FMX application that basically has a `TForm3D` inherited-from instance as the main form.
- Build a regular (2D) FMX cross-platform application and use a `TViewport3D` component to host 3D controls inside of it.

The choice among the two options largely depends on the kind of application you're building. The first option may be the best choice while building a 3D virtual environment. The user usually expects an immersive experience, with a first-person view. In this case, in games, the 3D-world simulation of players and some similar applications are typical use case examples.

The second option (a regular 2D application with a 3D scene container) can be more appropriate when you need to provide standard user interface controls to drive the business model of the application. There might be some settings or the user may need to input some parameters to let you render a 3D scene consequently. A model configurator (for a car seller) is a good example of this kind of application where business data (listings, available options, part details) is important and needs to be addressed through standard user controls (lists, grids, buttons, combo boxes, selectors, and more).

We'll head into the next section to learn how to actually build a 3D application using FMX components.

Building a 3D "Hello, world!" application

In the Delphi IDE, select **Create new Multi-Device Application** and choose **3D Application** from the dialog window that will pop up. You will see the dialog in the following screenshot, with the **3D Application** entry highlighted:

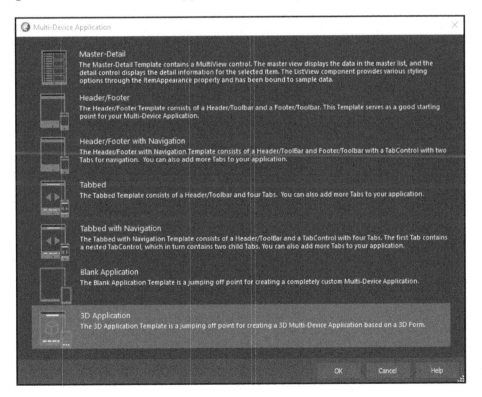

Figure 13.1

The IDE will prepare the new application by adding a form. Differently from what we are used to, this form inherits from the `FMX.Forms3D.TForm3D` class rather than the `FMX.Forms.TForm` class. It basically incorporates an instance of `FMX.Types3D.TContext3D` and implements the `FMX.Controls3D.IViewport3D` interface. This enables the form to act as a host for 3D controls.

In other words, the form will be used as a 3D container for our scene. However, many other aspects of the form are unchanged with respect to the `TForm` (2D) version. For example, you can change the `Color` property of the form from the default value (`White`) to a custom value (`Silver`) and you'll notice the change immediately in the Delphi IDE. The 3D FMX capabilities are fully integrated with the rest of the Delphi and FMX technologies.

Later in this chapter, we'll delve into how the rendering and 3D elements are managed in a 3D scene but for the moment, we are simply going to add our first 3D component to the form and see how it looks.

In the component palette, you will find a `TText3D` entry, in the **3D Shapes** category. Add a `TText3D` instance to your form and you'll see it show up right in the middle of the form. That's where the origin of our reference system lays, in the current view. That is due to a specific camera view to be used at design time, conveniently provided by the framework itself.

At first, you are not going to see anything else other than the theoretical boundaries of the `TText3D` instance. You need to give a value to the `Text` property of your `Text3D1` component in order to see the text actually rendered. In the following screenshot, you can see how your IDE should look if you set the `Width` property to `20` and the `Text` property to `Hello, World!`:

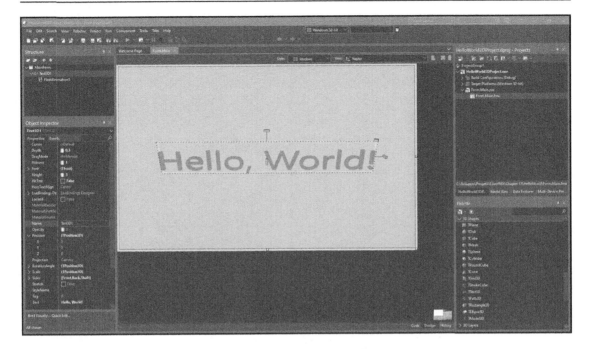

Figure 13.2

As you can see in the preceding screenshot, the design-time form editor is enabled with some different handles to size, position, and possibly rotate 3D objects.

You can find the preceding project in the `Chapter 13 | HelloWorld` folder in the GitHub repository associated with this book.

Also, you can guess the position and direction of the design-time camera used for rendering, that is, it is placed between you and the TText3D instance, somewhere above the ground level. The following schema shows how the **X**, **Y**, and **Z** directions are implemented in the FMX 3D environment:

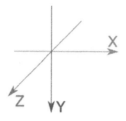

Figure 13.3

The thing to note in the preceding graph is that the **Y** axis is somehow reversed with respect to what we may feel is natural in the real world. Setting the Position.Y property of a 3D object to a positive value, in other words, means putting the object *below the horizon*. Also, the **Z** axis is *toward the screen*. Everything is relative, once the reference system is fixed, so you just need to know what the actual convention is.

Now we have a basic, non-empty, 3D scene. We could run the application and see what we are seeing at design time. Just to add a first dynamic element, we can try to manipulate some value of our 3D object (the Text3D1 component) in order to see it change at runtime. Each 3D object has Position and Rotation properties. Both are built of three different values as we are now in a 3D space. You can try to change the Rotation.Y value and see the object being rotated along the *y* axis.

As we saw in Chapter 10, *Orchestrating Transitions and Animations*, we can use FMX built-in animation support to drive the change of a value over time. Let's add TFloatAnimation inside the Text3D1 component and set its Property value to Rotation.Y. We want the value to range from -45 to 45 (degrees) within a duration of a couple of seconds.

We can set the Loop property to True and choose a nice Interpolation property value to achieve some nice effects (I've selected Quartic and I've set the AnimationType property to the InOut value). If you run the application, given that the Enabled property of our FloatAnimation1 component is set to True, you'll see the 3D **Hello, World!** text moving smoothly.

The following screenshot shows us a visual of the running application on the Windows platform, with the `Rotation.Y` value somewhere around 45 in value (positive rotation value changes are intended to be clockwise):

Figure 13.4

This is our first contact with the 3D capabilities of the FMX framework. A `TForm3D` instance acts as a container of a 3D text component. We are still in the big context of FMX so many concepts we have learned about throughout this book (such as parenthood, animations, rotations, opacity, and more) still apply.

In order to render the 3D scene at design time, FMX needs a dummy camera to act as the observer's point of view. The camera is itself conceived through a 3D component. Its position and mechanics have been set by the FMX framework builders. In order to fully understand what you are looking at while designing in the IDE, we need to introduce another basic component, that is, the `TDummy` component.

Understanding TDummy and the design-time camera

In the standard (2D) FMX environment, we are used to having `TLayout` instances acting as invisible containers. This lets the developer easily position and size objects (or groups of them) to achieve responsive UIs (as we discussed in `Chapter 9`, *Building Responsive UIs*). `TLayout` instances are invisible at runtime (and to the end user), yet they can be used to group other components and implement relative positioning and sizing. `TDummy` is the equivalent of `TLayout` in the 3D conception.

A `TDummy` component has a cubic shape and its boundaries are rendered only at design time. You can nest as many instances of `TDummy` as you like and you can size them as you prefer. They also can host other components and the contained component(s) will be relative to the container in terms of position, rotation, visibility, and other qualities (opacity, for example).

It is quite common to use a `TDummy` instance as the parent of all other components in the scene so that if you would like to rotate the scene, you'll simply have to rotate this `TDummy` instance and everything will move accordingly.

You can have as many `TDummy` instances as you need; there's theoretically no performance penalty in adding them while, at the same time, they can greatly simplify the life of the developer. For example, to implement the design camera of `TForm3D`, a couple of `TDummy` instances are used.

In the following screenshot (made with 3D modeling software called **SketchUp**), I've recreated the 3D scene of our `HelloWorld` demo project, adding the representation of the camera and the two `TDummy` objects used to properly set the camera position:

Figure 13.5

As you can see in the preceding screenshot, the first TDummy component (let's call it *D1*) is in the center of the scene and it is rendered as a transparent cube (no rotations applied). A second TDummy component (*D2*) is rendered in the color red and it is parented to the first one. It has the same size and (relative) position (0,0,0). It contains the camera component (*DC*), which has a relative position of (0,0,-20). *D2* is also rotated clockwise 20 degrees on the *x* axis. Given that *DC* is parented to *D2*, the rotation on *D2* also causes *DC* to be rotated as well, drawing an arc of 20 degrees and 20 units of radius.

This should make it clear what are you looking for in the designer while using a TForm3D component. Also, it provides a straightforward example of using (nested) TDummy objects to position an object (the camera) in the 3D space.

Of course, you can add as many cameras to the scene as you like. The TForm3D class has a Camera property to set which is the active one. Just remember to also set the UsingDesignCamera property to False once you have selected your camera by assigning the TForm3D.Camera property value.

In the next section, we are going to learn how to add and set up a viewport component (the TViewport3D instance) in order to add 3D rendering capabilities to a standard (2D) TForm descendant, without having to use TForm3D.

Setting up a 3D viewport

Now that we have had our first contact with the FMX TForm3D class, we can quickly introduce the second available way to add 3D capabilities to an FMX application. Many use cases for 3D-enabled (business) applications implies you have a regular (2D) UI that you want to enrich with some 3D graphics. For instance, you may want to use a region of your 2D UI to render a 3D scene.

The TViewport3D component acts as a container for 3D objects. You can place this container wherever in your 2D FMX UI, as you would do with a normal TLayout component. You can find the TViewport3D component under the **Viewports** category of the IDE component palette, as shown in the following screenshot:

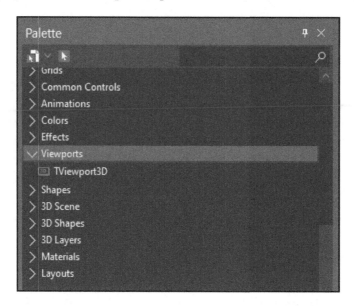

Figure 13.6

As you can see from the preceding screenshot, the **TViewport3D** component inherits from the FMX.Controls.TControl class and implements the FMX.Controls3D.IViewport3D interface (the same interface supported by TForm3D). It encapsulates a TContext3D component as well as a TCamera component, thus offering the same capabilities as a TForm3D instance. It can contain 3D objects, including cameras, lights, TDummy instances, and many others. There are three categories in the IDE component palette you may want to consider when looking for 3D components, as shown in the following screenshot:

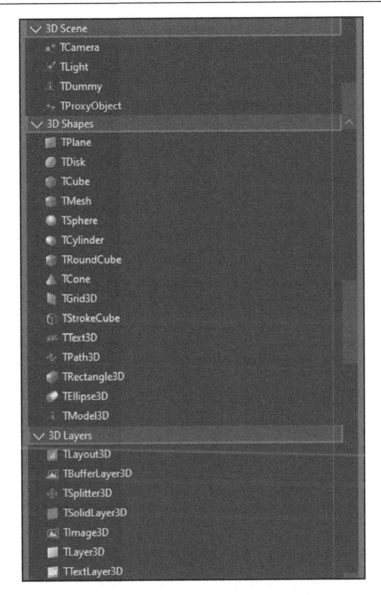

Figure 13.7

As you can see in the preceding screenshot, there are three categories in the IDE component palette:

- **3D Scene**: This contains components to set up your 3D scene, including lights and cameras.
- **3D Shapes**: This contains many basic shapes (such as `TPlane`, `TCube`, `TText3D`, and more) as well as more complex objects such as `TMesh` and `TModel3D`. The latter can be used to import 3D models from popular 3D graphics software (ASE, DAE, and OBJ formats are supported), theoretically letting you import whatever 3D object representation you like (more coverage is available in the official Embarcadero documentation: `http://docwiki.embarcadero.com/RADStudio/en/Importing_a_3D_Model_in_a_FireMonkey_Application`).
- **3D Layers**: This category includes components that are themselves containers of other objects. One of them, `TLayer3D`, is capable of hosting 2D components. This means you can mix 2D with 3D programming in FMX, using a single framework. We'll see an example later in this chapter.

As said, we can now build an FMX application that hosts a 3D scene. Just create an empty regular (2D) FMX application and add some components to your UI. As an example, we are going to introduce a `TModel3D` component to render a complex 3D object (a parrot). We are going to set up a scene where this model is in the center and we control a camera around it. The camera will move according to the user action and we'll also add a `TLight` component to let the user control the lighting of the scene.

Our application is made of two parts:

- Some UI (2D) controls to build the structure of our app and to implement the control settings of the scene (camera position, lights, and more).
- A `TViewport3D` component hosting all the 3D components (including the camera and the lights that we'd like to control through the 2D UI visual components).

The `Viewport` demo project has a main form, with a `TToolbar` component and a `TLayout` component hosting the 2D components. A `TViewport3D` instance is also present in the form. In the following screenshot, you can refer to the **Structure** view IDE window together with the **Form Designer** to understand the structure of the UI:

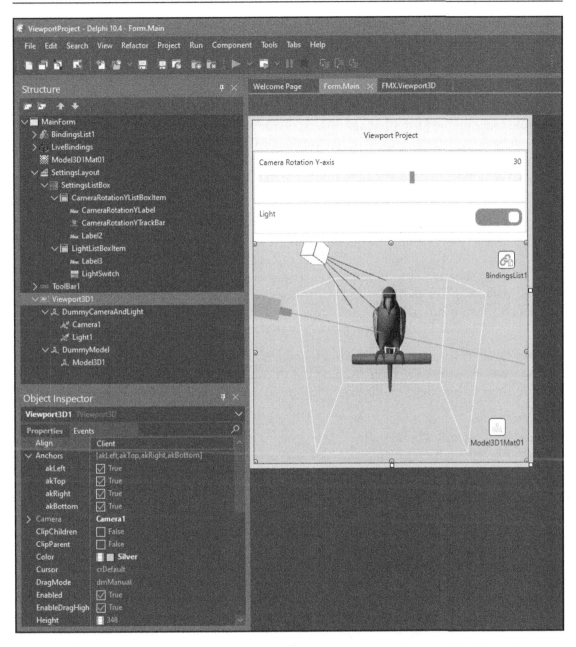

Figure 13.8

As you can see in the preceding screenshot, a `TListbox` instance has been used to host all the settings we want to make available to the user. It's a scrollable component, so in theory, we can have as many settings as needed without compromising the space available for the 3D scene.

The `Viewport3D1` component has its `Align` property set to `Client`, so it will fill up all the available space on the form (that also means on the mobile device's display). As explained before in this chapter, the use of `TDummy` can be very effective to group your 3D objects in the scene according to how they should relate to one another. We need a place to set the imported 3D model in the scene (and this is the reason we have a `DummyModel` component as a parent of our `TModel3D` instance). We also need a different reference system to set up a custom camera (`Camera1`) and an associated light (`Light1`).

For each aspect, we'd like the user to tweak, we have to add proper controls. You can spot a `TTrackbar` control (`CameraRotationYTrackBar`) that the user can use to set the `Rotation.Y` property value of our `DummyCameraAndLight` component. Rotating this `TDummy` instance, given that it is the `Parent` object of the `Camera1` and `Light1` components, will result in moving the camera and the light in a joint way (as if the camera has its own embedded light source, moving with the camera as a single object).

Another UI control that the user is provided with is a `TSwitch` component, which they can use to switch the light on and off. To bind the UI controls to the 3D ones, I've used **LiveBindings** technology (we discussed this topic in `Chapter 6`, *Implementing Data Binding*).

The first binding link is between the `CameraRotationYTrackBar.Value` property and the `DummyCameraAndLight.RotationAngle.Y` property. The second one is between the `LightSwitch` control and the `TLight` instance in the 3D scene. You can see the bindings in the following screenshot, showing the component editor of the involved `TBindingList` component:

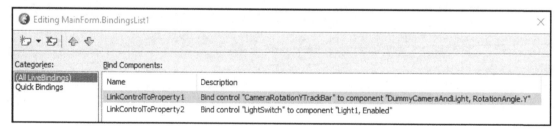

Figure 13.9

You can run this application and play with the `TTrackbar` and `TSwitch` components to see how the 3D scene is accordingly affected. We now have a nice, smooth application that can be a starting point for a typical product configurator app.

> Using what we learned in `Chapter 12`, *Exploring Cross-Platform Services*, we may want to also add gesture handling. It is surely the most wanted feature on mobile platforms because the user can interact with the 3D model in a very natural way and it should be trivial for you to implement it at this point in the book.

The following screenshot shows the application running on the Windows platform:

Figure 13.10

The preceding example is extremely meaningful because you are looking at a 2D "standard" multi-device application that hosts a 3D scene, mixing several technologies on several different platforms with a single code base. The following screenshot shows the same application running on my **Android 10** phone:

Figure 13.11

Now that we have introduced some of the most commonly used 3D components and we have learned how to set up 3D scenes in FMX applications, we can explore some other topics.

With the knowledge you have gained so far, it should be trivial to add a data persistence level (Chapter 5, *Using FireDAC in FMX Applications*) to show multiple 3D models and possibly tune in many more settings for the 3D scene (the kind of lights, camera position, zoom level, and more).

Understanding lights and materials

One of the most relevant aspects tied to the 3D rendering of a scene is the way lighting is handled. If we get close to what the real world looks like, the user will perceive that our application delivers a better experience for them. Obviously, dealing with lights and how they affect the rendering of every 3D object in the scene has a huge impact on the general complexity and, consequently, on the performance.

FMX has support for lights in 3D rendering. This means that if you can find a TLight component, then you can use it in the viewport of your form to represent a source of light. You can add multiple light sources to your scene, then position them properly, and see how this affects the rendering of other objects.

Learning about lights

The TLight class models a light source in the FMX framework. There are three different kinds of lights:

- **Spot**
- **Directional**
- **Point**

You can set the LightType property of a TLight instance to switch the light type for that instance. There are also a number of other details you can set up, including the positioning and orientation of the light source. For some types (that is, Spot) there are additional parameters, such as the spot cut-off angle (SpotCutOff property in degrees) and the light intensity (SpotExponent – the higher the value for this parameter, the more focused the light beam will be), that you can set.

In the following screenshot, you can see what happens when you switch off the light in the last project we discussed (the `Viewport` demo):

Figure 13.12

However, keep in mind that FMX does not provide a shadow-casting system. Instead, setting lights means defining the lightmap for the scene in order to determine how to render 3D objects according to their material.

Learning about the materials

There are three kinds of materials available in the FMX 3D framework:

- `TColorMaterialSource`: This is a simple solid color material.
- `TTextureMaterialSource`: This enables the use of a bitmap as filling.
- `TLightMaterialSource`: This implements a material (color- or texture-based), which is responsive with respect to the amount of light it is exposed to.

You can find the three aforementioned components in the component palette (in the **Materials** category). These are non-visual components you can add to your form and set up through the Object Inspector. Then, you can use them with 3D shapes or models by referencing them as values for the specific material-related properties of the object. For example, a `TCube` component has a `Material` property. A `TText3D` component has three different properties (`MaterialSource`, `MaterialBackSource`, and `MaterialShaftSource`) to let you diversify materials with respect to the sides of the 3D text object.

In this section, you learned how to build a 3D application with all the required basic elements, such as cameras, lights, materials, shapes, layers, components, and `TDummy` instances. You also should be relatively confident about the positioning and viewport features of an FMX 3D application.

In the next section, we are going to mix 2D and 3D objects in a different way. So far, we have seen 3D objects inside 2D UIs, but we'll also see how to add 3D effects to our 2D visual components.

Merging 3D and 2D visual objects

We have already seen in this chapter that FMX provides the ability to have a regular (2D) application containing a 3D scene (either within a `TForm3D` instance or through the use of a `TViewport3D` component).

There is another way to mix 2D and 3D visual components, that is, by trying to put regular (2D) components inside a 3D scene. There may be several use cases for this opportunity. For example, if your project is a 3D world simulator or **item configurator**, you may find yourself in need of having some data controls somewhere in the UI. Imagine you are building a product configurator and you want to provide a list of selectable options (that is, using a TListView component or a TListBox component) to the user without leaving the 3D scene.

The combination of FMX 3D capabilities that we are discussing in this chapter, together with the ability to render UI controls through the GPU, is very powerful. We just need to add the proper container to our 3D scene and we'll be able to add regular (2D) controls inside of it.

In this section, we will learn about the TLayer3D component and merging TFrameStand with the 3D visualization capabilities of the FMX framework.

Using the TLayer3D component

TLayer3D is one of the available 3D layers you can find under the **3D Layers** category in the IDE component palette. It is basically a bridge between the 3D and 2D world as it is actually a 3D visual component that can host 2D visual components.

You can make use of a TLayer3D instance as you would any other 3D FMX components. You can set its position (three-axis rotation included), size, scale, and any other available property that you would find in other 3D components. With the additional feature, this component can be a parent of, just to name a couple of possibilities, a TListView or a TLayout instance.

In the Mix3D2D demo project, you can see I've created a 3D application (using the TForm3D approach discussed earlier in this chapter) with some 3D objects. As you can see in the following screenshot, there are two TDummy instances, one holding the 3D scene (specifically a TProxyObject component), and a second one named DummyUI holding a couple of TLayer3D components:

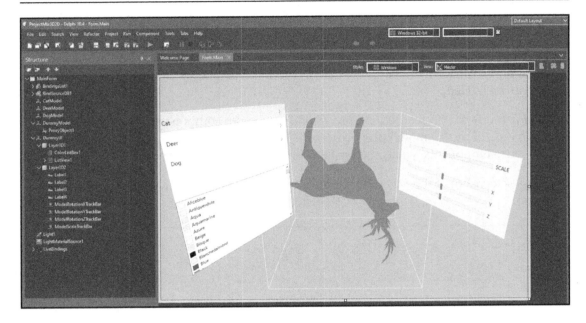

Figure 13.13

The TProxyObject component acts as a placeholder and can be used to render another 3D component (you can set which one through the TProxyObject.SourceObject property value) in a specific position. It is a handy way to switch the main subject of our scene without changing the position of actual components.

As you can see in the preceding screenshot, the application holds a dataset with some data about animals (a simple dataset actually), that is visually presented through the TListView instance hosted by the first TLayer3D component, on the left. In the same TLayer3D component, there is a TColorListBox instance that is used to change the color value of the TLightMaterialSource component used to render some imported 3D models of animals.

The 3D models have been imported at design time and stored directly in the FMX file of the main form, so they will be available on all platforms on which you may want to run the project.

 On the Windows platform (thus, in the Delphi IDE), there is an import procedure to load 3D object models from third-party software. It would require some attention (not too much) to make this feature also available on other platforms at runtime.

Data-binding has been implemented using LiveBindings technology between the `AnimalsTable` component (a `TDataModule` instance named `ModelsData` is a part of this project) and the `TListView` instance in the UI. A simple notification mechanism has been set up to notify the form when the current record has changed so that the corresponding 3D model can be loaded.

A set of controls has been added on the second `TLayer3D` component (on the right) for the manipulation of the 3D model (the proxy object actually) by the user. With the aid of some `TTrackbar` components, you can change the scale and rotate the model on the three axes.

Here is a screenshot of the **Mix3D2D** application running on the Microsoft Windows platform:

Figure 13.14

Without any effort, you can build the same application for Google Android. The following screenshot shows the application running on my smartphone:

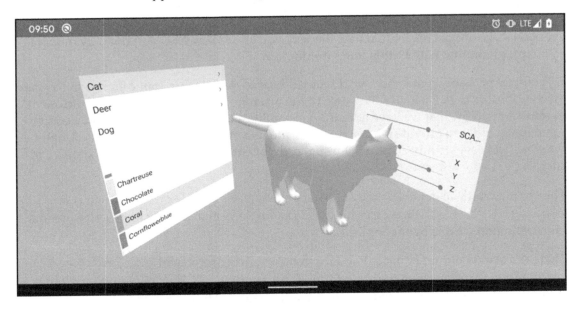

Figure 13.15

As you can see, I've selected the Cat entry on the list, changed the color to Coral, and tweaked the positioning and scaling of the model to have my cat properly placed in my 3D view.

If you want to improve this simple demo, you may consider adding some settings for the lights of the scene or adding a custom camera so that you may get a reasonable visualization even in portrait mode on a phone. Every FMX concept we have seen in the book for 2D applications is also available while building 3D applications. For example, you may want to add animations or effects to our controls. You may want to deal with mobile sensors and drive the positioning of the 3D model accordingly, and so on. The 3D context is just another part of the FMX framework; it is not set apart from the 2D components and functionalities.

Merging TFrameStand with 3D visuals

As you have seen, Chapter 8, *Divide and Conquer with TFrameStand*, was dedicated to TFrameStand (and its twin implementation about forms, TFormStand). These two simple yet powerful components may change the way you address mobile (and not only mobile) visual programming with Delphi and FireMonkey.

As you will probably remember, we discussed how to model your application using a state-machine abstraction. Each view is a state of the machine and actions/events are equivalent to transitions. Now that we have added 3D capabilities to our knowledge, we may want to use them in order to provide fancy visual transitions across views. We just learned that it is possible (and easy) to mix 2D and 3D visual components with FMX, thanks to components such as TViewport3D and TLayer3D.

The Stand3D official demo (https://github.com/andrea-magni/TFrameStand/tree/master/demos/Stand3D) showcases how you can implement a 3D transition across standard high-definition views of your application.

There is a stand definition (named new3d) in the Stands component (a TStyleBook instance) on the main form of the demo project. The following screenshot shows the structure of that stand (through the IDE's **Style Designer** window):

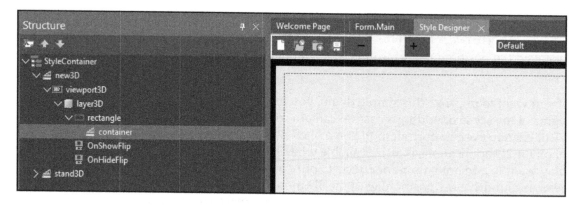

Figure 13.16

Feel free to refer back to `Chapter 8`, *Divide and Conquer with TFrameStand*, if you are not already familiar with `TFrameStand`. You should spot the `container` component, which is a `TLayout` instance, where the new view will be parented and made visible to the user. A `layer3D` component is visible in the structure together with the two animations used to flip the layer on the *x* axis, that is, `OnShowFlip` and `OnHideFlip`.

The following screenshot shows a visual of the Windows application during the transition (you may want to actually run the demo on your machine to appreciate the animation of course):

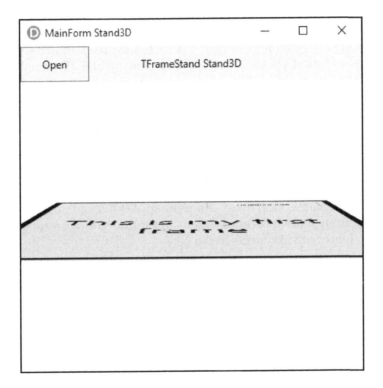

Figure 13.17

Once again, Firemonkey proves to be a very comprehensive framework where all the advanced capabilities we have seen in this book can be merged together in order to deliver high-quality visual applications across multiple platforms with a single code base.

The good separation we achieved using `TFrame/TFormStand` ensures we can focus alternatively on the UI aspects, including fancy animations and transitions (very important to deliver a modern user experience), and the application logic (which is never to be confused with the UI logic).

In this section, we learned how to use the `TLayer3D` component in a project. We also learned how to merge `TFrameStand` with 3D visuals, enriching the overall user experience and delivering it with limited effort and modern effects in your apps.

I really think FireMonkey enables developers aiming to build business applications in a reasonable amount of development time without failing to deliver a first-class UI and performance.

Summary

In this chapter, we have learned how to deal with 3D in the FMX framework. Having a high-level, component-based, cross-platform abstraction enables 3D visual programming. This is a huge benefit for the developer.

Apart from classic topics such as how to set up a 3D scene in our applications, we have seen how to mix 2D and 3D visual components in a single application. The FMX framework is very powerful and flexible at enabling 3D capabilities wherever needed (the whole form as a 3D surface or just a portion through the `TViewport3D` component) and at the same time allows mixing 3D effects in general 2D applications.

You now have the skills to develop many different applications taking advantage of 3D capabilities, that is, from simulation applications to product configurators, and from games to business applications with 3D effects in the UI.

Once again, FireMonkey proves to be a powerful tool for the multi-device, multi-platform developer.

Other Books You May Enjoy

If you enjoyed this book, you may be interested in these other books by Packt:

Delphi Programming Projects
William Duarte

ISBN: 978-1-78913-055-3

- Get to grips with the advanced features of RTL
- Understand how to deal with the paradigm change between multi platform projects
- Build rich interfaces with Google's Material Design features
- Understand how to implement design patterns in Delphi
- Turn a mobile device into a remote controller with app tethering technology
- Build a multi-database system using VCL

Delphi High Performance
Primož Gabrijelčič

ISBN: 978-1-78862-545-6

- Find performance bottlenecks and easily mitigate them
- Discover different approaches to fix algorithms
- Understand parallel programming and work with various tools included with Delphi
- Master the RTL for code optimization
- Explore memory managers and their implementation
- Leverage external libraries to write better performing programs

Leave a review - let other readers know what you think

Please share your thoughts on this book with others by leaving a review on the site that you bought it from. If you purchased the book from Amazon, please leave us an honest review on this book's Amazon page. This is vital so that other potential readers can see and use your unbiased opinion to make purchasing decisions, we can understand what our customers think about our products, and our authors can see your feedback on the title that they have worked with Packt to create. It will only take a few minutes of your time, but is valuable to other potential customers, our authors, and Packt. Thank you!

Index

Made in the USA
Columbia, SC
15 December 2020